Uncommon

Valor

THE EXCITING STORY OF THE ARMY

Edited by JAMES M. MERRILL

RAND McNALLY & COMPANY

Chicago   New York   San Francisco

Rand McNally wishes to thank the following sources who have kindly given permission for use of the photographs appearing in this book on the pages listed:
Air Force Museum, Wright-Patterson AFB, 363 (top); Arizona Pioneers' Historical Society, 231; Essex Institute, 65; Colonial Williamsburg, 31; Illinois State Historical Library, 119, 123, 219 (left); Indiana Historical Society Library, 75; New Hampshire Historical Society, 147 (top); The New-York Historical Society, endpieces, 51 (bottom), 147 (bottom), 163 (bottom), 219 (right), 283, 285, 299; New York Public Library, 43; Office of War Information, in the National Archives, 387, 393, 433; United States Signal Corps in the National Archives, 239, 249, 261, 271, 277, 281, 291 (bottom), 345, 363 (bottom); U.S. War Dept. General Staff in the National Archives, 291 (top); National Park Service, 207; Yale University Art Gallery, 51, 61, 111; West Point Museum Collections, 163 (top), 311; From *Second To None,* The Second United States Infantry Division-Korea, Vol. 1 (Tokyo, 1951) by Robert C. James, 465.

To those torchbearers, who knew the scent of
the sagebrush and the yucca that grew, my thirty-six
classmates who fought and died during World War II.

THE POOP SHEET

UNCOMMON VALOR endeavors to recapture the spirit of the United States Army by playing the spotlight on personalities. These include private and noncom, shavetail and brigadier general, the great and the near-great who shaped events, the obscure whose lives were touched by them. This book tells the story of the United States Army in the words of the men who served. They saw the British "a-comming" at Lexington and Concord, smashed the Redcoats at New Orleans, dodged through the bloody streets of Monterrey, faced Confederate bullets at Gettysburg, sloshed through the mud of the Philippines, scrambled over the top in France, and triggered the bomb releases in the flaming skies over Tokyo and Berlin. Some of the men who fought through America's wars, from Washington to Eisenhower, were destined to become Presidents of the United States.

In those long uneventful days of peace between wars, the average American mentally relegated the Regular Army to the status of an unglamorous organization off on distant posts or standing guard at picturesque forts, where they drilled a little, danced a good deal, and paraded on national holidays. But from the days of Lewis and Clark in the first years of the nineteenth century, the development and settlement of our country was largely through the agency of the Regular Army. By the sweat, muscle, and raw courage of its men, the Army conducted the preliminary explorations, built the roads, protected settlers, and drew the maps for the winning of the West. Beyond this, in crisis and disaster, the peacetime Army quashed insurrections, succored flood and earthquake victims, conquered tropical diseases, and pioneered aviation.

In the United States the majority of the men in the ranks have always been able to read and write. These soldiers scribbled letters, jotted in diaries, and meticulously made official reports. They described the Army to the folks back home, set down their daily routine in journals or, from the perspective of retirement, recalled the flash of guns and the smell of powder.

To paint the color and action of the past, to revive the clash of arms, I have riffled through countless personal letters, diaries, autobiographies, official correspondence, articles, unit histories, and recruiting pamphlets. Many of them are published here for the first time. The problem has not been what to include but what to exclude.

Raw recruit and thirty-year veteran have been asked to talk in their own words, write in the grammar and spelling that suits them best. These diaries and letters reflect their attitudes toward war, toward the enemy, toward life in the Army. These soldiers are not fond of flag-waving or mouthing the loud hurrah of patriotism. About their cause they say little. It is taken for granted. Earthiness and toughness are hallmarks of this male world—it shows in their language, their humor, and in their valor under fire.

This editor has done no more than arrange the letters and reports chronologically and, in prologues and notes, explain briefly the action. In accordance with accepted practice, I have deleted the trite and the unimportant and have broken up over-long paragraphs. The original meaning remains unaffected.

I am appreciative of the research grants from the Mershon Center on Education in National Security and the John and Dora Haynes Foundation, the latter through the auspices of Whittier College. For their encouragement I thank Dr. John H. Kemble of Pomona College, Dr. Brainerd Dyer of the University of California, Los Angeles, and Dr. Albert Upton, Dr. Benjamin Whitten, and Mrs. Ann Farmer, all of Whittier College. For their typing skills, I thank my students Linda Rawlinson and Michael Mitchell. Lastly, for help and support, I thank Ann, my wife.

JAMES M. MERRILL

Whittier, California

TABLE OF CONTENTS

I: 1775-1815

II: 1815-1861

III: 1861-1865

IV: 1865-1914

V: 1914-1941

VI: 1941-1945

VII: 1945-1962

LIST OF PHOTOGRAPHS

13

No one desires peace as much as the soldier for he must pay the greatest penalty in war.

GENERAL DOUGLAS MACARTHUR

Uncommon
Valor

CHAPTER I
1775-1815

To be prepared for war is one of the most effectual means of preserving peace

GEORGE WASHINGTON

The first blood in the American Revolution was spilled at Lexington in April, 1775. Following this clash of arms, the patriots recruited a ragtail army and appointed George Washington to command. The Americans, spurred by stern British actions, finally declared their independence in July, 1776.

The ill-disciplined troops of the Continental Army rankled their chief, and it was months before a core of several thousand hardened veterans could be whipped into line. This nucleus of experienced troops could not completely compensate for the inexperience of militia levies, the shortage of competent officers, the rivalry and bickering between the former colonies on military affairs.

Despite Washington's courageous generalship and tenacity and the multiple military blunders of the British, the patriots would have fought a longer, more arduous struggle for independence without French intervention. The colonials kept their revolution alive with secret French aid until 1778 when, after the American victory at Saratoga in the fall of 1777, the French came in openly as an ally. Spain and Holland also took up arms against Great Britain. Discovering the insurrection to be out of control, their army hemmed in at Yorktown, the British decided to come to terms with the rebels in 1781.

I

WE SEE THEM A-COMMING

On 18 April 1775 news leaked into Boston that American patriots were collecting military stores in Concord. British General Thomas Gage dispatched a strong detail of infantry to seize these munitions. After a night's march, the British entered Lexington and saw through the early morning haze a stern band of Minutemen standing across the Common. There was a shot. The British fired. Eight patriots slumped on the village green before the Minutemen scattered. The British trudged on to Concord where the yeoman farmers faced them at the bridge. After confiscating and igniting part of the hoard, the British trekked back to Boston. All along the road, from behind stone walls and ditches, the patriots took pot shots at the bright red coats. When Major Pitcairn and his soldiers finally made Boston, they had lost 247 in killed and wounded.

Three Minutemen, Sylvanus Wood, Amos Barrett, and James Stevens, set down their views of the action at Lexington and Concord.

[*Wood*]   I, Sylvanus Wood . . . on the morning of the 19th of April, 1775 . . . was an inhabitant of Woburn, living with Deacon Obadiah Kendall; that about an hour before break of day on said morning, I heard the Lexington bell ring, and fearing there was difficulty there, I immediately arose, took my gun, and, with Robert Douglass, went in haste to Lexington, which was about three miles distant. When I arrived there, I inquired of Captain [John] Parker, the commander of the Lexington company, what was the news. Parker told me he did not know what to believe, for a man had come up about half an hour before, and informed him that the British troops were not on the road. But while we were talking, a messenger came up and told the captain that the British troops were within half a mile. Parker immediately turned to his drummer, William Diman, and ordered him to beat to arms, which was done. Captain Parker then asked me if I would parade with his company. I told him I would. Parker then asked me if the young man with me would parade. I spoke to Douglass, and he said he would follow the captain and me.

By this time many of the company had gathered around the captain at the hearing of the drum, where we stood, which was about half way between the meeting-house and Buckman's tavern. Parker says to his men, "Every man of you, who is equipped, follow me; and those of you who are not equipped, go into the meeting-house and furnish yourselves from the magazine, and immediately join the company." Parker led those of us who were equipped to the north end of Lexington Common, near the Bedford road, and formed us in single file. I was stationed about in the centre of the company. While we were standing, I left my place, and went from one end of the company to the other, and counted every man who was paraded, and the whole number was thirty eight, and no more. Just as I had finished, and got back to my place, I perceived the British troops had arrived on the spot between the meeting-house and Buckman's, near where Captain Parker stood when he first led off his men. The British troops approached us rapidly in platoons, with a general officer on horseback at their head. The officer came up to within about two rods of the centre of the company, where I stood, the first platoon being about three rods distant. They there halted. The officer then swung his sword, and said, "Lay down your arms, you damned rebels, or you are all dead men—Fire!" Some guns were fired by the British at us from the first platoon, but no person was killed or hurt, being probably charged only with powder.

Just at this time, Captain Parker ordered every man to take care of himself. The company immediately dispersed; and while the company was dispersing and leaping over the wall, the second platoon of the British fired, and killed some of our men. There was not a gun fired by any of Captain Parker's company, within my knowledge. I was so situated that I must have known it, had any thing of the kind taken place before a total dispersion of our company. I have been intimately acquainted with the inhabitants of Lexington, and particularly with those of Captain Parker's company, and, with one exception, I have never heard any of them say or pretend that there was any firing at the British from Parker's company, or any individual in it, until within a year or two. One member of the company told me, many years since, that, after Parker's company had dispersed, and he was at some distance, he gave them "the guts of his gun."

After the British had begun their march to Concord, I returned to the Common, and found Robert Roe and Jonas Parker lying dead at the north corner of the Common, near the Bedford road, and others dead and wounded. I assisted in carrying the dead into the meeting-house. I then proceeded towards Concord with my gun, and when I came near the tavern in Lexington, now kept by Mr. Viles, I saw a British soldier seated on the bank by the road. I went to him, with my gun in readiness to fire, if he should offer to resist. I took his gun, cut-lass, and equipments from him, and meeting a Mr. Welch and another person, I delivered the prisoner to them.

After Welch arrived in Lexington with the prisoner, I understood that another prisoner was taken by Mr. John Flagg, and that they were conducted to Burlington and put under the care of Captain James Reed. I believe that the soldier who surrendered his gun to me was the first prisoner taken by the Americans on that day.[1]

[Barrett] . . . We at Concord heard that they was a-comming the Beel rong at 3 oclock for alaroum   as I was a minnit man I was soon in town and found my Capt and the Rest of my Compny at the post   it warnt long Before thair was other minit Compneys   one Compney I beleave of minnit men was raisd in a most every town to stand at a minits warning   be fore Sunrise thair was I beleave 150 of us and more of all that was thair—we thought we wood go and meet the Britsch   we marched Down to wards L[exington] about a mile or mile half and we see them a-comming   we halted and stayd till they got within about 100 Rods then we was orded to the about face and marchd before them with our Droms and fifes agoing and also the B[ritish]   we had grand musick   we marchd into town and over the north Bridge a litle more than half a mile and then on a Hill not far from the Bridge, whair we could see and hear what was agoing on— what the B[ritish] Came out after was to Destroy our Stores that we had got Laid up for our army. . . .

When we was on the hill by the Bridge thair was about 80 or 90 B[ritish] Came to the Bridge and their made a halt   after a while they begun to tair the plank of the Bridge mager Buttrick said if we wair all of his mind he wood Drive them away from the Bridge they should not tair that up we all said we wood go we then warnt loaded we wair all orded to Load—and had stricked orders not to fire till they fired firs then to fire as fast as we Could—we then marchd on Capt Davis minit Compney marchd first then Capt allens minnit compney the wone that I was in next we marchd 2 Deep it was a Long Corsay [causeway] Being round by the River Capt Davis had got I beleave within 15 Rods of the B[ritish] when they fired 3 gons one after the other I see the balls Strike in the River on the Right of me—as soon as they fired them they fired on us the balls whisled well—we then was all orded to fire that Could fire and not Kill our one men

It is straing that their warnt no more kiled but they fired to high Capt Davis was kiled and Mr. Osmore and anumber wounded we soon Drove them from the Bridge when I got over their was 2 Lay Dead and a nother allmost dead we Did not foller them their was 8 or 10 that was wounded and a Runing and Hobbling a Lout Lucking back to See if we was after them—we then Saw the Hull [whole] boddy a coming out of town we then was orded to Lay behind a wall that Ran over a hill and when they got ny anuff mager Buttrick Said He wood give the word fire but they Did not Come quite so near as he expected before they halted the Commanding officer orded the hull Battolion to halt and officers to the frount march the officers then marched to the front thair we Lay be hind the wall about 200 of us with our gons Cockd, Expecting every minnit to have the word to fire our orders was if we fired to fire 2 or 3 times and then Retreat if we had fired I beleave we Could Kiled allmost Every Officer—thairs was in the front but we had no orders to fire and their warnt agan [a gun] fired they staid about 10 minnits and then marched back and we after them after a while we found them a marching back towards Boston we was Soon after them when they got about mile half to a Road that comes from bedford and Bildrea [Bilrica] they was way laid and a quait many killd when I got thair was a grait many Layd dead and the Road was bloddy[2]

[*Stevens*] this morning a bout seven aclok we had alarum that the Reegerlers was gon to Conkord we gatherd to the meting hous

& then started for Concord   we went thro Tukesbary and in to Bilrica we stopt to Polords and eat some bisket & Ches on the common. we started & wen into Bedford and we herd the regerlers was gon back to Boston   we went through Bedford. we went in to Lecentown [Lexington]. we went to the metinghous and there we come to the distruction of the Reegerlers   thay cild eight of our men & shot a Canon Ball throug the metin hous. we went a long through Lecintown & we saw several regerlers ded on the rod & som of our men and three or fore housen was Burnt and som hoses and hogs was cild   thay plaindered in every hous thay could get in to thay stove in windows & broke in tops of desks   we met the men a coming back very fast   we went through Notemy [Menotomy now Arlington] & got into Cambridg

we stopt about eight acloke for thay say that the regerlers was got to Chalstown on to Bunkers hil and intrenstion   we stopt about two miles back from the college[3]

II

I CHOOSE TO DIE WHOLE

The countryside was ignited with rumors of British brutality at Lexington and Concord. All over New England, Americans like James Stevens, most of them with only a day or two of drill, swarmed the roads to Boston. In June they fought at Bunker's Hill and, as the year drew to a close, Washington's army was still before Boston. The British were forced to retire from the town but, in 1776, they wrested control of another major port, New York, and the command of the entrance to the Hudson River in the battles of Long Island and Harlem Heights.

Another aroused farm boy from Massachusetts, Park Holland, joined a brigade and marched off to defend New York. He recalls these experiences for his nephew.

Your father and I lived in the same neighborhood, and 1775 found us warm Whigs, or revolutionists, as we were then called. We were early enrolled as minutemen; but we did not enter actual service until 1776, when the state of Massachusetts was requested by Congress to raise a brigade of troops and march them immediately to New York. Without loss of time, in company with thirty of our neighbors and friends, we left our peaceful and retired homes, many of us for the first time in our lives; marched to Brookfield, where we joined the regiment commanded by Colonel Holman; and thence to New Haven, where we embarked for New York. We arrived there about the first of July, and remained in the city until a few days after the battle of Long Island. It was then agreed in council that the American troops should leave the city; which was done sometime in September.

The British, having notice of our intention, sent a number of armed vessels up both the North and the East River, with the intention of cutting off our retreat. Though they did not effect their purpose, they very much retarded our progress. However, with much difficulty we reached Harlem Heights, near the upper end of the island, and encamped. The next day we found that the enemy had landed a considerable force and were coming to give us battle. Having somewhat recruited, we lost no time in preparing to meet them, more mad than afraid. A battle soon commenced in earnest. Their front giving way, we rushed on and soon came up with the main body. A pretty severe engagement ensued; which ended in considerable loss on both sides, and the retreat of the British on board their vessels near Harlem Village. The principal part of our army now marched on to White Plains, where, under the command of Washington, we intrenched ourselves as well as we were able with our limited means, and made a short stand. We soon heard that the British forces were arming to meet us, with reinforcements from Frog's Neck or East Chester. A large detachment of our troops was immediately ordered to meet them.

We had proceeded but a mile, when, from a high ridge of land that we had ascended, the whole British force, ten or fifteen thousand strong, with heavy field artillery, lay in full view in the valley below. Here we halted, just within reach of their guns. The air was soon filled with balls, grapeshot and shells. Smallwood's regiment of Virginia troops lay in an opening in the ridge, and, on account of their exposed position, were cut to pieces in a horrible manner. Those of us who were posted on the highest part of the ridge suffered comparatively little, as they generally fired over us. The shells, however, annoyed us considerably. After a short time the cannonading ceased, and all at once their infantry appeared in solid columns in front of us. A warm fire of musketry on both sides took place, but after firing ten or twelve rounds, we discovered that they had flanked us both on the right and on the left.

We were now ordered to retreat, and the order was quickly obeyed. While descending the ridge the fire of the enemy did us little damage, as here, also, they generally fired over us. The loss on both sides amounted to several hundred, and neither party could claim much advantage.

In our rapid retreat down the hill a ball from the enemy broke the leg of a soldier just in advance of us; who, when we overtook him, begged us in mercy not to leave him to fall into the hands of the British, but dispatch him at once, if we could contrive no way to take him off the field. The whizzing of balls told us, in language not to be mistaken, that what we did must be done quickly. The planning of a litter being out of the question, I asked White, a neighbor of mine, to help raise him up, and take one arm while I took the other. Thus, with his broken leg dangling, we bore him safely down the hill, across a stream, and through the valley to a barn nearly, or quite, half a mile distant, which was fast filling with the wounded and dying.

Unused as we were, from our former lives of peace and retirement, to scenes like this, our hearts sickened within us on beholding so much suffering. The American army endured enough, as is well known, from many causes, but at this time from none more than the lack of skillful surgeons. Those we had were, many of them, young men from retired parts of the country, who had rarely seen a limb taken off in their lives, and of course they were ignorant. Many a brave fellow was losing a useful limb, and some their lives, through such mismanagement. We stood silently by our soldier, sad enough, to hear his fate decided. When his turn to be examined came, he was told that he must lose a leg or die. He promptly replied, "I choose to die whole, then; but not till you have bandaged and splintered my leg as best you can." Here we left him without knowing even his name. . . .

Of the five from my native town who were out in these two battles, two were killed. One, Perry, breathed his last on Harlem Heights; the other, whose name I do not remember, the drummer of the regiment, fell dead at White Plains.[4]

America to arms Repair
Honour & glory beat to war
Exert your selves with force and might
And shue how amarican Boys can fight
for to maintain their Charter rights
Huzza Brave Boys

Hark how the War like trumpets sounds
Whare there is Nought but Blood and Wounds
The Drums a Beating Colurs fling
Canon roring toris Dieing
these are the noble effects of War
Huzza Brave Boys

Ye that Rain masters of the serf
Shake off your youthful sloth and see
Well make the houty torys to know
the torters thay must undergo
When thay ingage their Mortle foe
Huzza Brave Boys

Display your Colours mount your guns
Bater their Castles fier their touns
United sons of amaricans fame
Let not your courage tame
We'll drive the torys back again
Huzza Brave Boys

Why then should be Danted at all
Sence we are ingaged in such a caus
As fiting for our rights and laws
& dying in so just a caus
We'll prove their fulle over throu
Huzza Brave Boys[5]

III

OVER THE RIVER WE WENT

*Washington and his troops escaped from Manhattan Island, re-
treated northward, and crossed the Hudson River into New Jersey. In*

the autumn of 1776, General William Howe, commanding the British forces, lost several chances to capture the American Army. Washington crossed the Delaware River to the Pennsylvania side before Howe's advance soldiers had reached the New Jersey bank. To strike the enemy, Washington recrossed the Delaware on the blustery Christmas night of 1776, and took a thousand Hessians at Trenton.

Enlisted man John Greenwood and General Washington describe the river crossing and the battle at Trenton.

[*Greenwood*]   Over the river we went in a flat-bottomed scow, and as I was with the first that crossed, we had to wait for the rest and so began to pull down the fences and make fires to warm ourselves, for the storm was increasing rapidly. After a while it rained, hailed, snowed, and froze, and at the same time blew a perfect hurricane; so much so that I perfectly recollect, after putting the rails on to the burn, the wind and the fire would cut them in two in a moment, and when I turned my face toward the fire my back would be freezing. However, as my usual acuteness had not forsaken me, by turning round and round I kept myself from perishing before the large bonfire. The noise of the soldiers coming over and clearing away the ice, the rattling of cannon wheels on the frozen ground, and the cheerfulness of my fellow-comrades encouraged me beyond expression, and, big coward as I acknowledge myself to be, I felt great pleasure, more than I now do in writing about it. After our men had all crossed—and there were not, as I could see, more than 200 of us— we began an apparently circuitous march, not advancing faster than a child ten years old could walk, and stopping frequently, though for what purpose I know not. During the whole night it alternately hailed, rained, snowed, and blew tremendously. I recollect very well that at one time, when we halted on the road, I sat down on the stump of a tree and was so benumbed with cold that I wanted to go to sleep; had I been passed unnoticed I should have frozen to death without knowing it; but as good luck always attended me, Sergeant Madden came and, rousing me up, made me walk about. We then began to march again, just in the old slow way, until dawn of day, about half-past seven in the morning. . . .

None but the first officers knew where we were going or what we were going about, for it was a secret expedition, and we, the bulk of the men coming from Canada, knew not the disposition of the army we were then in, nor anything about the country. This was not unusual, however, as I never heard soldiers say anything, nor ever saw them trouble themselves as to where they were or where they were led. It was enough for them to know that wherever the officers commanded they must go, be it through fire and water, for it was all the same owing to the impossibility of being in a worse condition than their present one, and therefore the men always liked to be kept moving in expectation of bettering themselves.

Between seven and eight o'clock, as we were marching near the town, the first intimation I received of our going to fight was the firing of a 6-pound cannon at us, the ball from which struck the fore horse that was dragging our only piece of artillery, a 3-pounder. The animal, which was near me as I was in the second division on the left, was struck in its belly and knocked over on its back. While it lay there kicking the cannon was stopped and I did not see it again after we had passed on. As we advanced, it being dark and stormy so that we could not see very far ahead, we got within 200 yards of about 300 or 400 Hessians who were paraded, two deep, in a straight line with Colonel Roll (Rall or Rahl), their commander, on horseback, to the right of them. They made a full fire at us, but I did not see that they killed any one. Our brave Major Sherburne ordered us to fall back about 300 yards and pull off our packs, which we accordingly did and piled them by the roadside. "Now, my boys," says he, "pass the word through the ranks that he who is afraid to follow me, let him stay behind and take care of the packs!" Not a man offered to leave the ranks, and as we never went back that way, we all lost our packs: at least I never heard anything of mine, and I had in it a beautiful suit of blue clothes, turned up with white and silver laced.

As we had been in the storm all night we were not only wet through and through ourselves, but our guns and powder were wet also, so that I do not believe one would go off, and I saw none fired by our party. When we were all ready we advanced, and, although there was not more than one bayonet to five men, orders were given to "Charge bayonets and rush on!" and rush on we did. Within pistol-shot they again fired point-blank on us; we dodged and they did not hit a man, while before they had time to reload we were within three feet of them, when they broke in an instant and ran like so many frightened devils into the town, which was at a short distance, we after them pell-mell. Some of the Hessians took refuge in a church at

Battlefield portrait showing George Washington at Trenton.

the door of which we stationed a guard to keep them in, and taking no further care of them for the present, advanced to find more, for many had run down into the cellars of the houses. I passed two of their cannon (26), brass 6-pounders, by the side of which lay seven dead Hessians and a brass drum. This latter article was, I remember, a great curiosity to me and I stopped to look at it, but it was quickly taken possession of by one of the drummers, who threw away his own instrument. At the same time I obtained a sword from one of the bodies, and we then ran on to join the regiment, which was marching down the main street toward the market. Just before we reached this building, however, General Washington, on horseback and alone, came up to our major and said, "March on, my brave fellows, after me!" and rode off.

After passing a number of dead and wounded Hessians we reached the other side of the town and on our right beheld about 500 or 600 of the enemy paraded, two deep, in a field. At the time we were marching in grand divisions which filled up the street, but as we got opposite the enemy we halted and, filing off two deep, marched right by them—yes, and as regular as a Prussian troop. When we had reached the end of their line we were ordered to wheel to the right, which brought us face to face six feet apart, at which time, though not before, I discovered they had no guns. They had been taken prisoners by another party and we had marched between them and their guns, which they had laid down. A few minutes afterward a number of wagons came behind us, into which the guns were placed, and the next thing ordered was to disarm the prisoners of their swords, with one of which every man was provided; these we also put in the wagons, but compelled the enemy to carry their cartridge-boxes themselves. Our regiment was then ordered to conduct them down to the ferry and transport them over to the other side; so we began the march, guarding the flanks or sides of the road.

The Hessian prisoners, who were all grenadiers, numbered about 900. I saw also a party of 300 or 400 who had got off, but how they did it I could not conceive. The scow, or flat-bottomed boat which was used in transporting them over the ferry, was half a leg deep with rain and snow, and some of the poor fellows were so cold that their underjaws quivered like an aspen leaf. On the march down to the boats, seeing some of our men were much pleased with the brass caps which they had taken from the dead Hessians, our prisoners, who were besides exceedingly frightened, pulled off those that they were wearing, and, giving them away, put on the hats which they carried tied behind their packs. With these brass caps on it was laughable to see how our soldiers would strut—fellows with their elbows out and some without a collar to their half-a-shirt, no shoes, etc.

The next day (December 27, 1776), being two days after our time was out, we received three month's pay—and glad was I. We were offered twenty-six dollars to stay six weeks longer, but as I did not enlist for the purpose of remaining in the army, but only through necessity, as I could not get to my parents in Boston, I was determined to quit as soon as my time was out. As our captain had been taken prisoner at the Cedars, I told my lieutenant (Edward Cumston) that I was going home. "My God!" says he, "you are not, I hope, going to leave us, for you are the life and soul of us and are to be promoted to an ensign." I told him I would not stay to be a colonel. I had the itch then so bad that my breeches stuck to my thighs, all the skin being off, and there were hundreds of vermin upon me, owing to a whole month's march and having been obliged, for the sake of keeping warm, to lie down at night among the soldiers who were huddled close together like hogs.

Leonard Parks, a young fifer-boy, and myself set off to cross the river for Newton. We were both sick, and I from weakness could hardly put one foot before the other, yet we trudged along together, with one blanket, expecting to reach Boston, the route we had to take being about 350 miles.[6]

[*Washington, 27, December, To The President of the Congress*] Sir: I have the pleasure of Congratulating you upon the success of an enterprize which I had formed against a Detachment of the Enemy lying in Trenton, and which was executed yesterday Morning. The Evening of the 25th I ordered the Troops intended for this Service to parade back of McKonkey's Ferry, that they might begin to pass as soon as it grew dark, imagining we should be able to throw them all over, with the necessary Artillery, by 12 O'Clock, and that we might easily arrive at Trenton by five in the Morning, the distance being about nine Miles. But the Quantity of Ice, made that Night, impeded the passage of the Boats so much, that it was three O'Clock before the Artillery could all get over, and near four, before the Troops took up their line of march.

This made me despair of surprising the Town, as I well knew we could not reach it before the day was fairly broke, but as I was certain there was not making a Retreat, without being discovered, and harassed on repassing the River, I determined to push on at all Events. I form'd my detachments into two divisions one to March by the lower or River Road, the other by the upper or Pennington Road. As the Divisions had nearly the same distance to March, I ordered each of them, immediately upon forcing the out Guards, to push directly into the Town, that they might charge the Enemy before they had time to form. The upper Division arrived at the Enemys advanced post, exactly at Eight O'Clock, and in three Minutes after, I found, from the fire on the lower Road that, that Division had also got up. The out Guards made but small Opposition, tho' for their Numbers, they behaved very well, keeping up a constant retreating fire from behind Houses. We presently saw their main Body formed, but from their Motions, they seemed undetermined how to act. Being hard pressed by our Troops, who had already got possession of part of their Artillery, they attempted to file off by a road on their right leading to Princetown, but perceiving their Intention, I threw a body of Troops in their Way which immediately checked them. Finding from our disposition that they were surrounded, and that they must inevitably be cut to pieces if they made any further Resistance, they agreed to lay down their Arms. The Number that submitted in this manner, was 23 Officers and 886 men. . . . Our loss is very trifling indeed, only two Officers and one or two privates wounded. . . . Immediately upon the begining of the Attack, all those who were not killed or taken, pushed directly down the Road towards Bordentown. These would likewise have fallen into our hands, could my plan have been compleatly carried into Execution. Genl. Ewing was to have crossed before day at Trenton Ferry, and taken possession of the Bridge leading out of Town, but the Quantity of Ice was so great, that tho' he did every thing in his power to effect it, he could not get over.

This difficulty also hindered General Cadwallader from crossing, with the Pennsylvania Militia, from Bristol, he got part of his Foot over, but finding it impossible to embark his Artillery, he was obliged to desist. I am fully confident, that could the Troops under Generals Ewing and Cadwallader have passed the River, I should have been able, with their Assistance, to have driven the Enemy from all their posts below Trenton. But the Numbers I had with me, being inferior to theirs below me, and a strong Battalion of Light Infantry at Princetown above me, I thought it most prudent to return the same Evening, with my prisoners and the artillery we had taken. . . . In justice to the Officers and Men, I must add, that their Behaviour upon this Occasion, reflects the highest honor upon them. The difficulty of passing the River in a very severe Night, and their march thro' a violent Storm of Snow and Hail, did not in the least abate their Ardour. But when they came to the Charge, each seemed to vie with the other in pressing forward, and were I to give a preference to any particular Corps, I should do great injustice to the others.[7]

IV

DADDY, THE INFANTRY MUSTN'T LEAVE

After routing the Hessians at Trenton, Washington skirted General Cornwallis' forces, which Howe had dispatched to capture the Americans, defeated a portion of the British at Princeton, and maneuvered his army into winter quarters near Morristown, New Jersey. The British returned to New York.

With possession of this city, the Redcoats in 1777 plotted the reconquest of the northern colonies. To sever New England from her sisters, Howe was to advance from New York City up the Hudson and make contact near Albany with General John Burgoyne's army, which was to march from Canada down the line of Lake Champlain, Lake George, and the Hudson River. Howe, whose orders to aid Burgoyne were delayed, had already embarked the bulk of his force on board transports in midsummer 1777 for Chesapeake Bay and an attack against Philadelphia. Left stranded, Burgoyne moved southward and gained an initial success at Fort Ticonderoga, which lay across his line of march. From then on misfortune piled upon misfortune. The difficulties of advancing a European-style army through heavily wooded country were immense. At Bennington, one foraging party met defeat from the stubborn Vermonters. Burgoyne stumbled forward. The Americans closed in. Near Saratoga in October, 1777, they defeated the Redcoats and forced Burgoyne to surrender to General Horatio Gates.

Park Holland, who after the battle of White Plains had returned to his Massachusetts farm, reenlisted for the duration. The account to his nephew continues, reconstructing the events at Saratoga as do the narratives of General James Wilkinson and Ebenezer Mattoon.

[*Holland*] Sometime in the winter of 1776–7 Congress proposed the raising of a permanent army, to be engaged for three years or during the war. Massachusetts was requested to raise fifteen regiments. The business progressed rather slowly; however, it was concluded before spring, and your father, who had been nominated a lieutenant, received enlisting orders. He offered me a sergeant-major's berth, if I would enlist; and, though heartily sick of a soldier's life, I did not hesitate, but, with twenty-four or five of my townsmen, enlisted for the war, well knowing the importance it would prove to the cause of liberty to have a permanent army. About the first of May we marched to Leicester, where we were enrolled by the muster master. Thence we proceeded to Bunker Hill barracks to be inoculated for the smallpox. About nine hundred entered the hospital, eight hundred of whom recovered. . . . Of course we suffered from want of attention. Our only food was water gruel, placed in the cook room a few feet from our barracks, where we went when we pleased, reached our hands through the window, and with a tin porringer took from a half-hogshead what we saw fit. Our salts were similarly arranged. Neither of them, as everybody knows, is very palatable, even when taken in small quantities from clean vessels. Some of the soldiers, who were feeble and delicate, died rather than take what was necessary of either; and our physicians, from having so much to do, were unable to see that their rules were obeyed; though no two men could make greater exertions than they did for our comfort and safety. We had a soldier from Cape Ann who, on finding how we were to fare, was soon among the missing. How the fellow escaped none could conjecture, as we were strictly guarded; but all cursed his memory as a deserter to the enemy. After we had recovered, as we were preparing to wash up, who should make his appearance but our deserter, Mr. Joplin, as large as life and in good health! It appeared that he did not like our treatment; so he crept through a water-course till past the guard, went to the village and bought a supply of pork and beans, built him a hut in the bushes, and there alone and unaided battled with the smallpox. He had come off victorious and was now ready for the British.

From the barracks we marched to Worcester, where we remained till news came, the first of July, that Ticonderoga had been evacuated and our northern army was retreating to Fort Edward. On receipt of this information we were despatched with all possible speed to Greenbush, east of Albany. Here we left our luggage and sick, taking with us only what was absolutely necessary, and proceeded as rapidly as possible to Ford Edward. From here we immediately sent a strong detachment, to reinforce our retreating army under command of General Schuyler; who joined General St. Clair at Hubbardton, not far from Skeenesboro. The next day they were attacked by the enemy and quite a number on both sides killed. . . . Your father and I were not in this skirmish, having been left at Fort Edward. General Schuyler, on his return down the river, destroyed the bridges and obstructed the roads in such a manner that the enemy were prevented from pursuing us closely. We remained at Fort Edward but a few days, while preparing for a further retreat down the river. Our next halt was at Fort Miller, where we left quite a number of our troops.

While we were at Fort Edward, two of our officers, Lieutenant Sawyer and Sergeant Rogers, thought they would visit some of their friends at Fort Miller. They had proceeded but about forty rods, when a dozen Indians came out of the woods and, in plain sight of us, killed them both and scalped them before we could reach the spot. When we arrived, there lay the bodies of our friends, who left us but a moment before in high glee and full of life and hope. A more horrid sight is rarely seen, even by a soldier, than was now presented to our view. Not an Indian was to be found. We bore the bodies of our friends back and buried them. . . .

Our prospects were not dark enough. There were foes in every direction; and, what was worst of all, we knew not when we were in greatest danger. To add to our perplexities, we were fast losing confidence in our commander, General Schuyler, though why this was the case it would be difficult to tell. He certainly did everything a man in his situation could do. But the situation of a retreating army is never a pleasant one; and, as often remarked, a commander is often blamed for misfortunes over which he could have had no control, and likewise praised for victories for which he was more indebted to fortunate circumstances than his own bravery or judgment. . . .

We continued our retreat down the river and encamped on Van Schoick's Island at the mouth of the Mohawk. . . . About this time took place the battle of Bennington and the defeat of St. Leger, which sent a thrill of hope and joy through every rank of the American army. Strong reinforcements of militia daily joining us, with a commander in whom we had perfect confidence (though perhaps no better than our former one), also added to our spirits and courage fresh energy. We turned our march up the river to meet General Burgoyne with a determination not to yield, gathering from the looks of our commanders, rather than their words, that we were playing an almost desperate game; that, if Burgoyne fought his way through, and joined the British army, as we knew was his intention, all would be lost. We arrived at Bemis Heights, within a few miles of the British camp at Saratoga. Here we made a firm stand till the nineteenth of September, when the enemy, finding themselves in a very critical situation, determined to force our lines in a desperate attempt to reach Albany. They accordingly marched out about noon and gave us battle. The engagement continued with vigor till sunset, when each army retired to camp, leaving the dead and some of the wounded on the field. The next morning, by mutual agreement, each army took away its own dead. Both sides claimed the victory, but neither had much ground for boasting. The action was a severe one on both sides, and the loss probably about equal; except that the officers suffered more on the British than on our side. Both armies lay pretty quiet till October 7.[8]

[*Wilkinson*]   On the afternoon of the 7th October, the advanced guard of the centre beat to arms; the alarm was repeated throughout the line, and the troops repaired to their alarm posts. I was at head quarters when this happened, and with the approbation of the General, mounted my horse to inquire the cause; but on reaching the guard where the beat commenced, I could obtain no other satisfaction, but that some person had reported the enemy to be advancing against our left. I proceeded over open ground, and ascending a gentle acclivity in front of the guard, I perceived about half a mile from the line of our encampment, several columns of the enemy, 60 or 70 rods from me, entering a wheat field which had not been cut, and was separated from me by a small rivulet; and without my glass I could distinctly mark their every movement. After entering the field, they displayed, formed the line, and sat down in double ranks with their arms between their legs. Foragers then proceeded to cut the wheat or standing straw, and I soon after observed several officers, mounted on the top of a cabin, from whence with their glasses they were endeavouring to reconnoitre our left, which was concealed from their view by intervening woods.

Having satisfied myself, after fifteen minutes attentive observation, that no attack was meditated, I returned and reported to the General, who asked me what appeared to be the intentions of the enemy. "They are foraging, and endeavouring to reconnoitre your left; and I think Sir, they offer you battle." "What is the nature of the ground, and what your opinion?" "Their front is open, and their flanks rest on woods, under cover of which they may be attacked; their right is skirted by a lofty height. I would indulge them." "Well, then, order on Morgan to begin the game."[9]

[*Mattoon*]   Our troops were immediately put under arms, and the lines manned. . . .

Capt. Furnival's company of artillery, in which I was lieutenant, was ordered to march towards the fire, which had now opened upon our picket in front, the picket consisting of about 300 men. While we were marching, the whole line, up to our picket or front, was engaged. We advanced to a height of ground which brought the enemy in view, and opened our fire. But the enemy's guns, eight in number, and much heavier than ours, rendered our position untenable.

We then advanced into the line of infantry. Here Lieutenant M'Lane joined me. In our front there was a field of corn, in which the Hessians were secreted. On our advancing towards the corn field, a number of men rose and fired upon us. M'Lane was severely wounded. While I was removing him from the field, the firing still continued without abatement.

During this time, a tremendous firing was heard on our left. We poured in upon them our canister shot, as fast as possible, and the whole line, from left to right, became engaged. The smoke was very dense, and no movements could be seen; but as it soon arose, our infantry appeared to be slowly retreating, and the Hessians slowly advancing, their officers urging them on with their hangers.

Just at this moment, an elderly man, with a long hunting gun, coming up, I said to him, "Daddy, the infantry mustn't leave, I shall be cut to pieces." He replied, "I'll give them another gun." The smoke then rising again, several officers, led by a general, appeared moving to the northward, in rear of the Hessian line. The old man, at that instant, discharged his gun, and the general officer pitched forward on the neck of his horse, and instantly they wheeled about, the old man observing, "I have killed that officer, let him be who he will." I replied, "you have, and it is a general officer, and by his dress I believe it is [General] Fraser." While they were turning about, three of their horses dropped down; but their further movements were then concealed by the smoke. . . .

The troops continuing warmly engaged, Col. Johnson's regiment coming up, threw in a heavy fire, and compelled the Hessians to retreat. Upon this we advanced with a shout of victory. At the same time Auckland's corps gave way.[10]

[*Wilkinson*] The ground which had been occupied by the British grenadiers presented a scene of complicated horror and exultation. In the square space of twelve or fifteen yards lay eighteen grenadiers in the agonies of death, and three officers propped up against stumps of trees, two of them mortally wounded, bleeding, and almost speechless; what a spectacle for one whose bosom glowed with philanthropy, and how vehement the impulse, which can excite men of sensibility to seek such scenes of barbarism! I found the courageous Colonel Cilley a straddle on a brass twelve-pounder and exulting in the capture—whilst a surgeon, a man of great worth, who was dressing one of the officers, raising his blood-besmeared hands in a frenzy of patriotism, exclaimed, "Wilkinson I have dipt my hands in British blood." He received a sharp rebuke for his brutality, and with the troops I pursued the hard pressed flying enemy, passing over killed and wounded until I heard one exclaim, "protect me Sir, against this boy." Turning my eyes, it was my fortune to arrest the purpose of a lad, thirteen or fourteen years old, in the act of taking aim at a wounded officer who lay in the angle of a worm fence. Inquiring his rank, he answered, "I had the honour to command the grenadiers"; of course, I knew him to be Major Ackland, who had been brought from the field to this place, on the back of a Captain Shrimpton of his own corps, under a heavy fire, and was here deposited, to save the lives of both. I dismounted, took him by the hand and expressed hopes that he was not badly wounded, "not badly," replied this gallant officer and accomplished gentleman, "but very inconveniently, I am shot through both legs; will you Sir have the goodness to have me conveyed to your camp?" I directed my servant to alight, and we lifted Ackland into his seat, and ordered him to be conducted to head-quarters.

[*Mattoon*] We proceeded but a short distance before we came upon four pieces of brass cannon, closely surrounded with the dead and dying; at a few yards further we came upon two more. Advancing a little further, we were met by a fire from the British infantry, which proved very fatal to one of Col. Johnson's companies, in which were killed one sergeant, one corporal, fourteen privates—and about twenty were wounded.

They advanced with a quick step, firing as they came on. We returned them a brisk fire of canister shot, not allowing ourselves time even to sponge our pieces. In a short time they ceased firing, and advanced upon us with trailed arms. At this juncture Arnold came up with a part of Brooks's regiment, and gave them a most deadly fire, which soon caused them to face about and retreat with a quicker step than they advanced.

The firing had now principally ceased on our left, but was brisk in front and on the right. At this moment, Arnold says to Col. Brooks (late governor of Massachusetts), "Let us attack Balcarras's works." Brooks replied, "No. Lord Auckland's detachment has retired there, we can't carry them." "Well, then, let us attack the Hessian lines." Brooks replies, "With all my heart." We all wheeled to the right and advanced.

No fire was received, except from the cannon, until we got within about eight rods, when we received a tremendous fire from the whole line. But a few of our men, however, fell. Still advancing, we received a second fire, in which a few men fell, and Gen. Arnold's horse fell under him, and he himself was wounded. He cried out, "Rush on, my brave boys." After receiving the third fire, Brooks mounted their works. When we entered the works, we found Col. Bremen dead, surrounded by a number of his companions, dead or wounded. We still pursued slowly; the fire, in the mean time, decreasing. Nightfall now put an end to this day's bloody contest.

41

During the day, we had taken eight cannon, and broken the centre of the enemy's lines.

We were ordered to rest until relieved from the camps. The gloom of the night, the groans and shrieks of the wounded and dying, and the horrors of the whole scene baffle all description.

[*Holland*] On the seventeenth of October, a day never forgotten by any one present, the British army marched out of camp and surrendered themselves as prisoners of war. It was a glorious day to us. The Tories throughout the country had tauntingly told us months before, that, when Burgoyne's army reached Albany, they would teach us to play "Yankee Doodle" in a way we should never forget. When all was arranged for the surrender, our army formed into lines, that we might have a fine view. When the music was ordered to strike up, it began with "Yankee Doodle."

V

FIRE CAKE AND WATER, SIR

To the south in the late summer of 1777, General Howe's advance against Philadelphia had been successful. All Washington's outnumbered forces could do was to delay the British at Brandywine Creek on 9 September. Less than three weeks later, Howe entered Philadelphia and, after the failure of Washington's thrust at Germantown, the tattered Americans went into miserable, ramshackle winter quarters at Valley Forge.

Surgeon Albigence Waldo of the Connecticut Line keeps a diary of the day-to-day hardships endured by the officers and men.

December 14—Prisoners and Deserters are continually coming in. The Army which has been surprisingly healthy hitherto, now begins to grow sickly from the continued fatigues they have suffered this Campaign. Yet they still show a spirit of Alacrity and Contentment not to be expected from so young Troops. I am Sick-discontented-and out of humor. Poor food—hard lodging—Cold Weather—fatigue—

THE YANKEE'S
RETURN FROM CAMP.

FATHER and I went down to camp,
　Along with Captain Gooding;
There we see the men and boys
　As thick as hasty-pudding.

CHORUS.

Yankee doodle keep it up,
　Yankee doodle dandy;
Mind the music and the step,
　And with the girls be handy.

And there we see a thousand men,
　As rich as 'Squire David;
And what they wasted every day,
　I wish it could be saved.
　　Yankee doodle, &c.

The 'lasses they eat every day,
　Would keep a house a winter;
They have as much that I'll be bound,
　They eat it when they're a mind to.
　　Yankee doodle, &c.

And there we see a swamping gun,
　Large as a log of maple,
Upon a duced little cart,
　A load for father's cattle.
　　Yankee doodle, &c.

And every time they shoot it off,
　It takes a horn of powder;
It makes a noise like father's gun,
　Only a nation louder.
　　Yankee doodle, &c.

I went as nigh to one myself,
　As 'Siah's under-pinning;
And father went as nigh again,
　I thought the deuce was in him.
　　Yankee doodle, &c.

Cousin Simon grew so bold,
　I thought he would have cock'd it;
It scar'd me so I streak'd it off,
　And hung by father's pocket.
　　Yankee doodle, &c.

But Captain Davis has a gun,
　He kind of clap'd his hand on't;
And stuck a crooked stabbing iron,
　Upon the little end on't.
　　Yankee doodle, &c.

And there I see a pumpkin shell,
　As big as mother's bason,
And every time they touch'd it off,
　They scamper'd like the nation.
　　Yankee doodle, &c.

I see a little barrel too,
　The heads were made of leather,
They knock'd upon it with little clubs,
　And call'd the folks together.
　　Yankee doodle, &c.

And there was Captain WASHINGTON,
　And gentlefolks about him;
They say he's grown so tarnal, proud,
　He will not ride without 'em.
　　Yankee doodle, &c.

He got him on his meeting clothes,
　Upon a slapping stallion;
He set the world along in rows,
　In hundreds and in millions.
　　Yankee doodle, &c.

The flaming ribbons in their hats,
　They look'd so tearing fine, ah;
I wanted plaguily to get,
　To give to my Jemima.
　　Yankee doodle, &c.

I see another snarl of men,
　A digging graves, they told me,
So tarnal long, so tarnal deep,
　They 'tended they should hold me.
　　Yankee doodle, &c.

It scar'd me so, I hook'd it off,
　Nor stopp'd, as I remember;
Nor turn'd about till I got home,
　Lock'd up in mother's chamber.
　　Yankee doodle, &c.

Sold, wholesale and retail, by L. DEMING, No. 62, Hanover Street, 2d door from Friend St. Boston.

Nasty Cloaths—nasty Cookery—Vomit half my time—smoak'd out of my senses—the Devil's in't—I can't Endure it—Why are we sent here to starve and freeze—What sweet Felicities have I left at home; A charming Wife—pretty Children—Good Beds—good food—good Cookery—all agreeable—all harmonious. Here all Confusion—smoke and Cold—hunger and filthyness—A pox on my bad luck. There comes a bowl of beef soup—full of burnt leaves and dirt, sickish enough to make a Hector spue. . . . There comes a Soldier, his bare feet are seen thro' his worn out Shoes, his legs nearly naked from the tatter'd remains of an only pair of stockings, his Breeches not sufficient to cover his nakedness, his Shirt hanging in Strings, his hair dishevell'd, his face meagre; his whole appearance pictures a person forsaken and discouraged. He comes, and crys with an air of wretchedness and despair, I am Sick, my feet lame, my legs are sore, my body cover'd with this tormenting Itch—my Cloaths are worn out, my Constitution is broken, my former Activity is exhausted by fatigue, hunger and Cold, I fail fast I shall soon be no more! and all the reward I shall get will be—"Poor Will is dead." People who live at home in Luxury and Ease, quietly possessing their habitations, Enjoying their Wives and Families in peace, have but a very faint idea of the unpleasing sensations, and continual Anxiety the man endures who is in a Camp, and is the husband and parent of an agreeable family. These same People are willing we should suffer every thing for their Benefit and advantage, and yet are the first to Condemn us for not doing more!! . . .

December 16—Cold Rainy Day, Baggage ordered over the Gulph of our Division, which were to march at Ten, but the baggage was order'd back and for the first time since we have been here the Tents were pitch'd, to keep the men more comfortable. Good morning Brother Soldier (says one to another) how are you? All wet I thank'e, hope you are so (says the other). The Enemy have been at Chestnut Hill Opposite to us near our last encampment the other side of Schuylkill, made some Ravages, kill'd two of our Horsemen, taken some prisoners. . . .

December 18—Universal Thanksgiving—a roasted Pig at Night. God be thanked for my health which I have pretty well recovered. . . . Our brethren who are unfortunately Prisoners in Philadelphia meet with the most savage and inhumane treatments that Barbarians are capable of inflicting. Our Enemies do not knock them in the head or burn them with torches to death, or flee them alive, or gradually dismember them till they die, which is customary among Savages and Barbarians. No, they are worse by far. They suffer them to starve, to linger out their lives in extreem hunger. One of these poor unhappy men, drove to the last extreem by the rage of hunger, eat his own fingers up to the first joint from the hand, before he died. Others eat the Clay, the Lime, the Stones of the Prison Walls. Several who died in the Yard had pieces of Bark, Wood, Clay and Stones in their mouths, which the ravings of hunger had caused them to take in for food in the last Agonies of Life! "These are thy mercies, O Brittain!"

December 21—(Valley Forge) Preparations made for hutts. Provisions Scarce. . . . A general cry thro' the Camp this Evening among the Soldiers, "No Meat! No Meat!"—the Distant vales Echo'd back the melancholly sound—"No Meat! No Meat!" Immitating the noise of Crows and Owls, also, made a part of the confused Musick.

What have you for your Dinner Boys? "Nothing but Fire Cake and Water, Sir." At night, "Gentlemen the Supper is ready." What is your Supper Lads? "Fire Cake and Water, Sir." Very poor beef has been drawn in our Camp the greater part of this season. . . .

December 22—Lay excessive Cold and uncomfortable last Night —my eyes are started out from their Orbits like a Rabbit's eyes, occasion'd by a great Cold and Smoke.

What have you got for Breakfast, Lads? "Fire Cake and Water, Sir." The Lord send that our Commissary of Purchases may live (on) Fire Cake and Water, 'till their glutted Gutts are turned to Pasteboard.

Our Division are under Marching Orders this morning. I am ashamed to say it, but I am tempted to steal Fowls if I could find them, or even a whole Hog, for I feel as if I could eat one. But the Impoverish'd Country about us, affords but little matter to employ a Thief, or keep a Clever Fellow in good humour. . . .

This Evening a Party with two field pieces were order'd out. At 12 of the Clock at Night, Providence sent us a little mutton, with which we immediately had some Broth made, and a fine Stomach for same. . . .

December 25, Christmas—We are still in Tents—when we ought to be in huts—the poor sick, suffer much in Tents this cold weather. But we now treat them differently from what they used to be at home, under the inspection of Old Women and Doct. Bolus Linctus. We give them Mutton and Grogg and a Capital Medicine once in a while, to start the Disease from its foundation at once. We avoid Piddling Pills, Powders, Bolus's Linctus's Cordials and all such insignificant matters whose powers are Only render'd important by causing the Patient to vomit up his money instead of his disease. But very few of the sick Men die.

December 26— . . . The Enemy have been some Days the west Schuylkill from Opposite the City to Derby. Their intentions not yet known. The City is at present pretty Clear of them. Why don't his Excellency rush in and retake the City, in which he will doubtless find much Plunder? Because he knows better than to leave his Post and be catch'd like a d—d fool cooped up in the City. He has always acted wisely hitherto. His conduct when closely scrutinised is uncensurable. Were his Inferior Generals as skillfull as himself, we should have the Grandest Choir of Officers ever God made. Many Country Gentlemen in the interior parts of the States who get wrong information of the Affairs and State of our Camp, are very much Surprized at G Washington's delay to drive off the Enemy, being falsely inform'd that his Army consists of double the Number of the Enemy's— such wrong information serves not to keep up the spirit of the People, as they must be by and by undeceiv'd to their no small disappointment—it brings blame on his Excellency, who is deserving of the greatest encomiums; it brings disgrace on the Continental Troops, who have never evidenced the least backwardness in doing their duty, but on the contrary, have cheerfully endur'd a long and very fatigueing Campaign. . . .

*December 28—*Yesterday upwards of fifty officers in Gen Greene's Division resigned their Commissions—Six or Seven of our Regiment are doing the like to-day. All this is occasion'd by Officers Families being so much neglected at home on account Provisions. Their Wages will not buy considerable, purchase a few trifling Comfortables here in camp, and maintain their families at home, while such extravagant prices are demanded for the common necessaries of Life—What then have they to purchase Cloaths and other necessaries with? It is a Melancholly reflection that what is of the most universal importance, is most universally neglected—I mean keeping up the Credit of Money.

The present Circumstances of the Soldier is better by far than the Officers—for the family of the Soldier is provided for at the public expence if the Articles they want are above the common price—but the Officer's family, are obliged not only to beg in the most humble manner for the necessaries of Life—but also to pay for them afterwards at the most exorbitant rates—and even in this manner, many of them who depend entirely on their Money, cannot procure half the material comforts that are wanted in a family—this produces continual letters of complaint from home.

When the Officer has been fatiguing thro-wet and cold and returns to his tent where he finds a letter directed to him from his Wife, fill'd with the most heart aching tender Complaints, a Woman is capable of writing. . . . What man is there—who has the least regard for his family—whose soul would not shrink within him? Who would not be disheartened? . . .

December 29—Snow'd all day pretty briskly. . . . So much talk about discharges among the officers—and so many are discharged—his Excellency lately expressed his fears of being left Alone with the Soldiers only. Strange that our Country will not exert themselves for his support, and save so good—so great a Man from entertaining the least anxious doubt of their Virtue and perseverance in supporting a Cause of such unparallel'd importance! ! . . .

December 30—Eleven Deserters came in to-day—some Hessians and some English—one of the Hessians took an Ax in his hand and cut away the Ice of the Schuylkill which was 1½ inches thick and 40 Rod wide and waded through to our Camp—he was ½ hour in the Water. They had a promise when they engag'd that the war would be ended in one year—they were now tired of the Service. . . .

1778, January 1 New Year—I am alive. I am well. Hutts go on briskly, and our Camp begins to appear like a spacious City. . . .

January 3— . . . To day his Excellency in Orders acquainted the Troops of the Congress's high approbation of their spirited perseverance and good Conduct this Campaign, that . . . the troops may be Supply'd with a greater quantity of Provision than they have been of late; and that a Month's Wages extraordinary shall be given to every Officer and Soldier who shall live in Hutts this Winter.

Good encouragement this, and we think ourselves deserving of it, for the hunger, Thirst, Cold and fatigue we have suffer'd this Campaign, altho' we have not fought much, yet the oldest Soldiers among us have called the Campaign a very severe and a hard one. . . .[11]

VI

NO, BY GOD . . . YOU SHOULD NOT STIR A STEP

In 1780 Americans were stunned when General Benedict Arnold turned traitor. He planned to sell out the stronghold of West Point, commanding the Hudson River. The plot was discovered completely by accident and Arnold escaped to the British, but Major John André, the British officer who was arranging the defection, was captured by three militiamen.

Colonel Alexander Hamilton, John Paulding of the militia, and General Washington relate the occurrences which uncovered Arnold's betrayal.

[*Hamilton*] From several circumstances the project seems to have originated with Arnold himself and to have been long premeditated. The first overture is traced back to some time in June last. It was conveyed in a letter to Col. Robinson: the substance of which was, that the ingratitude he had experienced from his country, concurring, with other causes, had intirely changed his principles, that he now only sought to restore himself to the favour of his king, by some signal proof of his repentance, and would be happy to open a correspondence with Sir Henry Clinton for that purpose. About this period he made a journey to Connecticut, on his return from which to Philadelphia, he solicited the command of West Point; alleging that the effects of his wound had disqualified him for the active duties of the field. The sacrifice of this important post was the atonement he intended to make. General Washington hesitated the less to gratify an officer who had rendered such eminent services, as he was convinced the post might be safely trusted to one, who had given so many distinguished specimens of his bravery. In the beginning of August, he joined the army, and renewed his application. The enemy, at this juncture, had embarked the greatest part of their force on an expedition to Rhode Island; and our army was in motion to compel them to relinquish the enterprise or to attack New York in its weakened state. The General offered Arnold the left wing of the army;

which he declined on the pretext already mentioned, but not without visible embarrassment. He certainly might have executed the duties of such a temporary command, and it was expected from his enterprising temper, that he would gladly have embraced so splendid an opportunity. But he did not choose to be diverted a moment from his favourite object, probably from an apprehension, that some different disposition might have taken place, which would have excluded him. The extreme solicitude he discovered to get possession of the post, would have led to a suspicion of the treachery, had it been possible from his past conduct to have supposed him capable of it.

The correspondence thus begun was carried on between Arnold and Major André, Adjutant General to the British army, in behalf of Sir Henry Clinton, under feigned signatures. . . .

The 20th. of last month [September] Robinson and André went up the River in the Vulture Sloop of War. Robinson sent a flag to Arnold with two letters; one to General Putnam inclosed in another to himself; proposing an interview with Putnam, or in his absence, with Arnold, to adjust some private concerns. The one to General Putnam was evidently meant as a cover to the other, in case by accident, the letters should have fallen under the inspection of a third person.

General Washington crossed the river, in his way to Hartford, the day these dispatches arrived. Arnold conceiving he must have heard of the flag, thought it necessary for the sake of appearances, to submit the letters to him and ask his opinion of the propriety of (comply)ing with the request. The General with his usual caution, though without the least surmise of the design, dissuaded him from it, and advised him to reply to Robinson, that whatever related to his private affairs, must be of a civil nature, and could only properly be addressed to the civil authority. This reference fortunately deranged the plan and was the first link in the chain of events that led to the detection. The interview could no longer take place, in the form of a flag, but was obliged to be managed in a secret manner.

Arnold employed one Smith to go on Board the Vulture the night of the 22d to bring André on shore. . . . André came ashore accordingly, and was conducted within a picket of ours to the house of Smith, where Arnold and he remained together in close conference all that night and the day following. At day light in the morning, the commanding officer at Kings ferry, without the privity of Arnold moved a couple of pieces of cannon to a point opposite to where the vulture lay and obliged her to take a more remote station. This event, or some lurking distrust, made the boatmen refuse to convey the two passengers back, and disconcerted Arnold so much, that by one of those strokes of infatuation, which often confound the schemes of men conscious of guilt, he insisted on André's exchanging his uniform for a disguise, and returning in a mode different from that in which he came. André who had been undesignedly brought within our posts in the first instance remonstrated warmly against this new and dangerous expedient. But Arnold persisting in declaring it impossible for him to return as he came, he at length reluctantly yielded to his direction. Smith furnished the disguise, and in the evening passed Kings ferry with him and proceeded to Crompond where they stopped the remainder of the night (at the instance of a militia officer) to avoid being suspected by him. The next morning they resumed their journey Smith accompanying André a little beyond Pine's bridge, where he left him. He had reached Tarry town, when he was taken up by three militia men, who rushed out of the woods and seized his horse.[12]

[*Paulding*]   Myself, Isaac Van Veart and David Williams, were laying by the side of the road, about a half a mile above Tarry Town, and about fifteen miles from King's-bridge, on Saturday morning, between nine and ten o'clock, the twenty third of September last [1780]. We had lain there about an hour and a half, as near as I can recollect, and saw several persons we were acquainted with, whom we let pass. Presently, one of the young men who was with me said, "There comes a gentleman-like looking man, who appears to be well dressed, and has boots on, who you had better step out and stop if you don't know him." On that I got up and presented my firelock at the breast of the person, and I told him to stand; and then I asked him which way he was going. Says he, "Gentlemen, I hope you belong to our party." I asked him "What party"; he said, "The lower party." Upon that I told him I did. Then he said, "I am a British officer out of the country, on particular business, and I hope you won't detain me a minute," and to show that he was a British officer, he pulled out his watch; upon which I told him to dismount. Upon that, he said, "My God, I must do anything to get 'along' ''; seemed to make a kind of a laugh out of it, and pulled out General Arnold's

Self-portrait of Major John André (*right*) and a powderhorn drawing depicting the story of the treason of Major André and Benedict Arnold.

Pass, which was to John Anderson, to pass all guards to White Plains and further. Upon that he dismounted, and says he, "Gentlemen you had best let me go, or you will bring yourselves in trouble, for, by your stopping of me you will detain the General's business"; and he said he was to go to Dobb's Ferry, to meet a person there, on the General's business. Upon that I told him I hoped he would not be offended, and I told him we did not mean to take anything from him; and told him there were many bad people going along the road, and I did not know but perhaps he might be one; and I asked him if he had any letters about him. He made answer, "No." Upon that, myself, or one of my comrades, though I think myself, told him to pull off his clothes, which he did. We searched his clothes, but could find nothing; and I told him to pull off his boots; he rather seemed backward of pulling them off; however, he pulled off one of them, and I felt at his foot, where I felt the papers in his stocking under his foot; then I told him to pull off the other boot, and when the other boot was off, I found other papers in his stocking, under his foot. Then I looked on the back of the papers, and I saw what the contents of them were, and I said to the young fellows who were with me, "This is a spy." One of the young fellows who were with me asked if he would give up his horse, saddle, and bridle, and watch, and a hundred guineas, if he would let him go. He made answer, "Yes, and whatever sum of money you will mention, or quantity of dry goods." And then I made answer, "No, by God, if you would give us ten thousand guineas, you should not stir a step." One of the young fellows winked at me, who had a mind to find out a little more, and I made answer to the lads who were with me to come along, for I would have nothing more to say to him, and we asked him some questions as we were going along the road, and [he] begged we would ask him none till he came to some officers, and then he would reveal the whole. We carried him to Colonel Jameson and there he took him into custody.[13]

[*Washington*] On my return from Hartford I met Chevalier Luzerne towards evening within about 15 miles of West Point, which I intended to reach that night, but he insisted upon turning back with me to the next public house; where, in politeness to him, I could not but stay all night, determining, however, to get to West Point to breakfast very early. I sent off my baggage and desired Colonel

Hamilton to go forward and inform General Arnold that I would breakfast with him. Soon after he arrived at Arnold's quarters, a letter was delivered to Arnold which threw him into the greatest confusion. He told Colonel Hamilton that something required his immediate attendance at the garrison which was on the opposite side of the river to his quarters; and immediately ordered a horse, to take him to the river; and the barge which he kept to cross, to be ready; and desired Major Franks, his Aid, to inform me when I should arrive that he was gone over the river and would return immediately. When I got to his quarters and did not find him there, I desired Major Franks to order me some breakfast; and as I intended to visit the fortifications I would see General Arnold there.

After I had breakfasted I went over the river, and inquiring for Arnold, the commanding officer told me that he had not been there. I likewise inquired at the several redoubts, but no one could give me any information where he was. The impropriety of his conduct when he knew I was to be there, struck me very forcibly, and my mind misgave me; but I had not the least idea of the real cause. When I returned to Arnold's quarters about two hours after, and told Colonel Hamilton that I had not seen him, he gave me a packet which had just arrived for me from Col. Jemmison, which immediately brought the matter to light. I ordered Colonel Hamilton to mount his horse and proceed with the greatest dispatch to a post on the river about eight miles below, in order to stop the barge if she had not passed; but it was too late. It seems that the letter which Arnold received which threw him in such confusion was from Col. Jemmison, informing him that André was taken and that the papers found upon him were in his possession. Col. Jemmison when André was taken with the papers, could not believe that Arnold was a traitor, but rather that it was an imposition of the British in order to destroy our confidence in Arnold. He, however, immediately on their being taken, despatched an express after me, ordering him to ride night and day till he came up with me. The express went the lower road, which was the road by which I had gone to Connecticut, expecting that I would return by the same route, and that he would meet me; but before he had proceeded far, he was informed that I was returning by the upper road. He then cut across the country and followed my track till I arrived at West Point. He arrived about two hours after and brought the above packet.

When Arnold got down to the barge, he ordered his men, who were very clever fellows and some of the better sort of soldiery, to proceed immediately on board the Vulture sloop of war, as a flag, which was lying down the river; saying that they must be very expeditious, as he must return in a short time to meet me, and promised them two gallons of rum if they would exert themselves. They did, accordingly; but when they got on board the Vulture, instead of their two gallons of rum, he ordered the coxswain to be called down into the cabin and informed him that he and the men must consider themselves as prisoners.

The coxswain was very much astonished, and told him that they came on board under the sanction of a flag. He answered that that was nothing to the purpose; they were prisoners. But the Captain of the Vulture had more generosity than this pitiful scoundrel, and told the coxswain that he would take his parole for going on shore to get his clothes, and whatever else was wanted for himself and his companions. He accordingly came, got his clothes and returned on board. When they got to New York, General Clinton, ashamed of such low and mean action, set them at liberty.[14]

[*Hamilton*] André was without loss of time conducted to the Head Quarters of the army, where he was immediately brought before a board of General officers, to prevent all possibility of misrepresentation or cavil on the part of the enemy. The Board reported, that he ought to be considered as a spy and according to the laws and usages of nations to suffer death; which was executed two days after.

Never perhaps did any man suffer death with more justice, or deserve it less. The first step he took after his capture was to write a letter to General Washington conceived in terms of dignity without insolence and apology without meanness. The scope of it was to vindicate himself from the imputation of having assumed a mean character for treacherous or interested purposes; asserting that he had been involuntarily an impostor, that contrary to his intentions, which was to meet a person for intelligence on neutral ground, he had been betrayed within our posts and forced into the vile condition of an enemy in disguise, soliciting only that to whatever rigor policy might devote him a decency of treatment might be observed, due to a person who though unfortunate had been guilty of nothing dishonorable. His request was granted in its full extent, for in the whole progress of the affair, he was treated with the most scrupulous delicacy. When brought before the Board of Officers, he met with every mark of indulgence and was required to answer no interrogatory, which could even embarrass his feelings. On his part, while he carefully concealed everything that might involve others, he frankly confessed all the facts relating to himself; and upon his confession without the trouble of examining a witness, the Board made their report. The members of it were not more impressed with the candor and firmness mixed with a becoming sensibility, which he displayed than he was penetrated with their liberality and politeness. He acknowleged the generosity of the behaviour towards him, in every respect, but particularly in this, in the strongest terms of manly gratitude. In a conversation with a Gentleman who visited him after his trial, he said he flattered himself he had never been illiberal; but if there were any remains of prejudice, in his mind, his present experience must obliterate them.

In one of the visits I made to him (and I saw him several times during his confinement) he begged me to be the bearer of a request to the General for permission, to send an open letter to Sir Henry Clinton. "I foresee my fate (said he) and though I pretend not to play the hero, or to be indifferent about life; yet I am reconciled to whatever may happen, conscious that misfortune, not guilt, has brought it upon me. There is only one thing that disturbs my tranquility—Sir Henry Clinton has been too good to me; he has been lavish of his kindness. I am bound to him by too many obligations and love him too well to bear the thought, that he should reproach himself, or that others should reproach him, on the supposition of my having conceived myself obliged by his instructions to run the risk I did. I would not for the world leave a sting in his mind, that should embitter his future days." He could scarce finish the sentence, bursting into tears, in spite of his efforts to suppress them; and with difficulty collected himself enough afterwards to add, "I wish to be permitted to assure him, I did not act under this impression, but submitted to a necessity imposed upon me as contrary to my own inclination as to his orders." His request was readily complied with. . . .

When his sentence was announced to him, he remarked, that since it was his lot to die there was still a choice in the mode which would make a material difference to his feelings, and he would be happy, if possible, to be indulged with a professional death. He made a second application by letter in concise, but persuasive terms. It was thought this indulgence being incompatible with the customs of war could not be granted and it was therefore determined in both cases to evade an answer to spare him the sensations, which a certain knowlege of the intended mode would inflict.

In going to the place of execution, he bowed familiarly as he went along to all those with whom he had been acquainted in his confinement. A smile of complacency expressed the serene fortitude of his mind. Arrived at the fatal spot, he asked with some emotion, *must I then die in this manner?* He was told it had been unavoidable. "I am reconciled to my fate (said he) but not to the mode." Soon however recollecting himself, he added, "it will be but a momentary pang," and springing upon the cart performed the last offices to himself with a composure that excited the admiration and melted the hearts of the beholders. Upon being told the final moment was at hand, and asked if he had any thing to say, he answered: "nothing, but to request you will witness to the world, that I die like a brave man." Among the extra ordinary circumstances that attended him, in the midst of his enemies, he died universally esteemed and universally regretted. . . .

VII

GROUND ARMS!

Faced with the task of restoring authority over some extensive area of American soil, the British turned to the southern colonies. They had captured Savannah in 1778, had taken Charleston two years later, and then moved into Virginia. To secure supplies from British ships, Lord Cornwallis led his army into Yorktown. But French naval forces, not British, controlled the waters off the Virginia Capes, and Washington's American and French troops hemmed his army in. Deprived of British sea power, the hideous truth dawned on Cornwallis. He was trapped. In October, 1781, he surrendered his command to Washington. The major fighting of the War of Independence was over. The revolutionists had triumphed.

Surgeon James Thacher describes the siege at Yorktown and the capitulation.

27th Sept. 1781.—We arrived at Yorktown yesterday from Jamestown, and have encamped within one mile of the enemy's line of redoubts.

28th.—The French troops have arrived and encamped on our left. Yorktown is situated on the south bank of the river, about fifteen miles from its entrance into Chesapeake bay. In this little village, Lord Cornwallis, with about seven thousand troops, has taken his station, and is endeavoring to fortify himself against the impending danger of our combined operations. His communication by water is entirely cut off by the French ships of war stationed at the mouth of the river, preventing both his escape and receiving succor from Sir Henry Clinton at New York. The allied army is about twelve thousand strong, exclusive of the militia, under Governor Nelson. The Americans form the right, and the French the left wing of the combined forces, each extending to the borders of the river, by which the besiegers form a half-circle round the town. His Excellency General Washington commands in person, and is assisted by Major-General Lincoln, Baron Steuben, the Marquis de la Fayette, General Knox, &c. The French troops are commanded by General the Count Rochambeau, a brave and experienced officer, having under him a number of officers of distinguished character. Unbounded confidence is reposed in our illustrious commanders, the spirit of emulation and military ardor universally prevails, and we are sanguine in our expectations that a surrender of the royal army must be his lordship's fate. A cannonade commenced yesterday from the town, by which one man was wounded, and I assisted in amputating his leg.

30th.—We were agreeably surprised this morning, to find that the enemy had, during the preceding night, abandoned three or four of their redoubts, and retired within the town, leaving a considerable extent of commanding ground, which might have cost us much labor and many lives to obtain by force. Our light infantry and a party of French were ordered to advance and take possession of the abandoned ground, and to serve as a covering party to our troops who are employed in throwing up breastworks. Considerable cannonading from the besieged in the course of the day, and four militia-men were wounded by a single shot, one of whom died soon after. . . .

October 1st and 2d.—Our troops have been engaged in throwing up two redoubts in the night time; on discovery, the enemy commenced a furious cannonade, but it does not deter our men from going on vigorously with their work. Heavy cannon and mortars are continually arriving, and the greatest preparations are made to prosecute the siege in the most effectual manner. . . .

7th.—A large detachment of the allied army, under command of Major-General Lincoln, were ordered out last evening for the purpose of opening intrenchments near the enemy's lines. This business was conducted with great silence and secrecy, and we were favored by Providence with a night of extreme darkness, and were not discovered before day-light. The working party carried on their shoulders fascines and intrenching tools, while a large part of the detachment was armed with the implements of death. Horses, drawing cannon and ordnance, and wagons loaded with bags filled with sand for constructing breastworks, followed in the rear. Thus arranged, every officer and soldier knowing his particular station, orders were given to advance in perfect silence, the distance about one mile. My station on this occasion was with Dr. Munson, my mate; in the rear of the troops; and as the music was not to be employed, about twenty drummers and fifers were put under my charge to assist me in case of having wounded men to attend. I put into the hands of a drummer, a mulatto fellow, my instruments, bandages, &c., with a positive order to keep at my elbow, and not lose sight of me a moment; it was not long, however, before I found to my astonishment that he had left me, and gone in pursuit of some rum, carrying off the articles which are indispensable in time of action. In this very unpleasant predicament, unwilling to trust another, I hastened with all speed to the hospital, about one mile, to procure another supply from Dr. Craik; and he desired that if the Marquis de la Fayette should be wounded, I would devote to him my first attention.

On my return I found Dr. Munson and my party waiting, but the troops had marched on and we knew not their route. We were obliged to follow at random, and in the darkness of night, hazarding our approach to the enemy. Having advanced about half a mile, of a sudden a party of armed men in white uniform rose from the ground, and ordered us to stop; they proved to be the rear-guard of the French. The officer demanded the countersign, which I was unable to give, and as we could not understand each others' language, I was detained under considerable embarrassment till an officer who could speak English was called, when producing my instruments and bandages, and assuring the French officer that I was surgeon to the infantry, he politely conducted me to my station. Our troops were indefatigable in their labors during the night, and before day-light they had nearly completed the first parallel line of nearly two miles in extent, besides laying a foundation for two redoubts, within about six hundred yards of the enemy's lines. At day-light the enemy, having discovered our works, commenced a severe cannonade, but our men being under cover, received no injury. A French soldier deserted to the enemy; after which, there was a constant firing against the French lines, and one officer was killed, and fifteen men were killed or wounded. In the latter part of the night it rained severely, and being in the open field, cold and uncomfortable, I entered a small hut made of brush, which the enemy had abandoned. Soon after, a man came to the door, and, seeing me standing in the centre, instantly drew his sword, and put himself in an attitude to plunge it into me. I called out *friend, friend,* and he as speedily, to my great joy, responded, "Ah, Monsieur, *friend,*" and returning his sword to its place, he departed. I think he was a French soldier, and it is doubtful whether he or myself was the most frightened.

8th and 9th.—The duty of our troops has been for several days extremely severe; our regiment labors in the trenches every other day and night, where I find it difficult to avoid suffering by the cold, having no other covering than a single blanket in the open field. We erected a battery last night in front of our first parallel, without any annoyance from the enemy. Two or three of our batteries being now prepared to open on the town, his Excellency General Washington put the match to the first gun, and a furious discharge of cannon and mortars immediately followed, and Earl Cornwallis has received his first salutation.

From the 10th to the 15th, a tremendous and incessant firing from the American and French batteries is kept up, and the enemy return the fire, but with little effect. A red-hot shell from the French battery set fire to the Charon, a British 44-gun ship, and two or three smaller vessels at anchor in the river, which were consumed in the night. From the bank of the river, I had a fine view of this splendid conflagration. The ships were enwrapped in a torrent of fire, which spreading with vivid brightness among the combustible rigging, and running with amazing rapidity to the tops of the several masts, while all around was thunder and lightning from our numerous cannon and mortars, and in the darkness of night, presented one of the most sublime and magnificent spectacles which can be imagined. Some of our shells, overreaching the town, are seen to fall into the river, and bursting, throw up columns of water like the spouting of the monsters of the deep.

We have now made further approaches to the town, by throwing up a second parallel line, and batteries within about three hundred yards; this was effected in the night, and at day-light the enemy were roused to the greatest exertions; the engines of war have raged with redoubled fury and destruction on both sides, no cessation day or night. The French had two officers wounded, and fifteen men killed or wounded, and among the Americans, two or three were wounded. I assisted in amputating a man's thigh.

The siege is daily becoming more and more formidable and alarming, and his lordship must view his situation as extremely critical, if not desperate. Being in the trenches every other night and day, I have a fine opportunity of witnessing the sublime and stupendous scene which is continually exhibiting. The bombshells from the besiegers and the besieged are incessantly crossing each others' path in the air. They are clearly visible in the form of a black ball in the day, but in the night, they appear like a fiery meteor with a blazing tail, most beautifully brilliant, ascending majestically from the mortar to a certain altitude, and gradually descending to the spot where they are destined to execute their work of destruction. It is astonishing with what accuracy an experienced gunner will make his calculations, that a shell shall fall within a few feet of a given point, and burst at the precise time, though at a great distance. When a shell falls, it whirls round, burrows, and excavates the earth to a considerable extent, and bursting, makes dreadful havoc around. I have more than once witnessed fragments of the mangled bodies and limbs of the British soldiers thrown into the air by the bursting of our shells. . . .

The enemy having two redoubts, about three hundred yards in front of their principal works, which enfiladed our intrenchment and impeded our approaches, it was resolved to take possession of them both by assault. The one on the left of the British garrison, bordering on the banks of the river, was assigned to our brigade of light-infantry, under the command of the Marquis de la Fayette. The advanced

corps was led on by the intrepid Colonel Hamilton, who had commanded a regiment of light-infantry during the campaign. The assault commenced at eight o'clock in the evening, and the assailants bravely entered the fort with the point of the bayonet without firing a single gun. We suffered the loss of eight men killed, and about thirty wounded. Major Campbell, who commanded in the fort, was wounded and taken prisoner, with about thirty soldiers, the remainder made their escape. . . .

During the assault, the British kept up an incessant firing of cannon and musketry from their whole line. His Excellency General Washington, Generals Lincoln and Knox, with their aids, having dismounted, were standing in an exposed situation waiting the result. Colonel Cobb, one of General Washington's aids, solicitous for his safety, said to his excellency, "Sir, you are too much exposed here. Had you not better step a little back?" "Colonel Cobb," replied his excellency, "if you are afraid, you have liberty to step back." The other redoubt on the right of the British lines was assaulted at the same time by a detachment of the French. Such was the ardor displayed by the assailants, that all resistance was soon overcome, though at the expense of nearly one hundred men killed and wounded. . . .

16th.—A party of the enemy, consisting of about four hundred men, commanded by Colonel Abercrombie, about four in the morning, made a vigorous sortie against two unfinished redoubts occupied by the French; they spiked up seven or eight pieces of cannon and killed several soldiers, but the French advanced and drove them from the redoubts, leaving several killed and wounded. Our New England troops have now become very sickly; the prevalent diseases are intermittent and remittent fevers, which are very prevalent in this climate during the autumnal months.

17th.—The whole of our works are now mounted with cannon and mortars; not less than one hundred pieces of heavy ordnance have been in continual operation during the last twenty-four hours. The whole peninsula trembles under the incessant thunderings of our infernal machines; we have leveled some of their works in ruins, and silenced their guns; they have almost ceased firing. We are so near as to have a distinct view of the dreadful havoc and destruction of their works, and even see the men in their lines tore to pieces by the bursting of our shells.

But the scene is drawing to a close. Lord Cornwallis, at length realizing the extreme hazard of his deplorable situation, and finding it in vain any longer to resist, has this forenoon come to the humiliating expedient of sending out a flag, requesting a cessation of hostilities for twenty-four hours, that commissioners may be appointed to prepare and adjust the terms of capitulation. Two or three flags passed in the course of the day, and General Washington consented to a cessation of hostilities for two hours only, that his lordship may suggest his proposals as a basis for a treaty, which being in part accepted, a suspension of hostilities will be continued till to-morrow.

18th.—. . . At an early hour this forenoon General Washington communicated to Lord Cornwallis the general basis of the terms of capitulation, which he deemed admissible, and allowed two hours for his reply. Commissioners were soon after appointed to prepare the particular terms of agreement. The gentlemen appointed by General Washington are Colonel Laurens, one of his aid-de-camps, and Viscount Noaille of the French army. They have this day held an interview with the two British officers on the part of Lord Cornwallis, the terms of capitulation are settled, and being confirmed by the commanders of both armies, the royal troops are to march out to-morrow and surrender their arms. . . .

19th.—This is to us a most glorious day; but to the English, one of bitter chagrin and disappointment. . . . At about twelve o'clock, the combined army was arranged and drawn up in two lines extending more than a mile in length. The Americans were drawn up in a line on the right side of the road, and the French occupied the left. At the head of the former, the great American commander, mounted on his noble courser, took his station, attended by his aids. At the head of the latter was posted the excellent Count Rochambeau and his suite. The French troops, in complete uniform, displayed a martial and noble appearance, their band of music, of which the timbrel formed a part, is a delightful novelty, and produced while marching to the ground a most enchanting effect. The Americans, though not all in uniform, nor their dress so neat, yet exhibited an erect, soldierly air, and every countenance beamed with satisfaction and joy. The concourse of spectators from the country was prodigious, in point of numbers was probably equal to the military, but universal silence and order prevailed.

It was about two o'clock when the captive army advanced through the line formed for their reception. Every eye was prepared to gaze on Lord Cornwallis, the object of peculiar interest and solicitude; but he disappointed our anxious expectations; pretending indisposition, he made General O'Hara his substitute as the leader of his army. This officer was followed by the conquered troops in a slow and solemn step, with shouldered arms, colors cased, and drums beating a British march. Having arrived at the head of the line, General O'Hara, elegantly mounted, advanced to his excellency the commander-in-chief, taking off his hat, and apologized for the non-appearance of Earl Cornwallis.

With his usual dignity and politeness, his excellency pointed to Major-General Lincoln for directions, by whom the British army was conducted into a spacious field, where it was intended they should ground their arms. The royal troops, while marching through the line formed by the allied army, exhibited a decent and neat appearance, as respects arms and clothing, for their commander opened his store, and directed every soldier to be furnished with a new suit complete, prior to the capitulation. But in their line of march we remarked a disorderly and unsoldierly conduct, their step was irregular, and their ranks frequently broken.

But it was in the field, when they came to the last act of the drama, that the spirit and pride of the British soldier was put to the severest test: here their mortification could not be concealed. Some of the platoon officers appeared to be exceedingly chagrined when giving the word *"ground arms,"* and I am a witness that they performed this duty in a very unofficer-like manner; and that many of the soldiers manifested a *sullen temper,* throwing their arms on the pile with violence, as if determined to render them useless. This irregularity, however, was checked by the authority of General Lincoln. After having grounded their arms and divested themselves of their accoutrements, the captive troops were conducted back to Yorktown, and guarded by our troops till they could be removed to the place of their destination.[15]

In the first decade of the nineteenth century, the Army explored the vast territory west of the Mississippi and struggled against the Indian menace in the wilderness of the Old Northwest.

Cornwallis resigning his sword at Yorktown. This photograph was taken from a pitcher with a copper luster.

VIII

OURS WAS A BLOODY VICTORY, THEIRS A BLOODY DEFEAT

White settlers were steadily infringing upon the redman's hunting grounds. After a series of treaties, culminating with the purchase of three million acres in 1809, pioneers pushed far up the valley of the Wabash River in Indiana. The Shawnee leader, Tecumseh, and his brother, "The Prophet," traveled from tribe to tribe trying to confederate the Indians from the Gulf to the Great Lakes. Headquartered at "Prophet's Town," they proclaimed the cession of 1809 invalid. Tecumseh's departure to organize the southern tribes gave the Governor of Indiana Territory, William Henry Harrison, his opportunity to inflict what he hoped would be a crushing defeat upon the hostiles. Plodding up the Wabash from Vincennes, Harrison's frontiersmen were surprised by a savage attack just before dawn on 7 November 1811. The Americans, averting defeat, rallied and beat off the attackers. They pressed on and, after the Indians had abandoned "Prophet's Town," they destroyed it.

Soldiers Adam Walker, Isaac Naylor, William Brigham, Sergeant Orr, and Charles Larrabee describe the expedition and the tide of battle at Tippecanoe.

This victory helped elect Harrison President of the United States in 1840 but, instead of ending the Indian wars, the defeat roused the redman to widespread attacks along the frontier.

[*Walker*] 27 September.—The army was embodied, consisting of between ten and twelve hundred men; and under the immediate command of Gov. Harrison, we took up our line of march from Vincennes, being well furnished with arms, ammunition and provision.

In this manner we proceeded on our march by the taps of the drums at the head of each column, to prevent the lines distancing each other too far. It was customary each morning, an hour before day-break, to rouse the troops from their slumbers, with three solitary taps of the drums of each line, when they turned out and formed in front of their tents, which was the line of battle in case of an attack; in this manner they stood to their arms until the beating of the Reveillee. This precaution was deemed a very necessary one, knowing it to be the time that the Indians generally choose to make their attacks, as the troops sleep more sound, and the sentinels become wearied and sleepy, and consequently less vigilant.

Oct. 3.—After a march of six days, through an uninhabited country, we arrived at a place on the banks of the Wabash, called Battelle des Illinois. Here we formed our encampment with the intention of tarrying a few weeks, to ascertain more correctly the disposition of the Prophet and his warriors. A Fort and Block-Houses were ordered to be built at this place, which gave sufficient employment to the militia. . . .

About this time many Indians came peaceably into camp, and held frequent Council, with the Governor; but all endeavors to effect an accommodation with the Prophet were vain—they still continued stubborn and refractory—and would not listen to any terms of peace made them by the Governor. Their lurking Indians were nightly prowling about our encampment, and alarming the sentinels on their posts. On the 20th Oct. in the evening, an Indian crept cautiously through the bushes, opposite one of the sentinels in the main guard and shot him through both thighs—the sentinel nearest to him, saw the flash of the rifle, and immediately presented his piece—snapped it twice—both times it missed fire!—The Indian made his escape—the camp was alarmed, and the troops called to arms. The Dragoons were instantly formed, and under the command of that gallant and spirited officer, Major Daviess, sallied out, and scoured the woods in the vicinity of the encampment; but no Indians could be found. The Dragoons in passing the line of sentinels, were fired upon by mistake, the sentinels supposing them to be the enemy (it being very dark) but fortunately no one was injured. We stood to our arms the whole of this night, while the Gov. and Col. Boyd were riding down the lines animating the troops to do their duty in case we were attacked.

Thus after a tedious course of negociations, and fruitless endeavors to effect by fair means, a redress of our wrongs, and the patience of the Governor and of the army being nearly exhausted, it was determined to give them some *weightier* reasons than had been heretofore offered, why peace should be concluded. Orders were therefore given for the army to be in readiness to march to the Prophet's town.

October 21.—We commenced our march from Fort *Harrison.* . . . Having a number of sick who were unable to proceed farther, a small block-house was erected, for their accommodation, and a Sergeant's guard was left for their protection.

Nov. 1.—We crossed the Vermillion river into the Indian possessions, at which time the weather became rainy and cold. Many Indians were discovered by our spies, lurking in the woods about us; supposed to be the scouts of the Prophet, watching our movements. After marching about fourteen miles, we crossed a small creek, and encamped on a high open piece of land: still rainy and cold. An alarm was here given by one of the sentinels, who fired on a Horse, which had strayed out of Camp.

November 3.—Continued on our march—came to an extensive level prairie, which took up the whole of this day in crossing—started up many deer, two of which we killed—also an animal called a prairie wolf. Nothing of importance transpired until——

November 6.—When our spies, who had ventured near the Indian village, returned, and informed the Governor we were within a few miles of the Prophet's town—We were ordered to throw off our knapsacks, and be in preparation for an attack. We advanced about 4 miles to the edge of a piece of woods, when we were ordered to break off by companies, and advance in single lines; keeping a convenient distance from each other to enable us to form a line of battle, should necessity require it—this was frequently done in the course of our advance toward the town, in consequence of the unevenness of the land, and the appearance of many favorable places for the enemy to attack us. In this manner we advanced very cautiously, until we came in sight of the Indian village, when we halted. The Indians appeared much surprized and terrified at our sudden appearance before their town; we perceived them running in every direction about the village, apparently in great confusion; their object however, was to regain in season their different positions behind a breastwork of logs which encircled the town from the bank of the Wabash. A chief came out to the Governor, begging of him not to proceed to open hostilities; but to encamp with the troops for that night, and in the morning they solemnly promised to come into camp and hold a council, and they would agree to almost any terms the Governor might propose; expressing their earnest desire for peace without bloodshed—but the treacherous villains merely made this promise to gain sufficient time to put their infernal scheme in execution. The Governor enquired of the chief where a situation suitable for encamping might be found; being informed, he dispatched three or four officers to examine the ground, who returned with a favorable report of the place—which was a piece of narrow rising ground, covered with heavy timber, running some length into a marshy prairie, and about three quarters of a mile north-west of the town. Here we encamped for the night, as near the form of a hollowsquare as the nature of the ground would admit. Being cool, cloudy weather, we built large fires in front of our tents, to dry our clothing, cook our provisions &c.[16]

[*Naylor*]　About ten o'clock at night Joseph Warnock and myself retired to rest, he taking one side of the fire and I the other, the other members of our company being all asleep. My friend Warnock had dreamed, the night before, a bad dream which foreboded something fatal to him or to some of his family, as he told me. Having myself no confidence in dreams, I thought but little about the matter, although I observed that he never smiled afterwards.

I awoke about four o'clock the next morning, after a sound and refreshing sleep, having heard in a dream the firing of guns and the whistling of bullets just before I awoke from my slumber. A drizzling rain was falling and all things were still and quiet throughout the camp. I was engaged in making a calculation when I should arrive at home.[17]

[*Brigham*]　At 3 o'clock I again took post; very dark and rainy. I had resumed my station about half an hour, when I heard a faint whistle, not far from Wm. Brown's post, as I supposed—he called to me; but I did not think it prudent to answer—however, after he had called several times, I answered "holloa"—says he, "look sharp"— (the usual word of *caution* between sentinels)—I kneeled down, with my gun on a charge. It was so very dark that no object could be discerned within three feet of me, and I could hear nothing except the rustling noise occasioned by the falling rain among the bushes. At this time, Brown, (being much alarmed) very imprudently left his post, and came towards me. I heard light footsteps—presented my gun, and should have fired upon him had he not that moment spoke, much agitated—"Brigham, let us fire and run in—you may depend on it there are Indians in the bushes." I told him not to fire yet for fear we should give a false alarm. While we were standing together, something struck in the brush near us, (I suppose an arrow)—we were both frightened and run in without firing—the Indians close upon our heels—we passed swiftly by Capt. Barton's tents.

[*Orr*] I was partly asleep, when some person rushed by and touched the corner of the tent—I sprang partly up—all was still. I jogged Corpl. Thomas, (who slept in the same tent) and asked, "if he did not hear somebody run by the tent?"—He said, "no—I've been asleep." I then laid down again, when something struck the top of the tent—Corpl. Thomas rose up, took his gun; in a moment three or four rifles were discharged at the very door of the tent, and an awful yell ensued—Thomas fell back on to me—I said, "Corpl. Thomas, for God's sake don't give back"—he made me no answer— for he was a dead man.—I got out of the tent as soon as possible— the men were in confusion, some in front and some in the rear of the tents firing—the Indians within a rod of us. Capt. Barton ordered the men to form instantly—they were too much broken, and no regular line could be formed; but they kept up a steady fire on the Indians, who fell back. Capt. Griger's company of militia, stationed near us, were in great confusion—they could hardly be distinguished from the Indians—I received a wound and was obliged to retire.[18]

[*Naylor*] I heard the crack of a rifle, followed by an awful Indian yell all around the encampment. In less than a minute I saw the Indians charging our line most furiously and shooting a great many rifle balls into our camp fires, throwing the live coals into the air three or four feet high.

At this moment my friend Warnock was shot by a rifle ball through his body. He ran a few yards and fell dead on the ground. Our lines were broken and a few Indians were found on the inside of the encampment. In a few moments they were all killed. Our lines closed up and our men in their proper places. One Indian was killed in the back part of Captain Griger's tent, while he was attempting to tomahawk the Captain. . . .

A young man, whose name was Daniel Pettit, was pursued so closely and furiously by an Indian as he was running from the guard fire to our lines, that to save his life he cocked his rifle as he ran and turning suddenly round, placed the muzzle of his gun against the body of the Indian and shot an ounce ball through him. The Indian fired his gun at the same instant, but it being longer than Pettit's the muzzle passed by him and set fire to a handkerchief which he had tied round his head.

[*Larrabee*]   the manner the indians faught was desperate   thay would rush with horid yelds in bodies upon the lines   being driven back, they would remain in perfect silance for a few seconds, then would whistle (on an instrument made for that purpose) and then commence the rush again, while others would creep up close to the lines on their hands and knees, and get behind trees for their support.[19]

[*Walker*]   One company of Indiana militia fell back in great disorder, but after some arduous exertions of their officers, they were again rallied and fought with a spirit that evinced a determination to escape the odium of cowardice. The battle had now become general, every musket and rifle contributed its share to the work of carnage. A few Indians had placed themselves in an advantageous situation on the left of the front line, and being screened from our fire by some large oak trees, did great execution in our ranks. The small company of U.S. Riflemen, commanded by Lieut. Hawkins, were stationed within two rods of these trees, and received the heaviest of their fire, but maintained the position in a most gallant manner, altho' the company of militia on their left were giving way in great disorder. Major Daviess, with a small detachment of dragoons attempted to dislodge them; but failed in the attempt, and was himself mortally wounded. Capt. Snelling, of the regulars, soon after made a desperate charge at the head of his company, with success, losing one man, who was tomahawked by a wounded Indian. The Indians fell back, and for a short time, continued the action at a distance—here was some sharp shooting, as they had greatly the advantage, by the light afforded them from our fires, which could not be entirely extinguished. We were well supplied with buck shot cartridges, which were admirably calculated for an engagement of this nature. The savages were severely galled by the steady and well directed fire of the troops. . . . The awful yell of the savages, seeming rather the shrieks of despair, than the shouts of triumph—the tremendous roar of musquetry—the agonizing screams of the wounded and dying, mingling in tumultuous uproar, formed a scene that can better be imagined than described. . . .

Capt. Baen, who had been with us but a few days, was shockingly mangled with the tomahawk—he was taken up in a delirious state, and died a short time afterwards. There was but one other instance of any person being tomahawked in this engagement; which was a private soldier of Capt. Snelling's company, upon a charge in the midst of the Indians.

Gen. Harrison received a shot through the rim of his hat. In the heat of the action, his voice was frequently heard and easily distinguished, giving his orders in the same calm, cool, and collected manner with which we had been used to receive them on a drill or parade.

[Naylor] Just after daylight the Indians retreated across the prairie toward their town, carrying off their wounded. This retreat was from the right flank of the encampment, commanded by Captains Spencer and Robb, having retreated from the other portions of the encampment a few minutes before. As their retreat became visible, an almost deafening and universal shout was raised by our men. "Huzza! Huzza! Huzza!" This shout was almost equal to that of the savages at the commencement of the battle; ours was the shout of victory, theirs was the shout of ferocious but disappointed hope.

The morning light disclosed the fact that the killed and wounded of our army, numbering between eight and nine hundred men, amounted to one hundred and eight. Thirty-six Indians were found near our lines. Many of their dead were carried off during the battle. . . . Ours was a bloody victory, theirs a bloody defeat.

Soon after breakfast an Indian chief was discovered on the prairie, about eighty yards from our front line, wrapped in a piece of white cloth. He was found by a soldier by the name of Miller, a resident of Jeffersonville, Indiana. The Indian was wounded in one of his legs, the ball having penetrated his knee and passed down his leg, breaking the bone as it passed. Miller put his foot against him and he raised up his head and said: "Don't kill me, don't kill me." At the same time five or six regular soldiers tried to shoot him, but their muskets snapped and missed fired. Major Davis Floyd came riding toward him with dragoon sword and pistols and said he "would show them how to kill Indians," when a messenger came from General Harrison commanding that he should be taken prisoner. He was taken into camp, where the surgeons dressed his wounds. Here he refused to speak a word of English or tell a word of truth. Through the medium of an interpreter he said that he was a friend to the white people and that the Indians shot him, while he was coming to camp to tell General Harrison that they were about to attack the army. He refused to have his leg amputated, though he was told that amputation was the only means of saving his life. . . . In accordance with his request he was left to die, in company of an old squaw, who was found in the Indian town the next day after he was taken prisoner. They were left in one of our tents.

At the time this Indian was taken prisoner, another Indian, who was wounded in the body, rose to his feet in the middle of the prairie, and began to walk towards the woods on the opposite side. A number of regular soldiers shot at him but missed him. A man who was a member of the same company with me, Henry Huckleberry, ran a few steps into the prairie and shot an ounce ball through his body and he fell dead near the margin of the woods. Some Kentucky volunteers went across the prairie immediately and scalped him, dividing his scalp into four pieces, each one cutting a hole in each piece, putting his ramrod through the hole, and placing his part of the scalp just behind the first thimble of his gun, near its muzzle. Such was the fate of nearly all of the Indians found dead on the battleground, and such was the disposition of their scalps.

The death of Owen, and the fact that Daviess was mortally wounded, with the remembrance also that a large portion of Kentucky's best blood had been shed by the Indians, must be their apology for this barbarous conduct. Such conduct will be excused by all who witnessed the treachery of the Indians, and saw the bloody scenes of this battle.

Tecumseh being absent at the time of battle, a chief called White Loon was the chief commander of the Indians. He was seen in the morning after the battle, riding a large white horse in the woods across the prairie, where he was shot by a volunteer named Montgomery, who is now living in the southwest part of this State. At the crack of his rifle the horse jumped as if the ball had hit him. The Indian rode off toward the town and we saw him no more. During the battle the prophet was safely located on a hill, beyond the reach of our balls, praying to the Great Spirit to give the victory to the Indians. . . .

We had about forty head of beef cattle when we came to the battle. They all ran off the night of the battle, or they were driven off by the Indians, so that they were all lost. We received rations for two days on the morning after the action. We received no more rations until the next Tuesday evening, being six days afterwards. The Indians having retreated to their town, we performed the solemn duty of consigning to their graves our dead soldiers, without shrouds or coffins. They were placed in graves about two feet deep, from five to ten in each grave.

General Harrison having learned that Tecumseh was expected to return from the south with a number of Indians whom he had enlisted in his cause, called a council of his officers, who advised him to remain on the battlefield and fortify his camp by a breastwork of logs around, about four feet high. This work was completed during the day and all the troops were placed immediately behind each line of the work when they were ordered to pass the watchword from right to left every five minutes, so that no man was permitted to sleep during the night. The watchword on the night before the battle was "Wide awake, Wide awake." To me it was a long, cold, cheerless night.

On the next day the dragoons went to Prophet's town, which they found deserted by all the Indians, except an old squaw, whom they brought into the camp and left her with the wounded chief before mentioned. The dragoons set fire to the town and it was all consumed, casting up a brilliant light amid the darkness of the ensuing night. I arrived at the town when it was about half on fire. I found large quantities of corn, beans and peas. I filled my knapsack with these articles and carried them to the camp and divided them with the members of our mess, consisting of six men. Having these articles of food, we declined eating horse-flesh, which was eaten by a large portion of our men.

[*Walker*] *Nov. 9.*—After destroying considerable of our baggage, in order to make room in the waggons for the conveyance of the wounded, we began our march on the return to Vincennes expecting the Indians would follow and attack us. Such an event was greatly to be dreaded; as we were nearly out of provisions, and had up-

General Harrison leading his troops at the Battle of Tippecanoe, 1811.

Sortie at Fort Meigs, War of 1812.

wards of a hundred and thirty wounded men to be attended to, who were painfully situated in the waggons, especially those who had broken limbs, by their continual jolting, on an unbeaten road through the wilderness.

Having suffered severely in consequence of the light afforded the Indians from our fires in the late attack, we adopted another method on our return, by building large fires some distance beyond the line of sentinels, while those in the encampment were extinguished on our retiring to rest; which in case of an attack, would have been of much service by placing the enemy between us and the fires. The sentinels on post at night having been frequently alarmed by lurking Indians, would place a stake in the ground about the height of a man, and hang their blanket and cap upon it, and retire a few paces behind some log or tree; as it had become hazardous for sentinels to walk their posts while the Indians were continually hovering about them. It was said that arrows had been found in some of the blankets put up in this manner, which is very probable, as they would approach within a few feet of a sentinel in the stillest night, without being discovered, as was the case at Fort Harrison, where a sentinel was shot down by an Indian, who had made his way through a thicket of bushes directly in front, and within twelve feet of the man on post.

On the 14th we arrived at the small block-house on the Vermillion river. . . .

We suffered much for the want of provisions during our march to this place. Many of the troops had made use of horse meat to satisfy their craving appetites for the last 5 days. Col. Miller, then at Fort Harrison, being apprized of our destitute situation, immediately dispatched a boat with fresh provisions to our relief, which fortunately arrived at the block-house nearly at the same time with the army. . . .

Nov. 19.—Arrived at Vincennes and immediately after were placed in excellent quarters, and every possible attention paid to the sick and wounded, by Gov. Harrison and Col. Boyd, who always evinced the most anxious solicitude for the welfare of their soldiers.

Angry western frontiersmen, inflamed by alleged British-sponsored Indian massacres, and southern planters, with maritime grievances against Great Britain, manipulated a declaration of war in 1812. With the United States woefully unprepared, its army ill-equipped and harassed by incompetent officers, the American invasions of Canada in 1812 and 1813 petered out despite extravagant boasts of quick victory. In 1814 the Redcoats assailed American soil and put the torch to Washington. The Americans whipped the enemy fleets on Lake Erie (1813) and on Lake Champlain (1814), but the tiny ocean-going Navy, although defeating the British in several brilliant single-ship victories, was virtually cancelled out. When peace came, the Redcoats had had the best of the fighting. Men-of-war tightly blockaded the American coasts, the enemy was poised to attack New Orleans, and British soldiers occupied about one-half of Maine and a larger area on the northwestern frontier. The United States happily accepted a restoration of the status quo in the Treaty of Ghent (1814).

IX

THE WHISKEY . . . FROZE HARD

In the spring of 1812 the War Department ordered an aging veteran of the Revolutionary War, Brigadier General William Hull, to march his troops through the wilderness from Dayton, Ohio, to Detroit to invade Upper Canada. Hull's force stumbled into Detroit in mid-July. Anxious lest his communications be impaired, the General asked the War Department to secure control of Lake Erie before he advanced further.

Meanwhile in the far Northwest, the British commander at St. Joseph's on the Sault forced the Americans at Michilimackinac to surrender on 17 July. At Detroit, Hull demanded the Americans at Fort Dearborn (Chicago) rush him reinforcements. The Indians captured part and tomahawked the rest of this detachment. Hull's anxiety increased. When the British general marched his troops in sight of Detroit and demanded surrender, the timid Hull capitulated without firing a shot. The invasion of Canada collapsed on 16 August 1812.

To militiaman Nathan Newsom and his friends congregating at

Urbana, Ohio, this surrender was "disgraceful," "horrid," "pitiful."
He tells of his day-to-day army life, the hardships of the wilderness,
and of an expedition into Indian country.

We had been at Urbana only very few days until the ever disgraceful and memorable act of Hull the traitor happened. The scene was horrid and pitiful. Some men who happened not to be convenient when Hull sold them, took their flight through the wilderness as they could, and passed by Urbana in small parties in the utmost despair. The company of Captain Brush were from the neighborhood of Chillicothe—they passed through Urbana to their homes in quite small parties for several successive days in the most abject appearance and lowness of spirit. Anger and indignation were apparent in the countenance of every man, at the infamous conduct of Hull, who had not only committed treason of the highest degree, but had put a blot on the fair character of the American people.

From the 20th of August to the 14th of September, nothing very extraordinary appeared—Urbana exhibited a scene of military preparation. Troops were coming and troops were going. We were daily trained to military discipline. . . .

Oct. 1st. On the first day of Oct., about ten o'clock A.M. we struck our tents, and after some concomical parade through the streets of Urbana, in the presence of and under the command of Governor Meigs, to which the private soldiers were apparently averse we left Urbana regulating our guard in order of march, the same as we expected to do, when we arrived in the enemy's country. . . . We pitched our tents that evening on an eastern branch of Mad river, called King's Creek, between three & four miles from Urbana. The men generally composing this army are volunteers, drafted men, or substitutes. An idea was held out to the volunteers when they volunteered, that so soon that they entered into the service for six months, $16 would be advanced to them for clothing; as also 2 months pay at $5 per month. But nearly two months expired before any pay could be drawn, at which time they received only two months pay. Many of the men being not prepared with winter clothing they attributed it to this disappointment, and considerable cursing and discontent was manifested by the troops. . . .

We were somewhere about 800 men strong when we left Urbana. Desertions were frequent, but with very little or no injury to the army, as none but the most trifling characters deserted. On the night of the 3d an express arrived stating that a large body of Indians were advancing, which created a great desire in the troops to meet them. All hands rose in the night and prepared to start early in the morning. And on the 4th, it being Sunday, we marched about 5 miles, crossed Mad river, and encamped on the bank. . . .

On the 7th October we struck our tents on the banks of Mad river, and marched up the river some miles, then turned a north direction from it to M'Pherson's Block house, where we encamped; it being 21 miles from Urbana. . . . Many Indian families arrived at M'Pherson's Block house on the same day we did, who had fled from the hostile Indians for protection to the army. . . . Many of their warriors have turned out with our spies and participate in our victories and in our defeats. They left their squaws and children here.

Most of our officers as well as the men are as yet destitute of the qualifications requisite in military life. . . .

On the 11th General Tupper returned to our encampment from the troops stationed under the command of General Harrison and Winchester. He had left us when we were stationed at Urbana to take the command of some troops in that quarter. . . .

On the 12th, we struck our tents at McPherson's Blockhouse and marched about 6 miles to Solomon's Town, a place evacuated by the Indians. . . .

On the 13th, . . . an Indian came into camp. He passed the guard by leave of the officer of the guard. He made some inquiry about the number of tents &c which created some suspicion in the men. He was put under guard. The officers were obliged to put him under a strong guard, for fear the soldiers would raise a mob and kill him. On the 14th, early in the morning; the officers sent for Captain Lewis, a notorious influential Indian, who had taken an active part in favor of the Americans, and it was supposed he had a knowledge of all friendly Indians in this part of the country. Lewis appeared, attended by several distinguished personages of the savage race, as also some of their squaws, who interested, attended on the occasion. Lewis, as well as the other Chiefs and squaws, claimed the prisoner Indian as one of the friendly party. The officers of course let him go. This act exasperated some of the inferior officers as well as the soldiers; Because some of the soldiers in the army who had been at Detroit and along the British line were willing to take their oath as to the identity of the before stated prisoner Indian;—and that they knew him to be a British Indian. Under these circumstances the commotions of the soldiers were such as really appeared dangerous to the army. . . . On the 15th two men were punished. They had to ride a rail in front of the line, carried by two men. Their crime was desertion.

On the 16th, two men were marched in front of the line, in conformity with their sentence. The one for complaining that the Indians were more respected and better treated by the commanding officers, than the soldiers. The other for getting drunk and sleeping on his post. . . .

On the night of the 21st, there were several guns fired in succession by the sentinels. It being about 9 o'clock. No individual could easy believe otherways, but that it was the beginning of a formidable attack by the Indians. Every man (some excepted) took hold of his arms, and ran with joy, thinking an opportunity was now offering to avenge himself of the savage enemies of his country. In a few minutes time every line was arrayed in battleform, and rushed on to meet the enemy; But on right examination no enemies were found. However, two or three sentinels asserted, that several men were seen by them out side of the line, and they did not answer when hailed; they fired on them conformable with their orders. On the 22d, the army was paraded in a hollow square. . . .

Three prisoners were brought up who were substitutes for drafted men; their crime was desertion. Their sentence was read to them and put into execution immediately after. They were stripped naked, their pantaloons excepted. Their backs were daubed with tar, to make a paper stick thereon, containing their crime in very large letters. Their hands and feet were tied together; and in this position they were hung by hand and feet to a rail and carried by the front of the lines; afterwards there left eye-brows were shaved. They were afterwards ordered to be taken to the guard-house, and there left hand kuffed, and on half rations, during four days, before liberated. On Friday 23d of October all hands (the guard and sick excepted) fell to forming what they called a brestwork. This mighty fortification was made out of brush, built square;—a road left open to each guard house. . . .

On the 24th as also the 25th, numbers of men were allowed to go into the woods with their rifles. They over run every part of the country adjacent to Soloman town in every direction a great distance.

From the great similarity of the surface of the country two men were lost; one of them encamped out from the army one night; the other encamped out two nights and had altogether lost himself. On the second day he accidentally met with a friendly Indian, named Joseph Lewis, about 18 or 20 miles from the army. The Indian displayed considerable friendship towards him, and shewed him which way the army was, in fact accompanied him, until they arrived near the army. The person so lost was Ensign Nathan Burwell. . . .

October 31st, about 8 or 9 o'clock A.M. we struck our tents and marched about 10 miles to M'Arthur's Block house.

November 1st, 2d, 3d and 4th teams were arriving every hour at M'Arthur's Blockhouse, loaded with flour, whiskey &c for the use of the army. In this time we moved about a ½ mile from our first encampment at the bridge, and encamped higher up on the banks of the Sciota. Here we erected a Brestwork with logs and brush. . . . We desire to mention that a bad habit at this time actuates the guard. Guns are fired almost every night by the sentinels at something or other, supposed by them as they say, to be Indians spying out our situation. This conduct has a bad effect on the wakefullness of the army. . . .

November 6th, 7th, 8th the fall rains continued almost without an interval. . . . By this continuation of rain every part of our encampment and even the surrounding country became a compleat mire of stagnated water. The water forced into the tents so that no place of rest nor comfort was to be found. The men fixed puncheons into their tents to keep the floors dry, and four guard houses were erected for the safety and comfort of the guard. Agues and intermittents became more general, and the army encreased to be more unhealthy during these long and almost steady rains.

On the 9th of November our spies arrived with a British prisoner of some distinction known by the name of Captain Clarke. He was taken near a post on the rapids of the Maumee river, which was held by the British and Indians at that place corroborated with what our spies asserted. They were circumstances which moved General Tupper to apply to the army in general for volunteers to go with him, surprise them, either by night or day, whatever time might be found the most suitable and to get possession. Six hundred and ninety-odd men immediately volunteered exclusive of the staff officers. In fact, the very flower of the army immediately, not withstanding the fatigue and great danger inevitable attending this expedition was fully stated to them. Every man made ready as fast as possible. The next day being the 10th of November, between 10 and 11 o'clock they paraded, formed themselves into marching order and started in high spirits amidst acclimation and shouting. There was such a prevalent certainty among some of the troops of being victorious at the rapids and thereby get in possession of provision, that one of the Captains only drew three days rations for their men to march 80 miles. The 10th we marched about fifteen miles to a block-house, known by the name of Fort Necessity or Mud fort. We took a cannon along with 6 horses hitched to the carriage on which it was mounted, but found it impossible on account of the miry road to take it along farther than the neighborhood of this blockhouse. . . .

On the 11th, we marched about 25 miles to where Findley's Blockhouse had formerly been, but the Indians had burned it down. . . .

On the 13th in the morning, being then on Carron river, 16 miles from the Rapids of the Maumee; The army was paraded in a suitable form, General Tupper appeared, delivered a short, but impressive, speech. The following is nearly a summary—we were now among the enemy, that our safety and the completing of our object depended on our profound silence, our perseverance, or fortitude, courage and valor. The discourse had the desired effect. Notwithstanding there were upward to seven hundred men, including officers, the most profound silence was observed. It was seldom you heard any human voice at all, louder than the breathe. . . . About 9 o'clock P.M. we arrived at the river about one mile above the place where we intended to ford it; but thinking it too soon to cross, the army closed up, some lay down on the top of others, or made every shift to keep warm. The wind blew hard and the weather grew excessive cold. We remained in this situation some hours in the most profound silence, and then marched to the fording cross. The wind continued hard, the cold was excessive and penetrating; the river appeared full and furious.

General Tupper was one of the first men that waded into and crossed the river. This conduct had the desired effect;—it animated the troops to that degree, that they marched into the river as fast as possible with an intention to cross. Some few reached the opposite shore safe, some weted their guns and ammunition; others were swept down the river by the violent force of the stream, lost their guns, and with some difficulty their lives were saved. Under these circumstances orders were given to return and many, assisted with horses to aid them to return again to the shore from which they came. However some men stayed on the Indian side of the river that night without kindling any fire, for fear the Indians would discover them.

On the next morning early, they were assissted with horses to cross the river, when they joined the army again. It being now Saturday the 14th November, in the morning the army put itself into a suitable position, and marched down the river to get opposite the British and Indian fort, with an intention to aggravate them to give us battle. Some of our men carefully left the lines and went in quest of Indian hogs, potatoes &c. A party of Indians, mounted on horses, killed and scalped four, others escaped with their lives to the army very narrowly. So soon as the Indians rightly discovered us, their horrid yells were shortly after heard almost every direction. Many of them, both on horses and on foot crossed the river at different places, and immediate preparation was made to give us battle. Their horrid yells, firing of guns, and advancing towards us, induced us to believe that a battle would immediately take place. We formed ourselves in suitable lines, gave them the war whoop, ran forward to meet them; but they stood us no fight. We dispersed them the whole day every direction, wherever they appeared to be the most formidable. We killed and wounded many more Indians than they did our men. . . .

Near sun down, all firing and yelling ceased, and the Indians had retreated out of sight and out of hearing:—we were entirely out of provisions. It was thought best to march homeward. . . . The ground was covered with snow which had fell during the time we were at the rapids. The weather continued excessive cold. Many were sick and could scarcely get along. Hunger and fatigue gave the army a ghostly appearance. . . . On Saturday morning when we left the banks to proceed down the river, three of our men were sick—two of them were so low, apparently helpless; the third was not so low, but what he might have done something towards his security. Two horses were left with them, but some unmerciful officer in the army, whether with or without authority from the general, we do not know, returned and took the horses, and left these three sick men entirely alone, exposed to the Tommahawk and scalping knife of the savages. . . .

On Sunday morning the 15th of November we started from Carron River, and on the evening we arrived at Finley's Blockhouse. . . .

On our return we found the army in a far worse state of health than we had left it. Two men were buried in our absence, and some waggon loads of sick conveyed to the hospital at Urbana, notwithstanding great numbers remained sick in the encampment. Three more died in a few days after our return.

From our return to the 27th of November nothing very material happened, except the army grew daily more unhealthy. . . .

November the 28th. . . . The situation of the army at this time presents an object of charity and every species of human misery. . . . Nearly one half of this army is reported sick, nearly the other half is known to be almost naked, notwithstanding winter is now among us with all its attendant horrors. The cold forces itself into the skin in spite of every effort;—hundreds of young men's constitutions are about getting ruined for life. Some of the sick lay in the last pangs of death with one bad little blanket—the amount total of all their bedding, not withstanding many of the officers markees are filled with blankets. What 'cause keeps the army together under such circumstances, under such preparations is hard to be accounted for; unless we attribute it to the exhorbitant wages, which many of our officers receive. Their number appears entirely too great in proportion to the quantity of privates, if even the privates were well and clothed. Whether government will continue to be duped and imposed upon by such conduct, time only can develope. . . . On the night of the 28th, a volunteer soldier in the company of Captain Calvin Shepard died. He was an inoffensive, innocent young man. He had caught a cold preceeding the commencement of a severe spell of weather, which laid him up. His clothes were intended for summer's wear and altogether unsuitable for the inclemency of this kind of weather. One little old blanket was the amount total of all his bedding. In this situation he remained many days, in the most excruciating agony without the requisite aid, and at last expired. His name was John Smith. On the 29th in the evening he was buried. . . .

December 3d. The army mostly moved to their new encampment, the encampments being mostly completed. The whole of the day continued cloudy, and on the night of the 3d it rained excessively the whole night, so that the water penetrated almost into every encampment. . . . From the 7th of this month until the 10th the weather continued cold and generally cloudy. It snowed more or less almost every day. The cold was so penetrating that the whiskey which was drawn by the soldiers from the commissary and not immediately drank, but preserved during the night in canteens, froze hard, and could not be used the next day, without the aid of fire. No Thermometer was in the army by which we can ascertain the degrees of coldness in this climate. However, we will leave it to the reader to decide, what causes this whiskey to freeze; If it is the intense coldness of this climate, or whether the commissaries are committing fraud in issuing whiskey to the soldiers of an inferior quality and almost destitute of spirits. . . .

On the 18th a quantity of shoes were issued by the Captains of companies, which had arrived at this place one or two days before. It was a happy circumstances for the men, as many of them had been without shoes for some time. These were the first clothes the men received from government. Those who were the most shoeless are now shod; but there are many clothes wanted or needed yet by the men to keep the cold from interferring with their healths. . . . Impatience and discontent are manifested and visible in every part of the encampment. Every day you may hear the men calculating how many days remain yet until their time of servitude in the army expires. They look forward to that day as a day of deliverance from bondage. Particularly those who have lost all confidence and respect for their officers, and believe them from their conduct to possess neither integrity nor competency to discharge the duties attached to their offices. . . . We are stationed here, so presumed by most to take an active part with the different armies, now stationed at various places all under the command of General Harrison, destined for the purpose of destroying Indians and the Invasion of Upper Canada. . . .[20]

X

THEY SHOT HIM DOWN;
AND . . . SCALPED HIM

General William Henry Harrison's forces were moving in three different divisions from the Ohio River toward Detroit. The Redcoats whipped one of the divisions at Frenchtown on the Raisin River, 22 January 1813, and another at Fort Meigs at the rapids of the Maumee, 5 May. After these setbacks, Harrison decided to avoid further action until American naval units could secure control of Lake Erie.

Reverend Thomas Dudley, and soldiers Elias Darnell and Timothy Mallary relate the horror of the Indian attack at Frenchtown.

[*Dudley*]   On the seventeenth day of January, 1813, a detachment of five hundred and fifty men, under command of Colonel William Lewis from the left wing of the Northwest Army, was ordered to Frenchtown, on the River Raisin, where it was understood a large number of British had collected, and were committing depredations on the inhabitants of that village. On the seventeenth, at night, the detachment encamped at the mouth of Swancreek, on the Maumee of the lake. On the eighteenth, they took up the line of march, meeting a number of the inhabitants retreating to the American camp, opposite to where Fort Meigs was subsequently built. Our troops inquired whether the British had any artillery, to which the reply was, "They have two pieces about large enough to kill a mouse." They reached the River Raisin about three o'clock in the afternoon; and, while crossing the river on the ice, the British began firing their swivels, when the American troops were ordered to drop their knapsacks on the ice.

Reaching the opposite shore, they raised a yell, some crowing like chicken-cocks, some barking like dogs, and others calling, "Fire away with your mouse cannon, again. . . ." Graves' Battalion was ordered to dislodge the enemy. . . . The right and center were ordered to remain where they were, in the open field, until Major Graves's command should force the enemy to the woods. . . . So soon as the right and center reached the woods, the fighting became general and most obstinate, the enemy resisting every inch of ground, as they were compelled to fall back. . . . About dusk, Major Graves was sent by Colonel Lewis, to stop the pursuit of the enemy and direct the officers commanding the right and center, who had been hotly engaged in the conflict and had killed many of the enemy, to return to Frenchtown, bearing the killed for interment, and the wounded for treatment. Nothing of importance occurred until the morning of the twentieth, when General Winchester, with a command of two hundred men, under Colonel Wells, reached Frenchtown. . . . The spies were out continually, and brought word that the enemy were advancing, in considerable force, to make battle. . . .

On the twenty-second, just as the reveille was arousing the troops, about daybreak, the first gun was fired. . . . The fighting became general along the line, the Artillery of the enemy being directed mainly to the right of our lines, where Wells's command had no protection but a common rail fence, four or five rails high. Several of the Americans, on that part of the line, were killed, and their fence knocked down, by the cannon balls, when General Winchester ordered the right to fall back a few steps and reform on the bank of the river, where they would have been protected from the enemy's guns. . . . Unfortunately, however, that part of the line commenced retreating, and reaching Hull's old trace, along the lane, on either side of which the grass was so high as to conceal the Indians. At this time, Colonels Lewis and Allen, with a view of rallying the retreating party endeavored to arrest their flight. Very many were made prisoners—among them, General Winchester, Colonel Lewis, Major Overton, etc. The firing was still kept up by the enemy on those within the pickets, and returned with deadly effect.

The Indians, after the retreat of the right wing, got around in the rear of the picketing, under the bank, and on the same side of the river, where the battle was raging, and killed and wounded several of our men. . . . Major Graves being wounded, Major Madison was now left in command, who, when the summons to surrender came, repaired to the room in which Major Graves and several other wounded officers were, to consult with them as to the propriety of surrendering. Our ammunition was nearly exhausted. It was finally determined to surrender, requiring of the enemy, a solemn pledge for the security of the wounded. If this was not unhesitatingly given, they determined to fight it out. . . . Our Madison replied to the summons, "We will not surrender without a guarantee for the safety of the wounded, and the return of side-arms to the officers"—we did not intend to be dishonored. The British officer haughtily responded: "Do you, Sir, claim the right to dictate what terms I am to offer?" Major Madison replied: "No; but I intend to be understood as regards the only terms on which we will agree to surrender."

Captain William Elliott, who had charge of the Indians, it was agreed, should be left with some men, who, it was said, would afford ample protection, until carryalls could be brought from Malden to transport the prisoners there; but the sequel proved they were a faithless, cowardly set. The British were in quite a hurry, as were their Indian allies, to leave after the surrender. Pretty soon, Captain Elliott came into the room where Major Graves, Captain Hickman, Captain Hart, and the writer of this—all wounded—were quartered. . . . He proposed borrowing a horse, saddle, and bridle, for the purpose of going immediately to Malden, and hurrying on sleighs to remove the wounded. . . . Begging us not to feel uneasy; that we were in no danger; that he would leave three interpreters, who would be an ample protection to us, he obtained Major Graves's horse, saddle, and bridle, and left; which was the last we saw of Captain Elliott.[21]

[Darnell] We passed this night under the most serious apprehensions of being massacred by the tomahawk or consumed in the flames. I frequently went out during the night to see if the house was set on fire. At length the long wished-for morn arrived, and filled each heart with a cheerful hope of being delivered from the cruelty of those merciless savages. We were making every preparation to be ready for the promised sleighs; but alas! instead of the sleighs, about an hour by sun a great number of savages, painted with various colors, came yelling in the most hideous manner! These bloodthirsty, terrific savages (sent here by their more cruel and perfidious allies, the British) rushed into the houses where the desponding wounded lay, and insolently stripped them of their blankets and all their best clothes, and ordered them out of the houses. I ran out of the house to inform the interpreters what the Indians were doing. At the door, an Indian took my hat and put it on his own head. I then discovered the Indians had been at the other house first, and had used the wounded in like manner.

As I turned to go back into the house, an Indian, taking hold of me, made signs for me to stand by the corner of the house. I made signs to him I wanted to go in and get my hat; for I desired to see what they had done with the wounded. The Indians sent in a boy who brought out a hat and threw it down to me, and I could not get in the house. Three Indians came up to me, and pulled off my coat. My feeble powers cannot describe the dismal scenes here exhibited. I saw my fellow soldiers, naked and wounded, crawling out of the houses to avoid being consumed in the flames. Some that had not been able to turn themselves on their beds for four days, through fear of being burned to death, arose and walked out and about through the yard. Some cried for help, but there were none to help them. "Ah!" exclaimed numbers, in the anguish of their spirit, "what shall we do?" A number, unable to get out, miserably perished in the unrelenting flames of the houses, kindled by the more unrelenting savages. Now the scenes of cruelty and murder we had been anticipating with dread during the last night, fully commenced. The savages rushed on the wounded, and in their barbarous manner, shot, and tomahawked and scalped them; and cruelly mangled their naked bodies while they lay agonizing and weltering in their blood.[22]

[*Dudley*]   The house in which Major Graves, Captains Hart and Hickman, and the writer were, had been occupied as a tavern. The Indians went into the cellar and rolled out many barrels, forced in their heads, and began drinking and yelling. Pretty soon, they came crowding into the room where we were, and in which there were a bureau, two beds, a chair or two, and, perhaps, a small table. They forced the drawers of the bureau, which were filled with towels, table-cloths, shirts, pillow-slips, etc. About this time, Major Graves and Captain Hart left the room. The Indians took the bed-clothing, ripped open the bed-tick, threw out the feathers, and apportioned the ticks to themselves. They took the overcoat, closebodied coat, hat, and shoes from the writer. When they turned to leave the room, just as he turned, the Indians tomahawked Captain Hickman, in less than six feet from me.

I went out on to a porch, next the street, when I heard voices in a room, at a short distance; went into the room where Captain Hart was engaged in conversation with the interpreter. He asked: "What do the Indians intend to do with us?" The reply was: "They intend to kill you." Hart rejoined: "Ask liberty of them for me to make a speech to them, before they kill us." The interpreters replied: "They can't understand." "But," said Hart, "you can interpret for me." The interpreters replied: "If we undertook to interpret for you, they will as soon kill us as you." It was said, and I suppose truly, that Captain Hart subsequently contracted with an Indian warrior, to take him to Amherstburg, giving him six hundred dollars. The *brave* placed him on a horse, and started. After going a short distance, they met another company of Indians, when the one having charge of Hart spoke of his receiving the six hundred dollars to take Hart to

Malden. The other Indians insisted on sharing the money, which was refused, when some altercation took place, resulting in the shooting of Hart, off the horse, by the Indian who received the money.

A few minutes after leaving the room, where I had met Hart and the interpreters, and while standing in the snow, eighteen inches deep, the Indians brought Captain Hickman out on the porch, stripped of clothing, except a flannel shirt, and tossed him out on the snow after which he breathed once or twice, and expired. While still standing in the yard, without coat, hat, or shoes, Major Graves approached me in charge of an Indian, and asked if I had been taken. I answered "No." He proposed that I should go along with the Indian who had taken him. I replied "No. If you are safe I am satisfied." He passed on, and I never saw him afterward. While standing in the snow, two or three Indians approached me at different times, and I made signs that the ball I received was still in my shoulder. They shook their heads, leaving the impression that they designed a more horrid death for me. I felt that it would be a mercy to me if they would shoot me down, at once, and put me out of my misery.

About this time, I placed my hand under my vest, and over the severe wound I had received, induced thereto by the cold, which increased my suffering. Another young warrior passed on, and made signs that the ball had hardly struck, to which I nodded assent. He immediately took off a blanket, (having two), and tied the sleeves around my shoulders, and gave me a large red apple. The work of death, on the prisoners, being well nigh done and the houses fired, he started with me, toward Detroit. After going a short distance, he discovered my feet were suffering, being without shoes; and he having on two pair of moccasins, pulled off the outer pair, and put them on my feet. Having reached Stonycreek, five miles from the battle-ground, where the British and Indians camped the night before the battle of the twenty-second of January—their camp fires were still burning, and many had stopped with their prisoners to warm—in a short time, I discovered some commotion among them. An Indian tomahawked Ebenezer Blythe, of Lexington. Immediately, the Indian who had taken me resumed his march; and soon overtook his father, whom I understood to be an old Chief. . . . There was the severest thunder-storm, that night, witnessed at that time of the year. The water ran under the blanket, and the ground being lower in the centre, around the fire, I awoke some time before day and found myself lying in the water, possibly two inches deep. Got up and dried myself as well as I could. About day-break, they resumed their march toward Detroit, stopping on the way and painting me again. We reached Detroit, about three o'clock in the afternoon.

[*Darnell*] The Indian who claimed me [after the battle] gave me a coat, and when he had got as much plunder as he could carry he ordered me, by signs, to march, which I did, with extreme reluctance, in company with three of the wounded and six or seven Indians. In travelling about a quarter of a mile, two of the wounded lagged behind about twenty yards. The Indians, turning round, shot one and scalped him. They shot at the other and missed him; he, running up to them, begged that they would not shoot him. He said he would keep up, and give them money. But these murderers were not moved with his doleful cries. They shot him down; and rushing on him in a crowd, scalped him. In like manner my brother Allen perished. He marched with difficulty after the wounded, about two or three hundred yards, and was there barbarously murdered. My feelings at the sight and recollection of these inhuman butcheries cannot be described. In addition to these deep sorrows for the mournful fate of my companions, and the cruel death of a dear brother, I expected every moment, for a considerable time, that the same kind of cruelty and death would be my portion. The Indians that guarded me and one of the wounded, observing our consternation, one that could talk English said, "We will not shoot you." This a little revived our hopes, that were almost gone; and he, having cut a piece, hide and all, of a dead cow, started. It is their common practice to kill a cow or hog, and take a piece and leave the rest.

In travelling two miles, we came to a house where there were two British officers; the Indian made a halt, and I asked one of the officers what the Indian was going to do with me; he said he was going to take me to Amherstburg (or Malden). I judged these villains had instructed the Indians to do what they had done. A few miles farther we came to the Indian encampment, where there were a great many hallooing and yelling in a hideous manner. I thought this my place of destiny. The Indian took off my pack, broiled a piece of meat and gave me part; this I ate merely in obedience to him. Then we started and arrived at Amherstburg, eighteen miles from Frenchtown. The other prisoners had just arrived. The British were firing their salute. The Indian took me into a house not far from the fort; it was probably their council house; it would have held five hundred. It was inhabited by a large number of squaws, children and dogs. They welcomed me by giving me some bread, meat and hominy to eat. After this an Indian asked me if I had a squaw; I told him not; he immediately turned round and talked to the squaws in Indian, while I sat in a pensive mood observing their motions. I discovered the squaws were pleased, by their tittering and grinning; one, I observed, had a great desire to express her joy by showing her teeth; but the length of time she had lived in this world had put it out of her power. I suspected, from their manoeuvres, I would have to undergo a disagreeable adoption (as other prisoners had done)—and, what was a task still more unpleasant, to be united in the conjugal band to one of these swarthy, disgustful animals.

The Indians asked me a few questions—where we had come from —how far it was—when we started—and if there were any more coming. In reply to these questions, I gave him but little satisfaction. After this they spread blankets down, and made signs for me to go to bed. I did, and soon fell asleep, as I was much fatigued and had not slept much for four nights past.

[*Mallary*] We proceeded on to their encampment, seven or eight miles from Detroit, on the River Rouge, which appeared to be headquarters. They were furnished at this place with bark wigwams; here was a large number of squaws and children, I supposed two thousand.

They here stripped off my clothes, and dressed me after the Indian manner. They shaved off my hair, except a small quantity on the top of my head, which they left for the purpose of rendering the task of scalping more easy. They bored my ears, which they supplied plentifully with ear-rings, frequently by hanging one in another, like the links of a chain. They wanted to bore my nose, but I objected, and they did not insist. They frequently painted my face one-half black and the other red, and frequently with red and black streaks.

Shortly after our arrival at these encampments, I was adopted into a Pottowatomie family that had lost a son in the battle at the River Raisin.

I was presented to this family by an Indian whose name was *Ke-wi-ex-kim*. He introduced me to my father and mother, brothers and sisters, and instructed me to call them by these respective appellations. My father's name was *Asa Chipsaw*, after whom they call me; they asked me if I had a squaw; I answered in the negative, at which they appeared well pleased, and brought me a squaw, urging me to marry her. I refused, and told them when I got well I would accede to the proposals; this they took as a great offence. After having made themselves acquainted with the situation of my wound, they made a tea of sassafras and cherrytree barks, which was the only drink I was permitted to take for fifteen days. . . .

They appointed me cook. I then had to undergo much fatigue in getting wood, &c., for they lent no assistance. Their customary way of cooking is to boil the meat and make soup, which they immediately devour without salt.

They have drunken frolics, whenever they can get any kind of spirits to drink. When these frolics take place the squaws hid me, to prevent them from murdering me. Once I was hid in some brush and deprived of food for four days, during which time there was a continual uproar in the camp, as though they had been killing each other.

The squaws, who frequently visited me, and to whom I as often applied for something to eat, informed me that there could be nothing had until the men got sober, who would then either kill provisions, or draw from Detroit. On the fourth day, when I had given up to perish, they brought me a piece of dog cooked without salt, and although you may feel squeamish when I mention it, yet it was to me the sweetest morsel that I ever recollect to have eaten.

During my stay with them I saw them take a number of scalps to Malden, for which they said they received from four to six dollars each, either in whiskey or store goods. They said they got thirty-seven scalps at the battle of the 18th and upwards of four hundred at that of the 22d January. I replied, that there were only ten scalped on the 18th. They said "Yankee d—d lie. . . ."[23]

(*Note*) Later Mallary escaped successfully and both Darnell and Dudley were paroled. Dudley exclaimed, "I was once more permitted to look on the much-loved flag of my country, and paroled and put across the Niagara-river, on American soil, then, with all my suffering, I felt that I could once more breathe freely."

XI

GOOD LORD, LIEUTENANT,
WHAT DOES ALL THIS MEAN?

*At Fort Meigs in early May, 1813, Reverend A. M. Lorraine,
General Harrison, and Lieutenant Joseph Underwood of the Kentucky militia, who was with the reinforcements, recount the siege.*

[*Lorraine*]   One afternoon two strangers, finely mounted, appeared on the western bank of the river, and seemed to be taking
a very calm and deliberate survey of our works. It was a strange
thing to see travellers in that wild country, and we commonly held
such to be enemies, until they proved themselves to be friends. So
one of our batteries was cleared and the gentlemen were saluted with
a shot that tore up the earth about them, and put them to a hasty
flight. If that ball had struck its mark, much bloodshed might have
been prevented; for we learned subsequently that our illustrious
visitors were [General] Proctor and Tecumseh. The garrison was
immediately employed in cutting deep traverses through the fort,
taking down the tents and preparing for a siege. The work accomplished in a few hours was prodigious. The grand traverse being completed, each mess was ordered to excavate, under the embankment,
suitable lodgings, as substitutes for our tents. Those rooms were shot
proof and bomb proof, except in the event of a shell falling in the
traverse and at the mouth of a cave.

The above works were scarcely completed before it was discovered
that the enemy, under cover of night, had constructed batteries on a
commanding hill north of the river. There their artillery men were
posted; but the principal part of their army occupied the old English
fort below. Their Indian allies appeared to have a roving commission,
for they beset us on every side. The cannonading commenced in
earnest on both sides. . . . One of our militia men took his station on
the embankment, and forewarned us of every shot. In this he became
so skillful, that he could, in almost every case, predict the destination
of the ball. As soon as the smoke issued from the muzzle of the gun,

he would cry out "shot," or "bomb," as the case might be. Sometimes he would exclaim, "Blockhouse No. 1," or "Look out, main battery"; "Now for the meathouse"; "Good-by, if you will pass." In spite of all the expostulations of his friends, he maintained his post. One day there came a shot that seemed to defy all his calculations. He stood silent—motionless—perplexed. In the same instant he was swept into eternity. . . . On the most active day of the investment, there were as many as five hundred cannon balls and bombs thrown at our fort. Meantime, the Indians, climbing up into the trees, fired incessantly upon us. Such was their distance, that many of their balls barely reached us, and fell harmless to the ground. . . . The most dangerous duty which we performed within the precincts of the fort, was in covering the magazine. Previous to this, the powder had been deposited in wagons, and these stationed in the traverse. Here there was no security against bombs; it was therefore thought to be prudent to remove the powder into a small block-house, and cover it with earth. The enemy, judging our designs from our movements, now directed all their shot to this point. Many of their balls were red-hot. Wherever they struck, they raised a cloud of smoke, and made a frightful hissing. An officer, passing our quarters, said, "Boys, who will volunteer to cover the magazine?" Fool-like, away several of us went. As soon as we reached the spot, there came a ball and took off one man's head. The spades and dirt flew faster than any of us had before witnessed.

In the midst of our job, a bombshell fell on the roof, and lodging on one of the braces it spun round for a moment. Every soldier fell flat on his face, and with breathless horror awaited the vast explosion which we expected would crown all our earthly sufferings. Only one of all the gang presumed to reason on the case. He silently argued that, as the shell had not bursted as quickly as usual, there might be something wrong in its arrangement. If it bursted where it was, and the magazine exploded, there could be no escape: it was death anyhow; so he sprung to his feet, seized a boat-hook, and pulling the hissing missile to the ground, and jerking the smoking match from its socket, discovered that the shell was filled with inflammable matter, which, if once ignited, would have wrapped the whole building in a sheet of flame. This circumstance added wings to our shovels, and we were right glad when the officer said, "That will do; go to your lines."[24]

[*Harrison*]   On the 1st, 2nd, and 3d May the fire was most insistant and tremendous 5½ and 8½ inch shells with 24 lb. ball fell in showers in our camp and would have produced the most unfortunate effect but from the great pains and labour which had been bestowed in the erection of Traverses which in a great degree shielded our Camp from the former. For the latter there was no prevention but that of taking the Batteries. About 12 o'clock last night [4 May] an officer arrived in a boat from Genl. Clay to inform me of his approach and that he would reach this place in two hours. I immediately determined upon a general sally and sent an officer to Genl. Clay directing him to land eight hundred men some short distance above, to attack and carry the battery, spike the cannon and destroy the artillery. The Genl. was unfortunately delayed longer than he expected in passing the Rapids and the detachment destined to make the attack did not reach the landing until near nine o'clock.[25]

[*Underwood*]   It being a damp, unpleasant morning, I was lying in the stern, wrapped in my blanket, not having entirely recovered from a severe attack of the measles. I learned that we were to land on the left bank, storm the British batteries erected for the purpose of annoying the fort; but what further orders were given, I did not ascertain. Shortly before we landed, we were fired upon by some Indians from the right bank of the river, and I understood that Captain Clarke was wounded in the head. The fire was returned from our boats, and the Indians fled, as if to give intelligence of our approach. We were formed on the shore in three parallel lines, and ordered to march for the battery at right angles with the river—the object being to surprise the enemy at their battery. Before we reached the battery, however, we were discovered by some straggling Indians, who fired upon us and then retreated. Our men, pleased at seeing them run, and perceiving that we were discovered, no longer deemed silence necessary, and raised a tremendous shout. This was the first intimation that the enemy received of our approach, and it so alarmed them that they abandoned the battery without making any resistance.[26]

[*Harrison*]   That confidence which always attends Militia when successful proved their ruin. Although there was time sufficient to return to the boats before a reinforcement arrived to the enemy, they remained upon the ground in spite of the repeated calls which we made across the River to bring them back and suffered themselves to be amused and drawn into the woods by some feint skirmishing whilst the British Troops and an immense body of Indians were brought up.

[*Underwood*]   When we came within a small distance of the river, we halted. The enemy at this place had gotten in the rear of our line, formed parallel with the river, and were firing upon our troops. Captain J. C. Morrison's company did not long remain in this situation. Having nothing to do, and being without orders, we determined to march our company out and join the combatants. We did so accordingly. In passing out, we fell upon the left of the whole regiment, and were soon engaged in a severe conflict. The Indians endeavored to flank and surround us. We drove them between one and two miles, directly back from the river. They hid behind trees and logs, and poured upon us, as we advanced, a most destructive fire. We were from time to time ordered to charge. The orders were passed along the lines, our field officers being on foot.

Shortly after this, Captain J. C. Morrison was shot through the temples. . . . I took charge of the company and continued the battle. We made several charges afterwards, and drove the enemy a considerable distance. At length orders were passed along the line directing us to fall back and keep up a retreating fire. As soon as this movement was made, the Indians were greatly encouraged, and advanced upon us with the most horrid yells. Once or twice the officers succeeded in producing a temporary halt and a fire on the Indians; but the soldiers of the different companies soon became mixed—confusion ensued—and a general rout took place. The retreating army made its way towards the batteries, where I supposed we should be able to form and repel the pursuing Indians. They were now so close in the rear, as to frequently shoot down those who were before me.

About this time I received a ball in my back, which yet remains in my body. It struck me with a stunning, deadening force, and I fell on my hands and knees. I rose and threw my waistcoat open to see whether it had passed through me; finding it had not, I ran on, and had not proceeded more than a hundred or two yards before I was made prisoner. In emerging from the woods into an open piece of ground, near the battery we had taken, and before I knew what had happened, a soldier seized my sword and said to me, "Sir! you are my prisoner!" I looked before me and saw, with astonishment, the ground covered with muskets. The soldier, observing my astonishment, said: "Your army has surrendered," and received my sword. He ordered me to go forward and join the prisoners. I did so. The first man I met whom I recognized, was Daniel Smith, of our company. With eyes full of tears, he exclaimed, "Good Lord, Lieutenant, what does all this mean?" I told him we were prisoners of war.

[*Harrison*] About one hundred and fifty only—out of nearly eight hundred effectives escaped to the boats. When the Ballance of Genl. Clay's force made its appearance and attempted to land above the garrison their flank was attacked by a large body of Indians I immediately ordered out a detachment consisting of part of the 19th U.S. Regt. about one hundred twelve months volunteers and some Militia. They however succeeded in driving the enemy entirely off. Pursuant to the plan which I had formed an attack was then made upon the Batteries on this side of the River by Col. Miller of the 19th Regt. This attack was also completely successful the enemy were driven from their works a number killed and two British officers and forty one privates brought into camp. This attack was intended to be simultaneous with that on the other side and it was nearly so. Notwithstanding the severe loss we have sustained in the Kentucky Militia the events of the day have been honorable to the American army.

XII

SEARCH FOR THE ENEMY & FIGHT HIM

Meanwhile, on the Niagara front, Americans and British fought no decisive battles in 1813, but on 27 April of that year, General Henry Dearborn in a hit-and-run raid struck York, the capital of Upper Canada. General Dearborn; Colonel Winfield Scott, who later won fame in Mexico; Private Sam Stubbs; and Dr. William Beaumont, who after the battle attended the wounded, describe the landing from transports and the assault.

[*Dearborn*] After a detention of some days, by adverse winds, we arrived off York yesterday morning, and at eight o'clock commenced landing our troops about three miles westward of the town, and one and a half from the enemy's works. The wind was high and in an unfavorable direction for our boats, which prevented the troops landing at a clear field. The unfavorable wind prevented as many of the armed vessels from taking such positions as would as effectually cover our landing as they otherwise would have done. Our riflemen first landed under a heavy fire from Indians and other troops. [British] General Sheaffe had collected his whole force in the woods near where the wind obliged our troops to land, consisting of about 700 regulars and militia, and 100 Indians. The contest was sharp and severe for near half an hour.

The enemy was repulsed by a far less number than their own, and as soon as General Pike landed with 7 or 800 men, and the remainder of the troops were pushing for the shore, the enemy retreated to their works.[27]

[*Scott*] According to the preparatory order, I [and my detachment were] to march 300 paces after affecting a landing, to halt & cover the army. I halted at the distance of 1000 yards for the first time. Here I was joined by Col. Miller (of the 6th) when I received my first order which was to "search for the enemy & fight him." Without other aid I passed in column back of the town to cut off the retreat of the enemy towards the head of the Lake, but finding he had fallen back towards the plain in front of St. George, I was in the right course to pursue. I soon got sight of my object & displayed into line, Miller on the left & no Genl. present to spoil my sport. The enemy not coming forwd. to meet me (we were 100 yds apart) I broke into the perpendicular echelon, right in front to dislodge him from behind a range of barracks between us. The enemy immediately retreated.

We pursued in column. 200 yds farther & I found myself opposite the fort (which was now between me & the river). Here I detached companies & marched with them to take the Fort (which I saw the British were abandoning). The army at this time was far in the rear & no Genl. yet up. Having taken 2 men who were flying from the Fort I was informed the remainder were about firing the magazine, & spiking the cannon. I quickened pace to prevent them.

Being on horseback I rode far ahead of my detacht; near to the fort, I took five other prisoners when a magazine blew up with a tremendous explosion.[28]

[*Stubbs*] We was pursuing 'um, when on a sudden, as if the whole earth was parting asunder and discharging from its bowels huge rocks and stones, a dredful explosion took place from the maggazeen, which the arch dogs had fixed for the purpose! And a serious exploshon it proved for us, I tell ye, for it killed one hundred of our men, including our brave commander General Pike. For my own part, I scaped with just my life as you may say, for a stone as big as your fist struck me on the head, and nocked off a piece of my scalp as broad as your hand! But, faith, this didn't mind much, but waddled on with the rest, over dead bodies as thick as cowslops, and soon got possesshon of the town.

The cowerdly British chief, General Scheaff, had thought it best to scamper off with his soldiers and Indians before we entered the town, so that I got but one fare shot at one of their copper-colour'd sanups, whose heels I soon made too light for his head, and would have scalpled the dog, but my captain would'nt allow it.[29]

[*Scott*] Genl. Boyd was now near me, & fell back telling me not to advance [into the fort], & indeed my prisoners assured me that 3 other magazines were about to explode. I went forwd *singly* & entered the fort 60 paces ahead of any American (my prisoners with me) & had the satisfaction to find the [British] colours yet flying. The British were so much hurried they left their work unfinished. The three remaining magazines were saved, three pieces of cannon remained unspiked & the flag shaft not quite cut down, by the retreating enemy. The halliards being cut away, by our shot from the opposite shore, & an axe laying by, I applied myself to work.

Genl. Porter now came up; gave a stroke or two with a second axe & I had the honour to take the colours of Fort George. Before this was over, Hindman was in, & extinguished the fuzes applied to the remaining magazines. . . .

I lost not a moment—having given Hindman orders, I galloped forward to join the column which, during the 15 minutes I had been absent, had pursued the retreating enemy who fled in every direction. I continued the pursuit 5 miles up the river—Miller alone (with the

6th) was with me. The Generals & the army, were yet in the village below me. I recd. several orders in these 5 miles to halt; but as these did not come thro' the proper channels I pursued my march. In sight of Queenston, however; I got an order from Maj. Genl. Lewis to halt & a reprimand for having gone so far.

It is universally acknowledged, that if we had been permitted to pursue, we might have defeated the enemy at Queenston where he had collected his force or at any rate have saved immense magazines which were there burned at his leisure. Just as I was about counter marching Boyd came up with the remainder of his Brigade which made us more than a match for a retreating enemy. But it was ordained otherwise.

[*Beaumont*]   Encampt in Garrison this night, mounting a guard 500 strong to secure our safety through the night. A most distressing scene ensues in the Hospital—nothing but the groans of the wounded and agonies of the Dying are to be heard.

The Surgeons wading in blood, cutting off arms, legs, and trepanning heads to rescue their fellow creatures from untimely deaths. To hear the poor creatures crying, "Oh, Dear! Oh, Dear! Oh, my God, my God! Do, Doctor, Doctor! Do cut off my leg, my arm, my head, to relieve me from misery! I can't live, I can't live!" would have rent the heart of steel, and shocked the insensibility of the most hardened assassin and the cruelest savage. It awoke my liveliest sympathy, and I cut and slashed for 48 hours without food or sleep.

My God! Who can think of the shocking scene when his fellow-creatures lie mashed and mangled in every part, with a leg, an arm, a head, or a body ground in pieces, without having his very heart pained with the acutest sensibility and his blood chill in his veins. Then, who can behold it without agonizing sympathy!

28th, 10 Ock. A.M. Just got time to suspend capital operation, whilst I can take a little refreshments to sustain life, for the first time since four o'clock yesterday. Return again to the bloody scene of distress, to continue dressing, Amputating and Trepanning. Dressed rising of 50 patients, from simple contusions to the worst of compound fractures, more than half of the last description. Performed two cases of amputation and one of trepanning. 12 Ock. P.M., retired to rest my much fatigued body and mind.[30]

XIII

MR. MADISON, THE ENEMY ARE NOW
AT BLADENSBURG

In June, 1814, a British force was on board transports with orders to destroy towns and districts in the Chesapeake region. American gunboats retired up the Patuxent River without offering opposition. An incompetent American general and 7,000 militia hastened from Washington to the nearby village of Bladensburg, Maryland, to meet the invaders. President Madison and some of the Cabinet rode out to see the action. After light casualties, the undisciplined militia scattered. Commodore Joshua Barney with 400 seamen and five cannon from the gunboats gallantly held off the British advance along the road, but their resistance soon collapsed and the Redcoats marched into the city on 24 August 1814, putting the torch to public buildings.

Scout William Simmons, General William Winder, and Lieutenant Colonel J. Lavall relate the action.

[*Simmons*] When the alarm was given that the enemy were on their march to this city, and it was expected that they would come by the way of the Eastern Branch bridge, I rode there under the wish to render all the service in my power to oppose them. When I arrived near the Eastern Branch, I found a few of the city and Georgetown uniform companies there, laying upon their arms, and understood that the President, the Secretary of War, and other officers, were at the house of a Mr. Minnifee, holding council. I rode down to the bridge, where there were a few sailors, with a piece or two of cannon in front of the bridge, who were to destroy the bridge in case the enemy approached. I rode back to the uniform troops, who, I found, were getting in motion to march to Bladensburg, to which way it was said that the enemy were coming. I immediately rode on towards Bladensburg with all expedition.

When I arrived upon the hill, on this side of the Bladensburg bridge, I observed Colonel Monroe, the then Secretary of State, just in the rear of our troops, which were posted on both sides of the road.

The cry was, that the enemy were coming. I observed to Mr. Monroe, that I would go on and see the enemy, and would let them know when they were coming. I rode into Bladensburg, and halted a few minutes at Ross's tavern, where there were a few militia men, from whom I could get no other information than that the enemy were coming on the river road. I proceeded to a height, a little west of Ross's tavern. After remaining there for some time, I observed, at a considerable distance, a great cloud of dust rise to a great degree, which satisfied me that they were coming in great force. When they approached to the foot of the hill, I fell back, and descended and, immediately after I crossed the bridge, I looked back, and found that the advance party of horse had got into the Annapolis road.

I was proceeding to our troops, to give information, when I met the President, General Armstrong, Colonel Monroe, and Mr. Rush, the Attorney General, considerably in advance of all our troops, going immediately into Bladensburg. I observed on meeting them, "Mr. Madison, the enemy are now in Bladensburg." He exclaimed, with surprise, "the enemy in Bladensburg!" and, at the same moment, they all turned their horses and rode towards our troops with considerable speed. I called out aloud, "Mr. Madison, if you will stop I will show them to you; they are now in sight." He paid no attention. . . . Our troops, before I could get up to them, began to fire, from the left of the line, with cannon and small arms, into the town of Bladensburg. I rode up the hill, expecting to find some of the Heads of Departments, to endeavor to get them to stop the firing, till it could be more effectual. I could not see the President or any of the gentlemen that were with him when I gave him the information. But I observed General Winder in the rear of the line, who I found to be the commanding officer. I informed him that I was just from Bladensburg; that they [the Americans] had commenced firing too early; and that, if they would reserve their fire for a few minutes, the British troops were then coming down the hill, and were about to form on the Annapolis road, when they would be able to do some execution. General Winder appeared to pay but little attention to what I said.

[*Winder*] [Our] advanced riflemen began to fire, and continued for half a dozen rounds, when I observed them to run back to the skirts of the orchard. They halted there, and seemed for a moment returning to their position, but in a few minutes entirely broke, and retired. I immediately ordered the fifth Baltimore regiment to advance. They promptly commenced this movement; but the rockets, which had, for the first three or four, passed very high above the heads of the line, now passed very close above the heads of Shutz's and Ragan's regiments. A universal flight of these two regiments was the consequence. This leaving the right of the fifth unsupported, I ordered it to halt; rode swiftly across the field toward those who had so shamefully fled, and exerted my voice to the utmost to arrest them. They halted; began to collect; and seemed to be returning to their places. An ill-founded reliance that their officers would succeed in rallying them, induced me to return to the fifth, its situation was likely to become very critical. When I had regained my position, I found the whole of these regiments (except a few of Ragan's, not more than forty, and as many perhaps of Shutz's) were flying in the utmost disorder.

[Our] advanced artillery had immediately followed the riflemen and retired by the left of the fifth. I directed them to take post on a rising ground in the rear. The fifth, and the artillery on its left, still remained, and I hoped that their fire would prevent [the British] advance. The enemy's light troops showed themselves and received the fire of this artillery and the fifth, which made them draw back. The cover to them was, however, so complete, that they were enabled to advance and take positions from which their fire annoyed the fifth considerably. A strong column of the enemy having passed up the road as high as the right of the fifth, and beginning to deploy into the field to take them in flank, I directed the artillery to retire to the hill and ordered the fifth regiment also to retire. This corps, which had heretofore acted so firmly, evinced the usual incapacity of raw troops to make orderly movements in the face of the enemy, and their retreat in a very few moments became a flight of absolute and total disorder.

[*Lavall*] All of a sudden our army seemed routed; a confused retreat appeared to be about in every corner of the battle ground, and the place we were occupying seemed to have been the one by which it was to be effected. They poured in torrents by us; my right wing being outside of the ravine, covered, unfortunately, a gate which it appeared was much wanted. An artillery company drove through before we could clear it; several of my men were crushed down,

104

horses and all, and myself narrowly escaped having my thigh broken by one of the wheels which nearly took me off my horse.

[*Winder*]   As soon as I found it vain longer to endeavor to turn the tide of retreat, I turned toward the positions occupied by Lieutenant Colonel Beall, Commodore Barney, and General Smith. The enemy had gained commanding positions, and was passing our right flank; his force pursuing on the left, had also advanced to a line with our left, and there was nothing there to oppose him. To preserve Smith's command from being pressed by fresh troops, who were coming on at the same time, I sent to General Smith to retreat. . . .

After accompanying the retreating army within two miles of the capitol, I rode forward.

In a few moments the Secretary of State and the Secretary of War joined me. I stated the diminution of my force, and that no reasonable hope could be entertained that we had any troops who could be relied on to make a resistance.

Both of these gentlemen concurred that it would subject my whole force to certain capture or destruction; and in its reduced and exhausted condition it was wise and proper to retire through Georgetown and take post in the rear of it, on the heights.

[*Lavall*]   Having [retreated and] arrived at the capitol, I formed my troop. It had been rumored that we were all to form near it; but, after remaining there half an hour, I saw no troops in the neighborhood. I was then informed that the President's house was the place before which the army was to be formed. I then marched through the avenue, and soon arrived before the President's house, but saw no army nor symptoms of any, which would indicate a probability of resistance. After remaining in that situation for about three quarters of an hour, I could not, nor would not, believe that the city was to be given up without a fight. When I received orders to follow the army, which it appeared had passed through Georgetown two hours before us, I then, sir, with a heart full of sorrow, grief, and indignation, ordered my troops to follow.

[*Simmons*]   I returned to the city, and stopped at the President's house, which I found entirely abandoned, excepting one white servant, who informed me that the President had returned from the battle ground, and that he had gone out of the city. I observed at the President's door two pieces of cannon, well mounted on travelling carriages, which had been fixed there for the defence of the house, under a guard of soldiers, for some time, which was also abandoned. This being late in the day, and the most of the retreating soldiers having passed by, there was, however, still some coming on, very much fatigued, and worn down with hunger and thirst. I stopped a number of them, and plied them with plenty of brandy, which I got the President's servant to bring forward from the house. I then prevailed upon the soldiery to remove the cannon, by hand, towards Georgetown, where they were saved from falling into the hands of the enemy, who took possession of the house soon after. This now being near night, and not seeing a single military man in the city, I retired a few miles in the country, where I soon was a spectator to the conflagration of the capitol, President's house, &c.[31]

Our Countries invaded, oheare the alarme
Turn out sons of tennessee and gird on your armes
We air sons of Columbia and straingers to fear
Sure heaven will smile on the brave Volenteere.

When wars and its thunders shall cease for to roar
Then we will returne and enjoy our stores
We'll train up our children their rights to revere
And when their invaded turn out Volenteere.[32]

XIV

THEY'RE COMIN' ON THEIR ALL FOURS!

The British force which had burned Washington and had been turned back at Baltimore, retired to a bay in the West Indies to reorganize during the fall of 1814 for an assault upon New Orleans.

After being reinforced, the British army, commanded by Sir Edward Pakenham, set out with six ships-of-the-line, fourteen frigates, many smaller ships, and eleven transports. To block this armada and hold the city, General Andrew Jackson relied upon 5,000 men, three-quarters of them militia, two 15-gun sloops-of-war at New Orleans, and seven gunboats on Lake Borgne.

On 14 December the British overpowered and sank the gunboats in the lake. The Redcoats moved up the bayou which almost connected Borgne with the Mississippi River and encamped at a plantation on the north bank, only a few miles from New Orleans. At daybreak on 8 January, American and British guns fired. The main battle of New Orleans had begun. Thousands of miles away at Ghent, the peace treaty, which ended the War of 1812, had already been signed. The victory at New Orleans, although of no military value, erased the humiliation of the previous American defeats.

As the crisis approached at New Orleans, Jackson addressed his troops:

To The Embodied Militia

Fellow-Citizens and Soldiers: The general, commanding in chief, would not do justice to the noble ardour that has animated you in the hour of danger, he would not do justice to his own feelings, if he suffered the example you have shewn to pass without publick notice. Inhabitants of an opulent and commercial town you have by a spontaneous effort shaken off the habits, which are created by wealth, and shewn that you are resolved to deserve the blessings of fortune by bravely defending them. Long strangers to the perils of war, you have embodied yourselves to face them with the cool countenances of veterans—and with motives of disunion that might operate on weak minds, you have forgotten the difference of language and the prejudices of national pride and united with a cordiality that does honour to your understandings as well as to your patriotism. Natives of the United States! they are the oppressors of your infant political existence, with whom you are to contend—they are the men your fathers conquered whom you are to oppose. Descendants of Frenchmen! natives of France! they are English, the hereditary, the eternal enemies of your ancient country—the invaders of that you have adopted, who are your foes. Spaniards! remember the conduct of your allies at St.

Sebastiens, and recently at Pensacola, and rejoice that you have an opportunity of avenging the brutal injuries inflicted by men who dishonour the human race.

Fellow citizens of every description! remember for what and against whom you contend. For all that can render life desirable—for a country blessed with every gift of nature—for property, for life—for those dearer than either, your wives and children—and for liberty, dearer than all, without which country, life, property, are no longer worth possessing: as even the embraces of wives and children become a reproach to the wretch who could deprive them by his cowardice of those invaluable blessings. You are to contend for all this against an enemy whose continued effort is to deprive you of the last of those blessings—who avows a war of vengeance and desolation, proclaimed and marked by cruelty, lust, and horrours unknown to civilized nations. . . .

To the Batallion of Uniform Companies

When I first looked at you on the day of my arrival I was satisfied with your appearance, and every day's inspection since has confirmed the opinion I then formed. Your numbers have increased with the increase of danger, and your ardour has augmented since it was known that your post would be one of peril and of honour. This is the true military spirit! this is the true love of country! you have added to it an exact discipline, and a skill in evolutions rarely attained by veterans; the state of your corps does equal honour to the skill of the officers and the attention of the men. With such defenders our country has nothing to fear. Every thing I have said to the body of the militia, applies equally to you—you have made the same sacrifices—you have the same country to defend, the same motive for exertion—but I should have been unjust had I not noticed as it deserved the excellence of your discipline and the martial appearance of your corps.

To the Men of Colour

Soldiers! From the shores of the Mobile I called you to arms—I invited you to share in the perils and to divide the glory of your white countrymen. I expected much from you, for I was not uninformed of those qualities that must render you so formidable to an invading foe —I knew that you could endure hunger and thirst, and all the hardships of war—I knew that you loved the land of your nativity and that, like ourselves you had to defend all that is most dear to man—but you surpassed my hopes; I have found in you, united to those qualities, that noble enthusiasm which impels to great deeds.

Soldiers—the President of the United States shall be informed of your conduct on this occasion, and the voice of the representatives of the American nation shall applaud your valour, as your general now praises your ardour. The enemy is near; his "sails cover the lakes"; but the brave are united; and if he finds us contending among ourselves, it will be for the prize of valour and the rewards of fame.[33]

General Jackson and an anonymous soldier in the ranks describe the battle of New Orleans.

[*Jackson*]   During the days of the 6th and 7th [January] the enemy had been actively employed in making preparations for an attack on my lines. With infinite labor they had succeeded on the night of the 7th in getting their boats across from the lake to the river, by widening and deepening the canal on which they had effected their disembarkation. It had not been in my power to impede these operations by a general attack: added to other reasons, the nature of the troops under my command, mostly militia, rendered it too hazardous to attempt extensive *offensive* movements in an open country, against a numerous and well disciplined army. . . .

In *my* encampment everything was ready for action, when, early on the morning of the 8th, the enemy after throwing a heavy shower of bombs and rockets, advanced their columns on my right and left, to storm my entrenchments. I cannot speak sufficiently in praise of the firmness and deliberation with which my whole line received their approach—*more* could not have been expected from veterans inured to war. For an hour the fire of the small arms was as incessant and severe as can be imagined. The artillery, too, directed by officers who displayed equal skill and courage, did great execution. Yet the columns of the enemy continued to advance with a firmness which reflects upon them the greatest credit. Twice the column which approached me on my left, was repulsed, and twice they formed again and renewed the assault.[34]

[*Soldier*]   Col. Smiley, from Bardstown, was the first one who gave us orders to fire from our part of the line; and then, I reckon, there was a pretty considerable noise. There were also brass pieces on our right, the noisest kind of varmints, that began blaring away as hard as they could, while the heavy iron cannon, toward the river, and some thousands of small arms, joined in the chorus and made the ground shake under our feet. I think he was from Knox County, Kentucky, but an Irishman born, came running along. He humped upon the breastwork and stopping a moment to look through the darkness as well as he could, he shouted with a broad North of Ireland brogue, "Shoot low, boys! shoot low! rake them—rake them! They're comin' on their all fours!"

It was so dark that little could be seen, until just about the time the battle ceased. The morning had dawned to be sure, but the smoke was so thick that every thing seemed to be covered up in it. Our men did not seem to apprehend any danger, but would load and fire as fast as they could talking, swearing, and joking all the time. All ranks and sections were soon broken up. After the first shot, every one loaded and banged away on his own hook. Henry Spillman did not load and fire quite so often as some of the rest, but every time he did fire he would go up to the breastwork, look over until he could see something to shoot at, and then take deliberate aim and crack away. Lieut. Ashby was as busy as a nailor and it was evident that, the River Raisin was uppermost in his mind all the time. He kept dashing about and every now and then he would call out, with an oath, "We'll pay you now for the River Raisin! We'll give you something to remember the River Raisin!" When the British came up to the opposite side of the breastwork, having no gun, he picked up an empty barrel and flung it at them. Then finding an iron bar, he jumped up on the works and hove that at them. . . .

It was near the close of the firing. About the time that I observed three or four men carrying [away the body of one of the men] or directly after, there was a white flag raised on the opposite side of the brestwork and the firing ceased.

The white flag, before mentioned, was raised about ten or twelve feet from where I stood, close to the brestwork and a little to the right. It was a white handkerchief, or something of the kind, on a sword or stick. It was waved several times, and as soon as it was perceived, we ceased firing. Just then the wind got up a little and blew the smoke off, so that we could see the field. It then appeared that the flag had been raised by a British Officer wearing epaulets. I was

110

RECT VIEW of the BATTLE *Near the City of* NEW ORLEANS, *on*
January 1815, Under the Command of Gen! And⁴ Jackson, *Over* 10,000 *British Troops,*
their most distinguished Generals were killed, & several wounded and upwards of 3,000 *of their chois*
Soldiers were killed, wounded, and made Prisoners, &c.

"A correct view of the Battle near the city of New
Orleans," under the com-
mand of General Andrew
Jackson, (*right*).

told he was a Major. He stepped over the brestwork and came into our lines. Among the Tennesseans who had got mixed up with us during the fight, there was a little fellow whose name I do not know; but he was a cadaverous looking chap and went by the name of Paleface. As the British Officer came in, Paleface demanded his sword. He hesitated about giving it to him, probably thinking it was derogatory to his dignity, to surrender to a private all over begrimed with dust and powder, and that some Officer should show him the courtesy to receive it. Just at that moment, Col. Smiley came up and cried, with a harsh oath, "Give it up—give it up to him in a minute!" The British Officer quickly handed his weapon to Paleface, holding it in both hands and making a very polite bow. . . .

When the smoke had cleared away and we could obtain a fair view of the field, it looked, at the first glance, like a sea of blood. It was not blood itself which gave this appearance but the red coats in which the British soldiers were dressed. Straight out before our position, for about the width of space which we supposed had been occupied by the British column, the field was entirely covered with prostrate bodies. In some places they were laying in piles of several, one on the top of the other. On either side, there was an interval more thinly sprinkled with the slain; and then two other dense rows, one near the levee and the other towards the swamp. About two hundred yards off, directly in front of our position, lay a large dapple gray horse, which we understood to have been Packenham's. . . .

When we first got a fair view of the field in our front, individuals could be seen in every possible attitude. Some laying quite dead, others mortally wounded, pitching and tumbling about in the agonies of death. Some had their heads shot off, some their legs, some their arms. Some were laughing, some crying, some groaning, and some screaming. There was every variety of sight and sound. Among those that were on the ground, however, there were some that were neither dead nor wounded. A great many had thrown themselves down behind piles of slain, for protection. As the firing ceased, these men were every now and then jumping up and either running off or coming in and giving themselves up.

Among those that were running off, we observed one stout looking fellow, in a red coat, who would every now and then stop and display some gestures toward us, that were rather the opposite of complimentary. Perhaps fifty guns were fired at him, but he was a good way off, without effect. "Hurra, Paleface! load quick and give him a shot. The infernal rascal is patting his butt at us!" Sure enough, Paleface rammed home his bullet, and taking a long sight, he let drive. The fellow, by this time was from two to three hundred yards off, and somewhat to the left of Packenham's horse, Paleface said, as he drew sight on him and then run it along up his back until the sight was lost over his head, to allow for the sinking of the ball in so great a distance, and then let go. As soon as the gun cracked, the fellow was seen to stagger. He ran forward a few steps, and then pitched down on his head, and moved no more. As soon as he fell, George Huffman, a big stout Dutchman, belonging to our Company, asked the Captain if he might go and see where Paleface hit him. The Captain said he didn't care and George, jumping from the brestwork over the ditch, ran over the dead and wounded until he came to the place where the fellow was lying. George rolled over the body until he could see the face and then, turning round to us, shouted at the top of his voice, "Mine Gott! he is a nagar!" He was a mulatto and he was quite dead. Paleface's ball had entered between the shoulders, and passed out through his breast. George, as he came back, brought three or four muskets which he had picked up. By this time, our men were running out in all directions, picking up muskets and sometimes watches and other plunder. One man who had got a little too far out on the field was fired at from the British brestwork and wounded in the arm. He came running back a good deal faster than he had gone out. He was not much hurt but pretty well scared.[35]

[*Jackson*] The enemy having hastily quitted a post which they had gained possession of, on the other side of the river, and we having immediately returned to it, both armies at present, occupy their former positions. Whether, after the severe losses he has sustained, he is preparing to return to his shipping, or to make still mightier efforts to attain his first object, I do not pretend to determine: It becomes me to act as tho, the latter were his intention. One thing, however, seems certain, that if he still calculates on effecting what he has hitherto been unable to accomplish he must expect considerable reinforcements; as the force with which he landed must, undoubtedly, be diminished by at least 3000. . . . There is little doubt that the commanding general Sir Edwd. Packingham [Pakenham] was killed and that majors general Kean and Gibbs were badly wounded.

[*Jackson, 13 February 1815*]   The enemy [has] retired to Ship Island in so cripled a condition as to have little to apprehend from a renewal of his attempts. . . .

I am sensible, however that we have a thousand times more causes to rejoice than to repine. Heaven, to be sure, has interposed most wonderfully on our behalf, and I am filled with gratitude when I look back to what we have escaped; but I greive the more that we did not, with more wisdom and more industry use the means with which she had blessed us. Again and again I must repeat, we have been always too backward with our preparations. When the enemy comes, we begin to think of driving him away; and scarecely before.

CHAPTER II
1815-1861

My wounded are behind me, and I will never pass them alive.

ZACHARY TAYLOR

Partly as a result of General Jackson's rousing victory at New Orleans, an outburst of nationalism ran through the United States. Americans seemed united in pride of country and in devotion to a common national purpose. The most obvious lesson of the struggle with Great Britain had been the weakness of the national defenses and the need for adequate protection against possible enemies lurking along the borders or across the Atlantic. Congress provided appropriations for a standing army of 10,000; the President appointed Jacob Brown and Andrew Jackson, each with the rank of major general, to command the northern and southern departments. Americans toughened coastal defenses, beefed up the coast guard, built new warships.

In the Southwest the Seminoles in Florida joined the Creeks in harassing settlers, which precipitated the Seminole War in 1817. General Jackson crushed the Indians with vigor.

Out West the flow of settlers into the Mississippi valley reached substantial proportions during the twenty years after the close of the War of 1812. This rapid growth brought many new states into the Union and the western vote was important in settling questions of Indian policies.

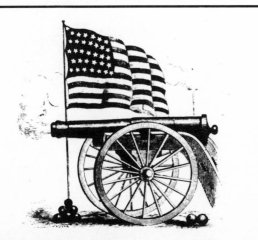

I

I HAD A GOOD MANY BLOODY STRUGGLES
WITH THE MUSQUETOES

*During President Jackson's Administration in the 1830's the
United States government signed nearly one hundred Indian treaties,
gobbled up several million acres of land, and pushed many thousand
unwilling redmen across the Mississippi River.*

*Chief Black Hawk of the Sauk and Fox attempted to hold his
ground at the mouth of the Rock River, Illinois. Settlers infringed on
his lands and, in 1831, Black Hawk retreated into Missouri country.
Facing famine and hostile Sioux, he returned the following spring
with 1,000 followers. The Illinois militia supported by the United
States Army, fearing hostile intent, chased the starving Indians up the
Rock River into the wilds of Wisconsin. When the redmen tried to
recross the Mississippi, Americans chopped them to pieces. Only 150
of the original 1,000 Indians succeeded in fording the river, and
Black Hawk himself was taken East to be exhibited.*

*Colonel Zachary Taylor and Lieutenant Robert Anderson report
on this affair. Later, in the United States House of Representatives,
Abraham Lincoln of Illinois made some wry observations on his part
in the Black Hawk War while poking fun at Senator Lewis Cass of
Michigan, the Democratic presidential nominee, who ran against
General Zachary Taylor in 1848.*

[*Taylor*]   I wrote you in Apl. from Louisville informing you that
my station had been fixed at Fort Snelling, for which place I was
then on the point of leaving—a few days before setting out I recd.
a letter from Genl. Atkinson that he was on the point of leaving

117

Jefferson Barracks for this section of country, to settle some Indian difficulties which had arisen among themselves, as well as to suppress some hostile movements of the Sac's, & Foxes against the whites, requesting me to join him as soon as practicable; on reaching St. Louis, I found the Genl. had left a short time before for Rock Island, where I joined him a few days afterwards. I found the Genl. preparing to pursue the hostile Indians who had a short time before crossed from the west, to the east side of the Mississippi into the state of Illinois, & ascended Rock River, & located themselves on it, about one hundred miles above its mouth, & about thirty above Dixons ferry . . . we set out in pursuit of the enemy with the six companies of the 6th. & four of the first Infy. amounting to about three hundred & twenty rank, & file in addition to the militia, the latter moving by land on horseback & the regulars on foot up rock river. . . . The regulars reached Dixons the ninth day after setting out, the militia two days before us; The day the militia reched that place, another detachment of militia, under the command of a Genl. Stillman, who had been several days at Dixons watching the movements of the Indians, attacked them, but on the Indians joining battle with them & killing one white man, they became panic struck, & fled in the most shameful manner . . . it is probable had it not been just at night when the attack was made on the Indians, that a very large proportion of the whites would have been killed, the cover of the night enabled them to get off. Immediately after this affair, the indians removed to the almost impenetrable marshes, & swamps on the head waters of Rock river, & in small parties commenced an indiscriminate massacre of men, women & children along the frontiers.

Immediately we moved up to where the enemy had been encamped, & finding they had dispersed, & the Genl. determined to drop down to Dixons ferry, as his provisions were nearly exhausted. . . . I accompanied the Volunteers to the upper settlements on the Illinois & Fox rivers, to protect them as far as practicable but we found the indians had preceeded us, & had murdered three entire families, with the exception of two young women who was carried off by them. You have no idea, nor can I describe the panic & distress produced by this, & other murders . . . the panic was not confined to women, & children, but prevailed among a large portion of the men of that part of the state, who fancied they saw an Indian in every bush, or behind every tree or stump, whenever they were

The Battle of Bad Axe in the Black Hawk War. Zachary Taylor (*below*) commanded troops in this war. *Right:* Chief Black Hawk of the Sauk and Fox.

out of sight of a Fort. On getting to a place called Ottawa on the Illinois river Genl. A—— joined us. . . . We commenced the pursuit of the Indians, & after I may say a forced march of near thirty days during which we suffered every privation & hardship common to our profession (owing to the impossibility of procureing transportation even for a full supply of provisions, in wading daily swamps, & marshes, & passing over a number of hills that in Europe would be termed mountains which before had never been passed by a white man even a trader, much less an army) we succeeded on the morning of the second inst. in overtaking them on the bank of the Mississippi. . . .[1]

[*Anderson*] The engagement (if a fight with Indians who are only seen when they raise to fire upon you or to fly is worthy of that term) and pursuit continued ten hours. The Indians were driven across the Missi. or killed. Our loss was 5 *regulars* killed—4 wounded —14 volunteers wounded. . . . The conjectures as to the probable loss of the Indians are various. Maney were killed in swimming the river —others in the morasses and high grass—whose bodies have probably not been found. I counted 8 warriors—7 women & 1 child—their losses I think exceeds or at least amounts to one hundred. The loss of the squaws and children gives great cause of regret but, fighting with an enemy who concealed themselves in the high grass and behind logs and the banks of the ravines and river—whose positions were designated by the flash and report of their guns individual safety required that our fire should be directed to every point where an Indian appeared.

When the fact is known, that the women urged their warriors to an opposition to the U. States telling them, "that the warriors had become women and were no longer men"—and when to this, is added the fact, that, some of our men were wounded by the squaws—we may think it less to be regretted than under other circumstances—39 women and children & 1 man were taken Prisoners on the battle field. The number of Prisoners & scalps taken near this Post by our troops and the friendly Indians probably amount to 65 (½ prisoners—½ killed). Black Hawk and some of his principle men—have escaped but as their forces are much diminished—it is probable that they will be overtaken by the Sioux who are in pursuit of them. Black Hawk will be brought in dead or alive.[2]

[*Lincoln*] By the way, Mr. Speaker, did you know I am a military hero? Yes sir; in the days of the Black Hawk war, I fought, bled, and came away. Speaking of Gen. Cass' career, reminds me of my own. I was not at Stillman's defeat, but I was about as near it, as Cass was to Hulls surrender; and, like him, I saw the place very soon afterwards. It is quite certain I did not break my sword, for I had none to break; but I bent a musket pretty badly on one occasion. If Cass broke his sword, the idea is, he broke it in desperation; I bent the musket by accident. . . . If he saw any live, fighting indians, it was more than I did; but I had a good many bloody struggles with the musquetoes; and although I never fainted from loss of blood, I can truly say I was often very hungry. Mr. Speaker, if . . . they shall take me up as their candidate for the Presidency, I protest they shall not make fun of me, as they have of Gen. Cass, by attempting to write me into a military hero.[3]

II

THE WEST POINTERS

On 4 July 1802 the United States Military Academy was opened at West Point with ten cadets present. For years the Academy was the only engineering school in the United States and, until after the Civil War, its graduates led many explorations, mapped out routes, constructed bridges, tunnels, ports, and directed most of the nation's civil engineering works. In the 1840's General Winfield Scott noted, "I give it as my fixed opinion, that but for our graduated cadets, the war between the United States and Mexico might, and probably would, have lasted some four or five years." In the Yankee Army during the Civil War, West Pointers rose rapidly as combat revealed the blunderings of the political generals. By 1865 all general officers of the Union line were Academy men. In every major battle West Pointers commanded the forces on at least one side, and usually on both.

During the generation before the Civil War, O. O. Howard, George Cushing, William Dutton, Ulysses S. Grant, and George Cul-

121

lum were cadets at the Point. Their comments here on life at the Academy are abridged from their letters. Strict chronology has not been followed in order to give a more general picture of the training during this era.

[*Howard*] Dear Mother—*I am here:* Came on Monday last, after having staid in N. York over the sabbath. I had a most beautiful sail up the river. Arrived here about 10. Nobody can form any idea of military discipline only those who *are* or have been subjected to it. But I will not tell you how I like, till my greenness has worn off, so that I may speak unbiased by the severity of my last "Drill". The companies are all in their encampment but will move to the *"barracks"*—i.e.—the place where they room. It is a glorious place here. Ladies & gentlemen here from all parts of the United States. My class about one hundred. Have not passed my examination yet. It is a change indeed from the Senior Class at College to the 4th Class here. I shall soon, however, be able to make myself at home. As a scholar I have not much doubt of "carrying the palm": But as a Soldier! the extreme neatness!—not a speck of rust on the gun or on your clothes. Not a drop of Liquor is sold or allowed on the Point, but a few & perhaps many get men to send it secretly to them from N. York, which they pay for during their vacation, so it is said. It cannot be drunk here as in College. Should an officer know of a young man's drinking, he is punished peremptorily & severely according to the military fashion.

If I had been here two months I should now begin to enjoy myself, but I expect to be a little homesick, until I get into the Barracks, where I can have my trunk and some Books, for here we are allowed neither while in the Camp. I sleep upon the tent-floor, upon the ground wrapped in my blanket. My health is good, my face long. My love to all my friends.

[*Cushing*] I supposed you would like to know how I like *"sogering"*—Horribly! Ah! Bah!—I am admitted—well.—Last Monday afternoon, at 4 o'clock we began to pitch tents, and in one hour 60 tents were pitched, sentinels posted & c. Three in a tent and our bed are merely a blanket and pillow on a slight wooden flooring within the tent.—it comes very hard to me now, and the old cadets persecute us most intolerably. I was pulled out of my tent last night about 3

"Lincoln the Soldier," in the Black Hawk War.

times and every other plebe undergoes the same. One fellow plebe the other afternoon went to the guard tent for picking his teeth with his pocket knife.—another on being asked for matches, and giving two or three was sent to the guard tent, for being *"penurious"*—all this is fun, you know. I take it easy—It being camp there is no studying—and when we are off duty we can read—play music & c—but we are confined to the camp and can't leave, without permission. I haven't seen mother for three days—this is a very beautifil place and on a fine sunny day to see the evening parade is nice—every motion is performed with lightning quickness—in drill—and the splendid band adds a great deal to the scene.

Monday I went with a squad to the library where all the professors &c were arranged in a dreadful semicircle—about 20 ft in front was a long array of black boards—"Cushing" up I jump—advance— and answered every question they put to me—then a few lines from a book was read and I wrote them down and in a better hand than this.—then I read a page from a book—and then went to the hospital to be examined by the surgeon—well thank God I passed all—and now am a West Point Cadet—

Camping out is awful hard work now. Such hot weather beats everything. We are drilled in the shade, but for all that when night comes I am fairly wilted down. I went to day into my first recitation in Tactics. I recited to Lieut. Nelson. You don't know how bad it makes one feel—I appear stupid—as I have to guess at more than half the questions, for I dislike to ask him to repeat—any how I'm in for 6 months, and if I pass then I will try to stay the 48 months.

I write this letter with no clothing on, save a chew in my mouth— it is tremendous hot. I was on guard and thought I should have died —I had to be in my thick uniform—hat, gloves &c—and was thus employed—toting a gun round to prevent the cadets from carrying off the sentry boxes. Among the orders given me the first time I went on guard was this—"Mr. Cushing" said the Corporal—"You are held responsible that no one shall set his watch by the sun dial after dark." The old cadets before our demerits commence run us. I can't write any funny things it is too hot.

Col. Walker in my opinion has no conscience, or he would not drill us every P.M. from 5 to 6½, and then march us on parade. I had to walk *all Sunday afternoon,* equipped as a sentinel before the Barracks—as a punishment for defacing public property. The said defacing consisting in reposing my heels on the iron table in my room, in which posture I was caught by "Old Sides," alias Lieut. Nelson— so that accounts for it.

I cant write as good a letter as I used to—as I am always thinking of Math. I have a nightmare every night almost of it. Gigantic X's and Y's, +'s and —'s squat on me, and amuse themselves in sticking me with equations, and pounding me on the head with developments. It's wusser than 'skeeters a darned sight. You can catch them, but its very hard work to catch mathematics, and I sometimes wish all the mathematicians from Archmiedes down to old Stinky (our present venerated instructor in the science of quantity) were jammed in a mortar, and something that rhymes with jammed, everlastingly.

Every third day I go to fence—we haven't yet had foils yet, but are being drilled in the positions. Mr. J—— is different from the other Professors in language at least—said he the other day, when something displeased him—"Can't you do right—Good Lord—I never see such a set of *plebes*." Blessed tattoo will beat in a few minutes, and then I can turn in—and "rest soldier rest"—until—Reviellie —I don't think much of reviellie, and haven't yet got reconciled to waking up at 5 o'clk—but *I MUST* or get *"skinned."*

[*Dutton*] At 5 A.M. which is ½ hour after the morning gun, the drums are beat by the barracks, & the cry given "fall in there," when we *all have* to be in the ranks or be reported. The roll is then called, we go to our rooms and have 15 minutes to roll up our blankets, put them up, wash, clean the room &c when *every thing must be in order*. We then remain in our rooms until the drums beat for breakfast again, if missing we are reported. We then march to the mess hall, & if one speaks, raises his hand, looks to the right or left we are reported, indeed, we are reported for every thing. I have been so fortunate as to escape—as yet. When we arrive at the tables, the command is given "take seats" and then such a scrambling you never saw. For breakfast we have the remains of the meat of the former day's dinner, with potato with considerable gravy—& not more than two thirds of them get a bit. Bread cut in chunks, butter & coffee. We have to eat as fast as we can, & before we get enough, the command is given "Squad rise." At dinner we have "Roast Beef" and boiled potato, & bread—no butter. At Tea, bread & butter & tea. We have to drill twice a day & a good many faint away, it is *terrible,* but I like the whole of it. After we have marched from tea, we stay in our room till ½ past 9 when we can go to bed if we choose, & at 10 every light must be out and after that the inspector happens in all times of night.

[*Cushing*]   I wish that in a week or two, you would write to Col. [Robert E.] Lee, [Superintendent], and signify your desire that he would permit me to come to New York next Christmas—as he has power to extend leave of absence at that time. I would like to come very much. I would like to know how it feels to be my own master. I would like to know how bread, tea, coffee and meat tastes—there is a little danger that I will be rampant, if I return to civilized life. But you can have a chain ready for me.

[Christmas]   The scene at the Mess Hall was rich. One cadet jumped on his table and sang and danced, and finished by kicking all the eatables off. Another was so blind drunk that he couldn't carve, and his turkey was taken away, and there he sat crying, and sobbing just like a little Sam—"Give my turkey, boo hoo, boo hoo." And all were singing and cursing, and every now and then a little fight varied the monotony of the scene. In the night the army officers gave us a serenade, and the band gave a grand concert in the fencing academy.

[New Years]   A dreadful fight took place in the mess hall, and the battalion was ordered out, before they had finished their dinner. Carving knives were used, and several first classmen were stabbed, but none were severely injured. One seized the steward of the Mess Hall by the throat and liked to have choked him to death.—another will be dismissed as he knocked down the officer of the Day and stripped off his coat and shirt, and fought desperately with a big carving knife in his hand, but was at last secured—liquor was at the bottom of it. It was very exciting, and if the battalion hadn't been turned out of the Hall, the fight would have spread. There was great excitement on parade this evening—as a very severe reprimand was read out in regard to the above occurrences. Two more Cadet Officers (Capts.) have been broke—I have had plenty of excitement the last few weeks—

126

[*Dutton*]   How easy it is to get "*demerits*," & when a person gets 200 in one year they are dismissed. We are inspected twice a day. Should anything be at all dirty or any of the brass mountings not perfectly bright, we get demerits, for not touching our hat to an officer when we must, for being late to any of the 6 roll calls, for not going thro' the manual properly & everything else. I had no idea the science of war was so complicated. 4 years seems short time enough to get through. Tomorrow I am on guard. It is the hardest work I ever done. You may think I do not like it here, if so you are mistaken. However I would like to see Mecklenburg & a field of corn or wheat or some such thing and would above all things like to get into Aunt Dorcus's cupboard a *moment*.

I will tell you what the things I have got have cost me. 1 Uniform coat, 1 fatigue coat, 1 forage cap, 1 dress cap, 7 pairs white pants, 7 pr white gloves, 2 pr socks, shaving soap, candles, sealing wax, & cleaning utensils—$39.38. These are things which will last me. You can form your own conclusions as to whether I can lay up anything or not. Our board comes to $9.25 per month. Our rooms in North Barracks where I am to room are *very* large & our fires are to be made for us before daybreak. We pay 50 cts a week for washing & sometimes have 20 pieces. We have now to scrub our trimmings.

[*Grant*]   On the 21st of June the Corps of Cadets marched into camp, with the exception of the second class which is on a Furlough untill the 28th of August next (I will be among the lot that get a leave of 2½ months next year, if I keep my health) where they are now tending to all the duties of a soldier. Since I entered the Academy which was thirteen months ago, there has been a great droping off of Cadets. My class consisted then of 82, now it is reduced to 49; and the higher classes have been droping off in the same manner but not quite so fast. The examinations are becoming stricter and the studies increased every year, so that now not ½ that enter are able to graduate, & one fourth of the remainder barely drag through. For my own part I hope to be able to graduate and understand my course perfectly, although many that study harder than I do, and write a much better letter than I can, are not able to pass a single examination. I believe I have told you of all the studies persued in my last years course but for fear I have not you will find them below. Here they are Algebra, and the first and second sections which I had the honor of being in,

General Theory of Equations of any degree. French, Plane Geometry, Plane Trigenometry, Spherical Trigenometry, Discriptive Geometry, & Mensuration of surfaces, and solids.

I will now give you an idea of how our standing is made out. In the first place the classes are divided off into sections of about 12 or 14 each, in each study, and every section has its teacher, and prepare there lessons, and recite them to him at a given hour every day, then the teacher gives each member a mark according to the way he recited. If he misses nothing he gets 3 that is the highest; if he does very well but hesitates a little on one question he gets 2¾ and so on; the worse he does the less he gets & if he know nothing he gets 0. These marks are then preserved untill the examination and with these and the way he recites at the examination his standing is made.

Dear Cousin we have a great deal of rough times here, drilling, walking post and pouring over our dry studies but then our time is not entirely spent in this dry and irksome way. On the evening of the 6th July we had a splendid *Ball*. The building where it was held is three stories high & about 300 by 75 feet in length and breadth; this was well filled by pretty faces from New York, Philadelphia, Albany, Troy, and lots of other places one of which is even West Point. Since that we have had three parties each week & will continue to have them untill the 28th August next when we will go to bonning. Give my respects to Grandmother and all the rest of the Bethel friends.

[*Cullum*] I commenced the other day with the intention of writing a long letter but was prevented from so doing by an order to attend, at the examination hall, to the running of the plebes through the gauntlet. It was quite a novel scene to me to be inquisitor at the same bar before which I have so often with fear and trembling awaited my own entrance. To see the poor devils puffing and sweating to answer a few simple questions in Arithmetic was, I am almost ashamed to say it, quite an amusing scene for me. One fellow, whom from his appearance I should judge old enough to have brought on a son, on being sent up to the black board to divide 5 by ⅔ began blabbering most tremendously. I felt almost tempted to kick him out of the Hall. Had he been in my section I think I should not have been very sparing of questions. Such a fellow is a putty boy for a soldier. Yesterday I was officer of the guard, and could not then finish my letter as I was obliged to be on the alert, for the whole twenty four hours during my tour of duty, visiting sentinels, instructing them in their duties, attending guard parades, receiving different officers &c &c. I can assure you I have been short with the plebes. Sometimes we get into Fort Clinton which is close by the line of posts, and flash powder at them, or wrap ourselves in sheets and then we cross their posts on our hands and feet making some undiscovered language, which they, poor simpletons, take to be ghosts or the devil himself. To their challenges of "Who comes there" we always answer something outlandish such as "Thunder and Lightning with an escort of two plebes," "The devil's chariot drawn by four mud turtles," or something of the kind. An old cadet the other night put on his accouterments, placed himself on the post of one of the plebes, as soon as his back was turned and immediately commenced challenging the plebe ordering him to advance and give the countersign, knowing which, he visited the other posts and played them a variety of tricks.

We are now instructing the Plebes in firing cannon which affords us no such quantity of amusement. Never being accustomed to hear so many pieces discharged at once so near them, they make as much fuss as though they had an arm or two shot off. Some get so frightened that it is almost impossible to get them again to their duty before ten minutes. As soon as the Artillery drill is over we attend the Laboratory where we are instructed in making all sorts of things for doing mischief such as cartridges, rockets, &c. &c. I am at present engaged in making Signal Rockets which are very pretty to see when set off, but I can assure you are not so pleasant to make, & I have a fine pair of blistered hands. At one o'clock we leave the laboratory to go to dinner.

I have talked long enough about man and books, let us turn to a more pleasing subject, that is those fair creatures, commonly called here the *feline* sex. I have been carrying on with those Misses, Mary and Harriet Keese who came down the river with me. They stayed here a month: were very pleasant and sociable and clean. One of them, not as pretty as her sister, which by the bye is not saying much, played and sung sweetly. I went to see them almost every day. In the evening they came over to hear the band and to see me of course. Although they were members of the church we had some jolly times together and I intend to have some more when I go to New York.

I took a fine number with them to the Cascade about ten days ago where we amused ourselves writing poetry which was quite laughable. I was walking with Henrietta until we came to some rough rocks, where she wished to try her skill in climbing down. I insisted helping her, but she said she wanted to show us that she could climb herself. After getting about half way down she sliped and tumbled down six or eight feet to the edge of a high bank, down which she would have undoubtedly fallen had I not have been active in catching her. I picked her up and found her uninjured except having her parasol broken to pieces, bonnet jammed up into the shape of a three cornered hat, and her collar torn to pieces as well as a few bruises and her ankle a little twisted. They are all gone and I'm alone.

I have just completed a day of toil and trouble. Since yesterday morning I have been studying my eyes almost out and have been buttoned up to the chin and girted so tight with sword and sash that I have not been able to breath freely till a few moments ago when I was relieved from duty as Officer of the Day. I must to my books with what remains of my eyes. Thanks be to God that he has carried me safely through seven plagues, may he in his goodness grant me a safe passage through the next, which stares me in the face in all its horrors. You have no idea, you cannot conceive of a true picture of a Cadets Examination. I can already feel the flesh crawling from my cheeks and my blood change color. I can see volume after volume marshalled against me and every line pointing a bayonet threatening me disappointment and disgrace.

Last night an order was published signed by that greatest of all jackasses, our worthy commander-in-chief, Gen. McComb, depriving all officers who have not done three years duty with their regiments of the privilege of being put on extra duty; prohibiting any officer from ever visiting Washington without special permission; but the worst of all is that we poor devils who graduate have our furloughs cut down from four to three months. I wish the old fool was sunk in the Potomac. It beats West Point tyranny.

Uncle wrote me some letters the other day to aid me in getting a situation in the Topographical Department for a few years, for which I am much obliged to him although they will be of no use in consequence of the orders I have just mentioned. I shall have to go to my post for three years after my present furlough expires without being able during that time to return home. The army, the army will never do for me. I can never submit to such law and being shut up in a prison house on sixty dollars a month without a wife. Oh no, this never getting married will never do for me.

[*Cushing*]   Oh! Lord, I was examined to day and passed the best
of any in the section, and made such a good mark, that I believe I
will go up a section—You had better believe I felt funny and queer,
when I stood up before the board, and old Church questioned me. I
did not miss *one* question, and then I had to solve something on the
board—so up I went and for two or three minutes I could not think
of the first thing, but I at last got it, and chalked it down. It was a
very easy demonstration, but I was glad I knew how to do it—if I
hadn't known I would have been found deficient—Prof. Bailey was
in the room, and I knew he would have felt bad if I didn't do well, so
I did well.

Now I have got six months more to stay before another examination, and I hope that I will do as well at that as I have at this.[4]

Hurrah! for the merry bright month of June,
    That opens a life so new,
When we doff the cadet, and don the Brevet,
    And change the gray for the blue.

This world we may find a very hard world,
    As we travel its mazes through,
But with right stout hearts we'll play our parts
    When we change the gray for the blue.

To the struggles of youth, to the mimic of war,
    To our sports, to our follies adieu!
We are now for the strife in the battle of life,
    We must change the gray for the blue.

And some will be bound to far Oregon's shore,
    And some to the famed Vera Cruz,
Will see Matamoras and the fair Signoras,
    Tho' not as "the Gray's" but the Blues.

When the bugle is calling on Mexico's plains
    May we all to our colors prove true,
Be cool and be steady with Old Rough and Ready,
    Nor tarnish the Gray nor the blue.[5]

During the early 1840's Mexicans were threatening the United States with war over the annexation of Texas which had gained its independence from Mexico in 1836. Thwarted from buying coveted California from the Mexicans, unable to reconcile other grievances with them, President Polk engineered a showdown in 1846 by ordering American troops close to the Mexican border. In the ensuing war, American soldiers vanquished the Mexicans everywhere—General Zachary Taylor at Monterrey and Buena Vista; General Winfield Scott at Cerro Gordo and elsewhere in his brilliant march toward Mexico City. In the Treaty of Guadalupe-Hidalgo (1848) the United States finally acquired California.

III

I AM AGOING TO ENLIST.

Fired by patriotism, Jacob Oswandel, a river boatman; Lew Wallace, who later fought in the Civil War and was the author of Ben Hur; and Nelson Huson, an Ohio farm lad, enlisted in the Army. Their diaries and letters tell of their emotions and experiences.

[*Oswandel*] We mentioned our intention of enlistment to Mr. Bently (a member of the company), who took us into the cabin and introduced us to the Captain as new recruits. The Captain shook hands, and expressed himself highly pleased that we had made up our minds to join his company, and he hoped that we would never have occasion to regret it. The roll-book was then laid upon the table, after which we signed it. The Captain then again shook hands, congratulated us in a neat and well appropriate speech. Lieut. Aquilla Haines, who also was present, shook hands and said that he knew from our motive and activity on board of the boat that we would make good soldiers, and as long as we obey orders, as soldiers should do, we will find no better officer in the regiment. We then left the cabin of the boat and followed our usual occupation on the boat until we arrived at Hollidaysburg.

During the day I informed my brother Frederick, who was also employed on the same boat, of what I had done and of my future destination. He seemed to be much surprised, and all he said was, well, I suppose you know your own business best, and all I can wish you is that you may keep your health, good luck, and a safe and triumphant return home again. The company of soldiers we have joined are entirely strangers to us, they (with the exception of a delegation of eight) hailing from the city of Philadelphia. Mr. Louis Bymaster and myself are both from Lewistown, Pa., and will no doubt feel a little *shyness* for a while, but I hope before long, and particularly when we get into camp, we may be well pleased with our choice.

Sunday, December 13, 1846.—This morning about 7 o'clock we arrived at Hollidaysburg, Pa., and for the first time took breakfast with the soldier company at Mr. Reynold's hotel. After breakfast I went back to the boat "Mary" to take a final good-bye of my brother and friends, and addressed them in these words, "Friends, I have enlisted and signed the United States muster roll to serve during the war with Mexico, and that I will not flinch or desert from it. Nay; I will go forward with the company, let the consequences be what they may, and fight for the good old State of Pennsylvania as long as my two arms swing." (Cheers.) "Again, I will state that you can all rest assured that I will not dishonor the old Keystone State. Nay, I will ever stand by its colors as long as there is breath of life within me." (Cheers.)

After this I shook hands with all my friends, and instructed my brother Frederick about my private affairs. I then joined our company, took the cars and ascended the Allegheny mountains, up five plains and five down. When we arrived at the top of the first plain, I looked back on the magnificent scene. The valley dotted with farm houses, the foaming and rapid Little Juniata River below us, presented a glorious view to the delighted eye. After the cars were attached to the engine and started, I, with the wave of my hand, bade good-bye to the "Mary," early scenes and exploits on and along the Juniata river. We arrived at Johnstown, Pa., about 4 o'clock, P.M., and by the invitation of the citizens we partook of a good supper.[6]

[*Wallace*] I found Adjutant-General Reynolds in a mood communicative. The mail of the day preceding had brought the Governor [of Indiana] an official notice that Congress, besides formally declaring war against Mexico, had appropriated ten million dollars to carry it on and authorized the President to call out fifty thousand volunteers. This was great news and I made haste to ask, "Will any of the troops be from Indiana?" "Yes, that is what is bothering me," the General replied. "We are asked to furnish three regiments and the business is entirely new. No form, no precedent, nothing for our guidance." I was shaking with excitement. Then I asked, "Can any one raise a company, or must authority be first had from the Governor?" "I suppose any one can go about it, only when raised it must, of course, be tendered to the Governor for regimental assignment and muster in." I went out resolved to raise a company if any one older or better known did not set about it.

There was much talk in Indianapolis about volunteering. Other parts of the State were showing activity. I bustled about interviewing members of the "Grays" and "Arabs." To my argument that the term of service was short, only one year, some of them with an earnestness implying personal experience replied that a year was ample time in which to die. Finally, in fear of the passing of the opportunity, I resolved to open a recruiting office myself. The town could not more than laugh at me.

So I took a room on Washington street and hired a drummer and fifer. Out of the one front window of the building I projected a flag, then a transparency inscribed on its four sides: "FOR MEXICO. FALL IN." I attacked the astonished public in the start. The first round was productive. A dozen or more fell into the procession. Within three days the company was full.

In the election of officers James P. Drake was chosen captain and John McDougal first lieutenant. The second lieutenancy was given to me. Upon acceptation by the Governor we were ordered to the general rendezvous at New Albany on the Ohio River.

In addition to the townfolk, the population of the entire country seemed present at our departure from Indianapolis. Lawyer John H. Bradley made an affecting farewell address. Mexico was a long way off, and the journey thither beset by dangers of sea and land. There were thousands who shook hands with us as with men never to return. We went in wagons to Edinburg, up to which a railroad had slowly crawled from Madison. The railroad was only so-called. In reality it was a tramway.

The solemnities of the public farewell scarcely moved me. That which excited sorrow in others did but stir my imagination. Nevertheless, a circumstance broke me down. We went on foot to the wagons. My father marched with me. He was in the prime of manhood. A soldier by education, he should have been at the head of the whole Indiana contingent. At my side, keeping step with me, he trudged along through the dust. The moment came for me to climb into the wagon. Up to that time he had kept silent, which was well enough, seeing I had only to look into his face to know he was proud of me and approved my going. Then he took my hand and said: "Good-bye. Come back a man." Instantly I gave him a shower of tears.[7]

[Huson] Dear father as I have a few lasure moments I think that I will improve it in writing a few lines to you to let you know whair I am and that I enjoy good helth I first went to cincinnatti I did not finde work to soot me and I hired aboard a steam boat and came down to New Orleans when I got here I thought that I would stop here a few days I have worked afew days since I have binn hear for two dollars a day comon work hands get two dollars per day I calculate to start this weak for Mexico the old saying is if nothing resked nothing had. I am agoing to enlist. I am agoing on my own accord as ther is several young men a gowing from here. We are a gowing to tampeco in Mexico. we think that we can make something thair if any whair if you wish to write direct your letters at Tampeco Mexoco.[8]

IV

THEM OHIOANS FIGHT LIKE *TIGERS!*

General Zachary Taylor nudged his force across the Rio Grande River after he had whipped the Mexicans in two minor engagements. His army, reinforced by additional men and munitions, pressed forward and, after a hard-fought battle, captured Monterrey, 21–23 September 1846.

This battle enhanced the reputations of Taylor and his son-in-law Colonel Jefferson Davis who, along with Private Carr White describe the American tactics and fighting.

[*Taylor*]   Having collected here [Camargo] a supply of provisions, forage, and ordnance stores, and judging from the newspapers that the people of the country were becoming impatient that the army under my orders should do something, I determined to move forward, and if practicable to take possession of Monterey, the capital of New Leon, and the most important city east of the Sierra Madre, commanding on this side the first and only road between the Gulf and that place for wheeled carriages by which the table lands of Mexico can be reached, a distance of near 400 miles. After raking and scraping the whole country for every pack mule, and collecting some 1,500 and their attendants (my principal means of transportation) I left Camargo on the 5th of September to join my advance at Serralvo, where I had thrown forward a small supply of provisions, forage, etc., and where I remained a few days for the arrival of some of the troops in the rear; on their joining I continued on and reached Monterey, distant from Serralvo about sixty-five miles, on the morning of the 19th with a little upwards of 6,000 men, about equal numbers of regulars and volunteers, with a small train of light artillery and one heavy mortar. I found the city naturally very strong, and well fortified, and occupied by a numerous garrison, between 7 and 8,000 regulars as admitted by Genl Ampudia, besides the citizens capable of bearing arms amounting to several thousand more, with forty-two pieces of artillery and an abundant supply of ammunition.

Finding the Mexican commander was determined not to hazard a general action in the field, but to confine himself to his strong works in and around the city, and having devoted the 19th and 20th to reconnoitering their works, and approaches, I determined to carry the place pretty much with the bayonet.[9]

[*White*]   The firing of small arms commenced on the extreme left by the Regulars & Baltimore Boys who charged on a little fort way down on the left. The head of the Baltimore Boys had two horses killed under him & was shot dead on the third himself. His command were very much cut up. In the very first charge they flew the track & by so doing broke the line threw all into confusion within fifty yards of the fort under a heavy fire of Grape, Canaster, & Musketry, killing many most gallant officers while trying to get the men into line of battle. This was one of the most unfortunate occurance that befell our forces that bloody day. I lost a young friend in that charge that I esteemed very much. . . . After the Baltimore Boys had got engaged Tennassee Boys & Mississippians started down the plain to engage with their Riffles.[10]

[*Davis*] . . . under a cross fire of artillery, we advanced in front of the fort upon our left, to a point within the range of the enemys musketry but beyond the effective fire of our rifles. Under orders to fill an interval which had been created upon my left, I ordered the Mississippi Riflemen to advance obliquely, by the left of companies to a line which I estimated as effectively near to the enemy, and then ordered the Battalion into line. The companies being directed when formed, to commence firing as in open order. In a few minutes the fire of the enemy had so far diminished as to indicate the propriety of a charge, and being without instructions, it was accordingly ordered. Lieut. Col. McClung sprung before his old Company, and called on them to follow him. The call was promptly answered. In an instant the whole regiment rushed forward, the flanks converging to an open embrasure which lay nearly before our centre, and it became a contest of speed who first should reach the fort. The enemy fled from the rear sally porte as we entered the front, leaving behind him his artillery, a considerable number of muskets, his dead, and wounded.

Passing immediately through the fort we found the enemy flying in disorder, some to a fortified stone building immediately in rear, others across the stream to the fort which stands beyond it. Our pursuit was so close that we reached the gate of the stone building before it was secured, and upon forcing it open the men inside fled behind the pilasters of the portico, and held up their hands in token of the sub- mission. An officer offered me his sword, and announced the surrender. I received it, and retired to select an officer to take charge of the prisoners, and receive their arms. Lieut Townsend of company "K" was directed to discharge this duty, and the pursuit of the enemy was immediately resumed. Leading those who had come up across the ford, we advanced within rifle range of the fort beyond the stream, and opened a fire upon such of the enemy as showed themselves above the wall, the intention being to storm the fort as soon as a sufficient number of our regiment came up.[11]

[*White*] Just as we entered Town Gen Hamer was back on the right & came dashing along down the line crying out at the top of his voice "Push on Boys! Close up! Close up! Close up!" all this time we were in a long run. hurrying down as fast as possible under a heavy shower of Grape & the road lined with dying men & horses, I recognized the old voice I had heard so often in the courthouse & on the stump & more especially what he pledged himself to give us a view of his red scalp in the hottest of the fight! all these reccollections crowded in my mind & I could not refrain from sheding tears & marching by the left flank I was leading the company I turned to them & said "Boys three cheers for Gen Hamer!" They were all fired by the same spirit & three heartier cheers never were given than we Brown Co Boys just as he passed us. We went down in town filed to the right & was going up street in a full run when we were met by Major Mansfield who had been making observations two days & nights & was intended by Gen Taylor to lead the attack as brave a man as ever lived too, He came limping up street wounded & bloody & told Gen Hamer for God Sake not to lead his men up their or he would have them all killed. We instantly countermarched & run down two or three squars, opposite a fort that was poring a deadly fire on us, where we filed to the right & had it not been that Capt George of the Butlar Boys disobeyed orders our Co. would have been the first over the ditch as it was we were the first whole company Capt George did not get more than six or eight of his Boys over before our whole company came up to the wall & with deliberate aim poped it into their yellow faces as fast as they stuck them above the wall. We fired on them there a while when Gen Hamer ordered us down further we then went down and took our position within 25 yds. of the fort. We almost silenced the firing of their small arms with our fatal fire for if a fellow stuck his head above the wall ten to one if you did not see their hands thrown up & tumble back dead. They soon [maneuvered] so they would not show their heads at all. They would stick the mussel of their guns over & fire without exposing anything but their hands.

All this time there were too cannon belching out the Grape & Canaster over our heads as thick as hail. but fortunately for us they over shot us every shot. if their fire had been well directed ten of us would not have got out of town alive. There were three Batteries poring their fire on us while occupying that position While there I saw very many of my friends fall some dead others mortally wounded. One poor fellow was shot right through the temples & in the forehead by my side & as he fell he brushed my side bloodying my sword & shirt;

at this point Col Mitchell Maj Gen Butlar our Adg & a number of our officers were wounded in fact the dead & dying were very thick around us. They run a cannon out in the street just below us, & compelled us to leave   We had order to leave sometime before our men fired on them so keen that the whole Regi had time to file around a cornor & take a position in another street.

I will here relate some compliments that were passed on us while engaged in that bloody street. . . . Said [one officer] "The Ohioans are as good troops as ever was taken into a field. Says the Kentuckians "Them Ohioans fight like *Tigers*." No Ohioan need ever be asshamed of our stand & conduct on the field that day. . . .

We receive orders from Gen Taylor to leave town & you know our Regiment must have been very much disorganized for every man took a position where could get a fire on the fort & not be wholy exposed himself   And when the order was given to retire the officers could not get their companies together. . . . just as we got out of town on the commons there was a shell lit right by our Co. I hallowed to the boys to scatter which they did & fell flat on the ground. It bursted without killing a man. We had not got organized & gone one hundred yards when the cry of Lancers! The Lancers! Being along the lines I looked to the left & it appeared as if they covered ten acres of ground, It was the prettiest sight I ever saw. They all came with their Lances at a rest, with a little flag 18 in. long & 12 in. wide flying most brilliantly. It was a matter of impossibility to form a hollow square in our situation. Gen. Hamer seeing that he ordered us to jump over a brush fens just to our right which was instantly done & every fellow had his gun leveled waiting their coming. But to our great dissatisfaction one of the Howitzers back on the palain guarded by the Legond threw a shell among them which bursted & killed some of them & scattered them in every direction   some that was far in advance came on as soon as they came up in point blank shot. some of our boys fired on them & tumbled every man of them not one got a way. If it had not of been for that shell we would have killed at least three hundred, & I dont believe we would have lost a man.

To our great mortification they lanced our wounded & their friends that were lying with them on the field & we could not go to their relief. We could see the murderers strike them with their lances as they were going on & look back to see if their murderous stroke had done its work of death. You have no idea how this galled us &

excited feelings of revenge Oh! how I could have buried the assassin's knife in their murderous brests if I had of had an opportunity. I dont blame the Texians for wanting to kill every one they come a cross. You in Ohio have no idea what provications those who fight them have to kill every one they meets.

We sent them a truce that evening to get permission to go under the fire of their forts & Batteries to gather up our dead & wounded the former to bury the latter to remove to the Hospital. Do you think they would grant it? No not they! They fired on every waggon that went down on the plain, & we could not get half our wounded off the field. And when night came on they sallied out under its covert, cut the throats of our wounded & stript off the clothing of every one they could find, & they never would let us bury our dead until Thursday after we had taken five or six of their Forts and had them completely in our hands. Thursday morning early before the firing commenced the Bugles commenced crying for quarters & one of their Col. came bearing a white Flag to Gen. Hamer. That day they surrender the Town all the ammunition—save seven rounds for their small arms & six pieces of cannon, which Taylor allowed them to take with them. . . . They have surrendered between thirty & forty pieces of cannon & one of the best Fortified cities on the western hemisphere. . . . We took into the field that morning forty four including the officers & in that number had none killed & but five wounded & not one of them mortal. One of the most remarkable circumstances I ever heard of. Remember we were under a cannonade from nine in the morning until five in the evening. Our Regamental colors was the first american flag ever waved in Monterey & it was shot down in the Bearers hand having the spear shot off & the staff just below the colors. I was standing right by his side touching elbows with him when it was shot down & it never got to touch the ground, it was caught a falling. . . .

Camp Near Montarey.
Nov. 8th 1846

Dear sister:

You would laugh If you could see how we soldiers live here. every felow has his knife fork Tin cup and plate we do our own cooking. we have got a great big Bake Oven. we bake 20 great Big loves at a time. we boil our victuals in a great big kettle, and every felow gows and gets his tin full of Coffee his plate full of Meat & soop we spread a Blanket down on the ground and every felow is like a Hungry Hog. we have fine times, all we have to do is to keep our guns & swords clean, and I tell you the way they shine is a show; we muster two hours each day, and then sweep up our quarters we then go and swing or play Ball or lay down in our tents and read. we have lots of fun. Oh! it is the prettiest sight you ever saw to see about two thousand soldiers all dressed alike with Bright and shining guns, swords, & belts white as snow, if you could see them marching and hear their music we have some of the Best swings you ever saw. we have ropes fixed in the tops of trees so that we can swing 20 feet into the air. we have a circus show here too. they are performing in the camp now. there are some little felows like Gip that can stand on their feet and ride as fast as their Horses can run. we have some little felows here not much larger than Gip that can beat the drum and play the fife as good as any body.

I have got a fine silk sash to sent to you. I was gowing to send by Capt. Johnston but he had his saddle Bags so full that he could not take it. I will send it by Adam who is gowing home in the course of a week or two, it is about four yards long and a half yard wide I gave four dollars and a half for it in the city of montarey. when you get it take good care of it. keep it as a relick of the great fight we had here. I have a fine silver mounted Bowie knife that I found on the Battle field the day of the fight. I picked up a fine sword on the Battle field which I still keep and ware every evening on dress parade. I could have picked up a dozen swords that were laying arond without scabords, but I had enough to do to handle the gun and sword I had. I shot eleven times at the Mexicans that day as deliberately as I ever shot at a squirel They shot at us all the time with their Big Canons and muskets, one poor felow by the name of pierson was shot right by my side the Ball went clar through him and within an inch of the heart. he felt as though he were dead but lived. I steped over the Bodies of a least 20 men who were either dead or wounded, I would not let myself sympathize with them for fear it would tend to intimidate. If I saw anything horible I would turn my eys away but after while I got so I could look at a dead man and feel no more sympathy than I would to see a dead dog. It was a terible time the Bulets whized arond us like so many Humin Birds. But I guess we whipe them at last.

You must write to me as soon as you get this. you must study hard. I will get some good Book for you as I go home. Tell Gip that he must study hard. Lem must study too. I want him to be as great a man as his namesake. he can if he will. Tell Gip and Lem they must keep good fires for Mother & little Liz—this winter & not lit them get cold. Gip and Lem are big enough to feed the cows & horses & they ought to do it. I am going to bring a wife home with me when I come.

Yours

Broth Carr

We were not many—we who stood
　　Before the iron sleet that day—
Yet many a gallant spirit would
Give half his years, if but he could
　　Have been with us at Monterey.

And on—still on our column kept
　　Through walls of flame its withering way;
Where fell the dead, the living stept,
Still charging on the guns which swept
　　The slippery streets of Monterey[12]

V

WHAT A HORRIBLE SIGHT A BATTLEFIELD IS

Back in Washington, President Polk was concerned by "Old Rough and Ready's" skyrocketing reputation. Already the Whigs talked of nominating Taylor for the Presidency in 1848. Polk approved General Winfield Scott's plan to shorten the war by landing at Veracruz and marching on Mexico City. Veracruz capitulated to Scott on 27 March 1847, and the Americans moved out for the capital of Mexico.

At the pass of Cerro Gordo, where Captain Robert E. Lee reconnoitered the trail to outflank the enemy, Scott gained victory over the Mexicans.

(Lee writes home)

Perote, April 25, 1847.

The advance of the American troops, under Generals Patterson and Twiggs, were encamped at the Plano del Rio, and three miles to their front Santa Anna and his army were intrenched in the pass at Cerro Gordo, which was remarkably strong. The right of the Mexican line rested on the river at a perpendicular rock, unscalable by man or beast, and their left on impassable ravines; the main road was defended by field works containing thirty-five cannon; in their rear was the mountain of Cerro Gordo, surrounded by intrenchments in which were cannon and crowned by a tower overlooking all—it was around this army that it was intended to lead our troops. I reconnoitered the ground in the direction of the ravines on their left, and passed around the enemy's rear.

On the 16th a party was set to work in cutting out the road, on the 17th I led General Twigg's division in the rear of a hill in front of Cerro Gordo, and in the afternoon, when it became necessary to drive them from the hill where we intended to construct a battery at night, the first intimation of our presence or intentions were known. During all that night we were at work in constructing the battery, getting up the guns, ammunition, etc., and they in strengthening their defenses on Cerro Gordo.

Soon after sunrise our batteries opened, and I started with a column to turn their left and to get on the Jalapa road. Notwithstanding their efforts to prevent us in this, we were perfectly successful, and the working party, following our footsteps, cut out the road for the artillery. In the meantime our storming party had reached the crest of Cerro Gordo, and, seeing their whole left turned and the position of our soldiers on the Jalapa road, they broke and fled. Those in the pass laid down their arms. General Pillow's attack on their right failed. All their cannon, arms, ammunition, and most of their men fell into our hands.

The papers cannot tell you what a horrible sight a field of battle is, nor will I, owing to my accompanying General Twigg's division in the pursuit, and being since constantly in the advance. I believe all our friends are safe. I think I wrote you that my friend Joe Johnston was wounded the day before I arrived at the Plano del Rio while reconnoitering. He was wounded in the arm and about the groin; both balls are out, and he was doing well and was quite comfortable when I left; the latter wound was alone troublesome. Captain Mason, of the rifles, was badly wounded in the leg, and General Shields was wounded in the chest; I have heard contradictory reports that he was doing well and that he was dead. I hope the former.

Jalapa is the most beautiful country I have seen in Mexico, and will compare with any I have seen elsewhere. I wish it was in the United States, and that I was located with you and the children around me in one of its rich, bright valleys. I can conceive nothing more beautiful in the way of landscape or mountain scenery. We ascended upwards of four thousand feet that morning, and whenever we looked back the rich valley was glittering in the morning sun and the light morning clouds flitting around us. On reaching the top, the valley appeared at intervals between the clouds which were below us, and high over all towered Orizaba, with its silver cap of snow.

The castle or fort of Perote is one of the best finished that I have ever seen—very strong, with high, thick walls, bastioned fronts, and deep, wide ditch. It is defective in construction and is very spacious, covers twenty-five acres, and although there is within its walls nearly three thousand troops, it is not yet full. Within the fort is a beautiful chapel, in one corner of which is the tomb of Guadalupe Victoria. There are various skulls, images, etc., in the sanctuaries. This morning I attended the Episcopal service within the fort. It was held on the parade. The minister was a Mr. McCarty, the chaplain of the Second Brigade, First Division. Many officers and soldiers were grouped around. I endeavored to give thanks to our Heavenly Father for all his mercies to me, for all the blessings he has bestowed upon me, for I know I fall far short of my obligations.

We move out tomorrow toward Pueblo. The First Brigade—Duncan's battery, light infantry and cavalry—form the advance. I accompany the advance. General Worth will remain a day or two with the remainder of his division until the Second Division, under General Twiggs, shall arrive. General Scott is still at Jalapa, Major Smith with him. I have with me Lieutenants Mason, Tower, and the Engineer Company. In advance, all is uncertain and the accounts contradictory. We must trust to an overruling Providence, by whom we will be governed for the best, and to our own resources.

(And, in a letter to his eldest son, dated the same day and place, Lee writes:)

I thought of you, my dear Custis, on the 18th in the battle, and wondered, when the musket balls and grape were whistling over my head in a perfect shower, where I could put you, if with me, to be safe. I was truly thankful that you were at school, I hope learning to be good and wise. You have no idea what a horrible sight a battle-field is.[13]

I am stumpless quite since from the shot
　　Of Cerro Gordo peggin',
I left behind, to pay Gen. Scott,
　　My grub, and gave my leg in.

I dare not turn to view the place
　　Lest Yankee toes should find me,
And mocking shake before my face
　　The Leg I Left Behind Me.

At Buena Vista I was sure
　　That Yankee troops must surrender,
And bade my men hurrah, for you're
　　All going on a bender.

That all my hopes and plans were dashed,
　　My scattered troops remind me,
But though I there got soundly thrashed,
　　I left no leg behind me.

Should Gen. Taylor of my track get scent,
　　Or Gen. Scott beat up my quarters,
I may as well just be content
　　To go across the waters.

But should that my fortune be,
　　Fate has not quite resigned me,
For in the museum I will see
　　The Leg I left Behind Me.[14]

VI

WHAT DO YOU PURPOSE NOW, GENERAL?

After Cerro Gordo, Scott's army continued on to Puebla where it remained for three months.
Reinforcements landing at Veracruz marched to join the encampment. General Franklin Pierce's diary gives a sampling of the guerilla tactics used by the Mexicans against the Americans.

Puente Nacionale, July 21. The brigade resumed its march yesterday, at three o'clock, and reached Paso de Orejas, three miles distant, where we encamped for the night. . . .

We left at four o'clock in the morning, and pursued our course uninterruptedly, until we reached Puente Nacionale. Anticipating, from rumors which had reached us upon the road, an attack at this place, and having no map of its defences, natural or artificial, I halted the entire command on the top of the long hill, which descends to the fork of the Antigua River. With a detail of two companies, I proceeded in person, two or three hundred yards, to an elevation on the right of the road, from which, with my glass, I could command a view of the bridge, the village, and the enemy's positions. There were a few lancers in the village, riding rapidly from one position to another, flourishing a red flag, and occasionally, as if in defiance, coming up to the barricade which they had thrown across the bridge. The main body of the enemy was posted behind a temporary breastwork on a bluff, a hundred and fifty feet high, commanding the whole bridge, and overhanging, as it were, the eastern arch. Their position could not be turned, as the heights continue precipitous from the water's edge, for a long distance below.

The tongue of land, dividing the fork referred to above from the main stream of the Rio del Antigua, rises to an immense height on the left; and on this eminence is a fortification, which, from the road, has the appearance of great strength. After crossing the bridge, the road turns suddenly to the left. Having satisfied myself that this fort, on the left, was not occupied, I sent forward Captain Dobbins with his

General Franklin Pierce at
Veracruz in the Mexican
War. *Below:* The battle at
the Heights of Monterey.

company, along the brow of the hill to the bank of the Antigua, opposite the village, with instructions, if possible, to cross the river above.

The passage above, like that below, being found impracticable, I rode forward to reconnoitre the enemy's works more closely, and to find on the left, if possible, a position for artillery. In this I was to a certain extent successful, and immediately ordered forward three pieces, two under the command of Captain Ridgeley, and one under Lieutenant Getty, of the Fourth Artillery. . . . The pieces swept the bridge, and dispersed the lancers from the village. Shots were also thrown at the heights to distract his fire from the advance, under Colonel Bonham, then awaiting my orders to cross. . . .

Under the discharge of the artillery of the enemy's works, the command was given to Colonel Bonham to advance. . . . Captain Holden's company, leading, rushed over the bridge with a shout; the captain, some paces in advance, leaped the barricade of brush and timber, his men following with great enthusiasm. Having crossed the bridge, he threw his company, under the cover of buildings, immediately beneath the bluff, and taking a narrow, steep path to the right, was in a few moments upon the summit, where the whole brigade greeted him with hearty cheers. The remainder of the command followed rapidly. In the mean time, with a view to cut off the retreat of the foe, Captain Dupreau, of the Third Dragoons, had leaped the barricade, dashed through the village, and, almost simultaneously with Captain Holden, planted the colors of his company upon the breastwork, from which the plunging fire had so recently ceased. The guerillas and lancers could hardly have waited, after the first shout of Holden's company, to see the effect of their own fire; for, before our first detachment reached their works, they were in full flight, beyond pursuit, in the dense chapperal of the mountains in their rear.

Colonel Bonham's horse was shot near me, and I received an escopette ball through the rim of my hat, but without other damage than leaving my head, for a short time, without protection from the sun. The balls spattered like hailstones around us, at the moment the column advanced; and it seems truly wonderful that so few took effect. . . .

The encampment was made in the village, for the night, thirty miles from Vera Cruz. Here General Santa Anna has a spacious and magnificent hacienda, in which I established my headquarters.

148

July 22. I left the princely hacienda of Santa Anna, at the Natural Bridge, this morning at four o'clock. The moment our picket guards were withdrawn, the enemy appeared on all the surrounding heights, but at distances too respectful to provoke any particular notice. I proceeded on the march. . . .

An old Spanish fort stands on a high eminence at the right of the road, commanding it in all directions, and overlooking the bridge. A bridge, about four hundred yards west of the main stream, had been barricaded, evidently with the intention of defending it. . . .

Removing the barricade at the small bridge, and proceeding about four hundred yards, we came to the Plan del Rio, over which there had been a bridge. It was a magnificent structure of art, combining great strength and beauty, a work of the old Spaniards, so many of which are found upon this great avenue from the coast. The fact that the main arch, a span of about sixty feet, had been blown up, first burst upon me as I stood upon the brink of the chasm, with a perpendicular descent of nearly a hundred feet to the bed of a rapid stream, much swollen by the recent rains. As far as the eye could reach, above and below, the banks on the west side, of vast height, descended precipitously, almost in a perpendicular line, to the water's edge.

This sudden and unexpected barrier was somewhat withering to the confidence with which I had been animated. The news having extended back along the line, my officers soon crowded around me. . . . "We have it before us now!" said Lieutenant Colonel Hebert. "The destruction of this magnificent and expensive work of a past generation could not have been ordered, but upon a deliberate and firm purpose of stern resistance." "This people have destroyed," said another, "what they never will rebuild." "What is to be done with this train?" "What do you purpose now, general?" "To have it closed up," I replied, "as compactly as possible tonight, and to cross to-morrow with every wagon!" But, I confess, there was no very distinct idea, in my own mind, how the thing was to be accomplished. . . .

A long hill descends from the west towards this river; the road is narrow, and there is no ground for an encampment or the packing of wagons. The wagons having been closed up, were of necessity left in the wood, making a line of more than a mile and a half in length. Thus disposed, every precaution was taken for the protection of the train, and the brigade was left to bivouac.

The growth, for miles around, was low and scrubby, affording no timber to reconstruct the arch; and it was perfectly apparent that no passage could be effected at the north. Lieutenant Thom, and two or three scientific officers with him, had been occupied from the time of our arrival in making a careful reconnoissance down the banks of the river, for two or three miles below. At dusk, they reported that the difficulties in that direction did not diminish, but that a road might probably be constructed down the bank, some hundred yards south of the bridge. Weary, and not in the most buoyant spirits, we all sunk to repose.

Early the next morning, I sent for Captain Bodfish, an officer of high intelligence and force of character. He had been engaged for many years in the lumber business, and accustomed to the construction of roads in the wild and mountainous districts of Maine. . . .

Being informed of the object for which he had been called, he retired, and, returning in half an hour, said that the construction of a road, over which the train might safely pass, was practicable. . . . "If you will give me five hundred men, I will furnish you a road over which the train can pass safely in four hours." The detail was immediately furnished; and, at the end of three hours, this officer reported to me that the road was ready for the wagons. Fortune favored us in more respects than one. The water in the river, which, in the rainy season, is a rapid and unfordable stream, fell one and a half feet from the time of our arrival to the hour of the completion of the work. . . .

Without removing an article from a single wagon, the entire train had passed, without accident, before the sun went down on the evening of the 23d. Here, on the east side of Plan del Rio, where there are barracks and many ranchos, we are comfortably quartered for the night.[15]

VII

THE LEGION OF STRANGERS

Severing communications with the coast on 7 August, Scott's troops reached the divide and saw the valley of Mexico before them.

*The army met stiff opposition at the battles of Contreras and Churu-
busco in mid-August. In the latter engagement, 1,056 Yankees fell
dead or wounded. The San Patricio battalion, a Mexican outfit composed of American deserters, inflicted the majority of the punishment
on Scott's infantry.*

*These deserters were captured and court-martialed. The proceed-
ings in the case of Private John Reilly, Scott's official correspondence
concerning twenty-nine of the ninety convicted by the court, and
personal accounts of the deserters' fate by two soldiers, George Ballan-
tine, a Britisher in the American Army, and George T. M. Davis,
are presented.*

Charge.
Desertion to the enemy.

Specification. In this that Private John Reilly of K Company, 5th
Infantry, did desert the service of the United States, from Camp opposite Matamoras, Mex., on the 12th of April 1846, and did afterwards enter the military service of Mexico, then at war with the
United States, and was captured bearing arms in the Mexican ranks
against the forces of the United States on the 20th of August 1847,
at the battle of Churubusco.

To which Charge and Specification the Prisoner pleaded *"Not
Guilty."*

Sergeant James M. Everstine, of K Company, 5th Infy., duly sworn
says—

The Prisoner now before the Court, deserted from the camp opposite Matamoras, on the 12th of April 1846, his name is Reilly; on
the day specified, the Prisoner had a pass written as he said to go to
church. He never returned. This is the first time I have seen him
since he deserted, I have been with the company ever since. The prisoner was a private of K Comp., 5th Infy., and I was at the time Corporal of the same company.

Ques. by Prisoner. What was my character while with the
company?

Answer. I never saw anything bad about the prisoner, I never
saw him in liquor more than once, to my recollection.

Ques. by Court. Where was the church which the prisoner could attend?

Answer. I never saw any church on the Texas side of the river.

Corporal Charles Franski, of K Compy., 5th Infy. duly sworn says—

The Prisoner Reilly, had a pass which I did not read, to go to church on the 12th of April, 1846; he never returned from that pass. He had a paper in his hand which I supposed was the pass.

Thomas O'Connor, a Mexican Prisoner, being duly sworn says—

I have been in Mexico about 9 years, I have been driving team the greater part of the time. I have been in the legion of strangers, not quite a month; I was never before a soldier. I recognize the prisoner before the Court, he is Captain John Reilly of the legion of strangers, a part of the Mexican Army. The prisoner was captured at the battle of Churubusco, the legion was near a church. The prisoner held the appointment of Captain, and was acting Major. When the legion marched to the field of battle, the prisoner was with it.

John Wilton a Mexican Prisoner duly sworn says—

The Prisoner before the court is Captain, acting as Major Reilly of the legion of strangers, in the Mexican service. He was captured after the battle at the same time that I was. He was with us, the legion, at the time of the fight against the American Army. This battle occurred about 7 or 8 days ago, it was the last battle fought.

Defence.

Captain Wm. Chapman, 5th Infty., duly sworn says—

I recollect the Prisoner when he was enlisted, just before we left Mackinac for Texas, in September '45. He served in our regiment from that time until the time of his desertion. To the best of my knowledge he was a quiet and very good man. I did not serve in the same company with him.

Capt. G. Deas, Asst. Adjt. Genl., duly sworn—

Ques. by Prisoner. Did Capt. Edw. Deas, when a prisoner at Matamoras write to you in relation to the prisoner?

Answer. I recd. a letter from my brother when he was a prisoner in Matamoras, a day or two after he crossed the river, which contained nothing more than an explanation of his object in crossing the river, and requesting me to settle his Commissary accounts & to send him some clothes and money. The prisoners name was not mentioned in the letter I recd. No other letter from him until the 18th of May when we crossed the Rio Grande with the Army. He said in that letter nothing about Reilly. He never said anything about Reilly except in one instance, and then he was not certain that the man was Reilly; the man he referred to was not a prisoner but a deserter— a tall man and an Irishman. He supposed this man to be Reilly.

Capt. M. E. Merrill, 5th Infantry duly sworn, says—
On Sunday morning about the 12th of April 1846, the prisoner came to me with a pass to attend the Catholic Church, saying that he was told that a Priest from Matamoras would hold the service in one of the buildings above camp on the Texas side, and I signed the pass for him. I have never seen him since until this day, and I have never heard from him that he was a prisoner at Matamoras.

Ques. by Prisoner. Will the Captain state what character I have in the company as a soldier?

Answer. His character was very fair. I don't recollect ever having to punish him in any way. He was in my company between 7 and 8 months.

Mr. H. R. Parker for the Defence duly sworn—
Ques. by Prisoner. What was my conduct towards the citizens of the United States in Mexico:

Answer. I know very little about it. The first place I saw Reilly was San Louis in March about the middle of the month, in this year. We were prisoners and were glad to see any one who could talk English. He was an officer at that time in the Mexican service. He came in and was interpreter to us when he came in and he brought us a bottle of liquor. Dr. Humphreys a Scotchman and Mr. Reilly got us permission to walk about the city for an hour in the evening and then we were shut up again. The next morning they started us to Mexico, & we were confined in the prison of St. Iago, for 3 months. After that I was permitted to stay in the city, at liberty for some time when we were all ordered into the interior. I did not want to go, and remained in the city. Mr. Reilly came to my room, showed me an order in Spanish, by which he was empowered to take up all the Americans who remained in the city but said that he would not trouble me, and that he did not want to trouble the Americans.

Ques. by Prisoner. Do you know of my getting papers of protection for any American citizens in Mexico?

Answer. Only from hearsay. The man who received the papers told me so.

Ques. by Court. Do you know whether Reilly ever persuaded any Americans to join the Mexican Army?

Answer. I was sent by Captain Smith, to see two teamsters, who were confined and said to be in want; on my way I met Mr. Reilly, who said that there were two Americans there who wanted to see some of the officers; when I went in, there were 4, 2 sailors and two teamsters. They all begun to complain that they could get nothing to eat, unless they enlisted. Reilly asked them, who told them they could get nothing to eat unless they enlisted; they answered that he did. He denied it, saying don't tell any damned lies, no one spoke until Mr. Reilly left.

The prisoners witnesses not appearing, and being beyond the jurisdiction of the Court, the prisoner proceeded with the defence.

I was never a deserter, I was captured by the Mexicans, at the time that I was on pass on Sunday morning. I went to hear service and was captured by the Mexicans, brought back as prisoner to Matamoras, to the presence of General Ampudia. Calling upon Captain Furlock as an Interpreter, and telling him that I was not a deserter, presenting my pass at the same time, and requesting him to tell General Ampudia that I was captured after coming from church. Likewise, General Ampudia by his order had me confined in the barracks of the Sappadores, in Matamoras, in order that I should have no communication whatever with the deserters, that had passed from the American camp; for the term of 19 days, I had been a prisoner, living upon 6 pence per day upon bread and water. On the 29th day of April, General Ampudia sent for me to his quarters. I told him that his country I did not know anything about. That I had lived for 2 years in the United States and served 7 months and 3 days in the ranks. Likewise that I being a British subject, that I hoped that the officers of the Army would consider me as a soldier and would relieve me in a few days afterwards.

Likewise on the 5th day of May, I had been escorted from the prison to the said General Ampudia, and has appointed Captain Furlock to ask me several questions concerning the camp of General Taylor and his men. The answers that I have made him, that I was neither a deserter or spy. That he should look to some further informants if he wanted any further information concerning the camp. Therefore on the 19th day of May General Ampudia has sent for me to his quarters and told me that if the Americans had caught me in Matamoras, that it was his opinion that General Taylor would have me shot. At the same time forced me on with the troops, tied as a prisoner, with my hands behind my back, till I came to Linares. At the same time the following day brought me as prisoner before him, asked me if I wished to take a 1st Lieutenants commission in the service of the Republic of Mexico. The answer that I made him, that in case that I took arms against the United States, that I was taking them against my brothers and countrymen. He has told me that as being an alien to the United States and Mexico both, I should suffer death; brought me out on the plaza, with my hands tied behind my back as a prisoner and sentenced me to be shot in 25 minutes from the time, to which General Arista rode upon horse-back and said to Ampudia, that no such business should take place while he was in command of the Army. At the same time said General Arista had sent one of his Aide-de-Camps to untie me, and marched me to his quarters.

General Arista has put several questions to me, enquiring whether the troops under General Taylor's command, was composed of Americans alone or not. I made him an answer that I did not come there for an informer, that I was taken a prisoner and hoped to be treated as such. He answered me that he saved me from being shot in the Plaza of Linares & that I should not make him any such answer. That he would turn me back to Ampudia's brigade and let Ampudia do as he liked with me. He marched me off under an escort of one officer, one sergeant and six men to the prison.

The following morning sent Captain Furlock to the prison, and advised me for to do something to save my life. I told Captain Furlock in return, to go to General Arista and tell him if he spared my life that I should deem to give him what informations he wanted. He sent a guard after me and marched me up to his quarters and told me that I should have two hours to consider upon what questions he should ask me.

I made him an answer that I should reply to his questions as far as I knew how. He asked me if I knew how many troops General Taylor had under his command. I made him an answer, that that was something I did not know, or no other private soldier in the ranks. He asked what they were composed of. I made him an answer that I considered them composed of all nations, that I had known some Irish, English, French, Germans in service. He asked me at the same time, by what means I came into the service. I told him that I was an alien to the ranks of the United States, and likewise to Mexico, that I was a subject of Great Britain. He told me that he would give me four days for to consider whether I should take arms in the defence of the Republic of Mexico or not. If not, that I should suffer the punishment that the remainder of my countrymen has suffered after the Battle of Labordee in Texas. That he had not considered me or no other foreigner entitled to take arms or to be a soldier in the ranks of the United States of America, therefore that he considered, that all foreigners who should be prisoners from them ranks should be treated as traitors to the Mexican Government. He gave orders that evening that I should be chained in the prison.

The following morning between the hours of 10 and 11 o'clock, General Arista has sent a Guard to march me back to his quarters. I had been brought back with my arms tied behind my back, like a criminal. He stept out into his hall and asked me a question whether I would take arms in defence of the Republic of Mexico or not. I made him an answer that I had never served as a private soldier in my lifetime, with the exception of 7 months and 3 days I had served in the American ranks. Therefore if I was sentenced to death as a British subject, that I would sooner serve as a commissioned officer and fight against my brothers and countrymen than to receive death. No consul belonging to Great Britain being in that part of the country at the time, I thought fit to accept of the commission for fear of being immediately shot. I accepted of it.

I requested some officers of the service of the United States for to convey me to General Taylor's tents, after the capitulation of Monterey; told me in a few minutes that they would call upon me and fetch me there, and at the same told me that they were afraid that I would be killed by the Texan Rangers. If I remember right Capt. Thornton, 2 Drags. was one, and Lieut. Dias of the Artillery was another, and a Colonel of the Texas Rangers was the third. They told me that they would call upon me at 4 o'clock in the afternoon, and I have never seen any of them since.

I have no further defence to make. Capt. Furlock who is my principal witness was in the City of Mexico when I left. I have written to him to bring him as a witness before this court, but have not heard of him or from him. Were he present he would sustain fully this defence.

The Court then closed and after deliberation find the prisoner PRIVATE JOHN REILLY of Company K, 5th Infantry,
>   GUILTY, of the Specification,
>   GUILTY, of the Charge
and do therefore sentence him *"To be hanged by the neck until he is dead."*

> Headquarters of the Army,
> *Tacubaya*, Sept. 8th 1847.

General Orders,⎫
                 ⎬
No. 281   ⎭

Proceedings of a General Court-Martial of which Colonel B. Riley, 2d Infantry, is President, convened at San Angel, Mexico, by General Orders No. 263, Headquarters of the Army.

Before the said court were tried the following named prisoners, Privates of the Army of the United States:

Note.	1. Henry Venator,	I	Company 2d Dragoons,
All these men	2. Francis Rhode,	I	Company 2d Dragoons,
convicted and	3. Thomas Riley,*	H	Company 3d Infantry,
sentenced to *be*	4. Wm. A. Wallace,	C	Company 3d Infantry,
hung—	5. Lawrence Macky,	K	Company 3d Infantry,
The *3 men* noted thus	6. Patrick Dalton,	B	Company 2d Infantry,
"*" deserted in	7. John Sheehan,	G	Company 5th Infantry,
April, 1846, before	8. John A. Myers,	G	Company 5th Infantry,
a condition of war	9. Henry Whistler,	E	Company 4th Artillery,
existed, and sen-	10. Henry Newer,#	D	Company 4th Artillery,
tence *commuted to*	11. Elizier S. Lusk,	C	Company 3d Infantry,
50 lashes; branding	12. James Spears,	D	Company 7th Infantry,
on cheek with letter	13. Dennis Conahan,	I	Company 7th Infantry,
"D"; to be con-	14. James Mc Dowell,	K	Company 7th Infantry,
fined till end of	15. James Mills,*	H	Company 3d Infantry,
war & then drummed	16. Martin Lydon,	D	Company 7th Infantry,
out of service.	17. Wm. H. Keeck,	F	Company 4th Artillery,
Like commutation of	18. Wm. Oathouse,	I	Company 2d Infantry,

157

sentences of the *4*
men marked thus *"∠"*—
Sentence of hanging
remitted in cases
of the *2 men* noted #.
The remaining *20*
men to be hung next
day after receipt
of order by Comd'r
of Post on Camp where
confined—

+ name not in-
cluded in list, at
end of order, of
those to be hanged,
but records show
that William O'Connor
was excuted.
& * sentence com-
muted to 50 lashes,
branding, &c.
∠ sentence remitted—
Remainder executed—

19. Henry Octker,   D   Company 4th Artillery,
20. Edwd. M. Herron,#   G   Company 4th Artillery,
21. Wm. O'Connor,+   K   Company 1st Artillery,
22. Andrew Nolan,   G   Company 4th Artillery,
23. Herman Schmidt,   D   Company 3d Infantry,
24. Hezekiah Akles,∠   H   Company 3d Artillery,
25. John Bartley,∠   H   Company 3d Artillery,
26. Alexander Mc Kee,∠   H   Company 3d Artillery,
27. John Reilly,*   K   Company 5th Infantry,
28. R. W. Garretson,   H   Company 3d Artillery,
29. John Bowers,∠   H   Company 3d Artillery.

Each and all charged with desertion to the enemy.

Each of the prisoners pleaded not guilty.

Sentences. The court found the above named prisoners severally Guilty as charged, and sentence each (two-thirds of the members of the court in every case concurring in the sentence) "to be hanged by the neck until he is dead."

2. The General-in-chief approves the foregoing proceedings and sentences, with the following exceptions: the cases of Thomas Riley, Company I, 5th Infantry, James Mills, Company H, same regiment, and John Reilly, Company K, 5th Infantry.

These three prisoners severally committed the crime of desertion, as charged, in the early part of April, 1846, At that date the United States were at peace with Mexico and all the world; for the present war did not break out, in fact, till a later date and was not recognized to exist by the Congress of the United States till the 13th of the following month.

No higher punishment can, therefore, be legally inflicted upon those atrocious offenders—T. Riley, J. Mills, and J. Reilly, than that prescribed for a state of peace, viz: fifty lashes with a raw-hide whip, well laid on the bare back of each, and their punishment is commuted accordingly, with the addition that each be branded on a cheek with the letter "D"; kept a close prisoner as long as this army remains in Mexico, and then be drummed out of the service.

So much of the punishment, in the case of Henry Newer, Company D, 4th Artillery, as relates to hanging is, on the recommendation of many members of the court, remitted and a like remission is made in the case of Edwd. M. Herron, Company G, same regiment, out of consideration for a son, a private in the same company who has remained faithful to his colors.

There being some slight circumstances of mitigation in the several cases of Hezekiah Akles, John Bartley, Alexander McKee, and John Bowers, all of Company H, 3rd Artillery, their sentences are commuted as in the case of T. Riley, J. Mills, and J. Reilly, above.

The remainder of the prisoners tried by the same court, and for the same crime . . . will be hung, according to their several sentences, between the hours of six and seven o'clock, in the forenoon, next after the receipt of this order, as may be arranged by the commander of the post or camp where the said prisoners may respectively be found.

By command of Major General Scott:

H. L. SCOTT,
A. A. A. Genl.[16]

(Scott also commuted the sentence of a number of other deserters sentenced to death by another court.)

[Ballantine] I sincerely pitied these poor fellows, many of whom I had reason to believe had been driven to the foolish step they had taken by harsh and cruel usage, operating on a sensitive and excitable temperment. The barbarous treatment which soldiers sometimes received from ignorant and brutal officers, and non-commissioned officers, on that campaign, were I to relate it in minute detail, would seem almost incredible. I have frequently seen foolish young officers violently strike and assault soldiers on the most slight provocation; while to tie them up by the wrist, as high as their hands would reach, with a gag in their mouths, was a common punishment for trivial offences. In fact such a bad state of feeling seemed to exist between men and officers throughout the service that I was not surprised that it should lead to numerous desertions. If our men had not known how utterly wretched was the condition of soldiers in the Mexican service, deserting to which was literally jumping out of the frying-pan into the fire, I believe that numerous as these desertions were they would have been infinitely more so. These deserters were considered a principal cause of the obstinate resistance which our troops met at Churubusco, two or three attempts of the Mexicans to hoist a white flag having been frustrated by some of them, who killed the Mexicans attempting to display it. The large number of officers killed in the affair was also ascribed to them, as for the gratification of their revenge they aimed at no other objects during the engagement.[17]

[*Davis*] Intense dissatisfaction, and an earnest remonstrance among the officers of the army in general, followed at the commutation of the sentences of the fourteen from death to whipping and branding, more particularly in the case of R[e]il[l]y, who was in command of the Mexican Battalion of St. Patrick, composed entirely of deserters from the United States Army, over one hundred strong; and who, from his rank at the time of his desertion, his general intelligence and influence, was believed by our officers to have been the principal cause of the desertion of the others. It was urged upon General Scott that it would be far preferable that every one of the rest of the forty-two condemned deserters should be pardoned rather than that Riley should escape death, more especially as we were in possession of the knowledge of the high estimate placed upon him as an officer by the enemy. The importance attached to saving his life was attested by the unwearied efforts that had been made by the whole Catholic priesthood within our lines to procure his liberation by exchange or ransom. It was held that if his life was spared from any cause it would, in their judgement, be attributed by the enemy to fear on our part, and its tendency would be to produce a more stubborn resistance. . . .

General Scott listened with dignified patience and courtesy to the arguments with which he was stormed to drive him from his position and induce him to abandon the modification he had made in the finding of the military tribunal that had condemned Riley to death. But the veteran, clear-headed, logical chief of our army was unmoved by the appeals made to him. He had set his feet upon the Articles of War and the laws of his country as upon a rock. With great terseness and eloquence of expression General Scott in a very few words disposed of all that had been urged against commuting Riley's death sentence, and put to confusion those who, in the best faith and with the most patriotic motives, had asked him to swerve from what he regarded to be the clearly defined spirit and letter of the Articles of War, and concluded by declaring that, sooner than the life of Riley should be taken, under the finding in his case of the military commission which had tried and condemned him to death, he (General

Scott) would rather with his whole army be put to the sword in the assault he was about to make upon the gates of the City of Mexico! . . .

On September 10th those of the condemned whose sentence was death were hung. The fourteen that were to be whipped and branded, were tied up to trees in front of the Catholic church on the plaza, their backs naked to the waistband of the pantaloons, and an experienced Mexican muleteer inflicted the fifty lashes with all the severity he could upon each culprit. Why those thus punished did not die under such punishment was a marvel to me. Their backs had the appearance of a pounded piece of raw beef, the blood oozing from every stripe as given. Each in his turn was then branded, and after digging the graves of those subsequently hung, the fourteen were drummed out of camp to the tune of the "Rogues' March." I should have prefaced this revolting scene with the statement that all the generals, with their respective staffs, were required to be present, but for which order nothing on earth could have influenced my witnessing what I did.

The sixteen who were executed at our camp were launched into eternity at one and the same moment, each being dressed in the uniform of the enemy in which he had been captured, the white caps being drawn over their heads. The scaffold was about forty feet in length, consisting of heavy stringpieces of timber supported by large square uprights, one at each end and a third in the middle, mortised into the stringer; it was fourteen feet high and erected upon an open plain or field. Two prisoners were placed at the extreme end of a transportation wagon, to which was attached a pair of our fleetest, best-broken mules, which were handled by the most expert drivers in the service. The teams were alternately headed to the east and west, with the ends of the wagons to which they were attached arranged in line, with mathematical precision, directly under the nooses suspended from the stringer. The drivers were mounted upon the saddle-mule of each team, ready to make an instantaneous start at the tap of a drum as the signal. In the front of the prisoners were arranged five Catholic priests in their canonicals, with a crucifix in one hand, engaged in appropriate devotional services, from the time the prisoners were stationed at the tail end of the wagons until they were swung off. Seven out of the sixteen hung being communicants of the Roman Catholic Church, their bodies after death were delivered into the custody of the priests to be buried in consecrated ground; the other nine were buried immediately under the scaffold where they were hung. They all, but one, died without a struggle; the exception, who was named Dalton, was literally choked to death. The remaining were executed at Miscoac, under the direction of Colonel Harney, who was in command of that place; but as I did not witness the execution I can enter into no details as to what transpired.

The prisoner who was pardoned owed his deliverance from death to a singular and touching incident. He was an old man of three score years, and had been a loyal and faithful soldier for many years in the United States army until he was tempted and fell under the evil influence and example of Riley. In the same company with himself was his eldest son, who had attained the meridan of the allotted period of man's life, and was still in service to his country. The son had refused to desert, or to become a traitor to his flag. This circumstance was brought to the notice of General Scott mainly through my instrumentality, but without any expectation or design that it would in any way influence the action that followed. The deserter condemned to death was unconditionally pardoned, and the only reason assigned by General Scott for this act of unexpected clemency was given in these few words: "In the hour of the greatest temptation the son was loyal and true to his colors." I was privileged to communicate to the father condemned to death his reprieve and its cause, and when I said to him that "he had been ransomed through the loyalty of his son to the flag of his country," the condemned prisoner dropped upon his knees, exclaiming: "This is worse than death! I would rather have died!" I looked upon the poor wretch with pity, but without the power of speech to reply; it was the last time I ever saw him, but the whole scene in his prison, saved as if by fire, is as vivid as in the hour when it occurred.[18]

VIII

UNDER A BRILLIANT SUN, I ENTERED THE CITY

General Scott himself gives a vivid description of his army's triumphal entry into Mexico City.

"Moving up to Battle," in the Mexican War. General Winfield
Scott (*below*) was one of the heroes of this war.

At about four o'clock next morning (September 14), a deputation of the city council waited upon me to report that the Federal Government and the army of Mexico had fled from the capital some three hours before, and to demand terms of capitulation in favor of the church, the citizens, and the municipal authorities. I promptly replied, that I would sign no capitulation; that the city had been virtually in our possession from the time of the lodgments effected by Worth and Quitman the day before; that I regetted the silent escape of the Mexican army; that I should levy upon the city a moderate contribution, for special purposes; and that the American army should come under no terms, not *self*-imposed—such only as its own honor, the dignity of the United States, and the spirit of the age, should, in my opinion, imperiously demand and impose. . . .

At the termination of the interview with the city deputation, I communicated, about daylight, orders to Worth and Quitman to advance slowly and cautiously (to guard against treachery) toward the heart of the city, and to occupy its stronger and more commanding points.

Quitman proceeded to the great *plaza* or square, planted guards, and hoisted the colors of the United States on the national palace. . . .

Soon after we had entered, and were in the act of occupying the city, a fire was opened upon us from the flat roofs of the houses, from windows and corners of streets, by some two thousand convicts, liberated the night before, by the flying Government—joined by, perhaps, as many Mexican soldiers, who had disbanded themselves and thrown off their uniforms.

This unlawful war lasted more than twenty-four hours, in spite of the exertions of the municipal authorities, and was not put down till we had lost many men, including several officers, killed or wounded, and had punished the miscreants. . . .

Under a brilliant sun, I entered the city at the head of the cavalry, cheered by Worth's division of regulars drawn up in the order of battle in the Alameda, and by Quitman's division of volunteers in the grand plaza between the National Palace and the Cathedral—all the bands playing, in succession, "Hail Columbia," "Washington's March," "Yankee Doodle," "Hail to the Chief," etc. Even the inhabitants, catching the enthusiasm of the moment, filled the windows and lined the parapets, cheering the cavalcade as it passed at the gallop.

IX

COLONEL LEE AT HARPER'S FERRY

During the 1850's the slavery issue strained the nation's unity.
In 1859 avid abolitionist, John Brown, dreamed of making war against
"the peculiar institution" with an army of fugitive blacks and stubborn
whites. Heading a contingent of thirteen white men and five Negroes,
John Brown captured the federal arsenal at Harper's Ferry, Virginia,
on the night of 16 October 1859, hoping to distribute guns and am-
munition to the slaves and lead a revolt. The mayor was shot down
and Brown took prominent townsfolk hostage. The governor of Vir-
ginia ordered out the militia and pleaded with Washington for help.
John Brown holed up in a railroad roundhouse and defended his
band. In the evening, when Colonel Robert E. Lee arrived with a
detachment of United States Marines, just four of the abolitionists were
unwounded. The marines forced an entrance the next day and seized
the enfeebled force.
Colonel Lee sends his official report to the War Department.

I made preparations to attack the insurgents at daylight. But for
the fear of sacrificing the lives of some of the gentlemen held by them
as prisoners in a midnight assault, I should have ordered the attack at
once. Their safety was the Subject of painful consideration, & to prevent if possible, jeopardizing their lives, I determined to summon the
insurgents to surrender. As soon after daylight as the arrangements
were made, Lt. JEB Stuart 1st Capn, who had accompd me from
Washington as Staff Offr, was dispatched under a flag with a written
summons. . . .

Hd Qrs: Harpers Ferry
18th Oct 1859

Colonel Lee U.S.A. Comm the troops sent by the President of the
U.S. to suppress the insurrection at this place; demands the surrender
of the persons in the Armory buildings.

If they will peaceably surrender themselves & restore the pillaged property, they shall be kept in safety to await the orders of the President.

Col Lee represents to them in all frankness that it is impossible for them to escape; that the Armory is surrounded on all sides by troops, & that if he is compelled to take them by force he cannot answer for their safety.

(Signed) R E LEE
Col Comm
U.S. Troops

Knowing the character of the leader of the insurgents, I did not expect it would be accepted. I had therefore directed that the volunteer troops under their respective commanders should be paraded on the lines assigned them outside of the Armory, & had prepared a storming party of 12 marines under their Commander Lt. Green, & had placed them close to the Engine house, secure from its fire. Three marines were furnished with sledge hammers to break in the doors, & the men were instructed how to distinguish our citizens from the insurgents & to attack with the bayonet, & not to injure the blacks detained in custody, unless they resisted. Lt. Stuart was also directed not to receive from the insurgents any counter-proposition. If they accepted the terms offered, they must immediately deliver up their arms, & release their prisoners. If they did not he must on leaving the Engine house, give me the signal. My object was, with a view of saving our citizens, to have as short an interval as possible, between the summons & attack.

The summons as I had anticipated was rejected. At the concerted signal, the storming party moved quickly to the door & commenced the attack. The fire engines within the house had been placed by the besieged close to the doors. The doors were fastened by ropes, the spring of which prevented their being broken by the blows of the hammers. The men were therefore ordered to drop the hammers & with a portion of the reserve to use as a battering ram, a heavy ladder, with which they dashed in a part of the door & gave admittance to the storming party. The fire of the insurgents up to this time had been harmless. At the threshold one marine fell mortally wounded. The rest led by Lt. Green & Major Russell, quickly ended the contest. The insurgents that resisted were bayoneted. Their leader John Brown was cut down by the sword of Lt. Green, & our citizens were protected by both officers & men. The whole was over in a few minutes. . . .

From the information derived from the papers found upon the persons, & among the baggage of the insurgents, & the statement of those now in custody, it appears that the party consisted of 19 men; 14 white & 5 black. That they were headed by John Brown, of some notoriety in Kansas, who in June last located himself in Md: at the Kennedy farm, where he has been engaged in preparing to capture the U. S. works at Harpers Ferry. He avows that his object was the liberation of the slaves of Va. & of the whole South; & acknowledges that he has been disappointed in his expectations of aid from the black as well as white population, both in the Southern & Northern States. The blacks whom he forced from their homes in this neighborhood, as far as I could learn, gave him involuntary assistance. . . . The result proves that the plan was the attempt of a fanatic or madman, which could only end in failure; & its temporary success was owing to the panic & confusion he succeeded in creating, by magnifying his numbers.[20]

X

IN GREAT EVENTS WE MUST CHOOSE ONE WAY OR ANOTHER

John Brown was tried, convicted of treason against the Commonwealth of Virginia, and hanged on 2 December 1859. Abraham Lincoln was elected President of the United States in November, 1860. South Carolina seceded from the Union in December.

Before hostilities actually broke out, men were choosing sides. In January, 1861, William Tecumseh Sherman takes his stand.

My dear Sir,

I take it for granted you have been expecting for some days the accompanying paper from me. I have repeatedly and again make known to General Graham and Dr. Smith that in the event of a severance of the Relations hitherto existing between the Confederated States of this Union, I would be forced to choose the Old Union. It is barely possible that all states will secede South and North, that new combinations will result, but this process will be one of time and uncertainty. I cannot with my opinions await this subsequent development.

I have never been a Politician and therefore undervalue the excited feelings and opinions of Present Rulers, all over the Land, but I do think if the People cannot execute a form of Government like the Present, that a worse one will result.

I will keep the Cadets as quiet as is possible. They are nervous, and I think the interest of the State requires them here, guarding this property, and acquiring the Knowledge which will be useful for your State in after times—when I leave, which I now regard certain. . . . I entertain the kindest feelings to all, and would leave the State with much regret—only in Great Events we must choose one way or another.

Truly yr friend
W. T. SHERMAN

Louisiana State Seminary of Learning and
Military Academy, January 18th, 1861[21]

CHAPTER III
1861-1865

Wherever the enemy goes let our troops go also
ULYSSES S. GRANT

The North-South conflict erupted in 1861. By April the first group of southern states had seceded peacefully from the Union. The Confederates galvanized the North into retaliatory measures by bombarding federally-held Fort Sumter in South Carolina. The war for the Union had begun. The superiority of the North in manpower and resources was overwhelming. The total population of the South was 8,700,000 (of whom 3,500,000 were slaves), while the Union had a total of 22,700,000. In railroad facilities, industrial establishments, liquid capital, foodstuffs, the Yankees likewise possessed a decided advantage. The Confederacy relied upon her competent generals, the superior training of her volunteers, the defensive character of the war, and the value of her cotton exports. The Confederacy hoped that dependency on cotton imports and sympathy with the southern position would cause Great Britain to tip the balance in her favor.

The process of dragooning the South back into the Union was slow. President Lincoln, forced to employ trial-and-error in selecting capable military leadership, finally discovered Ulysses S. Grant. General Sherman pushed on relentlessly in Georgia and the Carolinas, corroding civilian morale as he battled the South's uniformed defenders. Grant's devastating punches in Virginia compelled the Confederates to surrender in the spring of 1865.

I

FORT SUMTER

When the Union attempted to reinforce Fort Sumter in Charleston Harbor in April, 1861, it resulted in the southern bombardment of the Yankee-held bastion on 12 April.

Captain Abner Doubleday, a West Pointer who had fought in the Mexican War, and who is sometimes called the "father of baseball," was second-in-command at Fort Sumter.

About 4 A.M. on the 12th I was awakened by some one groping about my room in the dark and calling out my name. It proved to be Anderson, who came to announce to me that he had just received a dispatch from Beauregard, dated 3:20 A.M., to the effect that he should open fire upon us in an hour. Finding it was determined not to return the fire until after breakfast, I remained in bed. As we had no lights, we could in fact do nothing before that time except to wander around in the darkness and fire without an accurate view of the enemy's works.

As soon as the outline of our fort could be distinguished, the enemy carried out their programme. It had been arranged, as a special compliment to the venerable Edmund Ruffin, who might almost be called the father of secession, that he should fire the first shot against us from the Stevens battery of Cummings Point. . . . Almost immediately afterward a ball from Cummings Point lodged in the magazine wall and by the sound seemed to bury itself in the masonry about a foot from my head, in very unpleasant proximity to my right ear. This is the one that probably came with Mr. Ruffin's compliments. In a moment the firing burst forth in one continuous roar, and large patches of both

171

the exterior and interior masonry began to crumble and fall in all directions. . . .

Nineteen batteries were now hammering at us, and the balls and shells from the ten-inch columbiads, accompanied by shells from the thirteen-inch mortars which constantly bombarded us, made us feel as if the war had commenced in earnest.

When it was broad daylight, I went down to breakfast. I found the officers already assembled at one of the long tables in the mess hall. Our party were calm and even somewhat merry. . . .

When this frugal repast was over, my company was told off in three details for firing purposes, to be relieved afterward by Seymour's company. As I was the ranking officer, I took the first detachment and marched them to the casemates which looked out upon the powerful iron-clad battery of Cummings Point.

In aiming the first gun fired against the rebellion I had no feeling of self-reproach, for I fully believed that the contest was inevitable and was not of our seeking. . . .

Our firing now became regular and was answered from the rebel guns which encircled us on the four sides of the pentagon upon which the fort was built. The other side faced the open sea. . . . When the immense mortar shells, after sailing high in the air, came down in a vertical direction and buried themselves in the parade ground, their explosion shook the fort like an earthquake. . . .

The firing continued all day without any special incident of importance, and without our making much impression on the enemy's works. They had a great advantage over us as their fire was concentrated on the fort which was in the center of the circle, while ours was diffused over the circumference. Their missiles were exceedingly destructive to the upper exposed portion of the work, but no essential injury was done to the lower casemates which sheltered us. . . .

From 4 to 6½ A.M. [April 13] the enemy's fire was very spirited. From 7 to 8 A.M. a rain-storm came on, and there was a lull in the cannonading. About 8 A.M. the officers' quarters were ignited by one of Ripley's incendiary shells or by shot heated in the furnaces at Fort Moultrie. [Lieutenant Colonel Ripley commanded Confederate-held Fort Moultrie in Charleston Harbor.] The fire was put out but at 10 A.M. a mortar shell passed through the roof and lodged in the flooring of the second story, where it burst and started the flames afresh. This, too, was extinguished; but the hot shot soon followed each other so rapidly that it was impossible for us to contend with them any longer. It became evident that the entire block, being built with wooden partitions, floors, and roofing must be consumed, and that the magazine, containing three hundred barrels of powder, would be endangered; for even after closing the metallic door, sparks might penetrate through the ventilator. The floor was covered with loose powder where a detail of men had been at work manufacturing cartridge-bags out of old shirts, woolen blankets, etc.

While the officers exerted themselves with axes to tear down and cut away all the woodwork in the vicinity, the soldiers were rolling barrels of powder out to more sheltered spots and were covering them with wet blankets. The labor was accelerated by the shells which were bursting around us; for Ripley had redoubled his activity at the first signs of a conflagration. We only succeeded in getting out some ninety-six barrels of powder, and then we were obliged to close the massive copper door and await the result. A shot soon after passed through the intervening shield, struck the door, and bent the lock in such a way that it could not be opened again. We were thus cut off from our supply of ammunition but still had some piled up in the vicinity of the guns. Anderson officially reported only four barrels and three cartridges as on hand when we left.

By 11 A.M. the conflagration was terrible and disastrous. One-fifth of the fort was on fire, and the wind drove the smoke in dense masses into the angle where we had all taken refuge. It seemed impossible to escape suffocation. Some lay down close to the ground, with handkerchiefs over their mouths, and others posted themselves near the embrasures, where the smoke was somewhat lessened by the draught of air. Every one suffered severely. I crawled out of one of these openings and sat on the outer edge, but Ripley made it lively for me there with his case-shot which spattered all around. Had not a slight change of wind taken place, the result might have been fatal to most of us.

Our firing having ceased and the enemy being very jubilant, I thought it would be as well to show them that we were not all dead yet, and ordered the gunners to fire a few rounds more. I heard afterward that the enemy loudly cheered Anderson for his persistency under such adverse circumstances.

. . . The roaring and crackling of the flames, the dense masses of whirling smoke, the bursting of the enemy's shells and our own which were exploding in the burning rooms, the crashing of the shot, and the sound of masonry falling in every direction, made the fort a pandemonium. When at last nothing was left of the building but the blackened walls and smoldering embers, it became painfully evident that an immense amount of damage had been done. . . .

About 12:48 P.M. the end of the flagstaff was shot down and the flag fell. . . .

About 2 P.M. Senator Wigfall, in company with W. Gourdin Young, of Charleston, unexpectedly made his appearance at one of the embrasures, having crossed over from Morris Island in a small boat rowed by negros. He had seen the flag come down, and supposed that we had surrendered in consequence of the burning of the quarters. . . . An artillery-man serving his gun was very much astonished to see a man's face at the entrance, and asked him what he was doing there. Wigfall replied that he wished to see Major Anderson. The man, refused to allow him to enter until he had surrendered himself as a prisoner and given up his sword. . . . Wigfall, in Beauregard's name, offered Anderson his own terms, which were, the evacuation of the fort, with permission to salute our flag and to march out with the honors of war, with our arms and private baggage, leaving all other war material behind. As soon as this matter was arranged, Wigfall returned to Cummings Point. . . .

All of the preliminaries having been duly adjusted, it was decided that the evacuation should take place the next morning. . . . We slept soundly that night for the first time, after all the fatigue and excitement of the two preceding days.

The next morning, Sunday, the 14th, we were up early, packing our baggage in readiness to go on board the transport. The time having arrived, I made preparations, by order of Major Anderson, to fire a national salute to the flag. . . .

The salute being over, the Confederate troops marched in to occupy the fort. The Palmetto Guard, Captain Cuthbert's company, detailed by Colonel De Saussure, and Captain Hollinquist's Company B, of the regulars, detailed by Colonel Ripley, constituted the new garrison under Ripley. . . . Anderson directed me to form the men on the parade ground, assume command, and march them on board the transport. I told him I should prefer to leave the fort with the flag flying and the drums beating "Yankee Doodle," and he authorized me to do so. As soon as our tattered flag came down and the silken banner made by the ladies of Charleston was run up, tremendous shouts of applause were heard from the vast multitude of spectators; and all the vessels and steamers, with one accord, made for the fort.[1]

II

I THEREFORE TENDER MY RESIGNATION

A few days after the bombardment of Fort Sumter, although he had been offered the command of the Union field army, Robert E. Lee tendered his resignation from the United States Army to General Scott. In a letter to his sister, Lee explained his decision.

Arlington, Va., April 20, 1861

GENERAL:

Since my interview with you on the 18th inst. I have felt that I ought no longer to retain my commission in the Army. I therefore tender my resignation, which I request you will recommend for acceptance. It would have been presented at once but for the struggle it has cost me to separate myself from a service to which I have devoted all the best years of my life and all the ability I possessed.

During the whole of that time—more than a quarter of a century—I have experienced nothing but kindness from my superiors, and the most cordial friendship from my comrades. To no one, General, have I been as much indebted as to yourself for uniform kindness and consideration, and it has always been my ardent desire to meet your approbation. I shall carry to the grave the most grateful recollections of your kind consideration, and your name and fame will always be dear to me.

Save in defense of my native State, I never desire again to draw my sword. Be pleased to accept my most earnest wishes for the continuance of your happiness and prosperity, and believe me,

Most truly yours,
R. E. LEE

My Dear Sister:

. . . We are now in a state of war which will yield to nothing. The whole South is in a state of revolution, into which Virginia, after a long struggle, has been drawn; and though I recognize no necessity for this state of things, and would have forborne and pleaded to the end for redress of grievances, real or supposed, yet in my own person I had to meet the question whether I should take part against my native State. With all my devotion to the Union, and the feeling of loyalty and duty of an American citizen, I have not been able to make up my mind to raise my hand against my relatives, my children, my home. I have, therefore, resigned my commission in the Army, and save in defense of my native State—with the sincere hope that my poor services may never be needed—I hope I may never be called upon to draw my sword. . . .[2]

III

MY DEAR MINNIE

A week before the first battle of Bull Run, 21 July 1861, the first major clash of the war, William Tecumseh Sherman took time from his duties to write a moving letter to his daughter.

Sunday morning, July 14, 61
My dear Minnie,
. . . War is a terrible thing. Especially when as now we are fighting people like Mrs. Turner and thousands of others whom I used to know as kind of good friends; and they thinking they are defending their country, their homes and families against foreign invaders—so my Dear Child don't get in the habit of calling hard names of Rebels, Traitors, but remember how easy it is for People to become deceived and drawn in step by step, till war, death and destruction are upon them. . . .
I have under my command two Regiments of New York Volunteers here just by Georgetown, and three Regiments of Volunteers about a mile out, where there is a large field in which to drill them. We are all daily waiting for orders to march into Virginia. . . . I have a great deal to do. Reports to receive and make, orders to give, and to drill 4000 men is hard work. My voice is now very hoarse. . . . We have

to get along with as few Regulars as possible as these officers are needed elsewhere,—scattered all over the land. When we march I will have a horse, and a servant named John Hill, two mounted soldiers near me called orderlies, and I will make John lead a pack horse with some blankets and provisions for the party. The soldiers carry each a blanket, pair of socks, and his musket, 40 cartridges, and 3 days provisions. . . . We must fight and subdue those in Arms against us and our Government. . . .

This is a strange war—and God Grant it may never be felt near you all. In the quiet of Lancaster I believe you are better off than anywhere else and I am glad you all like it so. You and Lizzy must write often. Let mamma read this to you. Tell Willy I would like to show him some real soldiering here, but he will see enough of them in his day.

Your papa
W. T. Sherman[3]

IV

THE OHIOANS

Four future Presidents from the state of Ohio served in the armies of the Union. In the following selections, William McKinley, then a lad of 18, describes camp life and a march in search of Johnny Reb; Rutherford B. Hayes, in the same outfit, tells of his first brush with the enemy; James A. Garfield recounts his battle with the Confederates in Kentucky; Ulysses S. Grant writes about the capture of Fort Donelson on the banks of the Cumberland River in Tennessee, his first important victory. In Grant's battle description, General Wallace is the same Lew Wallace who was active in raising a company during the Mexican War.

(McKinley)

Camp Chase, June 20, 1861

Companies are arriving almost every day, evincing the fact that Ohio is bound to share the trophies of coming conquest, and have her name immortalized in the annals of history as a firm supporter of freedom, and free institutions. Yesterday a company, numbering one hundred and two, from Chillicothe, arrived here, all fitted out and uniformed; they made rather an imposing appearance. We have not received our uniform as yet, but think we will get them the last of this week. Grey uniforms have already been proffered the Twenty-Third Regiment, but our Colonel refuses to accept them. He will take none but "blue. . . ."

Some of our boys are rather unwell, and unable to perform military duty. This is owing to a change of diet and different mode of living. The best of care is being taken of them, and they will soon be effective soldiers. As far as I can learn, there has been, and is, but little sickness among the thousands of soldiers now collected here. For the past week it has been exceedingly warm and sultry, we have been wishing for rain. . . .

Our boys are all determined to stand by the stars and stripes, and never give up until their lives are sacrificed, or the Government placed on a firm and solid foundation.

To-day quite a number of letters were received from Poland [Ohio], which made the soldiers' hearts leap for joy.

Last Sabbath we received five numbers of the Register, and you can scarcely imagine the anxiety of the boys to get a sight of them. The company divided themselves up into squads, and one of the number read to them. Our heartfelt thanks are due you, Mr. Editor, for the satisfaction your paper gave our hungry minds.

[*Camp Chase, 6 July 1861*] Present indications plainly declare that the conflict cannot long continue. The probable duration of the war we do not pretend to discuss. Let time reveal the glad day when this conflict shall pause—when the broken bands of this once glorious Union shall be united—when our Government shall be established on a foundation too strong to be shaken by aspiring demagogues and traitorous rebels.

The 4th of July, the illustrious day of our National Independence, has passed. The occasion was appropriately celebrated by the soldiery collected at Camp Chase.

At 9 o'clock A.M. the Twenty-Third Regiment assembled on the parade ground by order from head-quarters, and there formed a hollow square. The Declaration of Independence was read, followed by our favorite national air, "Hail Columbia," by the regimental brass band.

Lieut. Col. Matthews addressed the Regiment in a brief yet pointed manner. He concluded by proposing three cheers for the Union, which was promptly responded to by the soldiers. The parade was then dismissed, with orders that there would be none of the usual duties performed that day. It might be proper here to remark, that none of the soldiers were permitted to leave the camp.

In the evening we had quite a display of fire-works. Sky-rockets ascended in great numbers, roman candles illuminated the encampment, and the sound of the musket was heard. The display, grand indeed, closed by the ascension of two splendid balloons. Slowly the airships wended their solitary course upward, until they were removed far from our view. At 9 o'clock P.M. a picket guard, numbering about fifty, was sent out of the encampment, to arrest soldiers who had broken guard, or otherwise disobeyed laws of the camp. Before the light of day, nearly fifty had been arrested and lodged in the guard-house.

[*Camp Chase, 19 July 1861*] We have received a fatigue suit, canteens, knapsacks and caps, and today we will receive all of our underclothing. Our fatigue uniform includes pants and coat; color of coats, indigo blue; color of pants, sky blue; they are very good for a fatigue suit, and add greatly to the appearance of the Regiment; they did not come until they were greatly needed. . . .

[*Weston, Va. 16 August 1861*] During the past week, the wing of our Regiment which remains here, has been compelled to perform an unusual amount of duty caused by the absence of some of our Regiment. Our labors, however, will be somewhat lessened in the future. Last Friday morning our picket guard returned to camp possessed of quite a fearful story about the enemy lurking around a bridge at which they were stationed. This report caused considerable excitement in camp, and together with the fact that one of the 23d Regiment has been shot in the hand while on picket guard was quite sufficient to cause a sensation among the soldiers and incite a desire to give the rascals their dues, should they be discovered.

Accordingly four of our company, independent of the regular detailed guard, volunteered on the following night, to share in the fun, fight or anything which might chance to be their fate. Corporals Johnson and Halliger, another member of our Company and myself, composed the number. Before the sun has sunk in the western horizon, we had commenced our silent march, and soon nothing could be heard but the dulcet strains of the bullfrog, or what we sometimes imagined to be the suppressed signs of a scouting rebel. While on our way we frequently halted, brought our muskets to a "ready," and were almost in the act of firing, when an itinerant porker, or one of the canine species, would appear from the thick underbush by the wayside.

We at last reached our desired station, amidst the darkness of a clouded night, Corporal Halliger, J. B. Frame, and myself, were placed in a cornfield on the road leading from Weston to Sutton, and about two miles and a half from the first mentioned place, while the rest of our party were stationed in an adjoining bridge and on the opposite side of the road from us. . . .

We had to keep our ears wide open and our eyes "peeled," as the enemy was expected to appear, in some shape before morning. But finally morning's dawn approached, without affording us an opportunity to discharge our loaded muskets. . . .

One of our pickets took the occasion to remark, that it was impossible for him to sleep, owing to the continuous and nocturnal biting of the mosquitos. We returned to our quarters with the firm determination that the enemy must be a little more numerous before we should volunteer to go picketing again. I have been out since, but not as a volunteer, and returned with a similar experience.

[*Camp at Buckhannon, 22 August 1861*] On Saturday, 17th, we took up our march for Bulltown, Braxton County, Va., and while on our way met with quite a serious incident. When about three miles from the town, our ranks were fired into from a neighboring hill by a concealed foe. Some five reports were heard; only three shots, however, taking effect. The result of this ambuscade was, that Corporal Becker was shot through the back, John Robison in the neck. . . .

No sooner were these reports heard, than the Company commenced mounting the towering hill, in pursuit of the assassins, but ere we had reached the place of firing, the skulking, blood-thirsty rebels had retreated to some secret place. . . . So we continued our march until we reached Bulltown, where we encamped for the night.[4]

(*Hayes*)

Gauley River, 8 Miles South of Summersville,
September 11, 1861.

Dear Lucy:—

Well, darling, we have had our first battle, and the enemy have fled precipitately. I say "we," although it is fair to say that our brigade, consisting of the Twenty-third, the Thirtieth (Colonel Ewing), and Mack's Battery had little or nothing to do, except to stand as a reserve. The only exception to this was four companies of the Twenty-third, Captains Sperry, Howard, Zimmerman, and Woodward, under my command, who were detailed to make an independent movement. I had one man wounded and four others hit in their clothing and accoutrements. You will have full accounts of the general fight in the papers. My little detachment did as much real work—hard work—as anybody. We crept down and up a steep rocky mountain, on our hands and knees part of the time, through laurel thickets almost impenetrable, until dark. At one time I got so far ahead in the struggle that I had but three men. I finally gathered them by a halt, although a part were out all night. We were near half an hour listening to the cannon and musketry, waiting for our turn to come.

You have often heard of the feelings of men in the interval between the order of battle and the attack. Matthews, myself, and others were rather jocose in our talk, and my actual feeling was very similar to what I have when going into an important trial—not different nor more intense. I thought of you and the boys and the other loved ones, but there was no such painful feeling as is sometimes described. I doubted the success of the attack and with good reason and in good company. The truth is, our enemy is very industrious and ingenious in contriving ambuscades and surprises and entrenchments but they lack pluck. They expect to win, and too often do win, by superior strategy and cunning. Their entrenchments and works were of amazing extent. During the whole fight we rarely saw a man. Most of the firing was done at bushes and log and·earth barricades.

We withdrew at dark, the attacking brigades having suffered a good deal from the enemy and pretty severely from one of those deplorable mistakes which have so frequently happened in this war—viz., friends attacking friends. The Tenth and Twenty-eighth (Irish and Second German of Cincinnati) fired on each other and charged doing much mischief. My detachment was in danger from the same cause. I ran upon the Twenty-eighth, neither seeing the other until within a rod. We mutually recognized, however, although it was a mutual surprise. It so happened, curiously enough, that I was the extreme right man of my body and Markbreit the left man of his. We had a jolly laugh and introductions to surrounding officers as partners, etc.

The enemy were thoroughly panic-stricken by the solid volleys of

McCook's Ninth and the rifled cannon of Smith's Thirteenth. The Tenth suffered most. The enemy probably began their flight by a secret road soon after dark, leaving flag, ammunition, trunks, arms, stores, etc., etc., but no dead or wounded. Bowie knives, awful to look at, but no account in war; I have one. One wagon-load of family stuff—a good Virginia plain family—was left. They were spinning, leaving rolls of wool, knitting, and making bedquilts. I enclose a piece; also a pass— all queer.

They (the enemy) crossed the Gauley River and are said to be fortifying on the other side. . . .

I have no time to write to other friends. The men are now talking to me. Besides, I want to sleep. Dearest, I think of you and the dear ones first, last, and all the time. I feel much encouraged about the war; things are every way looking better. We are in the midst of the serious part of a campaign. Goodbye, dearest. Pass this letter around—bad as it is. I have no time to write to all. I must sleep. On Sunday last, I rode nineteen hours, fifty to sixty miles, crossed a stream with more water than the Sandusky at this season at Mr. Valette's from thirty to forty times—wet above my knees all the time and no sleep for thirty-six hours; so "excuse haste and a bad pen," as Uncle says.

Affectionately,

R. B. Hayes[5]

(*Garfield, at Middle Creek in eastern Kentucky, 9–10 January 1862*)

At 8 o'clock we reached the mouth of Abbott's Creek, 1 mile below Prestonburg. I found that the enemy was encamped on the creek 3 miles above, and had been supplying himself with meal at a stream-mill in the vicinity. I sent back an order to Paintsville to move forward all our available force, having learned that another boat load of stores had arrived. I encamped on the crest of a wooded hill, where we slept on our arms in the rain till 4 o'clock in the morning, when I moved up Abbott's Creek 1 mile and crossed over to the mouth of Middle Creek, which empties into the Big Sandy opposite Prestonburg. Supposing the enemy to be encamped on Abbott's Creek, it was my intention to advance up Middle Creek and cut off his retreat, while the cavalry should attack his rear. I advanced slowly, throwing out flankers and feeling my way cautiously among the hills. At 8 o'clock in the morning we reached the mouth of Middle Creek, where my advance began a brisk skirmishing with the enemy's cavalry which continued till we had advanced 2½ miles up the stream to within 1,000 yards of the forks of the creek, which I had learned the enemy were then occupying.

I drew up my force on the sloping point of a semicircular hill, and at 12 o'clock sent forward 20 mounted men to make a dash across the plain. This drew the enemy's fire, and in part disclosed his position. The Fifty-fourth Virginia Regiment (Colonel Trigg) was posted behind the farther point of the same ridge which I occupied. I immediately sent forward two Kentucky companies to pass along this crest of the ridge, and one company Forty-second Ohio, under command of Capt. F. A . Williams, to cross the creek, which was nearly waist-deep, and occupy a spur of the high rocky ridge in front and to the left of my position.

In a few minutes the enemy opened a fire from one 6 and one 12 pounder. A shell from the battery fell in the midst of my skirmishers on the right, but did not explode. Soon after the detachment on the left engaged the enemy, who was concealed in large force behind the ridge. I sent forward a re-enforcement of two companies to the right, under Major Burke, of the Fourteenth Kentucky, and 90 men, under Major Pardee, of the Forty-second Ohio, to support Captain Williams. The enemy withdrew his Fifty-Fourth Virginia across the creek, and sent strong re-enforcements to the hills on the left. About 2 o'clock I ordered Colonel Cranor, with 150 men from the Fortieth and Forty-second Ohio and Twenty-second Kentucky, to re-enforce Major Pardee. Meantime the enemy had occupied the main ridge to a point nearly opposite the right of my position, and opened a heavy fire on my reserve, which was returned with good effect. In order more effectually to prevent his attempt to outflank me I sent Lieutenant-Colonel Monroe, of the Twenty-second Kentucky, with 120 of his own and the Fourteenth Regiment, to cross the creek a short distance below the point I occupied, and drive back the enemy from his position. This he did in gallant style, killing 15 or 20. Inch by inch the enemy, with more than three times our number, were driven up the steep ridge nearest the creek by Colonel Cranor and Major Pardee.

At 4 o'clock the re-enforcement under Lieutenant Colonel Sheldon, of the Forty-second Ohio, came in sight, which enabled me to send forward the remainder of my reserve, to pass around to the right and endeavor to capture the enemy's guns, which he had been using against us for three hours, but without effect. During the fight he had fired 30 rounds from his guns, but they were badly served, as only one of his shells exploded, and none of his shot, not even his canister, took effect. At 4:30 he ordered a retreat. My men drove him down the slopes of the hills, and at 5 o'clock he had been driven from every point. . . . It was growing dark, and I deemed it unsafe to pursue him, lest my men on the different hills should fire on each other in the darkness. The firing had scarcely ceased when a brilliant light streamed up from the valley to which the enemy had retreated. He was burning his stores and fleeing in great disorder. Twenty-five of his dead were left on the field, and 60 more were found next day thrown into a gorge in the hills.[6]

(*Grant, at Fort Donelson in Tennessee, February, 1862*)

I was very impatient to get to Fort Donelson because I knew the importance of the place to the enemy and supposed he would reinforce it rapidly. I felt that 15,000 men on the 8th would be more effective than 50,000 a month later. I asked Flag-officer Foote, therefore, to order his gunboats still about Cairo to proceed up the Cumberland River and not to wait for those gone to Eastport and Florence; but the others got back in time and we started on the 12th [February, 1862]. . . .

I started from Fort Henry with 15,000 men, including eight batteries and part of a regiment of cavalry, and, meeting with no obstruction to detain us, the advance arrived in front of the enemy by noon. That afternoon and the next day were spent in taking up ground to make the investment as complete as possible. . . . The troops were not intrenched, but the nature of the ground was such that they were just as well protected from the fire of the enemy as if rifle-pits had been thrown up. Our line was generally along the crest of ridges. The artillery was protected by being sunk in the ground. The men who were not serving the guns were perfectly covered from fire on taking position a little back from the crest. The greatest suffering was from want of shelter. It was midwinter and during the siege we had rain and snow, thawing and freezing alternately. It would not do to allow camp-fires except far down the hill out of sight of the enemy, and it would not do to allow many of the troops to remain there at the same time. In the march over from Fort Henry numbers of the men had thrown away their blankets and overcoats. There was therefore much discomfort and absolute suffering.

During the 12th and 13th, and until the arrival of Wallace and

Thayer on the 14th, the National forces, composed of but 15,000 men, without intrenchments, confronted an intrenched army of 21,000 without conflict further than what was brought on by ourselves. Only one gunboat had arrived. There was a little skirmishing each day, brought on by the movement of our troops in securing commanding positions; but there was no actual fighting during this time except once, on the 13th, in front of McClernand's command. That general had undertaken to capture a battery of the enemy which was annoying his men. Without orders or authority he sent three regiments to make the assault. The battery was in the main line of the enemy, which was defended by his whole army present. The assault was a failure, and the loss on our side was great for the number of men engaged. . . . Up to this time the surgeons with the army had no difficulty in finding room in the houses near our line for all the sick and wounded; but now hospitals were overcrowded. Owing, however, to the energy and skill of the surgeons the suffering was not so great as it might have been. The hospital arrangements were as complete as it was possible to make them, considering the inclemency of the weather and the lack of tents, in a sparsely settled country where the houses were generally of but one or two rooms.

On the return of Captain Walke [commanding one of the gunboats] to Fort Henry on the 10th, I had requested him to take the vessels that had accompanied him on his expedition up the Tennessee, and get possession of the Cumberland as far up towards Donelson as possible.

He started without delay, taking, however, only his own gunboat, the Carondelet, towed by the steamer Alps. Captain Walke arrived a few miles below Donelson on the 12th, a little after noon. About the time the advance of troops reached a point within gunshot of the fort on the land side, he engaged the water batteries at long range. On the 13th I informed him of my arrival the day before and of the establishment of most of our batteries, requesting him at the same time to attack that day so that I might take advantage of any diversion. The attack was made and many shots fell within the fort. The investment on the land side was made as complete as the number of troops engaged would admit of. . . .

The plan was for the troops to hold the enemy within his lines, while the gunboats should attack the water-batteries at close quarters and silence his guns if possible. Some of the gunboats were to run the batteries, get above the fort and above the village of Dover. I had ordered a reconnaissance made with the view of getting troops to the river above Dover in case they should be needed there. That position attained by the gunboats it would have been but a question of time—and a very short time, too—when the garrison would have been compelled to surrender.

By three in the afternoon of the 14th Flag-officer Foote was ready, and advanced upon the water batteries with his entire fleet. After coming in range of the batteries of the enemy the advance was slow. I occupied a position on shore from which I could see the advancing navy. The leading boat got within a very short distance of the water battery, not further off I think than two hundred yards, and I soon saw one and then another of them dropping down the river, visibly disabled. Then the whole fleet followed and the engagement was closed for the day. . . .

The enemy had evidently been much demoralized by the assault, but they were jubilant when they saw the disabled vessels dropping down the river entirely out of the control of the men on board. I only witnessed the falling back of our gunboats and felt sad enough at the time over the repulse. . . . The sun went down on the night of the 14th of February, 1862, leaving the army confronting Fort Donelson anything but comforted over the prospects. The weather had turned intensely cold; the men were without tents and could not keep up fires where most of them had to stay. Two of the strongest of our gunboats had been disabled, presumably beyond the possibility of rendering any present assistance. I retired this night not knowing but that I would have to intrench my position, and bring up tents for the men or build huts under the cover of the hills.

On the morning of the 15th, before it was yet broad day, a messenger from Flag-officer Foote handed me a note, expressing a desire to see me on the flag-ship and saying that he had been injured the day before so much that he could not come himself to me. . . .

When I reached the fleet I found the flag-ship was anchored out in the stream. A small boat, however, awaited my arrival and I was soon on board with the flag-officer. He explained to me in short the condition in which he was left by the engagement of the evening before, and suggested that I should intrench while he returned to Mound City with his disabled boats, expressing at the time the belief that he could have the necessary repairs made and be back in ten days. . . .

When I left the National line to visit Flag-officer Foote I had no idea that there would be any engagement on land unless I brought it on myself. The conditions for battle were much more favorable to us than they had been for the first two days of the investment. From the 12th to the 14th we had but 15,000 men of all arms and no gunboats. Now we had been reinforced by a fleet of six naval vessels, a large division of troops under General Wallace and 2,500 men brought over from Fort Henry belonging to the division of C. F. Smith. The enemy, however, had taken the initiative. Just as I landed I met Captain Hillyer of my staff, white with fear, not for his personal safety, but for the safety of the National troops. He said the enemy had come out of his lines in full force and attacked and scattered McClernand's division, which was in full retreat. The roads, were unfit for making fast time, but I got to my command as soon as possible. The attack had been made on the National right. I was some four or five miles north of our left. The line was about three miles long. In reaching the point where the disaster had occurred I had to pass the divisions of Smith and Wallace. I saw no sign of excitement on the portion of the line held by Smith; Wallace was nearer the scene of conflict and had taken part in it. He had, at an opportune time, sent Thayer's brigade to the support of McClernand and thereby contributed to hold the enemy within his lines.

I saw everything favorable for us along the line of our left and center. When I came to the right appearances were different. The enemy had come out in full force to cut his way out and make his escape. McClernand's division had to bear the brunt of the attack from this combined force. His men had stood up gallantly until the ammunition in their cartridge-boxes gave out. There was abundance of ammunition near by lying on the ground in boxes, but not all of our commanders had been educated to the point of seeing that their men were constantly supplied with ammunition during an engagement. When the men found themselves without ammunition they could not stand up against troops who seemed to have plenty of it. The division broke, but most of the men, only fell back out of range of the fire of the enemy. It must have been about this time that Thayer pushed his brigade in between the enemy and those of our troops that were without ammunition. At all events, the enemy fell back within his intrenchments and was there when I got on the field.

I saw the men standing in knots talking in the most excited manner.

No officer seemed to be giving any directions. The soldiers had their muskets but no ammunition, while there were tons of it close at hand. I heard some of the men say that the enemy had come out with knapsacks, and haversacks filled with rations. They seemed to think this indicated a determination on his part to stay out and fight just as long as the provisions held out. I turned to Colonel J. D. Webster, of my staff, and said: "Some of our men are pretty badly demoralized, but the enemy must be more so, for he has attempted to force his way out, but has fallen back: the one who attacks first now will be victorious and the enemy will have to be in a hurry if he gets ahead of me." I determined to make the assault at once on our left. It was clear to my mind that the enemy had started to march out with his entire force, except a few pickets, and if our attack could be made on the left before the enemy could redistribute his forces along the line, we would find little opposition except from the intervening abatis. I directed Colonel Webster to ride with me and call out to the men as we passed: "Fill your cartridge-boxes, quick, and get into line; the enemy is trying to escape, and he must not be permitted to do so." This acted like a charm.

The men only wanted someone to give them a command. We rode rapidly to Smith's quarters, when I directed him to charge the enemy's works in his front with his whole division, saying at the same time that he would find nothing but a very thin line to contend with. The general was off in an incredibly short time, going in advance himself to keep his men from firing while they were working themselves through the abatis intervening between them and the enemy. The outer line of rifle-pits was passed, and the night of the 15th General Smith, with much of his division, bivouacked within the lines of the enemy. There was now no doubt but that the Confederates must surrender or be captured the next day. . . .

Before daylight General Smith brought to me the following letter from General Buckner:

Headquarters, Fort Donelson
February 16, 1862

Sir:

In consideration of all the circumstances governing the present situation of affairs at this station, I propose to the Commanding Officer of the Federal forces the appointment of Commissioners to agree upon terms of capitulation of the forces and fort under my command, and in that view suggest an armistice until 12 o'clock to-day.

I am, sir, very respectfully,

Your ob't se'v't,

S. B. Buckner
Brig. Gen. C. S. A.

To this I responded as follows:

Headquarters Army in the Field,
Camp near Donelson,
February 16, 1862

General S. B. Buckner,
Confederate Army.

Sir:

Yours of this date, proposing armistice and appointment of Commissioners to settle terms of capitulation, is just received. No terms except an unconditional and immediate surrender can be accepted. I propose to move immediately upon your works.

I am, sir, very respectfully,

Your ob't se'v't,
U. S. Grant
Brig. Gen.

To this I received the following reply:

Headquarters, Dover, Tennessee,
February 16, 1862.

To Brig. Gen'l. U.S. Grant,
U. S. Army.

Sir:

The distribution of the forces under my command, incident to an unexpected change of commanders, and the overwhelming force under your command, compel me, notwithstanding the brilliant success of the Confederate arms yesterday, to accept the ungenerous and unchivalrous terms which you propose.

I am, sir,

Your very ob't se'v't,
S.B. Buckner
Brig. Gen. C.S.A.[7]

V

BLOODHOUNDS AND BUSHWHACKERS

In the same year that Grant dislodged the enemy at Fort Donelson, a band of federal soldiers in disguises infiltrated the South and stole a locomotive in an ill-fated attempt to cut an important Rebel supply line. The story of "the great locomotive chase" has been retold many times.

The Confederates hanged the leader, James J. Andrews, and seven others. Eight escaped from prison at Atlanta, 16 October 1862, and made their way back to Union lines. Six others were exchanged as prisoners of war the following year. All the participants were given the first Congressional Medals of Honor ever awarded.

Two days before his execution, Andrews writes to friends in Flemingsburg, Kentucky. As Corporal Wilson Brown fled from prison, he paired off with Private William Knight, and the two pushed northward. Brown tells of this escape in his memoirs.

June 5th, 62

D. S. McGavic, Esq.
Flemingsburg, Ky.

Dear Sir:
You will doubtless be surprised to hear from me from this place & more surprised to hear that I am to be executed on the 7th.

First: For attempting to capture and run a train of cars from the western and Atlantic R.R. To Huntsville, Alabama for the youse of General Mitchell. I had a party of twenty one detailed men from the 2.21 and 33 Ohio Regiments with me. We succeeded in getting possession of the train and traveled with it some eighty or eighty-five miles when on account of one extra train being on the road, we were compelled to abandon the train, the party scattering and trying to make our way back on foot, the whole party however, were captured. I was taken on the 14th day of April. I am satisfied that I could very easily have goten away had they not put a pack of Doggs on my trail, it was impossible to elude them, I was tried by Court Marshall and Rec'd my sentence on the last day of May. One week before the time set for my examination.

On Monday morning the 2nd I made an attempt to escape I succeeded in getting out of prison and ran by the guard, they shot at me but not hiting me, the whole country was immediately swarmed with soldiers. I succeeded in eluding them until Tuesday about two o'clock, when I was recaptured and will be executed on Saturday. The sentence seems a hard one for the crime proven against me, but I suppose the court that tride me thought otherwise.

I have now calmly submitted to my fate and have been earnestly engaged in preparing to meet my God in place and I have found that piece of mind and tranquility of sole that even astonishes myself. I never supposed it possible that a man could feel so entire a change under simelar circumstances. How I would like to have one hours chatt with you, but this I shall never have in this life but hope and prey we may meet in Heaven where the troubles and trials of this life never enter, what the fate of the balance of the party will be, I am unable to say, but I hope they will not share the fate of their leader, if they ever return some two or three of them will call on you and the rest of the friends and I hope you will receive them kindly, they are noble fellows and will give you a full history of the affair.

Please acquaint my friends of my fate. I shall try to wright to some two or three more before my execution. Tell J. B. Jackson should there be any claims that I neglected to settle to pay them and keep the horse. I dont think there are any but there may be; in regard to the other matters, do exactly as instructed before I left I have rec'd. no letters from Fleminsburg, since I left, I wrote several but never rec'd. any answers.

Please read this letter to Mrs. Eckles and tell her that I have thought of her kindness many times and that I hope we may meet in Heaven where we shall enjoy the presence of the Lord together forever. Give my kindest regards to Mr. Eckles also. According to the source of nature it will not be long until we shall meet in that happy country, Blessed thoughts.

Remember me also to the young ladies of Flemingsburg, especialy to Miss. Kate Wallingford and Miss. Nannie Baxter. Hoping we may meet in that better country, I bid you along and last farewell.

J. Andrews[8]

(Brown)

Knight and I were partners en route from Atlanta to Somerset, Kentucky, four hundred miles distant. When they moved us to Atlanta, they removed our chains thinking we were so far from Union lines that we would not attempt to escape. In this they were mistaken.

After elaborate planning, we seized the keeper of the prison when he came to our cell to feed us, and rushed out upon the guards and quickly disarmed six of them, took their guns and started to run for the woods, one mile away. Knight and I ran like greyhounds.

We had to kill a man who tried to stop us with a club as we entered the woods. No sooner were we inside than we heard bloodhounds. The Rebs were surging close. We headed north from Atlanta, stopping only to take a bearing from the sounds of the hounds.

We were determined not to die on a Rebel scaffold. We climbed a small hill ahead of the hounds, and used rocks to kill four of the ten while the Rebs were yelling: "Halt, you Yankee devils, halt halt. Shoot the engine thieves, don't take one alive." This made us move along.

Fortunately none of their bullets hit us. With the North Star as our guide we followed a course we mapped out before we broke out of prison.

All we had with us to eat were crusts of bread from the prison; we knew if we could get into the mountains we could find berries, which we did. The first night out we hid in a cave in the side of a mountain, having shaken off the hounds by wading a stream for a distance.

We slept, not awaking until after sundown. We decided to travel at night, hide by day. Our feet were sore from the beginning, and our clothes almost in tatters from the start. But we thought only of freedom and getting back to our lines.

I killed a coon with a club the first day out and we ate it raw and without salt. It strengthened us. The second night out we could still hear shots and bloodhounds.

By the third day our shoes had given out and we wrapped our feet in rags. We headed for the big mountains of Georgia and the land we hiked through was barren, sparsely settled and unfit for cultivation.

We finally reached the mountains, the top covered with beautiful grass and shaded with pine and cedar trees. We found a spring and some chestnut trees full of nuts. We loaded ourselves quickly of them and they kept us from starving. That day we met an old, old man who had built himself a stone cabin in the mountains. Here we stayed for two days, allowing our feet a rest, and getting lots of sleep with him as a lookout.

We were anxious to get into eastern Tennessee because most of these people were loyal to the Union.

[After several days of trudging through the mountains they came to a valley. They decided to take a chance and approach a house for food and a night's lodging. The man and woman received them with suspicion, seemed to accept them when told they were the "engine thieves" and fed them supper. After they ate they were shown to a room to spend the night. Awakened in the night, they discovered they had been betrayed.]

The door was thrown open and in stalked the old man of the house and two other long legged six footers, each carrying a rifle. One of them said to us: "We got you Yanks, do you surrender?" "Yes," we replied. But when they leaned their guns against the wall and turned to get a rope to tie us, we grabbed their guns and made our escape, taking the two newcomers as prisoners.

We stopped to rest some miles from the house. The two tried to jump up and we had to kill them. We took their shoes and continued our flight. The next day we slept, undisturbed, in a barn. We would have starved to death if we hadn't been able to find chestnuts along the way.

The next night I lost Knight. We had lain down to rest and when I woke up, Knight was gone. I called, got no answer. So I decided to go forward, hoping I'd run in to him.

I soon came to a river and found it was the Halsteen. Suddenly I noticed a spot where the mud on the bank was smoothed over and letters written on it. In the mud was written—I got lost from you, keep on a northeast course, I go slow. This was good news. All of a sudden I heard a rifle shot and hounds, and men yelling.

A man came running toward me and I recognized Knight. "Come on," he yelled, "the Rebs are after me." We ran into a thicket. We were surrounded. Coming out with our arms up, we surrendered. As luck would have it, they were Union sympathizers.

The leader gave us two seven shooters and 40 rounds of cartridges, told us Rebs were after them and we could help fight them off.

Soon 10 bushwhackers appeared. We lay in wait until they were within five rods, then we opened fire. They ran, we pursued and wiped out all of them.

Pleased, the captain of the group of Union sympathizers set us in the right direction after giving us the revolvers and a good supply of ammunition and described a house where we could get food.

The pangs of hunger impelled us rapidly in the direction of the house, five miles distance. Arriving we were greeted by a barking dog; then a man appeared, heard our story, and invited us to supper.

Before we were through eating two of the boys in the family came running into the house shouting "the —— Rebs are coming." They brought out guns, passed them around and prepared for the raid.

The Rebs, well mounted, dashed into the lane, carbines in hand. We poured a volley into them that caused a hasty retreat. In following them we found one, wounded, by the roadside. We brought him to the house. Something about him looked familiar. I asked Knight what he thought. Knight said the man looked like one of the guards at the Atlanta prison.

We asked him if he guarded the raiders at Atlanta. He admitted he did, and showed us a scar on his head where, he said, one of the raiders dealt him a blow that sent him whirling. He told us he wanted to join the army, but at Knoxville he discovered the outfit there were not Confederate soldiers, but bushwhackers, plundering the country-side. We said we hoped he would recover and join the Union army and fight for God's people.

The head of the house was John Flint and his whole family were Unionists. They fed us well and after several days we thanked them and continued our journey.

Knight wrote in a little book the names of loyal people we might find on our way through Tennessee. One family was named Wamic, and we had a description of their house.

After walking for about 10 miles we sat down and ate from provisions the Flints had given us. Then not far from the mountains we ran across a road that was marked by fresh horse tracks—a party of bush-whackers for sure.

We hid and prepared to watch for their return. We didn't have to wait long. Soon we saw retreating Rebels, followed closely by a force of cavalry who were cutting them down right and left.

We waited until they were out of hearing, then walked out on the road and found two unconscious graycoats. We relieved them of their

Winchester rifles. We were now in possession of two rifles and 35 rounds of ammunition. We could fight if necessary. A few miles further on we came to a clearing and saw a house like the description of Wamic's.

Two armed men confronted us near the house. We told them we were the engine thieves, trying to get back to Somerset, Kentucky. They greeted us friendly like and invited us to join them until they made sure no bushwhackers were in the area.

Sure enough, two of the graycoats turned up. We shot one and took the other prisoner. We were going to hang him, but he asked to be shot. But before we could fire, he dropped dead. We figured he died of fright.

Then we went to the Wamic house, were introduced and told them our experiences, which they insisted on hearing before supper.

It was here we met Captain Sterling, leader of a group of loyalists fighting bushwhackers. He asked us to join them and we did. For a week we stayed in a cave near the Wamic house as the captain and his boys went on a roundup to increase their forces.

Then one day we got word the captain wanted us at the house.

The captain and his men were busy making preparations for the raid and were much pleased at the idea of having two of the engine thieves in their gang. "We are going to try to break up a band of Rebel bushwhackers that had been terrorizing the loyal element of east Tennessee," he told us. We rode for about three hours, then the captain said it was only 20 miles to the Rebel position, that we'd wait until midnight, then charge.

We rode to within 10 miles of the Rebel camp, examined our firearms and waited. We had 58 men armed with repeating rifles and navy revolvers and felt confident. We drank some applejack and prepared to rush the Rebs like a Kansas blizzard.

At midnight we dashed to within sight of their campfires, finding no guards. We rode straight into their camp and found them fast asleep. But they woke up and fired into us, wounding several. We cut them down with our sabers. Some of the 80 in camp got away and fired on us from the fringes. We followed, and after a fierce battle, we wiped them out.

The captain then turned his attention to us and escorted us for 10 miles toward Somerset, our destination.

We turned our horses over to the captain and thanked him for his interest in us and set out on foot toward Somerset, some 80 miles away.

We traveled in low swampy land, with big ponds and lakes, said to be infested with large snakes. We didn't see any, though, and had to forage for a living, not having brought provisions with us. Frequently we sank up to our knees in mud and water and the mosquitoes pursued us like a pack of bloodhounds. After hours and hours of walking we came out of the swamp and onto dry ground.

We hoped to reach the mountains soon. From high on a hill we looked into a valley and saw some fine houses and barns. Almost starved, we decided to chance it and ask for food.

A dog, roaring like a lion, met us at the first house, but the man called him off and after finding out we were the engine thieves, invited us in, introduced us to his wife and two daughters and said his boys were hunting and would be back shortly. Their name was Smith.

Smith told us we were 60 miles from Somerset and that the woods were full of Rebel bushwhackers. After the boys returned we had supper.

After we ate we showed them our rifles, which made their eyes sparkle.

The old man asked us to tell them about our escape from Atlanta prison. We told them eight of our gang were executed near Atlanta and we escaped. They were amazed and seemed pleased to meet the two of the engine thieves.

Suddenly one of the boys standing near the window said, "yonder comes some armed men on horseback; get your guns and we will have a fight."

We all sprang up. I looked out and saw about 20 greasy Rebs. I noticed they had flintlock rifles and squirrel hoot guns and appeared intoxicated. They dismounted and came up, knocked on the door, then when nobody opened it, shot a volley into the house.

We stayed silent. Then they broke the door open and four heads appeared in the hall. Bang went two Winchesters and the heads disappeared. We heard curses and yelling. They rushed us. We shot six of them and then they ran, mounted and galloped off. We thought they were going after reinforcements.

Billy Smith, the son, said he'd go get help while we buried the dead. It was noon the next day we sat down to dinner and the women were afraid the Rebs would come back and burn the house down. We figured out how we'd protect the house, and set guard to wait for their return.

That night the moon was bright as 19 of us faced 25 or 30 of the enemy. We surprised them and the volley turned them into a fast retreat. We found four dead Rebs and two mortally wounded.

At breakfast we were refreshed and ready for an emergency, dividing our party into two squads; one to scout for turkey and the other to guard.

The hunting party got a deer and that night we had a feast. But after eating we set up a guard again. I told Knight: "I'm getting tired of this life; it seems that we are constantly throwing ourselves into danger to defend someone else. I propose after tonight's fight, we leave and try to join our old 21st Ohio and then we can go into battle with good backing."

That night Bill Smith returned from scouting with a Reb who said he was friendly disposed to us. So we swore him into our gang. He told us a gang of 40 or 45 were coming and that they were drunk but well armed. We set up an advance guard and waited.

Soon we were warned of the approach of the band. We waited until they were within 10 rods of us, then fired and charged. We chased the cowards but found none dead, nor any wounded. We thought this was odd. We examined our guns and found they had been tampered with.

Sure enough, in the Reb's cartridge box we found blank cartridges and a little thing called a wormer, a screw made to draw loads from guns.

The Rebel started to tremble like a leaf. He confessed, so we tied him to a tree and riddled him with bullets.

Next morning we shook hands and, taking provisions Mrs. Smith provided, we started again by foot toward Somerset.

After several hours we ate. As daylight was fading, we started to push forward when a voice sang out, "Halt, who comes there?" We halted but did not answer and crack went a rifle ball close to my head. We did not return the fire, but did a quick retreat. We figured we were being ambushed by some rebs who saw us leave the Smith house.

We made up our minds long ago never to be taken alive. We knew the party surrounding us was numerous. We were about 18 miles from the Smith house and figured if lucky we could get back. We kept retreating until we figured we were some place near the Smith place.

I proposed to Knight that one of us stay while the other try to get help at the Smith's. We drew straws and Knight won the right to go.

After Knight left I sat there alone. I usually was cheerful but now

I had a strange feeling. The strain was getting too much and I thought we would never reach our lines. Men's voices aroused me and I started to run to escape discovery. Three shots rang out and a bullet went through the calf of my leg. It bled a lot and I knew I couldn't go far, so I climbed up a tree. I wrapped my leg in a piece of my shirt, then I must have dozed off. Voices again aroused me and I found men standing all around the base of the tree. Things looked very bad for me, but apparently they didn't see me. Some voices sounded like Indians. But after awhile nothing happened. I fell asleep. I awoke to hear and see a bloodhound looking up at me. The men were gone. I thought to tempt the dog with some meat I had. I took a piece and when he went for the meat I plunged my knife in him. The noble animal dropped with hardly a whine.

I peered through the bushes and saw swarthy men with long hair—Indians without doubt. They came close to the tree. I grabbed my rifle, but after they talked awhile, they left.

The next thing I knew I heard a bugle—Knight had returned with the men from the Smith house. I knew if Knight heard my rifle he would recognize it, and it might too draw the enemy back so our boys could mop them up. My plan worked like a charm.

The band from the Smiths, led by a captain named Logan, and about 50 greasy bushwhackers locked in battle, not far from my tree. Soon the Rebs were retreating. Knight found me. By that time I was weak from the bullet in my leg. They decided to carry me back on a stretcher to the Smith house. After tying up my wound, they started to carry me back. At the Smith house they washed my wound and redressed it and put me to bed.

Two Rebs had been taken prisoner and held in the Smith house—down the hall from my bedroom. I felt uneasy because although I had my gun by the bed, I felt too weak to use it. However, nothing happened the first two days, and I was beginning to feel better.

The captain was keeping the Rebs prisoners hoping to get information from them. The third night he came out smiling—"I found out about another band of bushwhackers," he said, adding, "they said they'd lead us to them if I will free them."

By that time I was almost recovered. But the fourth night there was a lot of commotion and Knight came running into my room to tell me the prisoners escaped but had been recaptured.

That night I heard someone walking in the hall and it didn't sound like the guard. There was a knock on the door. I asked who it was. The voice said, "Jack Smith." "You don't sound like Jack," I said. The door was kicked in and it was one of the Rebel prisoners. Just as he had a knife to my throat, in rushed the captain and the boys and subdued him.

I had tried to shoot the Reb, but I couldn't get him in line. The gun went off, but I missed. The captain said he had heard the shot and came running. The captain and the boys soon had him swinging from a rope. His companion had escaped after they had killed their guard.

As we were pondering these things, we got bad word. A Rebel deserter told the captain and Bill Smith that his gang had captured Knight and another of the boys who had gone out hunting, and had them tied to the ground and were going to roast them alive.

It was midnight, and we soon prepared to leave to rescue Knight and the other boy. We all mounted and by 4 A.M. were near the camp.

The captain detailed six men to reconnoiter the position of the enemy. In two hours they returned and reported they got close enough to see Knight and his companion bound to stakes flat on their backs and the Rebs asleep.

We prepared to attack and soon were dashing into the camp. We cut them down as fast as we came to them. Those who escaped our onslaught fled, leaving only Knight and the other man. We soon severed their ropes.

We found a good supply of food—bacon, rice, corn meal and sweet potatoes. I gathered these together as the rest of the gang tried to hunt down the rest of the Rebs.

We got Knight's Winchester back and a lot of ammunition. Then we returned to the house and started to prepare to leave for Somerset.

Although the captain wanted to escort us all the way, we said we'd follow our original plan and slip through alone. We left the next day. We came to an open field and could see a large house and a big frame barn. We debated, then decided to investigate. We flattened on the ground and watched movements. Suddenly a squad in gray uniforms, about 40, marched off over the very course we were pursuing, and disappeared.

We agreed it must be a Rebel headquarters and the troops had gone off on a scout. We crawled through underbrush and got to the barn. We found a Saratoga trunk and in it two suits of gray uniforms. We took them and crept out.

We schemed this way: We would don the uniforms, go to the house and pass ourselves off as part of the 18th Georgia regiment, hunting for the escaped Andrews Raiders.

We changed into the uniforms and after the troops returned we went up to the house. They let us in, eyed us sharply and inquired where we hailed from. "From Atlanta," said I. "We were guarding the engine thieves who stole the train at Big Shanty. We are after them now with orders to shoot them down on sight."

The leader said, "Is that so? We understand two of them are enroute to Somerset, Kentucky, and we are trying to head them off. They are desperate men—equal to a regiment, we're told."

The captain told us it was 40 miles to Somerset and he was posting guards on the road to head off the two engine thieves. Then he said we should get some sleep, he'd wake us early, so we could join them. As soon as everything was quiet, we sneaked to the stable, soon had the horses out in the lane and were ready to be off toward Somerset. The enemy was both in front and back of us and we had to be careful.

We met no trouble and made good time, expecting to reach Somerset in four or five hours. We knew we'd be arrested by union pickets as we neared Somerset.

We were anxious to see some boys in blue and figured we could explain our gray uniforms, even though our boys thought the Raiders were all dead.

Suddenly we were saluted by a volley and discovered a squad of Rebel cavalry coming for us. We emptied our Winchesters among them and dashed away, losing them.

Not long afterward we spotted men in blue uniforms advancing from the direction of Somerset. The main body halted and at our signal of surrender two guards advanced. "Confederate soldiers, I presume," said one. "No sir," we replied. "We stole the uniforms and the horses to get to Somerset where we hoped to find a squad of Union soldiers. We are part of the Andrews Raiders."

"Well," said the officer, "we will take you to Somerset and turn you over to authorities where your case will be investigated."

We remounted and rode with them to Somerset, reaching there about dark. . . .

Our hearts rejoiced next morning when many officers and soldiers came to see us at the guardhouse. From them we found out that the 21st Ohio was in camp at Nashville, Tennessee.[9]

VI

OH, GOD! WHAT A COSTLY WAR!

Eastward from Tennessee on the Virginia front the Federals were faltering. Rebels halted General McClellan's peninsular campaign during the spring of 1862. By the time his troops arrived back on the Potomac, Lee was preparing a fall offensive into Maryland. On 9 August his advanced detachments defeated the Yankees at Cedar Mountain and, three weeks later, Stonewall Jackson severely punished the Union army at Second Bull Run. Lee crossed the Potomac on 4 September and marched into Maryland.

Union and Confederate armies met head on at Antietam on 17 September. The result was a hard-fought but indecisive engagement. The Rebel army moved back into Virginia, but the ever-cautious McClellan failed to follow-up immediately.

Nurse Clara Barton, founder of the American Red Cross, served at Antietam.

The battle commenced on the right and already with the aid of field-glasses we saw our own forces, led by "Fighting Joe" (Hooker), overborne and falling back.

Burnside commenced to send cavalry and artillery to his aid, and, thinking our place might be there, we followed them around eight miles, turning into a cornfield near a house and barn, and stopping in the rear of the last gun, which completed the terrible line of artillery which ranged diagonally in the rear of Hooker's army. That day a garden wall only separated us. The infantry were already driven back two miles, and stood under cover of the guns. The fighting had been fearful. We had met wounded men, walking or borne to the rear for the last two miles. But around the old barn there lay, too badly wounded to admit of removal, some three hundred this early in the day, for it was scarce ten o'clock.

We loosened our mules and commenced our work. The corn was so high as to conceal the house, which stood some distance to the right, but, judging that a path which I observed must lead to it, and also that surgeons must be operating there, I took my arms full of stimulants and bandages and followed the opening.

Arriving at a little wicker gate, I found the dooryard of a small house, and myself face to face with one of the kindest and noblest surgeons I have ever met, Dr. Dunn, of Conneautville, Pennsylvania.

Speechless both, for an instant, he at length threw up his hands with "God has indeed remembered us! How did you get from Virginia here so soon? And again to supply our necessities! And they are terrible. We have nothing but our instruments and the little chloroform we brought in our pockets. We have torn up the last sheets we could find in this house. We have not a bandage, rag, lint, or string, and all these shell-wounded men bleeding to death."

Upon the porch stood four tables, with an etherized patient upon each, a surgeon standing over him with his box of instruments, and a bunch of green corn leaves beside him. . . .

Thrice that day was the ground in front of us contested, lost, and won, and twice our men were driven back under cover of that fearful range of guns, and each time brought its hundreds of wounded to our crowded ground.

A little after noon, the enemy made a desperate attempt to regain what had been lost. Hooker, Sedgwick, Dana, Richardson, Hartsuff, and Mansfield had been borne wounded from the field and the command of the right wing devolved upon General Howard.

The smoke became so dense as to obscure our sight, and the hot, sulphurous breath of battle dried our tongues and parched our lips to bleeding.

We were in a slight hollow, and all shells which did not break over our guns in front came directly among or over us, bursting above our heads or burying themselves in the hills beyond.

A man lying upon the ground asked for a drink. I stopped to give it, and, having raised him with my right hand, was holding him.

Just at this moment a bullet sped its free and easy way between us, tearing a hole in my sleeve and found its way into his body. He fell back dead. There was no more to be done. I have never mended that hole in my sleeve. I wonder if a soldier ever does mend a bullet hole in his coat?

The patient endurance of these men was most astonishing. As many as could be were carried into the barn, as a slight protection against random shot. Just outside the door lay a man wounded in the face, the ball having entered the lower maxillary on the left side and lodged among the bones of the right cheek. His imploring look drew me to him, when, placing his finger upon the sharp protuberance, he said, "Lady, will you tell me what this is that burns so?" I replied that it must be the ball which had been too far spent to cut its way entirely through.

"It is terribly painful," he said. "Won't you take it out?"

I said I would go to the tables for a surgeon. "No! No!" he said, catching my dress. "They cannot come to me. I must wait my turn, for this is a little wound. You can get the ball. There is a knife in your pocket. Please take the ball out for me."

This was a new call. I had never severed the nerves and fibers of human flesh, and I said I could not hurt him so much. He looked up, with as nearly a smile as such a mangled face could assume, saying, "You cannot hurt me, dear lady, I can endure any pain that your hands can create. Please do it. It will relieve me so much."

I could not withstand his entreaty and, opening the best blade of my pocket-knife, prepared for the operation. Just at his head lay a stalwart orderly sergeant from Illinois who had a bullet directly through the fleshy part of both thighs. He had been watching the scene with great interest and, when he saw me commence to raise the poor fellow's head, and no one to support it, with a desperate effort he succeeded in raising himself to a sitting posture, exclaiming as he did so, "I will help do that." Shoving himself along the ground he took the wounded head in his hands and held it while I extracted the ball and washed and bandaged the face.

I do not think a surgeon would have pronounced it a scientific operation, but that it was successful I dared to hope from the gratitude of the patient.

I assisted the sergeant to lie down again, brave and cheerful as he had risen, and passed on to others.

Returning in half an hour, I found him weeping, the great tears rolling diligently down his manly cheeks. I thought his effort had been too great for his strength and expressed my fears. "Oh! No! No! Madam," he replied. "It is not for myself. I am very well, but," pointing to another just brought in, he said, "this is my comrade, and he tells me that our regiment is all cut to pieces, that my captain was the last officer left, and he is dead."

Oh, God! what a costly war! This man could laugh at pain, face death without a tremor, and yet weep like a child over the loss of his comrades and his captain.

At two o'clock my men came to tell me that the last loaf of bread had been cut and the last cracker pounded. We had three boxes of wine still unopened. What should they do?

"Open the wine and give that," I said, "and God help us."

The next instant an ejaculation from Sergeant Field, who had opened the first box, drew my attention, and, to my astonished gaze, the wine had been packed in nicely sifted Indian meal.

If it had been golddust it would have seemed poor in comparison. . . .

Of twelve boxes of wine which we carried, the first nine, when opened, were found packed in sawdust, the last three, when all else was gone, in Indian meal. . . .

This was an old farmhouse. Six large kettles were picked up and set over fires, almost as quickly as I can tell it, and I was mixing water and meal for gruel.

It occurred to us to explore the cellar. The chimney rested on an arch, and, forcing the door, we discovered three barrels and a bag. "They are full," said the sergeant, and, rolling one into the light, found that it bore the mark of Jackson's army. These three barrels of flour and a bag of salt had been stored there by the rebel army during its upward march. . . .

All that night my thirty men (for my corps of workers had increased to that number during the day) carried buckets of hot gruel for miles down the line to the wounded and dying where they fell.

This time, profiting by experience, we had lanterns to hang in and around the barn, and, having directed it to be done, I went to the house and found the surgeon in charge, sitting alone, beside a table, upon which he rested his elbow, apparently meditating upon a bit of tallow candle which flickered in the center.

Approaching carefully, I said, "You are tired, Doctor." He started up with a look almost savage, "Tired! Yes, I am tired, tired of such heartlessness, such carelessness!" Turning full upon me, he continued: "Think of the condition of things. Here are at least one thousand wounded men, terribly wounded, five hundred of whom cannot live till daylight, without attention. That two inches of candle is all I have or can get. What can I do? How can I endure it?"

I took him by the arm, and, leading him to the door, pointed in the direction of the barn where the lanterns glistened like stars among the waving corn.

"What is that?" he exclaimed.

"The barn is lighted," I said, "and the house will be directly."

"Who did it?"

"I, Doctor."

"Where did you get them?"

"Brought them with me."

"How many have you?"

"All you want—four boxes."

He looked at me a moment, turned away without a word, and never alluded to the circumstances, but the deference which he paid me was almost painful. . . .

Darkness brought silence and peace, and respite and rest to our gallant men. As they had risen, regiment by regiment, from their grassy beds in the morning, so at night the fainting remnant again sank down on the trampled blood-stained earth, the weary to sleep, and the wounded to die.[10]

VII

THE CREST IS SAFE!

Lee followed his victory at Chancellorsville in May, 1863, by a second attempt to invade the North. It ended disastrously at Gettysburg. There on 1 July the bloody three-day horror began. The first day the Union army faltered, rallied on Cemetery Ridge. Along that line the Yankees dug in as rapidly as they arrived from the south and east. The Confederates maintained an encircling position, their right on Seminary Ridge, parallel to Cemetery Ridge.

Lee with his army at full strength determined to storm the Union lines. At 1 P.M., 3 July, Confederate artillery unleashed a deafening roar. Union cannon let loose. For an hour the artillery lashed out at each other. Suddenly, the thunder stilled. Lee ordered Pickett's, Pettigrew's, and Trimble's divisions, 15,000 strong, to assault the Union center. From Cemetery Ridge the blue coats spotted three gray lines emerge from the woods three-quarters of a mile away and march into the valley. When the Rebels were less than halfway across, Union cannon opened up. Nearer, the gray line came under a withering fire. The flank divisions evaporated. Pickett's division kept moving. Yankee muskets erupted. A Confederate general jumped the stone wall into Union lines. A hundred Rebels followed. For a fleeting moment the Confederate battle flag fluttered on the crest of Cemetery Ridge. Union lines closed for the kill, shooting down or capturing the hundred. The remnants of Pickett's division struggled back to their lines. The battle of Gettysburg had been won.

Frank Aretas Haskell of the Sixth Wisconsin, after enduring the cannonade, watched Pickett's charge and helped turn back the enemy.

At three o'clock almost precisely the last shot hummed, and bounded and fell, and the cannonade was over. The purpose of General Lee in all this fire of his guns was to disable our artillery and break up our infantry upon the position of the Second Corps, so as to render them less an impediment to the sweep of his own brigades and divisions over our crest and through our lines. . . . The artillery fight over, men began to breathe more freely, and to ask, What next, I wonder? The battery men were among their guns, some leaning to rest and wipe the sweat from their sooty faces, some were handling ammunition boxes and replenishing those that were empty. Some batteries from the artillery reserve were moving up to take the places of the disabled ones; the smoke was clearing from the crests. There was a pause between acts. We have passed by the left of the Second Division, coming from the First; when we crossed the crest the enemy was not in sight, and all was still—we walked slowly along in the rear of the troops, by the ridge cut off now from a view of the enemy in his position, and were returning to the spot where we had left our horses. . . . We were near our horses when we noticed Brigadier General Hunt, Chief of Artillery of the Army, near Woodruff's Battery, swiftly moving about on horseback, and apparently in a rapid manner giving some orders about the guns . . . . In a moment we met Captain Wessels and the orderlies who had our horses. Captain Wessels was pale, and he said, excited: "General, they say the enemy's infantry is advancing." We sprang into our saddles, a score of bounds brought us upon the all-seeing crest. . . .

None on that crest now need be told that *the enemy is advancing.*

Every eye could see his legions, an overwhelming resistless tide of an ocean of armed men sweeping upon us! Regiment after regiment and brigade after brigade move from the woods and rapidly take their places in the lines forming the assault. Pickett's proud division, with some additional troops, hold their right; Pettigrew's (Worth's) their left. The first line at short interval is followed by a second, and that a third succeeds; and columns between support the lines. More than half a mile their front extends; more than a thousand yards the dull gray masses deploy, man touching man, rank pressing rank, and line supporting line. The red flags wave, their horsemen gallop up and down; the arms of eighteen thousand men, barrel and bayonet, gleam in the sun, a sloping forest of flashing steel. Right on they move, as with one soul, in perfect order, without impediment of ditch, or wall or stream, over ridge and slope, through orchard and meadow, and cornfield, magnificent, grim, irresistible.

All was orderly and still upon our crest; no noise and no confusion. The men had little need of commands, for the survivors of a dozen battles knew well enough what this array in front portended, and, already in their places, they would be prepared to act when the right time should come. The click of the locks as each man raised the hammer to feel with his fingers that the cap was on the nipple; the sharp jar as a musket touched a stone upon the wall when thrust in aiming over it, and the clicking of the iron axles as the guns were rolled up by hand a little further to the front, were quite all the sounds that could be heard. Cap-boxes were slid around to the front of the body; cartridge boxes opened, officers opened their pistol-holsters. Such preparations, little more was needed. The trefoil flags, colors of the brigades and divisions moved to their places in rear. . . . General Gibbon rode down the lines, cool and calm, and in an unimpassioned voice he said to the men, "Do not hurry, men, and fire too fast, let them come up close before you fire, and then aim low and steadily." The coolness of their General was reflected in the faces of his men. Five minutes has elapsed since first the enemy have emerged from the woods—no great space of time surely, if measured by the usual standard by which men estimate duration—but it was long enough for us to weigh some of the elements of mighty moment that surrounded us. . . .

Our skirmishers open a spattering fire along the front, and, fighting, retire upon the main line—the first drops, the heralds of the storm, sounding on our windows. Then the thunders of our guns, first Arnold's then Cushing's and Woodruff's and the rest, shake and reverberate again through the air, and their sounding shells smite the enemy. The General said I had better go and tell General Meade of this advance. To gallop to General Meade's headquarters, to learn there that he had changed them to another part of the field, to dispatch to him by the Signal Corps in General Gibbon's name the message, "The enemy is advancing his infantry in force upon my front," and to be again upon the crest, were but the work of a minute. All our available guns are now active, and from the fire of shells, as the range grows shorter and shorter, they change to shrapnel, and from shrapnel to canister; but in spite of shells, and shrapnel and canister, without wavering or halt, the hardy lines of the enemy continue to move on.

The Rebel guns make no reply to ours, and no charging shout rings out to-day, as is the Rebel wont; but the courage of these silent men amid our shots seems not to need the stimulus of other noise. The enemy's right flank sweeps near Stannard's bushy crest, and his concealed Vermonters rake it with a well-delivered fire of musketry. The gray lines do not halt or reply, but withdrawing a little from that extreme they still move on. And so across all that broad open ground they have come, nearer and nearer, nearly half the way, with our guns bellowing in their faces, until now a hundred yards, no more, divide our ready left from their advancing right.

The eager men there are impatient to begin. Let them. First, Harrow's breastworks flame; then Hall's; then Webb's. As if our bullets were the fire coals that touched off their muskets, the enemy in front halts, and his countless level barrels blaze back upon us. The Second Division is struggling in battle. The rattling storm soon spreads to the right, and the blue trefoils are vieing with the white. All along each hostile front, a thousand yards, with narrowest space between, the volleys blaze and roll; as thick the sound as when a summer hailstorm pelts the city roofs; as thick the fire as when the incessant lightning fringes a summer cloud.

When the Rebel infantry had opened fire our batteries soon became silent, and this without their fault, for they were foul by long previous use. They were the targets of the concentrated Rebel bullets, and some of them had expended all their canister. But they were not silent before Rhorty was killed, Woodruff had fallen mortally wounded, and Cushing, firing almost his last canister, had dropped dead among his guns shot through the head by a bullet. The conflict is left to the infantry alone.

Unable to find my general when I had returned to the crest after transmitting his message to General Meade, and while riding in the search having witnessed the development of the fight, from the first fire upon the left by the main lines until all of the two divisions were furiously engaged, I gave up hunting as useless. . . . The conflict was tremendous, but I had seen no wavering in all our line. Wondering how long the Rebel ranks, deep though they were, could stand our sheltered volleys, I had come near my destination, when—great heaven! were my senses mad? The larger portion of Webb's brigade— my God, it was true—there by the group of trees and the angles of the wall, was breaking from the cover of their works, and, without orders or reason, with no hand lifted to check them, was falling back, a fear-stricken flock of confusion! The fate of Gettysburg hung upon a spider's single thread! . . .

My sword, that had always hung idle by my side, the sign of rank only in every battle, I drew, bright and gleaming, the symbol of command. . . . All rules and all proprieties were forgotten; all considerations of person, and danger and safety despised; for, as I met the tide of these rabbits, the damned red flags of the rebellion began to thicken and flaunt along the wall they had just deserted, and one was already waving over one of the guns of the dead Cushing. I ordered these men to "halt," and "face about" and "fire," and they heard my voice and gathered my meaning, and obeyed my commands. On some unpatriotic backs of those not quick of comprehension, the flat of my sabre fell not lightly, and, at its touch their love of country returned, and, with a look at me as if I were the destroying angel, as I might have become theirs, they again faced the enemy. General Webb soon came to my assistance. He was on foot, but he was active, and did all that one could do to repair the breach, or to avert its calamity. The men that had fallen back, facing the enemy, soon regained confidence in themselves, and became steady.

This portion of the wall was lost to us, and the enemy had gained the cover of the reverse side, where he now stormed with fire. But Webb's men, with their bodies in part protected by the abruptness of the crest, now sent back in the enemies' faces as fierce a storm. Some scores of venturesome Rebels, that in their first push at the wall had dared to cross at the further angle, and those that had desecrated

Cushing's guns, were promptly shot down, and speedy death met him who should raise his body to cross it again.

At this point little could be seen of the enemy, by reason of his cover and the smoke, except the flash of his muskets and his waving flags. These red flags were accumulating at the wall every moment, and they maddened us as the same color does the bull. Webb's men are falling fast, and he is among them to direct and encourage; but, however well they may now do, with that walled enemy in front, with more than a dozen flags to Webb's three, it soon becomes apparent that in not many minutes they will be overpowered, or that there will be none alive for the enemy to overpower. Webb has but three regiments, all small . . . and he must have speedy assistance, or this crest will be lost. Oh, where is Gibbon? where is Hancock?—some general—anybody with the power and the will to support that wasting, melting line? No general came, and no succor! I thought of Hayes upon the right, but from the smoke and war along his front, it was evident that he had enough upon his hands, if he stayed the inrolling tide of the Rebels there. Doubleday upon the left was too far off and too slow, and on another occasion I had begged him to send his idle regiments to support another line battling with thrice its numbers, and this "Old Sumpter Hero" had declined.

As a last resort I resolved to see if Hall and Harrow could not send some of their commands to reinforce Webb. I galloped to the left in the execution of my purpose, and as I attained the rear of Hall's line from the nature of the ground and the position of the enemy it was easy to discover the manner of this gathering of Rebel flags in front of Webb. The enemy, emboldened by his success in gaining our line by the group of trees and the angle of the wall, was concentrating all his right against and was further pressing that point. There was the stress of his assault; there would he drive his fiery wedge to split our line. . . . Not a moment must be lost. Colonel Hall I found just in rear of his line, sword in hand, cool, vigilant, noting all that passed and directing the battle of his brigade. The fire was constantly diminishing now in his front, in the manner and by the movement of the enemy that I have mentioned, drifting to the right. "How is it going?" Colonel Hall asked me, as I rode up. "Well, but Webb is hotly pressed and must have your support, or he will be overpowered. Can you assist him?" "Yes." "You cannot be too quick." "I will move my brigade at once." "Good." He gave the order, and in briefest time I saw five friendly colors hurrying to the aid of the imperilled three; and each color represented true, battle-tried men, that had not turned back from Rebel fire that day nor yesterday, though their ranks were sadly thinned, to Webb's brigade, pressed back as it had been from the wall, the distance was not great from Hall's right. The regiments marched by the right flank. Col. Hall superintended the movement in person. . . . The movement, as it did, attracting the enemy's fire, and executed in haste, as it must be, was difficult; but in reasonable time, and in order that is serviceable, if not regular, Hall's men are fighting gallantly side by side with Webb's before the all important point. I did not stop to see all this movement of Hall's, but from him I went at once further to the left, to the 1st brigade. Gen'l Harrow I did not see, but his fighting men would answer my purpose as well . . . all men that I could find I took over to the right at the double quick.

As we were moving to, and near the other brigade of the division, from my position on horseback I could see that the enemy's right, under Hall's fire, was beginning to stagger and to break. "See," I said to the men, "See the chivalry! See the gray-backs run!" The men saw, and as they swept to their places by the side of Hall and opened fire, they roared, and this in a manner that said more plainly than words—for the deaf could have seen it in their faces, and the blind could have heard it in their voices—*the crest is safe!*[11]

VIII

I MOVED MY MEN AT THE DOUBLE-QUICK

Gettysburg had stemmed the tide. In the spring of 1864 Grant sledgehammered his way toward Richmond. General Sherman with his legions pushed off from Chattanooga in early May bound for the railroad center of Atlanta, Georgia. At first the defensive skill of General Joe Johnston and his Confederate army held the Yankees in a series of severe battles at Resaca, 13–16 May, New Hope Church, 25–28 May, and Kenesaw Mountain, 27 June.

Around Resaca, a sleepy Georgia town, Johnston had formed a horseshoe-shaped defense line protected by hills, swamps, and ravines.

To one Union brigade fell the task of silencing an especially obnoxious Rebel battery commanding the approach to Resaca. Colonel Benjamin Harrison received orders that the Seventieth Indiana was to storm the hill. He describes the engagement in his official report.

In our new position we were informed that our brigade, supported by the other brigades of our division, was expected to assault the enemy's rifle-pits, and without delay our brigade was formed. My regiment leading, passed from the crest of an intrenched ridge, occupied by our forces, across an open field in the valley and up a steep and thickly wooded hill to the assault of the enemy's breastworks, whose strength, and even exact location, was only revealed by the line of fire which, with fearful destructiveness, was belched upon our advancing column. I moved my men at the double-quick and, with loud cheers, across the open space in the valley in order sooner to escape the enfilading fire from the enemy's rifle-pits on our right and to gain the cover of the woods, with which the side of the hill against which our assault was directed was thickly covered. The men moved on with perfect steadiness and without any sign of faltering up the hillside and to the very muzzles of the enemy's artillery, which continued to belch their deadly charges of grape and canister, until the gunners were struck down at their guns.

Having gained the outer face of the embrasures, in which the enemy had four 12-pounder Napoleon guns, my line halted for a moment to take breath. Seeing that the infantry supports had deserted the artillery, I cheered the men forward, and with a wild yell they entered the embrasures, striking down and bayoneting the rebel gunners, many of whom defiantly stood by their guns till struck down. Within this outer fortification, in which the artillery was placed, there was a strong line of breast-works, which was concealed from our view by a thick pine undergrowth, save at one point, which had been used as a gateway. This line was held by a rebel division of veteran troops, said to be of Hood's command. When we first entered the embrasures of the outer works the enemy fled in considerable confusion from the inner one, and had there been a supporting line brought up in good order at this juncture the second line might have easily been carried and held. My line having borne the brunt of the assault, it was not to be expected that it could be reformed for a second assault in time. The enemy in a moment rallied in rear of their second line, and poured in a most destructive fire upon us, which compelled us to retire outside the first line to obtain the cover of the works.

At this point some confusion was created among our forces in and about the enemy's works by a cry that the enemy was flanking us. This caused many to retire down the hill, and had for a time the appearance of a general retreat. I strove in vain to rally my men under the enemy's fire on the hillside, and finally followed them to a partially sheltered place behind a ridge to our left, where I was engaged in separating my men from those of other regiments and reforming them preparatory to leading them again to the support of those who still held the guns we had captured, when I was informed that General Ward was wounded, and was ordered to assume command of the brigade and reform it, which duty I discharged and then urgently asked General Butterfield for permission to take it again to the works we had carried and still held, and bring off the guns we had captured. This was refused, and by his order the brigade was placed in a new position on a hill to the left of the point at which we had assaulted, to assist in repelling an attack made by the enemy.

To sum up the account of the day's fight, I will add that detachments from my regiment, and, I believe, from each of the other regiments of the brigade, held the rebels from re-entering and taking the guns we had captured until they were brought off at night by a detail from the First and Second Brigades.[12]

IX

MARCH TO THE SEA

On 1 September 1864 the Confederates evacuated Atlanta and, on the following day, Sherman's force entered the city. In mid-November the general launched his march to the sea. While Rebel strength in Georgia and Tennessee collapsed, Sherman and his "bummers" moved toward the coast, ripping up railroad lines and foraging on Georgia farms and plantations. The Union army entered Savannah on 21 December, and then turned into the Carolinas.

Sherman himself recounts that march to the sea.

About 7 A.M. of November 16th we rode out of Atlanta by the Decatur road, filled by the marching troops and wagons of the Fourteenth Corps; and reaching the hill, just outside of the old rebel works, we naturally paused to look back upon the scenes of our past battles. We stood upon the very ground whereon was fought the bloody battle of July 22d, and could see the copse of wood where McPherson fell. Behind us lay Atlanta, smoldering and in ruins, the black smoke rising high in air, and hanging like a pall over the ruined city. . . .

Then we turned our horses' heads to the east; Atlanta was soon lost behind the screen of trees, and became a thing of the past. Around it clings many a thought of desperate battle, of hope and fear, and that now seem like the memory of a dream; and I have never seen the place since. The day was extremely beautiful, clear sunlight, with bracing air, and an unusual feeling of exhilaration seemed to pervade all minds—a feeling of something to come, vague and undefined, still full of venture and intense interest. Even the common soldiers caught the inspiration, and many a group called out to me as I worked my way past them, "Uncle Billy, I guess Grant is waiting for us at Richmond!" Indeed, the general sentiment was that we were marching for Richmond, and that there we should end the war, but how and when they seemed to care not; nor did they measure the distance, or count the loss of life, or bother their brains about the great rivers to be crossed, and the food required for man and beast, that had to be gathered by the way. There was a "devil-may-care" feeling pervading officers and men, that made me feel the full load of responsibility, for success would be accepted as a matter of course, whereas, should we fail, this "march" would be adjudged the wild adventure of a crazy fool. I had no purpose to march direct for Richmond by way of Augusta and Charlotte, but always designed to reach the sea-coast first at Savannah or Port Royal, South Carolina, and even kept in mind the alternative of Pensacola.

The first night out we camped by the road-side near Lithonia. Stone Mountain, a mass of granite, was in plain view, cut out in clear outline against the blue sky; the whole horizon was lurid with the bonfires of rail-ties, and groups of men all night were carrying the heated rails to the nearest trees, and bending them around the trunks. Colonel Poe had provided tools for ripping up the rails and twisting them when hot; but the best and easiest way is the one I have described, of heating the middle of the iron-rails on bonfires made of the cross-ties, and then winding them around a telegraph-pole or the trunk of some convenient sapling. I attached much importance to this destruction of the railroad, gave it my own personal attention, and made reiterated orders to others on the subject.

The next day we passed through the handsome town of Covington, the soldiers closing up their ranks, the color-bearers unfurling their flags, and the bands striking up patriotic airs. The white people came out of their houses to behold the sight, spite of their deep hatred of the invaders, and the negroes were simply frantic with joy. Whenever they heard my name, they clustered about my horse, shouted and prayed in their peculiar style, which had a natural eloquence that would have moved a stone. I have witnessed hundreds, if not thousands, of such scenes; and can now see a poor girl, in the very ecstasy of the Methodist "shout," hugging the banner of one of the regiments, and jumping up to the "feet of Jesus."

I remember, when riding around by a by-street in Covington, to avoid the crowd that followed the marching column, that some one brought me an invitation to dine with a sister of Sam. Anderson, who was a cadet at West Point with me; but the messenger reached me after we had passed the main part of the town. I asked to be excused, and rode on to a place designated for camp, at the crossing of the Ulcofauha-chee River, about four miles to the east of the town. Here we made our bivouac, and I walked up to a plantation-house close by, where were assembled many negroes, among them an old, gray-haired man, of as fine a head as I ever saw. I asked him if he understood about the war and its progress. He said he did; that he had been looking for the "angel of the Lord" ever since he was knee-high, and, though we professed to be fighting for the Union, he supposed that slavery was the cause, and that our success was to be his freedom. I asked him if all the negro slaves comprehended this fact, and he said they surely did. I then explained to him that we wanted the slaves to remain where they were, and not to load us down with useless mouths, which would eat up the food needed for our fighting-men; that our success was their assured-freedom; that we could receive a few of their young, hearty men as pioneers; but that, if they followed us in swarms of old and young, feeble and helpless, it would simply load us down and cripple us in our great task. . . .

It was at this very plantation that a soldier passed me with a ham on his musket, a jug of sorghum-molasses under his arm, and a big piece of honey in his hand, from which he was eating, and, catching my eye, he remarked *sotto voce* and carelessly to a comrade, "Forage liberally on the country," quoting from my general orders. On this occasion, as on many others that fell under my personal observation, I reproved the man, explained that foraging must be limited to the regular parties properly detailed, and that all provisions thus obtained must be delivered to the regular commissaries, to be fairly distributed to them that kept their ranks.

From Covington the Fourteenth Corps (Davis's) with which I was traveling, turned to the right for Milledgeville, via Shady Dale. General Slocum was ahead at Madison with the Twentieth Corps, having torn up the railroad as far as that place, and thence had sent Geary's division on to the Oconee, to burn the bridges across that stream, when this corps turned south by Eatonton, for Milledgeville, the common "objective" for the first stage of the "march." We found abundance of corn, molasses, meal, bacon, and sweet-potatoes. We also took a good many cows and oxen, and a large number of mules. In all these the country was quite rich, never before having been visited by a hostile army; the recent crop had been excellent, had been just gathered and laid by for the winter. As a rule, we destroyed none, but kept our wagons full, and fed our teams bountifully.

The skill and success of the men in collecting forage was one of the features of this march. Each brigade commander had authority to detail a company of foragers, usually about fifty men, with one or two commissioned officers selected for their boldness and enterprise. This party would be dispatched before daylight with a knowledge of the intended day's march and camp; would proceed on foot five or six miles from the route traveled by their brigade, and then visit every plantation and farm within range. They would usually procure a wagon or family carriage, load it with bacon, corn-meal, turkeys, chickens, ducks, and every thing that could be used as food or forage, and would then regain the main road, usually in advance of their train. When this came up, they would deliver to the brigade commissary these supplies thus gathered by the way. Often would I pass these foraging parties at the roadside, waiting for their wagons to come up, and was amused at their strange collections—mules, horses, even cattle, packed with old saddles and loaded with hams, bacon, bags of corn-meal, and poultry of every character and description.

Although this foraging was attended with great danger and hard work, there seemed to be a charm about it that attracted the soldiers, and it was a privilege to be detailed on such a party. Daily they returned mounted on all sorts of beasts, which were at once taken from them and appropriated to the general use; but the next day they would start out again on foot, only to repeat the experience of the day before. No doubt, many acts of pillage, robbery, and violence, were committed by these parties of foragers, usually called "bummers"; for I have since heard of jewelry taken from women, and the plunder of articles that never reached the commissary; but these acts were exceptional and incidental. I never heard of any case of murder or rape; and no army could have carried along sufficient food and forage for a march of three hundred miles; so that foraging in some shape was necessary. The country was sparsely settled, with no magistrates or civil authorities who could respond to requisitions, as is done in all the wars of Europe; so that this system of foraging was simply indispensable to our success. By it our men were well supplied with all the essentials of life and health, while the wagons retained enough in case of unexpected delay, and our animals were well fed. Indeed, when we reached Savannah, the trains were pronounced by experts to be the finest in flesh and appearance ever seen with any army. . . .

Habitually we started from camp at the earliest break of dawn, and usually reached camp soon after noon. The marches varied from ten to fifteen miles a day, though sometimes on extreme flanks it was necessary to make as much as twenty, but the rate of travel was regulated by the wagons; and, considering the nature of the roads, fifteen miles per day was deemed the limit.

The pontoon-trains were distributed in about equal proportions to the four corps, giving each a section of about nine hundred feet. The pontoons were of the skeleton pattern, with cotton-canvas covers, each boat, with its proportion of balks and chesses, constituting a load for one wagon. By uniting two such sections together, we could make a bridge of eighteen hundred feet, enough for any river we had to traverse; but habitually the leading brigade would, out of the abundant timber, improvise a bridge before the pontoon-train would come up, unless in the cases of rivers of considerable magnitude, such as the Ocmulgee, Oconee, Ogeechee, Savannah, etc.

On the 20th of November I was still with the Fourteenth Corps, near Eatonton Factory, waiting to hear of the Twentieth Corps; and on the 21st we camped near the house of a man named Vann; the next

One of General Sherman's "bummers."

A BUMMER.

Pencil drawing from a sketch book during Civil War.

I Got Drunk

day, about 4 P.M., General Davis had halted his head of column on a wooded ridge, overlooking an extensive slope of cultivated country, about ten miles short of Milledgeville, and was deploying his troops for camp when I got up. There was a high, raw wind blowing, and I asked him why he had chosen so cold and bleak a position. He explained that he had accomplished his full distance for the day, and had there an abundance of wood and water. He explained further that his advance-guard was a mile or so ahead; so I rode on, asking him to let his rear division, as it came up, move some distance ahead into the depression or valley beyond. Riding on some distance to the border of a plantation, I turned out of the main road into a cluster of wild-plum bushes, that broke the force of the cold November wind, dismounted, and instructed the staff to pick out the place for our camp.

The afternoon was unusually raw and cold. My orderly was at hand with his invariable saddle-bags, which contained a change of under-clothing, my maps, a flask of whiskey, and a bunch of cigars. Taking a drink and lighting a cigar, I walked to a row of negro-huts close by, entered one and found a soldier or two warming themselves by a wood-fire. I took their place by the fire, intending to wait there till our wagons had got up, and a camp made for the night. I was talking to the old negro woman, when some one came and explained to me that, if I would come farther down the road, I could find a better place. So I started on foot, and found on the main road a good double-hewed-log house, in one room of which Colonel Poe, Dr. Moore, and others, had started a fire. I sent back orders to the "plum-bushes" to bring our horses and saddles up to this house, and an orderly to conduct our headquarters wagons to the same place. In looking around the room, I saw a small box, like a candle-box, marked "Howell Cobb," and, on inquiring of a negro, found that we were at the plantation of General Howell Cobb, of Georgia, one of the leading rebels of the South, then a general in the Southern army, and who had been Secretary of the United States Treasury in Mr. Buchanan's time. Of course, we con-fiscated his property, and found it rich in corn, beans, pea-nuts, and sorghum-molasses. Extensive fields were all round the house; I sent word back to General Davis to explain whose plantation it was, and instructed him to spare nothing. That night huge bonfires consumed the fence-rails, kept our soldiers warm, and the teamsters and men, as well as the slaves, carried off an immense quantity of corn and pro-visions of all sorts. . . .

The next morning, November 23d, we rode into Milledgeville, the capital of the State, whither the Twentieth Corps had preceded us; and during the day the left wing was all united, in and around Milledgeville. From the inhabitants we learned that some of Kilpatrick's cavalry had preceded us by a couple of days, and that all of the right wing was at and near Gordon, twelve miles off, the place where the branch railroad came to Milledgeville from the Macon & Savannah road. The first stage of the journey was, therefore, complete, and absolutely successful.[13]

X

MANY, MANY ARE THE HEARTS
MADE GLAD THIS DAY

By early 1865, Lee's position in Virginia was precarious. Caught in a pincer between the armies of Grant and Sherman, he had no food supply. Lee evacuated Petersburg, abandoned the defense of Richmond, and marched out toward Lynchburg, his men ragged and half-starved. Grant captured General Richard S. Ewing's corps in early April and surrounded what was left of the forlorn Rebel forces.

At Appomattox Court House on 9 April, Lee and 13,000 troops— all that remained of the once-proud Army of Northern Virginia— capitulated. ·The war between the states, to all intents and purposes, was over. A Billy Yank in the First Michigan writes home of the surrender.

> *Bivouac 1st Mich Vol Infty*
> *On the Glorious Field where*
> *Genl Bob Lee Surrenderd*
> *Sunday Aprl. 9th 1865 at 3:20* PM

My dear Friends at Home

I am so "happy" I dont know what to say. You know I dont *drink* but I *realy* think, I should like a cup of tea at about this time. Well at last we have realy broke the "Back Bone" of the Rebelion. We have had a hard Time of it I assure you, but I feel *well repaid.*

Many are bare foot as the country is rough and stoney. The Soles of my Boots are worn off and for the past two days I have marched with my feet wound in pieces of cotton tenting. My feet are quite sore but I was bound to see the "Last Ditch" and Believe to have found it, for I now con-sider the Rebelion virtualy over.

Why! I feel as though I was almost home. Yesterday our cavalry captured five Trams of cars, five hundred Wagons and 42 pieces of artilery. We travailed most all night to get up and support the cavalry and with our legs accomplished the object, and got here just in time as the enemies Infantry was driving back our cavalry and would have escaped south had we not blocked the game by getting on their only road. Lee and his army was marching South between two ranges of hills with the 2nd and 6th Corps pressing him in the rear while our corps and a part of the 24th Corps with the cavalry by circutious rout on the left flank got this position. There is a small town called Appa-mattox Court Hous where Lee, Grant, and Sheridan, met to arrange the terms of the surrender. The Surrender is a conditional one, but might have been "Unconditional" If Grant had required it, but I think it is, and should be the policy of *all in authority,* to concilate as far as pocible without sacrifizeing our own honor. The conditions so far as I can learn are these. Officers and Men are to retain their personal effects, the former their side arms, and all to be paroled on the field.

The best of it is the Rebs are as pleased over the affair as are we, and when the surrender was made known to them *cheer* after *cheer* wen up along their whole line. Their "Southern pride" is thorougly humbled, and I think a majority of them will be better citizens than before.

What an event-ful week the past has been. One week ago yester day the 5th corps and Cav. took the South Side R.R. there by *turn-ing the key* to Petersburg and Richmond and last night the same force with a part of the 24 Corps again Turned the Key that *locked Lee in.* All the old Army of the Potomac has ever lacked was good leaders. But thanks to the powers that be that want was supplied at the proper time and you see the result. I cant realize the state of affairs it all seem like a dream. Perhaps it is well I cant, for it might derange me. I Do believe the past week has been the happiest of my life, the thought that the Army of the Potomac has at last accomplished what it has so long bled and sweat for. Little Royal, Saml. Scott, and Hobart Smit are all here and safe, each doing his duty to the last.

The Bands are playing and the armies are cheering "Sweet Home" "When Johney comes marching home again" and Hail to the Chief seem to be the prevailing pieces.

Many, many are the hearts made glad this day, and many more will be by the news. I suppose you are all crazy with joy up North, if you are not, you should be. On the 5th inst I saw Sute Ives and Bro. Sam, but have not heard from them since. The weather is very fine and has been since we started, favoring us very much. We are have-ing *Mich. May weather,* and the trees are budding. I have had no letters that wer written since my return, but expect some No more Now.

Monday Morning the 10th

Last night it rained a littled and is still lowry. Many rumors but nothing official. I have-not seen Genl Lee yet. The work of turning in arms and parole-ing will commence this morning and will probably tak two or three days. Rumor says our corps is going to Linch burg. No mail going out yet. Goo-by all—Billey

Evening

We have just been notified that the mail leaves Hdtrs in an hour.

All quiet and nothing startling to relate. Our army and the Rebs are visiting very cordialy. Many of the Rebs are ove take ing supper with our men.   they have a keen relish for a cup of Yankee Coffee. It is regular jubilee for both armies—A Big Thing—

Remember me to all enquireing friends if they *are loyal.*

Love to each and all the family

Do write one and all

Adieu

William[14]

P.S. this is a specimen of Reb paper

CHAPTER IV
1865-1914

Only those are fit to live, who do not fear to die
THEODORE ROOSEVELT

During the decades following the Civil War the militant Kiowa, southern Arapaho, Cheyenne, and Comanche were determined to arrest the advance of American settlers into the Great Plains and intermountain valleys. Each new influx of pioneers drove the Indian to warfare which generated renewed outrage and chastisement. At times as many as 30,000 troops took the field to defend the white men moving along the Missouri River and westward. The Sioux nation, powerful and skillfully led, constituted one of the most difficult problems for the Army command. In 1876 the slaughter of General George Custer's force on the Little Big Horn River shocked the nation. The Army slowly contained the Sioux and, by 1880, the northern frontier was relatively quiet. But the cost in lives and money had been high.

I

GERONIMO!

In the southwest, ten years of violence ended in the capture of the Apache chief, Geronimo, and the practical destruction of the tribe. But during the summer of 1885 Geronimo and Nachez escaped and resumed their war against the settlers. Captain Henry Ware Lawton with a picked force of seasoned troops trailed the Indians into Mexico in a driving and successful campaign. The Army shuttled Geronimo and other war leaders off to Fort Marion, Florida. Captain Lawton, in letters to his wife, depicts that campaign in Mexico and the capture.

[*21 June*]   We are going a long way down in Mexico now, and we have been very hard at work climbing mountains and following trails. I am now resting near a large ranch were I can get feed for my animals, and waiting the arrival of fresh troops and supplies for the coming three months, when I shall go on down to the Sierra Madres. It is very hot indeed and anything but pleasant, but *somebody* must do something and I am going to try to do it. So far we have had no chance. The Indians have been moving about in small parties, not stopping at all, and we have been chasing them. Now I think they have gone to make a permanent camp and we may have some chance of finding them. The Mexicans here had a small fight with a few of them the other day and got back a girl who had been taken prisoner near Calabasas. I was only eight miles away at the time but did not know of it. I would have given anything to have gotten the girl myself. . . .

[*22 June*] The mountains over this way are very rough and water is very scarce in them, and we have made more dry camps than I ever made before, and we were making such long hard marches that both animals and men showed the hard work, and I was compelled to stop and rest and give them something to eat. . . .

[*26 June*] We arrived at this place on the Sonora river all right. It is not a very nice place but we got some feed for our animals and that is what we need most. . . . I wish you would send me out one of my *old* blouses. —The one I brought with me is entirely worn out. I have a pair of old shoulder straps I can put on myself. . . . Mr. Benson got in to my camp last night and Mr. Brown with the Indians and Infantry will be here today. I will then send the Infantry and scouts out on the trail and move the Cavalry and pack train over to Campas, where the wagons will be, for supplies. Night before last some of the men got drunk and a couple of them got into a fight and one stabbed the other and is very badly hurt. . . .

[*11 July*] We marched the morning of the 9th and went into camp on Tepache creek very early in the day. The scouts being out looking for, or rather following, the trail which I had myself found, Dr. Wood and I rode to the town of Tepache. We did not know how far it was from us but knew the direction and trail to it. We found it was ten miles away. I heard of the Indians; got dinner, horses fed, some fig leaves, and two Mexican guides, and we then returned to camp, arriving just at dark, The next morning we started early and followed the trail, which still led South, until about 1 o'clock, when the Infantry began to suffer for water, and we had found none on the trail. Our guides knew of no water nearer than nine miles, and I was very much worried when one of the Mexican guides whom I had hired at Tepache, told me he knew where there usually was water in the rocks nearby. He went to the place to see and fortunately found enough for us, and I went in camp there last night.

I had left orders at Oposuri for Walsh with the Cavalry and pack-train to remain there until I sent for them, and you may imagine my surprise when they came marching into camp, but I found that Mr. Freinor, with whom I had left the order . . . got drunk and lost it, and as I had told Mr. Walsh to come on with the supplies and Cavalry on my trail unless I left him other orders, as he had not received *other orders,* he came on, following my trail. I was very, very sorry, as I wanted the Cavalry to rest and the horses to get some food and strengthened up for work later, and as there is no grass in the country, they could not stand it long, and besides I am so poorly supplied with rations that I cannot take my whole command in the field at once, as they only send me ten days' meat at a time, and I have to have part of the men where they can get fresh beef.

[*14 July*] I have been told by all my commanding officers that I can have *anything* I want but I have not yet been given *anything* I have asked for, not even a sufficient supply of rations, but I thought the matter over and decided to send Walsh and the pack-train back to Oposuri, and after taking from him all his supplies, I started him back. My scouts went out ahead and the morning of the 11th I started on their trail; made a short march and camped in a beautiful grove of palm trees, fine water and lots of grass. The scouts were still out ahead of me, and the next morning I again started early and made a long march. Reached the Yaqui river, crossed it twice and camped. The scouts being out of rations were in camp ahead of me. Just before we reached the river the trail we were following, which was of only three animals, came into a very large one of some 20 animals. This pleased me as I felt sure I was right and that the small parties were coming together and that I would find the main camp. In this camp the scouts only waited to cook some food and then went on ahead again.

I remained with the command all night. I speak of the command as something large. It consists of 19 Infantry and a pack-train. This march and camp was the 12th. The morning of the 13th we again started early, the trail leading up the river. The country is the worst mountains you can imagine, and the river runs through the roughest kind of canyons, and we had a hardtime getting our pack mules along. As I have said, the scouts were a long away ahead, and I did not expect to see any of them until the next day. I did not wish to make a long march as I did not want to get too close to the scouts, and about 12 o'clock I was looking for a good place to camp when I saw two scouts running towards me from the front. They were wet with perspiration, and handed me a note, saying the scouts had come on the hostiles' camp and would attack it at once, and for me to bring up the Infantry at once; that the camp was about eight miles from us.

I started at once with the Infantry and was guided by the scouts to the top of a high mountain, from which we could see the horses in the Indian camp, and in a few minutes I heard several volleys fired and the Indians shouting. I started the Infantry down towards them, but when we got there our scouts were in the camp and found no hostiles. They had taken alarm in time to make their escape, but left everything they had, horses, camp outfit, provisions, and everything, leaving on foot, and barely having time to make their escape. I was so disappointed as to be almost sick, for here was the chance we had been looking for so long, and it slipped from me without my being able to do anything to prevent it. The whole party were evidently together as the scouts estimated the number in camp, men, women and children (and there were some of each) at at least thirty.

I could not see or communicate with Lt. Brown, as he was so far ahead of me, but his plan was good. He was to go by a circuitous route around the camp and attack from above, and I, with the Infantry, was to be in position on a mountain below and in rear, expecting the Indians to retreat towards me, which would all have been beautiful if they had not discovered us and slipped out and left us to surround a deserted camp. I could cry, Mame, if it would do any good, and I know Gen'l Miles will be terribly disappointed and will probably think I have been careless or negligent, and we have worked *so hard* and under such trying circumstances, it seems too bad to fail and now it is all to do over again, only a hundred times more difficult, as the hostiles know we are after them and will watch all our movements, and I had so hoped I could finish the war and come home, but now no one can tell how much longer it will take. It is also very discouraging to my men.

It is hard for you to realize the hard work we have to do. The worst is the heat—from 120 to 130, and sometimes when we are down in the deep canons, it seems as though we just could not endure it. Yesterday when we were climbing the mountain back of the Indian camp, I thought I would faint and get real sick, and only the fact that I *must* keep going made me do so. Well, I will start again and do my best, but I am sometimes awfully worried. I hope I can wind the thing up soon. . . . We now are about six miles below the mouth of the Arros river on the Yaqui river. The Indians have crossed the river, but we have not been able to follow the trail far enough to know where they have gone.

[*16 July*] It was nearly dark the evening of the 14th before the courier left camp, and after he went away I went to bed after taking a

Captain Henry N. Lawton
with Army detachment and
Indian prisoners of war,
1886. *Right:* Geronimo
and Natchez, youngest son
of Cochise at Fort Bowie,
1886.

good bath in the river. Huber had washed all my soiled clothes and I was fresh and clean, so to speak. We do not keep so awfully clean out here. In fact, we cannot as we have nothing to sit on but the ground; cannot wear anything but underclothing on account of the heat, and they are so wet through with sweat all the time. Yesterday morning the scouts went out again to follow the trail and came in before noon with very unsatisfactory reports, and I was quite annoyed with them, and in the afternoon I moved camp up the Yaqui river towards the mouth of the Arros, to where the hostiles had crossed.

This morning I took the trail and followed it to this point. The country is very, very rough and we were until 10 o'clock going only eight miles, but the heat is so intense we suffer severely with the violent exercise we have to take. We all have to go on foot of course. No animal could carry a person safely over this country. One of the worst features of the country is that the mountains are covered with thick bushes which come just over ones head without shading and the sun shines on us and there is not a *breath* of air, and the water runs off of us so that our clothes are wet and our shoes full. We have been traveling due East today, which brings us about eight miles from the Yaqui river East and about the same distance South of the Arros. . . .

We have suffered a great deal for water and have had really no grass except at long intervals, and we appreciate such a camp as this. The water is rain water and in tanks, or holes, in the rocks. Since the rains have commenced we are better supplied with water, but frequently now go a long way without any. I shall remain here tomorrow and send the scouts ahead as I want the mules to have the advantage of the good grass. We have had one rain today but did not get wet. It drizzled all night last night and looks as though it would tonight. We do not get wet, but it is hot and muggy and sticky, and we can't sleep, and we sweat so we might as well be in the rain. I forgot to tell you we are in the land of parrots—not the small ones, but the great big green and red fellows. Hundreds of them fly about us every day and make the most awful noise, and they shriek all night. They are very wild and fly very high, but it seems funny to have parrots flying about wild. . . .

[*27 July*] Just think, it is almost August, and nearly three months since I left the Post, and the prospect of returning is not much better than the day I left except that *everything must* come to an end sometime, and on that principle this war must end sooner or later in some way. . . .

[*29 July*] I got the clothing you sent me all right. The shirts are bully but I think you have got yourself in trouble. They are so good I will just have you make *all* my shirts After this. . . .

[*30 July*] I put on one of the new shirts this morning. They are rather too small for me. The tails hardly come down far enough and the sleeves only a little below the elbows, but I can wear them. I am sending a couple of scouts (white men) out tonight to hear anything they can of the Indians. I am beginning to fear I may have trouble finding them. I hope we will soon be able to bring them in. We had no rain last night, and I got a small piece of musquitobar from Mr. Walsh and made a cover for my face, so I slept firstrate. This morning we are busy arranging our supplies and getting ready to start out again, which we will do as soon as Brown is heard from. . . .

[*31 July*] Brown has just got back; has been gone five days and found nothing. I shall start in the morning to look up the country and will go South East up the Aros River. I am awfully afraid we will have trouble getting the trail again. The Indians have been keeping very quiet, committing no depredations I can hear of, and it makes it all the harder to know where to look for them. They may be very close to us, lying up, or may have gone a great way off. Still they must get something to eat from someplace, and when they do, we must certainly hear of them.

Well, old woman! I am well; have just had a good cup of bean soup and bread and bacon and a can of pears. . . . I would like to be home, but I shall never ask to be sent in, and want to stay until Geronimo is killed or surrenders. I would feel that I was not trusted if I was ordered in. . . .

[*2 August*] Mr. Brown with the scouts got back late in the evening and reported seeing the pony-and cattle-trail; followed it to where it entered the Aros river, but that the river was so high they could not cross. I went down myself this morning, and Dr. Wood, the chief of scouts, Lt. Brown and two Indians swam across the river and saw where the trails came out on the other side, but the river is so high and running so swiftly that I cannot cross, so we returned to our camp. We will remain here until tomorrow when I will move down the river, and if I cannot cross, will remain until the water is lower. . . .

[*4 August*] We moved down to the river in the morning and found it had risen instead of falling as I had wished and expected. I at once got Smith at work making a raft, and Dr. Wood and I got a rope across the river. We had some trouble but finally got everything all right without any accident, and I crossed my two white scouts to go into the settlements North of the river to gather news, and Dr. Wood with the Chief of Scouts and 22 Indian scouts with two days' rations to look after trails and signs on that side. Mr. Brown has a sore toe and cannot go out with the scouts. I don't know what I would do if it was not for Dr. Wood. He is the best officer I ever had with me. If I had three or four, or rather if *all* my officers were like him, I would catch Geronimo in short order. . . . Lt. Parker and Lt. Gatewood came into my camp while I was working at the raft. I was very glad to see them, but too busy to talk much. They are camped about four miles from me. Lt. Gatewood stayed all night with me and is with me now. He has two Indians who are to go to Geronimo and ask him to surrender. Gatewood does not know what to do, as he says he cannot get his Indians to the hostiles if I insist upon fighting them. I will do all I can, however, to get Geronimo in my way and have the war over. I think Gatewood will send his Indians along with my scouts and when we come near a camp, let them go ahead and try to get them to surrender. . . .

[*5 August*] I am anxious to be out on the trail again, and the longer we have to wait, the harder it will be to find the trail, and I am so anxious to stir the rascals up a little during this bad weather. I think it would make them wish to talk peace when the chance is offered them. Now that I have Gatewood with me, and he has authority to communicate with them and offer them a chance to surrender, I have great hopes of winding up the war soon. All I want now is to find the trail again. . . .

[*6 August*] I had Smith yesterday try to make another raft of palm logs. They are all the big timber that grows near here. Well, I did, and Smith had a lot of fine straight logs cut, and when he rolled them into the river, they sank like stones, so that scheme had to be abandoned. He made the raft we have been using, but it was too small and did not answer our purpose. That is, we could cross a few things but it would not do for crossing the whole command, so this morning I took some men myself and gathered some logs from drift piles and made a fine large raft that we can use to cross any amount

of stuff, which works beautifully. Parker marched today and Gatewood moved into my camp. The scouts, with Dr. Wood, returned
about 3 p.m. very tired, having marched on foot over the mountains
30 miles, and having marched 70 since leaving camp, and very hungry
as they had nothing to eat today. They found and heard of nothing.
The hostiles seem to have absolutely vanished. . . .

[8 August] We have everything packed up and ready to start.
The river has not fallen sufficiently to be fordable, so we must cross
on a raft. The scouts sent to Sahuaripa have not yet returned so I
don't know what news they will bring. I am in the meantime starting
for the South West with Lt: Gatewood's Indians as guides. . . .

[9 August] We ferried ourselves across the river on a raft and got
started on our march at 11 o'clock. We had marched only about eight
miles when I met the scouts I sent to Sahuaripa for news, and who
had not returned, and they brought news that the hostiles had gone a
long way West instead of East as I had imagined. They were near
Ures, some 200 miles West of here the 23rd. It seems they took a
sudden turn back West as soon as the heavy rains washed out their
trails, so I could not find and follow them, and just flew out of the
country, as they must have gone all that distance on foot in at most
eight days. It is so long since they were where I have just heard of
them, and the distance is so great that I would not be justified in going
over there, so I have just stopped and sent scouts over there and in
other directions to get later news. I think now they will go North,
and that I will have to retrace my steps. I have sent to my supply
camp for 15 days' more rations, so I will be in condition to go anywhere, which will supply me until the 15th of September. . . .

[13 August] We lay in camp the 11th and nothing occurred to
vary the monotony, and the morning of the 12th (yesterday) I crossed
the river on the raft and moved out to this camp, which is one of my
old camps. . . . I left camp yesterday feeling better than I had for
sometime, but just before I got into camp, I commenced feeling badly
at the stomach and had to get off my mule and lie down. I was taken
vomiting and purging and was never so sick in my life, and I think
the Dr. was a good deal alarmed. I fainted twice and had to be carried to my bed after it was made down. I was sick all night and have
been in bed all day today, but this evening a courier came in bringing
news of the Indians; that they had crossed North of me towards the
Sierra Madres, and I must start out in the morning. I think I shall be

able to stand the march although I am very weak. I am glad, however, to hear something of the hostiles, and glad to get after them again. . . .

[*19 August*]   The morning of the 17th I started towards Oputo and marched to within six miles of the place. . . . Early the next morning, the 18th, we marched towards Nacozari where the hostiles had been last heard of. We made quite a long march and camped about half way. Soon after I got into camp some Mexicans came along with a burro pack-train from Nacozari and told me the hostiles had gone towards Frontares and that while near that place some had called to the people in the town from a hill and said they would like to surrender and come in. I at once sent Lt. Gatewood with his two Indians who are to go into Geronimo's camp, on to Frontares to see if they could find and talk with the hostiles and get them to surrender, and this morning I started, changing my course towards Frontares to find and follow the trail. . . . There should be some troops from Arizona on the trail before this as they would have only a short distance to march, but I have heard of none. Today we crossed the summit of a mountain range from which we could see the mountains in Arizona. I felt when I looked at them like old Moses when he looked at the promised land. . . .

[*26 August*]   . . . Just before I got into camp yesterday I got a note from Gatewood telling me his Indians had come to Geronimo's camp and that he had met Geronimo and was then talking to him. This morning Geronimo with 12 or 13 of his men came in to my camp and I have been talking with him all the morning. We had a very affectionate hug when we met and a lively, good, natural talk. He says he and all his people are anxious to make peace but he wants to see and make peace with General Miles. I shall write General Miles a full report. I feel now the war may soon be over for I am sure Geronimo will surrender to General Miles if he works it right. They all want to come in but want to make as good terms for themselves as they can. While I am waiting to hear from the General will camp here and Geronimo will camp near me, and I will feed him, and if the General will talk with him, he will go with me to the point they agree upon, and I hope then everything will soon be over. . . .

We will reach San Bernardino tomorrow, and I hope they will soon be off my hands and I can come home. The Mexicans have been troubling me some which is the reason for my hurrying across the line.[1]

236

The United States hip-hip-hurrahed into a war with Spain in 1898. Butcher, baker, candlestick maker rushed to the colors to free Cuba from Spanish treachery while the bands thundered "The Stars and Stripes Forever."

In the Philippines, Admiral George Dewey's warships clobbered the Spanish fleet and shore defenses in Manila Bay, while in Cuba, the Army, unprepared, its food spoiled, its guns inferior, stumbled ashore without opposition in late June. The war was brief, decisive.

II

TEDDY ROOSEVELT, ROUGH RIDER

American land forces in Cuba fought a few skirmishes. One of these victories produced a hero. Colonel Theodore Roosevelt and his Rough Riders stormed up Kettle and San Juan Hills, two of the elevations commanding Santiago, while the American Navy blockaded a Spanish fleet inside the harbor. When the bottled-up ships raced for freedom on 3 July, they were obliterated in four hours. The war in Cuba was over.

Colonel Roosevelt writes of his historic charge.

The instant I received the order I sprang on my horse and then my "crowded hour" began. The guerillas had been shooting at us from the edges of the jungle and from their perches in the leafy trees, and as they used smokeless powder, it was almost impossible to see them, though a few of my men had from time to time responded. We had also suffered from the hill on our right front, which was held chiefly by guerillas, although there were also some Spanish regulars with them, for we found their dead. I formed my men in column of troops, each troop extended in open skirmishing order, the right resting on the wire fences which bordered the sunken lane. Captain Jenkins led the first squadron, his eyes literally dancing with joyous excitement.

I started in the rear of the regiment, the position in which the colonel should theoretically stay. Captain Mills and Captain McCormick were both with me as aides; but I speedily had to send them off on special duty in getting the different bodies of men forward. I had intended to go into action on foot as at Las Guasimas, but the heat was so oppressive that I found I should be quite unable to run up and down the line and superintend matters unless I was mounted; and, moreover, when on horseback, I could see the men better and they could see me better. . . .

The Ninth Regiment was immediately in front of me, and the First on my left, and these went up Kettle Hill with my regiment. The Third, Sixth, and Tenth went partly up Kettle Hill (following the Rough Riders and the Ninth and First), and partly between that and the blockhouse hill, which the infantry were assailing. General Sumner in person gave the Tenth the order to charge the hills; and it went forward at a rapid gait. The three regiments went forward more or less intermingled, advancing steadily and keeping up a heavy fire. Up Kettle Hill Sergeant George Berry, of the Tenth, bore not only his own regimental colors but those of the Third, the color-sergeant of the Third having been shot down; he kept shouting, "Dress on the colors, boys, dress on the colors!" as he followed Captain Ayres, who was running in advance of his men, shouting and waving his hat. The Tenth Cavalry lost a greater proportion of its officers than any other regiment in the battle—eleven out of twenty-two.

By the time I had come to the head of the regiment we ran into the left wing of the Ninth Regulars, and some of the First Regulars, who were lying down; that is, the troopers were lying down, while the officers were walking to and fro. The officers of the white and colored regiments alike took the greatest pride in seeing that the men more than did their duty; and the mortality among them was great.

I spoke to the captain in command of the rear platoons, saying that I had been ordered to support the regulars in the attack upon the hills, and that in my judgment we could not take these hills by firing at them, and that we must rush them. He answered that his orders were to keep his men lying where they were, and that he could not charge without orders. I asked where the colonel was, and as he was not in sight, said, "Then I am the ranking officer here and I give the order to charge"—for I did not want to keep the men longer in the open suffering under a fire which they could not effectively return. Naturally the captain hesitated to obey this order when no word had been received from his own colonel. So I said, "Then let my men through, sir," and rode on through the lines, followed by the grinning

Rough Riders, whose attention had been completely taken off the Spanish bullets, partly by my dialogue with the regulars, and partly by the language I had been using to themselves as I got the lines forward, for I had been joking with some and swearing at others, as the exigencies of the case seemed to demand. When we started to go through it proved too much for the regulars, and they jumped up and came along, their officers and troops mingling with mine, all being delighted at the chance. When I got to where the head of the left wing of the Ninth was lying, through the courtesy of Lieutenant Hartwick, two of whose colored troopers threw down the fence, I was enabled to get back into the lane, at the same time waving my hat, and giving the order to charge the hill on our right front. Out of my sight, over on the right, Captains McBlain and Taylor, of the Ninth, made up their minds independently to charge at just about this time; and at almost the same moment Colonels Carroll and Hamilton, who were off, I believe, to my left, where we could see neither them nor their men, gave the order to advance. But of all this I knew nothing at the time. The whole line, tired of waiting, and eager to close with the enemy, was straining to go forward; and it seems that different parts slipped the leash at almost the same moment. . . .

By this time we were all in the spirit of the thing and greatly excited by the charge, the men cheering and running forward between shots, while the delighted faces of the foremost officers, like Captain C. J. Stevens, of the Ninth, as they ran at the head of their troops, will always stay in my mind. As soon as I was in the line I galloped forward a few yards until I saw that the men were well started, and then galloped back to help Goodrich, who was in command of his troop, get his men across the road so as to attack the hill from that side. Captain Mills had already thrown three of the other troops of the regiment across this road for the same purpose. Wheeling around, I then again galloped toward the hill, passing the shouting, cheering, firing men, and went up the lane, splashing through a small stream; when I got abreast of the ranch buildings on the top of Kettle Hill, I turned and went up the slope. Being on horseback I was, of course, able to get ahead of the men on foot, excepting my orderly, Henry Bardshar, who had run ahead very fast in order to get better shots at the Spaniards, who were now running out of the ranch buildings. . . . Some forty yards from the top I ran into a wire fence and jumped off little Texas, turning him loose. He had been scraped by a couple of bullets, one of which nicked my elbow, and I never expected to see him again. As I ran up to the hill, Bardshar stopped to shoot, and two Spaniards fell as he emptied his magazine. These were the only Spaniards I actually saw fall to aimed shots by any one of my men, with the exception of two guerillas in trees.

Almost immediately afterward the hill was covered by the troops, both Rough Riders and the colored troopers of the Ninth, and some men of the First. There was the usual confusion, and afterward there was much discussion as to exactly who had been on the hill first. The first guidons planted there were those of the three New Mexican troops, G, E, and F, of my regiment, under their captains, Llewellen, Luna, and Muller, but on the extreme right of the hill, at the opposite end from where we struck it, Captains Taylor and McBlain and their men of the Ninth were first up. Each of the five captains was firm in the belief that his troop was first up. As for the individual men, each of whom honestly thought he was first on the summit, their name was legion. One Spaniard was captured in the buildings, another was shot as he tried to hide himself, and a few others were killed as they ran. . . .

No sooner were we on the crest than the Spaniards from the line of hills in our front, where they were strongly intrenched, opened a very heavy fire upon us with their rifles. They also opened upon us with one or two pieces of artillery, using time fuses which burned very accurately, the shells exploding right over our heads.

On the top of the hill was a huge iron kettle, or something of the kind, probably used for sugar-refining. Several of our men took shelter behind this. We had a splendid view of the charge on the San Juan blockhouse to our left, where the infantry of Kent, led by Hawkins, were climbing the hill. Obviously the proper thing to do was to help them, and I got the men together and started them volley-firing against the Spaniards in the San Juan blockhouse and in the trenches around it. We could only see their heads; of course this was all we ever could see when we were firing at them in their trenches. Stevens was directing not only his own colored troopers, but a number of Rough Riders; for in a mêlée good soldiers are always prompt to recognize a good officer, and are eager to follow him.

We kept up a brisk fire for some five or ten minutes; meanwhile we were much cut up ourselves. Gallant Colonel Hamilton was killed, and equally gallant Colonel Carroll wounded. When near the summit Captain Mills had been shot through the head, the bullet destroying the sight of one eye permanently and of the other temporarily. He would not go back or let any man assist him, sitting down where he was and waiting until one of the men brought him word that the hill was stormed. Colonel Veile planted the standard of the First Cavalry on the hill, and General Sumner rode up. He was fighting his division in great form, and was always himself in the thick of the fire. As the men were much excited by the firing, they seemed to pay very little heed to their own losses.

Suddenly, above the cracking of the carbines, rose a peculiar drumming sound, and some of the men cried: "The Spanish machine-guns!" Listening, I made out that it came from the flat ground to the left, and jumped to my feet, shouting aloud: "It's the Gatlings, men, our Gatlings!" Lieutenant Parker was bringing his four Gatlings into action, and shoving them nearer and nearer the front. Now and then the drumming ceased for a moment; then it would resound again, always closer to San Juan hill, which Parker, like ourselves, was hammering to assist the infantry attack. Our men cheered lustily. We saw much of Parker after that, and there was never a more welcome sound than his Gatlings as they opened. It was the only sound which I ever heard my men cheer in battle.

The infantry got nearer and nearer the crest of the hill. At last we could see the Spaniards running from the rifle-pits as the Americans came on in their final rush. Then I stopped my men for fear they should injure their comrades, and called them to charge the next line of trenches, on the hills in our front, from which we had been undergoing a good deal of punishment. Thinking that the men would all come, I jumped over the wire fence in front of us and started at the double; but, as a matter of fact, the troopers were so excited, that they did not hear, or did not heed me; and after running about a hundred yards I found I had only five men along with me. Bullets were ripping the grass all around us, and one of the men, Clay Green, was mortally wounded; another, Winslow Clark, a Harvard man, was shot first in the leg and then through the body. He made not the slightest murmur, only asking me to put his water canteen where he could get at it, which I did; he ultimately recovered. There was no use going on with the remaining three men, and I bade them stay where they were while I went back and brought up the rest of the brigade. This was a decidedly cool request, for there was really no possible point in letting them stay there while I went back; but at the moment it seemed per-

fectly natural to me, and apparently so to them, for they cheerfully
nodded, and sat down in the grass, firing back at the line of trenches
from which the Spaniards were shooting at them. Meanwhile, I ran
back, jumped over the wire fence, and went over the crest of the hill,
filled with anger against the troopers, and especially those of my own
regiment, for not having accompanied me. They were quite innocent
of wrong-doing; and even while I taunted them bitterly for not having
followed me, it was all I could do not to smile at the look of injury
and surprise that came over their faces, while they cried out: "We
didn't hear you, we didn't see you go, Colonel; lead on now, we'll sure
follow you." I wanted the other regiments to come too, so I ran down
to where General Sumner was and asked him if I might make the
charge; and he told me to go and that he would see that the men
followed.

By this time everybody had his attention attracted, and when
I leaped over the fence again, with Major Jenkins beside me, the men
of the various regiments which were already on the hill came with a
rush, and we started across the wide valley which lay between us and
the Spanish intrenchments. Captain Dimmick, now in command of the
Ninth, was bringing it forward; Captain McBlain had a number of
Rough Riders mixed with his troop, and led them all together; Captain
Taylor had been severely wounded. The long-legged men like Greenway,
Goodrich, Sharp-shooter Proffit, and others, outstripped the rest of us,
as we had a considerable distance to go. Long before we got near
them the Spaniards ran, save a few here and there, who either surrendered or were shot down. When we reached the trenches we found
them filled with dead bodies in the light blue and white uniform of the
Spanish regular army. There were very few wounded. Most of the
fallen had little holes in their heads from which their brains were
oozing; for they were covered from the neck down by the trenches. . . .

There was very great confusion at this time, the different regiments
being completely intermingled—white regulars, colored regulars, and
Rough Riders. General Sumner had kept a considerable force in reserve
on Kettle Hill, under Major Jackson, of the Third Cavalry. We were
still under a heavy fire and I got together a mixed lot of men and
pushed on from the trenches and ranch-houses which we had just tak-
en, driving the Spaniards through a line of palm-trees, and over the
crest of a chain of hills. When we reached these crests we found ourselves overlooking Santiago.[2]

Thousands of miles from Cuba in the Philippines on 13 August 1898, American ground forces supported by Emilio Aguinaldo's Filipinos marched into Manila and hoisted the Stars and Stripes.

Aguinaldo, revolting against Spanish control of the Philippines in 1896, had aided American forces hoping that he would be installed as president of a new republic. Angry that the United States intended to hold the islands after the war with Spain, Aguinaldo's passion boiled over into insurrection.

III

THE ENGINE HAS JUST BROKEN DOWN

To maintain order in the Philippines and suppress Aguinaldo, Washington dispatched additional troops. Lieutenant Colonel Webb C. Hayes of the 31st Volunteer Infantry, son of a former President of the United States, pens his misadventures on board a transport bound for Manila.

2761 Miles West of Honolulu
17 Nov., 1899

. . . I have pitched my hammock on the Poop Deck of the ship and when the ship rolls as it does all the time, and a little more, I swing out over the beautiful blue Pacific. (Having Lt. Ralph Myer's fate in mind I am particularly careful to strap myself in the hammock before I go to sleep.) The ship has very limited deck room and we are very much crowded, especially at night, as nearly all the men are obliged to sleep on deck as it is frightfully hot in the hold where they are packed, since the failure of the electric plant which not only lighted the ship but also (and far more important) operated the electric fans necessary to keep the foul air in motion. . . . The Poop Deck is at the stern of the ship, just over the screw and as it was thought that the churning thereof would tend to soothe any sick or disabled, the hospital was located thereon. Outside of the five hospital corps men, I was the only occupant of the Poop Deck but now we have two men down with the fever and the soothing fumes of ether which have been administered to a poor sailor undergoing an operation almost lulls me to sleep as I swing in my hammock directly over and not two feet above a soldier lying on the deck who is suspected of having the smallpox by our Crank Doctor, who is literally a smallpox crank. I am an immune and a scoffer on the subject of smallpox and don't propose to be driven away by smallpox or the Doctor. My five weeks spent in the smallpox camp at Angel Island gave me a contempt for both the disease and the doctors. The engine has just broken down again and I must see what can be done. . . .

Well, I've had forty-eight of the liveliest hours of my experience. The engine bolts had become loosened, the journals hot and the machinery and the pumps had temporarily collapsed, stopping the ship, and how she did roll! We blew signals to our consort, the Peking which was just in sight on the horizon, and flew signals "Assistance Wanted." The Peking, some ten miles away, finally noticed that we had changed our course through drifting and when she could make out our signals how she did come a booming. The sea was high and our boats too small and old so I signalled the Peking to send a boat and I would come on board and explain the cause of the accident. They came for me in a life boat rowed by five Chinamen and what a trip I had. Calling in state in the middle of the Pacific in a rolling sea is great, only I didn't have any cards with me. After returning, the chief engineer, finally got things partially in shape and we started up again. After running perhaps an hour—bang, and the ship machinery stopped, the firemen and coal passers came rushing up and we found that our utterly incompetent chief engineer had opened a sea valve and before it could be closed some 30 tons of water had flooded the engine and fireroom, effectually closing operations—with hot steam and hot water galore, shutting down the Refrigerator apparatus and blowing out a plug in our water condenser. We at once signalled the Peking to "stand by ready to assist" and took account of stock with liabilities as follows:

No more water—condensing plant broken down
No more ice—ice plant broken down
No more fresh meat—ice plant broken down
No more light—electric plant broken down
No more fresh air—electric plant broken down
No more full speed, only ½ speed possible, if any.
2000 Miles to Manila, 600 miles to Guam and 3 miles to land at bottom of the Pacific.

Assets.

2000 gals. of water in reserve (daily consumption 1000 gals) 400 soldiers of 31st Inf. with worlds of nerve and ingenuity and six weeks rations uncooked.

Of course all the Bilge pumps were clogged and we had to bail out that 30 tons of water in buckets from the bottom of a rolling boat. At 4 A.M. I ordered out one Company, Co. I, and we took possession of the engine department as the ship's crew had fled or were exhausted. I headed the procession of soldiers and we literally went down into the bowels of the Sea. I would not dare describe the next four hours if I could, as you apparently think my tame description of the smallpox camp at Angel Island as well as the names of the two Hospitals "Hell" and "Purgatory" bordered on the sacrilegious, which it did not. . . .

Monday Nov 20th 1899 222 Miles
9 A.M. Honolulu Water 700 gals Condensed 860 gals.
. . . The Ther. in the ship showed 52° Fah. and Dr Hainer condemned the 282 lbs fresh meat and I ordered it thrown overboard. Chief Engineer McDonald *finally* confessed that the Starboard Boiler leaked so much that the steam could not be kept up besides filling the fire room with Boiling Water. On the recommendation of Ch. Eng. I directed that the Starboard Boilers be cooled off and the ship and condenser run by Port Boiler with Ice Plant abandoned and signaled this to Col Pettit on Peking. At 1:30 *Fire* was found in Port Coal Bunkers next to Boilers and under ships pantry. Sailing Crew & Officers & Men from Co L went at it and apparently drowned it out but it kept smouldering and burnt out three or four times. Signalled about fire. The Sailors and Soldiers were almost suffocated 1st Mate Barneson & 2nd Mate Hughes scorched and Capt Gilmer and myself with soldiers had it hot enough. The Heat and confined smoke was most suffocating and finally I ordered 3 men from each of the 4 companies to shovel all the coal out of the Bunker down into a lower Bunker near fireroom. When this was done I found that one side and ceiling deck were wooden and burned through to iron lining next to Port Boiler. Tried to signal to Col Pettit but Peking would not answer. We were barely moving while fighting the fire and Peking was far ahead. Peking stopped and we passed her but she would not answer signals. Probably too far off. We gradually increased speed. What can happen next? 1st Ship Scuttled and Drowned out. Then Fire. . . .

Tuesday, November 21st. 1899 225 Miles
9 A.M. Fresh Water 1700 Condensed 1130 gal. No Ice.
We have lost the Peking. She was in sight until 4 A.M. but would
not answer our Flag Signals all afternoon nor Lamp Wig Wag at dusk
when I tried to signal that Fire was out but to "Stand By" "Dont
know what *can* happen next." During night Sergeant Ferguson of Co
L got into Starboard Boiler and plugged her up so that steam was
raised in both Boilers and ship was soon making nearly 12 knots. Ship
officers hoisted Blue Lights and later fired rockets to indicate our increased speed to Peking but we soon lost her astern. . . .

Wednesday 260 miles November 22d, 1899.
9 A.M. Fresh Water 1700 gals condensed 1020 gals.
No sign of Peking and we must push on for nearest land at North
end Luzon 360 miles from Manilla. 2 severe tropical rain & wind
storm last night were rather frightful while they lasted but cooled the
air and smoothed the high waves. The soldiers who sleep on deck since
the failure of the Electric Plant to operate the Fans, were all driven
below and I was about the only one remaining on deck to sleep in my
Santiago-Hunting bed with its Phillipine Rain cover. The last storm
burst on me while asleep and before I could get my "cover" unrolled
my traps were blown helter skelter off the ship but strange to say my
campaign hut landed in a life boat hanging off the ships side and was
handed back to me this morning by Capt. Burchfield. . . .

Thursday November 23d, 1899   *Friday 70 Miles at noon.*
Made 250 Miles at noon.   *November 24th, 1899.*
It is impossible to describe the storm of Thursday and Friday. . . .
The ship tossed and rolled and water began coming into the fire rooms
and Coal Bunkers so fast that the ship's Engineer and firemen abandoned their posts, the steam ran down and we were soon tossing at the
Mercy of the Wind and Waves. Mr Barneston with the Sailing Crew
tried to secure everything on deck and Battoned Down the Hatches to
keep the water out, took in all the awnings and even removed my
hammock in the Guard Room Our Soldiers eventually got the Boiler
pressure up and we ran spasmatically all day. We had no Mess in the
Saloon but served Coffee and hard tack to the men below decks. Our
jib sail was soon carried away and we started into what turned out to
be the wildest night of my experience. We had three companies on

247

duty bailing, passing Coal, and firing. About 2 AM Friday morning the 3rd Officer sent for me from the Bridge (I was sleeping in the Guard room) and said he had sighted the Peking. He brought signal lights and I fired one which was soon answered. A little later the Peking signaled us and we answered. She stood by us all Friday, once or twice steaming around us as we tossed in the waves, not being able to keep up steam except for brief intervals during the day.

It was a wild day and the storm seemed to increase at nightfall. I lay down without undressing in the Guard Room.

Tuesday November 28th, 1899.

We cast anchor off Manilla at about 2 A.M. At 8 A.M. Col Pettit, Adjt Philip and Quartermaster Sharpley came along side in a QM boat and I joined them to Call on Major General Otis and report our safe arrival.[3]

IV

THE WAY I WORKED THAT GUN OF MINE
WASN'T SLOW

Newly arrived in the Philippines, a soldier in the ranks writes home of his experiences against Aguinaldo's troops.

Well Mother, our fighting is over with and I am kind of glad of it but I tell you I never expected to come out of it with out a scratch. We cleaned up every thing on the Island of Panay, a week ago Sunday and then we got orders to go to this Island as part of Auguandoldas Army was here. Well we got here Saturday and started to land under one of the worst fires that we have been in yet. The bullets dropped in the water around us just as though you took a handful of beans or small stones and throwed in-to the water. We had three Gunboats with us and we had to land right under their fire and Ma I tell you it was terrible the noise of the guns and the shrieks of the wounded Filipinos. This was part of Auganauldo's Army and I tell you it is a big feather in our hats for it is the first

surrender that is where they came right in and layed down their guns and every thin, and that is just what they did this A.M. At 11:35 we fell in and they had to March up in front of us and lay down their arms and I tell you it was a sight, lots of the men, I mean the Filipinos cryed—I tell you I could never surrender.

I captured an officer and I got his sword and gun, but gave the gun away as I couldn't fool with it but I got the sword it is about 2½ ft long and as sharp as a razor and a point on it like a neddle and I took the bayonet. I tell you the noise of those big guns off from the Gun boats and the screaching of those big shells over our heads kind of worked up my fighting blood and the way I worked that gun of mine wasn't slow.

Well I could tell or write to you about the fights that we have had for one whole day, but I want to get this off for I think that there is a little gun boat going to Manila today and I just want to let you know that I never got a scratch and that I am feeling fine.

Well Ma we will have an easy time here after we get settled down and it is a pretty little place, surrounded on three sides by high mountains and on the other side is the Ocean. I can toss a stone from our quarters into the Ocean, but we have got to fix the roof as it looks like a sieve from bullet holes and the other day when it rained every thing flooded around.

today is the first day that I have had on dry clothes for 3 months for we were always wading through rice fields or crossing Rivers or else we were soaking wet from swet. Good By

I wish we had that Mr. Riley of the 1st Baptist Church here. What we would do to him would be plenty—turn him loose and let the natives have him for a while, and I bet that he would have a different opinion of them and of him self—he could pray and be hanged for all the good it would do him, the Rebel, that is all he is and I would sooner go to the Salvation Army than to go to his church. The idea of a Preacher praying for the success of the Filipinos and that the American troops would not have success, but would have a safe return home. I tell you that there would be but a mighty few that would ever get home, he might as well pray for the end of the earth, for as long as the government furnishes us with guns and ammunition the devil himself will or can't ever hold us. He's a *FOOL*—there is no danger of him ever getting his nose where it might get shot off, I would like to see a couple of Bolo men get a hold of him they would give him something to pray about, if that is what he is looking for.

We came here to lick these niggers and I think that we came very near doing it, they started it and we will finish it no mater what Mr Riley and the rest of his cold *footed gang* think about it. If Mr. Riley don't keep his face closed, we will go over and take a wack at England and give him something to pray about, I am going to keep that paper so that there won't be any chance to deny it.[4]

V

THIS MAN SIGISMUNDO

The Filipino Insurrection settled into guerilla warfare and brigandage. Emilio Aguinaldo was so skillful in the art of deception that few of his own soldiers knew the exact location of his headquarters. General Frederick Funston relates how he discovered Aguinaldo's whereabouts and the march that resulted in his capture. Deprived of leadership, the Filipino resistance started to crumble.

HEADQUARTERS FOURTH DISTRICT,
DEPARTMENT OF NORTHERN LUZON.
San Isidro, Province of Nueva Ecija.
May 6th, 1901.

The Adjutant General,
Department of Northern Luzon.
SIR:

I have the honor to make the following report of the recent expedition under my command to Palanan, Province of Isabela.

On January 8th of the present year a native who gave his name as Cecilio Sigismundo presented himself to 1st Lieut. J. D. Taylor, 24th Infantry, commanding the station of Pantabangan, Nueva Ecija, and said that he had been sent by Emilio Aguinaldo to deliver important despatches to Baldomero Aguinaldo, Urbano Lacuna, Pablo Tecson, Simon Tecson, Teodoro Sandico and other insurgent chiefs.

This man stated that he had left Aguinaldo and a number of his officers with an escort of soldiers at Palanan, Province of Isabela, Jany. 14th, and accompanied by twelve armed men had traveled by way of Casiguran and San Jose de Casignan, a small town in the vicinity of Baler. When near the latter place he had encountered a detachment of American troops belonging to that station and two of his detachment had been either killed or captured. Upon arrival at Pantabangan he reported to the local Presidente who had formerly acted in such capacity for the insurgents, in order that he might be facilitated on his journey. This man told him that he was now acting with the Americans and advised him to present himself to Lieut. Taylor, giving up his correspondence. This the man did at once. Lieut. Taylor after hearing the man's story, and looking over the correspondence, telegraphed the Adjutant general of the District a brief account of the man's story and the nature of the correspondence. In reply he was instructed to send the man and captured letters with all possible haste to these Headquarters.

Upon arrival I questioned the man thoroughly and he did not vary from his original story.

Among the correspondence given up by this man were about twenty letters from Aguinaldo or some of the officers with him to insurgents in various parts of Luzon. There was also a considerable number of letters from soldiers of Aguinaldo's escort to their friends.

A letter to Baldomero Aguinaldo was in cipher and was worked out with much difficulty as we did not have the key. This letter instructed Baldomero Aguinaldo, then presumably in the Province of Cavite to take command of the central Provinces of Luzon, and as soon as possible to select four hundred armed men from various bands and send them to the writer, Emilio Aguinaldo. The bearer of the despatches, the man Cecilio Sigismundo was to tell him the exact whereabouts of Emilio Aguinaldo and was to serve as guide for the first detachment of the expected re-enforcements. This man in reply to a question stated that he had received instructions from Aguinaldo to conduct to Palanan any insurgent soldiers who might be sent there.

The fact that Aguinaldo would be expecting re-enforcements guided by this man suggested to me the plan for his capture.

Sigismundo stated that Aguinaldo was living in the small town of Palanan, Isabela, about due east of the town of Ilagan, and only two leagues from the coast. He stated that the only trail leading from Palanan to the valley of Cagayan was very carefully watched by outposts and that any attempt to capture Aguinaldo by ordinary methods would surely fail, as he would receive warning of the approach of a hostile force in sufficient time to retire to the heavily wooded mountains which surrounded the town. The man stated that a surprise by a party landing in boats on the coast near the town could not be effected for the reason that the Balugas, savages, living along the beach would quickly warn the insurgents.

My plan for the expedition to attempt the capture of Aguinaldo is shown by the following letter to your Headquarters.

> *San Isidro, Province of Nueva Ecija.*
> February 12th 1901.

The Adjutant General,
> Department of Northern Luzon.
> Manila, P.I.

SIR:

I have the honor to suggest the following plan for the capture of Aguinaldo who from recent developments is known to certainly be at Palanan, Province of Isabela. . . .

My plan is to take a company of Macabebes to Manila, arm them with mausers and remingtons, dress them partly in insurgent uniform and partly in the clothing of the country, take one of the Navy light-draft gunboats and be landed at night on east coast of Luzon, south of Casiguran. Four or five officers would be with them, carried along as supposed prisoners, until the time came for action. I would take Natividad and several other ex-insurgent officers who would act as officers of the column, until time came to throw off the disguise. Upon arrival at Casiguran which we would do by marching along the beach, we would call on the Presidente (an insurgent) to supply us with necessaries. This man facilitated Sigismundo, and would send forward a letter signed by Natividad that we were re-enforcements from Nueva Ecija coming in obedience to his orders.

I believe that we could deceive him until we were in his presence and the rest would be easy. Up to this time the American officers would be prisoners nominally. It is not likely that Aguinaldo knows that Natividad has presented himself, but still considers him in his service. The native Sigismundo is more than willing to play his part.

All details can be worked out satisfactorily and plan ought to succeed though there is no doubt that great hardships will be endured. It should be done before Aguinaldo learns that his courier has presented himself and given up the letters. It would be necessary to pay the Tagalos who go as supposed officers pretty liberally, contingent on success. If the plan is approved may I be notified by wire in order to make preparations.

Respectfully,

(*Signed.*)   Frederick Funston,
Brigadier General, U. S. V.

The Department Commander ordered me to Manila for consultation and approved the plan, as did also the Division Commander who arranged with Admiral Commanding the Asiatic Station to secure the services of a naval vessel to transport the expedition. The necessity for me to return to San Isidro for several days caused a delay in the departure of the expedition and it was not until March 6th that we embarked on the United States Ship Vicksburg, Commander E. B. Barry, Commanding.

Before going on the Vicksburg all necessary preliminaries had been arranged. From Company D, First Battalion Macabebe Scouts eighty-one men had been selected by the Company Commander, Captain R. T. Hazzard, 11th Cavy., U. S. V. These men were chosen because of their superior physique and intelligence and their ability to speak Tagalo. Captain Hazzard went in command of the company assisted by his brother, 1st Lieut. O. P. M. Hazzard. . . . The question of finding several Tagalos of undoubted reliability to be passed off as the officers of this supposed insurgent force was one of great difficulty. It was found necessary to abandon the original intention to use Joaquin Natividad.

The men chosen were all well known to me personally. They were all ex-insurgent officers who had since their capture or surrender served us in various ways. Hilario Placido who was the nominal chief of the force with rank of Lieut. Colonel was an ex-insurgent Major who had been captured at Jaen, Nueva Ecija. He had been released after several months confinement after taking the oath of allegiance. Lasaro Segovia, palmed off as a Captain was a full blooded Spaniard, formerly a first sergeant in the Spanish Army and later a lieutenant with the insurgents. He had presented himself to me at San Isidro in

May 1900 and had since done excellent service as a guide. Dionisio Bato and Gregorio Cadhit were ex-insurgent lieutenants who had been with us about three months. The former had been captured and the latter had surrendered. Cecilio Sigismundo also accompanied the expedition. None of the above mentioned natives, except Segovia and Sigismundo, knew our object until after the Vicksburg had sailed.

In addition to Captain Hazzard and Lieut. Hazzard, the two officers of the Macabebe company, I selected Captain Harry W. Newton, 34th Infantry, U. S. V., and 1st Lieutenant B. J. Mitchell, 40th Infantry, U.S.V., to accompany me. Captain Newton was chosen because of his having once visited Casiguran Bay where we expected to land. . . .

During the voyage from Manila the natives, both Tagalos and Macabebes, were carefully instructed in the part that they were to play. It was impressed upon them that they were to represent a band of insurgents of Lacuna's command on their way to join Aguinaldo in Isabela. The story that en-route they had fallen in with a small detachment of Americans and had taken five prisoners, which they were carrying with them, was gone over time and again so that they would be able to repeat it. They were warned that any treachery or disobedience of orders would be punished by the summary execution of the offenders.

On October 24th, 1900, while scouting in the vicinity of Gapan, Nueva Ecija, I had surprised the insurgent chief Lacuna, in his camp, and had captured, among other things, some writing paper which already bore his headquarters seal. On this paper two letters were written to Aguinaldo over the carefully forged signature of Lacuna.

One of these letters was dated February 24th, 1901, at Bulac, a place in the mountains east of Penaranda. In it Lacuna acknowledged the receipt of Aguinaldo's letters of January 13th and 14th, and thanked him for the confirmation of his (Lacuna's) appointment as brigadier general made sometime previously by Alejandrino.

It will be remembered that the letters of Aguinaldo referred to had fallen into our hands and had never been seen by Lacuna.

This letter also indulged in the usual rhetoric employed by the insurgent chiefs in their correspondence and gave a glowing account of the progress of the campaign from the standpoint of Lacuna.

Another letter supposedly from the same place but dated February

28th, was prepared stating that the writer had just received a communication from Baldomero Aguinaldo ordering him to send one of his best companies under a reliable chief to Emilio Aguinaldo in Isabela.

In accordance with these orders he was sending this force under Lieut. Colonel Hilario Placido. The latter, he stated, had been captured by the Americans a year ago and after his release had lived in Jaen, but had recently taken to the field again when ordered to do so by Lacuna. This was included in the letter for fear that Aguinaldo might have heard that Placido had been captured by the Americans and had taken the oath of allegiance. The letter also stated that Aguinaldo's courier, Cecilio Sigismundo, was with Lacuna and would accompany the column. These two letters were dictated by me but written by Segovia. We were in possession of a number of samples of Lacuna's signature and had previously succeeded in executing a very neat forgery of his autograph at the end of each one of the two sheets.

The Vicksburg with all lights screened and under low head of steam passed Cape San Ildefonso at the entrance to Casiguran Bay at 9:00 P.M. of the 13th, and at 1:00 A.M. anchored near the west shore about ten miles farther up. Boats were lowered and the expedition put on the beach, rapidly and quietly. The disembarkation was completed by 2:00 A.M. One of the Macabebes accidentally injured himself in disembarking and had to be left on the ship. Another hid himself in the hammock netting and was overlooked. Each one of the American officers carried on his person in the form of a roll a half blanket containing a towel, comb and extra pair of socks.

The Macabebes carried no blankets lest suspicion would be aroused, the insurgents not using them. Each one had on his person a day's ration of rice. The Americans were dressed as private soldiers in campaign hat, blue shirt, khaki trousers and leggings and wore no insignia of rank. The night was dark with occasional rain squalls. The Vicksburg steamed out to sea as soon as the disembarkation had been completed and sailed for Baler. I had arranged with Commander Barry that he was to visit the town of Casiguran four days later with the pretext that he was searching for some American prisoners who had been carried off by some insurgents.

This was not only for the purpose of aiding in carrying out the deception but to take us on board in case our identity had been discovered at Casiguran, as in that event any further effort would be useless. The vessel was to meet us finally at Palanan Bay on the 25th.

We remained quietly on the beach until daylight when we marched a short distance to find fresh water, and prepared breakfast.

At seven A.M. we resumed the march in a northerly direction up the west side of Casiguran Bay. The coast line was extremely irregular, being indented by numerous bays, and while it is doubtful if it is more than ten miles in an airline from the place of our disembarkation to the town of Casiguran, it took certainly twenty miles of marching at a very conservative estimate. At its head Casiguran Bay broadens out into a fine circular basin four miles in diameter.

We waded about a dozen streams, and owing to the fact that for a portion of the distance at high tide there was no space between the water and the mango jungles, we did some five miles of wading in salt water. At noon we found concealed in the bushes a small canoe, or "banca." In order to send a courier ahead so that the inhabitants of the town would not be frightened away by the approach of a body of armed men, we made use of this. Hilario Placido wrote a note to the Presidente of the town stating that he was in command of a column of Filipino troops bound north and would reach Casiguran in the evening. He instructed the Presidente to arrange for quarters and food for the command and to send a guide out of town to meet us.

Gregorio Cadhit and Cecilio Sigismundo accompanied by two armed Macabebes left us at noon in the canoe and as they were able to go straight across the head of the bay reached the town in two hours.

They delivered Placido's note to the Vice-Presidente, the Presidente himself being absent with Aguinaldo at Palanan. That individual was completely deceived and bestirred himself to carry out his orders. At four P.M. we met the guide sent out from the town and an hour later, having reached the head of the Bay, entered the forest. At half past six o'clock after an extremely hard all-day march we reached the town. Many people came to see the American prisoners. In order that nothing might be suspected the Macabebes made a great show of guarding us closely. The Vice-Presidente met the column and conducted us to several buildings which he had ordered vacated. We five Americans were kept in a room in one of the houses under guard and during the three nights passed in Casiguran slept on the floor.

The supposed officers of the detachment occupied another room in the same house. But little rice is raised at Casiguran, so that the people acting under orders of the Vice-Presidente brought us cracked corn, sweet potatoes and a few chickens. We learned here that there was a feast planned at Palanan on the 22nd. Also, the very disquieting information that Tinio with four hundred armed men had just joined Aguinaldo. This created something of a panic among the Macabebes, but during the night we saw some of them privately and made them believe that we could win anyhow by means of a surprise. As developed afterwards there was no truth in this story about Tinio. Although Placido was the supposed Commanding Officer of the detachment, the man on whom I most depended to hoodwink the vice-presidente and other people of Casiguran was the energetic and versatile Spaniard, Segovia.

From time to time I sent for him and surreptitiously gave him instructions regarding what I wished done. He was a man of courage and resource, and his knowledge of the Filipinos and of the Tagalo dialect made his services indispensable. . . .

It will be remembered that before landing we had prepared two letters to Aguinaldo over the forged signature of Lacuna. We now carefully prepared a letter to Aguinaldo for the signature of Placido. This communication stated that the writer in accordance with orders received from his chief, General Urbano Lacuna, had left the latter's camp near Buloc, mountains of Penaranda, to report to Aguinaldo with a company under Captain Lasaro Segovia. En-route while crossing the main range and on the trail between Pantabangan and Baler, he had surprised a detachment of ten American soldiers who were making maps and had killed two and wounded three which latter he had ordered sent to the American commander at Pantabangan.

The remaining five had been taken prisoners and were en-route with him. As it was evident that the unannounced approach would alarm Aguinaldo and cause him to get out of the way for the time being I instructed Placido and Segovia to obtain messengers to carry the three letters to Aguinaldo at Palanan, ninety miles up the coast.

These men, two Tagalos and a Baluga, left Casiguran at daybreak of the sixteenth and reached Palanan two days ahead of us. The letters taken through by these men threw Aguinaldo completely off his guard.

The question of obtaining quickly a sufficiently large supply of portable food for our seven days march to Palanan was a serious one. The people of Casiguran live mostly on fresh fish and sweet potatoes. The former could not be carried for any distance for obvious reasons and the latter were too heavy and bulky.

The Vice-Presidente told Placido that by sending up the valley he could in four or five days get a sufficient quantity of cracked corn for the march. Delay was out of the question, as the Vicksburg was to to be in Palanan Bay to meet us on the 25th. Accordingly with what cracked corn that could be obtained on short notice, about four hundred pounds, and a small quantity of dried carabao (buffalo) meat, we left Casiguran at eight A.M., March 17th, the Vice Presidente and principal men of the town accompanying us for a couple of miles. Our food which was about four days short ration was carried by twelve natives of Casiguran. On account of the difficulties of the trail their loads were necessarily light. These pack-bearers also served as guides, as Sigismundo's knowledge of the trail was not sufficiently definite. The presence of the twelve pack-bearers in the column made it incumbent on us during the whole of the march to continue to carry out the fiction that we were insurgent soldiers with American prisoners.

The Macabebes played their part well and made a pretence of closely guarding the Americans; and, when in hearing of the pack-bearers, often spoke to them harshly. It was evident that if anyone of those men suspected a trick he would hasten on to Palanan and give warning, after which there could be but little hope that any of us would ever get out of the country.

Our route after leaving Casiguran was first east and then northeast for five hours along a muddy trail through dense woods until we reached the sea and thence along the beach in a general northerly direction. This portion of the coast appears on maps to be comparatively unbroken, but this is merely because it has never been surveyed.

It is, as a matter of fact, very much indented, which greatly increases the distance to be travelled between any two points on the coast. The country is extremely mountainous and everywhere heavily wooded. In places the cliffs come down sheer to the sea, necessitating a detour through the mountains to reach the beach again.

The beach is generally of soft, fine sand though we had two days over boulders of various sizes, most tiresome and painful marching.

Our program for each day was to leave camp at daybreak without breakfast and march until ten A.M., when we would stop for the first meal of the day, resuming the march at one P.M. and continuing until darkness when we would go into camp and prepare supper. Because of the fearful nature of some portions of the trail we could not make an average of more than a mile and a half an hour. Rivers were numerous and had to be waded. Several times we narrowly escaped disaster in these swift mountain streams. It rained almost continuously day and night. All were soaked to the skin during the entire march and were compelled to sleep on the ground in their wet clothing.

Every effort was made to have the food hold out as long as possible, but the Macabebes in spite of all precautions managed to eat up all the dried meat in the first two days. We helped out our small rations on small fish caught by the men in their hands and with shell fish and snails. The country is uninhabited except by a few savages who kept out of our way. At six P.M. of the 22nd, after six days of hard marching we reached the spot where the trail for Palanan leaves the sea and starts inland. Here we found an old Tagalo in charge of several Balugas building a couple of small sheds which he told us were for the American prisoners and their guard. He also had a letter for Placido from Colonel Simeon Villa, Aguinaldo's Chief of Staff, instructing him to proceed to Palanan leaving the prisoners under a guard of a non-commissioned officer and ten soldiers. The prisoners were under no circumstances to be brought to Palanan lest they learn of Aguinaldo's whereabouts. This brought about a most difficult complication which it was absolutely necessary to overcome, but we were encouraged to know that our ruse was succeeding and that there was apparently no suspicion as to our identity.

Since leaving Casiguran we had been living on short rations and but two meals a day. During all of the 22nd we had had no food. This privation was telling on many, some twenty of the Macabebes being so weak that without food they would be unable to continue the march to Palanan, a distance of only eight miles. I discussed the situation with Segovia and had the latter prepare a letter to forward to Aguinaldo acknowledging receipt of his orders to leave the prisoners with a guard at this point. The letter stated that the instructions would be complied with and continued by requesting that food be at once sent to us in order that the march could be resumed. This message was sent to Palanan by a Baluga. During the night we American officers

Emilio Aguinaldo, leader of
the Philippine Insurrection
after capture (*right*). Soldiers ferrying guns across
river during the Insurrection.

held a secret conference and arranged a plan to avoid compliance with the orders that we be left behind and not brought to Palanan. So fearful were we of doing something that would arouse suspicion that we thought it best not to march with the column when it left camp in the morning lest this apparent disregard of orders by Placido alarm Aguinaldo and his officers. The old Tagalo who was constructing the two sheds knew that the prisoners were to be left with him and accordingly it was necessary to deceive him for fear that he would send a courier to Palanan with the news that the Americans had not been left behind. In the morning several Balugas arrived from Palanan with enough cracked corn to give all a sufficient meal.

The main part of the column under Placido and Segovia took up the march for Palanan at eight A.M., leaving the Americans behind with a very intelligent Macabebe corporal and ten privates. In accordance with arrangements previously made by us, in about an hour, two of the Macabebes who had gone on up the Palanan trail came running back with a note in Tagalo from Segovia to the corporal of the guard stating that orders had just been received from Palanan changing his previous instructions regarding the prisoners and that they were to follow the column to the town. The Macabebe corporal on receiving this written order showed it to the man in charge of the house building, and thus completely allayed his suspicion. We were then ordered to fall in and started out on the trail toward Palanan.

The general direction was north-westerly. The trail was narrow and muddy and through dense woods the entire distance. A branch of the Palanan river was crossed and re-crossed many times by wading.

We had no guide but were merely following in the trail of the main body of the command. About half way to Palanan we met a Macabebe sergeant and a private coming hastily back on the trail with the startling information that a detachment of ten armed insurgent soldiers had been met coming out from Palanan to take charge of the prisoners in order that the guard over them might go to Palanan.

Segovia with great presence of mind had detained these men in conversation and had sent back the two men to warn us of the danger.

It was by all means necessary to avoid these men as an encounter would have been almost inevitable and there was danger that the sound of firing would be heard in Palanan. Upon receiving the warning we hastened to conceal ourselves in the jungle near the trail.

The ten insurgents soon passed down the trail going to the coast but apparently did not suspect our presence. A few moments after they had passed we slipped into the trail behind them and continued on the way to Palanan. We purposely did not attempt to gain on the main column as we knew that the river was broad and deep and had to be crossed in one boat capable of holding but ten men. It was important that we should not reach the river until most of the column had already crossed lest some insurgent officer sent out from Palanan would see the Americans and warn Aguinaldo that his orders were being disobeyed. Our progress as well as that of the main body was extremely slow because of the weakened condition of all which made it necessary to halt every half hour.

At a few moments of three P.M. we cautiously approached the Palanan river, here about a hundred yards wide, and saw the town on the other side. The last boatload had crossed and the Macabebes were sending the boat back for us. The Macabebes started up into the town and we heard a few shots followed by scattered firing. We hastily crossed the river and running up into the town found that the Macabebes were somewhat demoralized and firing wildly in every direction. They were gotten under control with some difficulty. Aguinaldo's guard of about fifty armed and neatly uniformed men had been drawn up to receive the re-enforcements and on being fired into broke and ran, a few of them returning the fire as they retreated. Aguinaldo with his officers had awaited in his quarters. Placido and Segovia entered the house to report their arrival and after a short conversation, Segovia stepped outside the house and ordered the Macabebes who had just come up from the river bank to open fire on the insurgents who were standing in line at a distance of about fifty yards. The Macabebes were so excited and nervous that their fire was very ineffective. But two of the insurgents were killed, the remainder in their flight throwing away eighteen rifles and a thousand rounds of ammunition.

As soon as Segovia had given the order he ran back into the house and opened fire on the officers surrounding Aguinaldo. He wounded Villa and Alhambra. The latter jumped out of the house into the river and was not seen again. Villa on being wounded surrendered, as did also Santiago Barcelona, Aguinaldo's treasurer.

The five remaining officers escaped from the house and swam the river. Placido seized Aguinaldo and told him that he was a prisoner of the Americans. At this juncture the Americans arrived on the scene and gave their attention to getting the Macabebes under control and protecting the prisoners from them. One Macabebe was lightly wounded by a gun-shot in the forehead.

No attempt was made to pursue the fleeing insurgent soldiers as such an effort could have no result they having scattered in all directions through the jungle. We at once dressed Villa's wounds and made him as comfortable as possible. The three captured officers were confined in one of the rooms of the house while we American officers with Segovia and the Tagalos occupied the other two rooms. The prisoners were treated with every possible consideration, although very closely watched. There was constantly in the room with them an officer and three guards while there was a sentry outside of the house under each window. The Macabebes were quartered in the building where the insurgent troops had been.

There was found in the town a sufficient quantity of cracked corn, rice and sweet potatoes for the needs of all, and from the time of our arrival at Palanan there was no suffering from hunger.

All the inhabitants of the town fled immediately after the firing began and not one was seen during the remainder of our stay. . . .

The twenty-second, the day before our arrival, was Aguinaldo's birthday, and the town had been decorated with flowers and ornaments of bamboo in honor of the occasion. These decorations were still in place when the town was entered by us.

The night of the twenty-third passed without event, and all day of the twenty-fourth was spent in recovering from the hardships and fatigues of the march. The feet of many of the Macabebes were so worn and bruised that they could scarcely walk, and Segovia was suffering greatly from an abscess in his left foot. I had arranged with Commander Barry that the Vicksburg meet us on the twenty-fifth at Palanan Bay, six miles north-east of the town.

On the morning of that day we started marching down the Palanan river to the sea in a northeasterly direction. There was a multiplicity of trails leading in every direction. Houses with small fields and gardens were seen here and there but all the occupants had fled. Our prisoners knew but little of the route to be followed, and we lost considerable time by taking wrong trails.

Shortly after noon we reached the coast and sighted the Vicksburg coming in. Signals were exchanged and the ship came to anchor about two miles from the shore. Boats were lowered and after two hours of hard and dangerous work we were taken off from the beach.

Frederick Funston
Brigadier General, U.S.A.
Commanding.[5]

VI

BUILDING NO. 2

After the war with Spain, a disorganized Cuba presented multiple problems. A United States military government was established under General Leonard Wood, the same officer who helped track down Geronimo. Through his genius, strides were made in government, finance, education, and public health. Under his administration, Dr. Walter Reed, of the Army Medical Corps, and others, launched a war against yellow fever with American soldiers acting as human guinea pigs.

In a report, Reed writes of his experiments.

We believe that the general consensus of opinion, both of the medical profession and of the laity, is strongly in favor of the conveyance of yellow fever by fomites. The origin of epidemics, devastating in their course, has been frequently attributed to the unpacking of trunks and boxes that contain supposedly infected clothing; and hence the efforts of health authorities, both State and national, are being constantly directed to the thorough disinfection of all clothing and bedding shipped from ports where yellow fever prevails. To such extremes have efforts at disinfection been carried in order to prevent the importation of the disease into the United States that during the epidemic season all articles of personal apparel and bedding have been subjected to disinfection, sometimes both at the port of departure and at the port of arrival, and this has been done whether the articles have previously been contaminated by contact with yellow fever patients or not. The mere fact that the individual has resided even for a day in a city where yellow fever is present has been sufficient cause to subject his baggage to rigid disinfection by the sanitary authorities.

To determine, therefore, whether clothing and bedding which have been contaminated by contact with yellow fever patients and their discharges can convey this disease is a matter of utmost importance. Although the literature contains many references to the failure of such contaminated articles to cause the disease, we have considered it advisable to test by actual experiment on nonimmune human beings the theory of the conveyance of yellow fever by fomites, since we know of no other way in which this question can be finally determined.

For this purpose there was erected at Camp Lazear a small frame house consisting of one room 14 by 20 feet and known as "Building No. 1," or the "Infected clothing and bedding building." The cubic capacity of this house was 2,800 feet. It was tightly ceiled with "tongue-and-grooved" boards and was well battened on the outside. It faced to the south and was provided with two small windows, each 26 by 34 inches in size. These windows were both placed on the south side of the building, the purpose being to prevent, as much as possible, any thorough circulation of the air within the house. They were closed by permanent wire screens of 0.5 mm. mesh. In addition sliding glass sash were provided within and heavy wooden shutters without; the latter intended to prevent the entrance of sunlight into the building, as it was not deemed desirable that the disinfecting qualities of sunlight, direct or diffused, should at any time be exerted on the articles of clothing contained within this room. Entrance was effected through a small vestibule, 3 by 5 feet, also placed on the southern side of the house. This vestibule was protected without by a solid door and was divided in its middle by a wire-screen door, swung on spring hinges. The inner entrance was also closed by a second wire-screen door. In this way the passage of mosquitoes into this room was effectually excluded. During the day and until after sunset the house was kept securely closed, while by means of a suitable heating apparatus the temperature was raised to 92° to 95° F. Precaution was taken at the same time to maintain a sufficient humidity of the atmosphere. The average temperature of this house was thus kept at 76.2° F. for a period of sixty-three days.

November 30, 1900, the building now being ready for occupancy, three large boxes filled with sheets, pillow slips, blankets, etc., contaminated by contact with cases of yellow fever and their discharges were received and placed therein. The majority of the articles had been taken from the beds of patients sick with yellow fever at Las Animas Hospital, Havana, or at Columbia Barracks. Many of them had been purposely soiled with a liberal quantity of black vomit, urine, and fecal matter. A dirty "comfortable" and much-soiled pair of blankets, removed from the bed of a patient sick with yellow fever in the town of Quemados, were contained in one of these boxes. The same day, at 6 P.M., Dr. R. P. Cooke, acting assistant surgeon, United States Army, and two privates of the Hospital Corps, all nonimmune young Americans, entered this building and deliberately unpacked these boxes, which had been tightly closed and locked for a period of two weeks. They were careful at the same time to give each article a thorough handling and shaking in order to disseminate through the air of the room the specific agent of yellow fever, if contained in these fomites. These soiled sheets, pillowcases, and blankets were used in preparing the beds in which the members of the Hospital Corps slept. Various soiled articles were hung around the room and placed about the bed occupied by Doctor Cooke.

From this date until December 19, 1900, a period of twenty days, this room was occupied each night by these three nonimmunes. Each morning the various soiled articles were carefully packed in the aforesaid boxes and at night again unpacked and distributed about the room. During the day the residents of this house were permitted to occupy a tent pitched in the immediate vicinity, but were kept in strict quarantine.

December 12 a fourth box of clothing and bedding was received from Las Animas Hospital. These articles had been used on the beds of yellow fever patients, but in addition had been purposely soiled with bloody stools of a fatal case of this disease. As this box had been packed for a number of days, when opened and unpacked by Doctor Cooke and his assistants, on December 12, the odor was so offensive as to compel them to retreat from the house. They pluckily returned, however, within a short time and spent the night as usual.

December 19 these three nonimmunes were placed in quarantine for five days and then given the liberty of the camp. All had remained in perfect health, notwithstanding their stay of twenty nights amid such unwholesome surroundings.

During the week, December 20–27, the following articles were also placed in this house, viz, pajamas suits, 1; undershirts, 2; nightshirts, 4; pillow slips, 4; sheets, 6; blankets, 5; pillows, 2; mattresses, 1. These articles had been removed from the persons and beds of four patients sick with yellow fever and were very much soiled, as any change of clothing or bed linen during their attacks had been purposely avoided, the object being to obtain articles as thoroughly contaminated as possible.

From December 21, 1900, till January 10, 1901, this building was again occupied by two nonimmune young Americans, under the same conditions as the preceding occupants, except that these men slept every night in the very garments worn by yellow-fever patients throughout their entire attacks, besides making use exclusively of their much-soiled pillow slips, sheets, and blankets. At the end of twenty-one nights of such intimate contact with these fomites, they also went into quarantine, from which they were released five days later in perfect health.

From January 11 till January 31, a period of twenty days, "Building No. 1" continued to be occupied by two other nonimmune Americans, who, like those who preceded them, have slept every night in the beds formerly occupied by yellow-fever patients and in the nightshirts used by these patients throughout the attack, without change. In addition, during the last fourteen nights of their occupancy of this house they have slept each night with their pillows covered with towels that had been thoroughly soiled with the blood drawn from both the general and capillary circulation, on the first day of the disease, in the case of a well-marked attack of yellow fever. Notwithstanding this trying ordeal, these men have continued to remain in perfect health.

The attempt which we have therefore made to infect "Building No. 1" and its seven nonimmune occupants, during a period of sixty-three days, has proved an absolute failure. . . .

The question here naturally arises, How does a house become infected with yellow fever? This we have attempted to solve by the erection at Camp Lazear of a second house, known as "Building No. 2," or the "Infected Mosquito Building." This was in all respects similar to "Building No. 1," except that the door and windows were placed on opposite sides of the building so as to give through-and-through ventilation. It was divided, also, by a wire-screen partition, extending from floor to ceiling, into two rooms, 12 by 14 feet and 8 by 14 feet respectively. Whereas, all articles admitted to "Building No.

1" had been soiled by contact with yellow-fever patients, all articles admitted to "Building No. 2" were first carefully disinfected by steam before being placed therein.

On December 21, 1900, at 11.45 A.M., there were set free in the larger room of this building fifteen mosquitoes—*C. fasciatus*—which had previously been contaminated by biting yellow-fever patients, as follows: 1, a severe case, on the second day, November 27, 1900, twenty-four days; 3, a well-marked case, on the first day, December 9, 1900, twelve days; 4, a mild case, on the first day, December 13, 1900, eight days; 7, a well-marked case, on the first day, December 16, 1900, five days—total, 15.

Only one of these insects was considered capable of conveying the infection, viz, the mosquito that had bitten a severe case twenty-four days before; while three others—the twelve-day insects—had possibly reached the dangerous stage, as they had been kept at an average temperature of 82° F.

At 12 noon on the same day John J. Moran, a nonimmune American, entered the room where the mosquitoes had been freed, and remained thirty minutes. During this same time he was bitten about the face and hands by several insects. At 4.30 P.M. the same day he again entered and remained twenty minutes, and was again bitten. The following day at 4.30 P.M. he, for the third time, entered the room, and was again bitten.

On December 25, 1900, at 6 A.M., the fourth day, Moran complained of slight dizziness and frontal headache. At 11 A.M. he went to bed, complaining of increased headache and malaise, with a temperature of 99.6° F., pulse 88; at noon the temperature was 100.4° F., the pulse 98; at 1 P.M., 101.2° F., the pulse 96, and his eyes were much injected and face suffused. He was removed to the yellow-fever wards. He was seen on several occasions by the board of experts and the diagnosis of yellow fever confirmed.

The period of incubation in this case, dating from the first visit to "Building No. 2," was three days and twenty-three hours. If reckoned from his last visit it was two days and eighteen hours. There was no other possible source for his infection, as he had been strictly quarantined at Camp Lazear for a period of thirty-two days prior to his exposure in the mosquito building.

During each of Moran's visits two nonimmunes remained in this same building, only protected from the mosquitoes by the wire-screen partition. From December 21, 1900, till January 8, 1901, inclusive—eighteen nights—these nonimmunes have slept in this house, only protected by the wire-screen partition. These men have remained in perfect health to the present time.

Thus at Camp Lazear of 7 nonimmunes whom we attempted to infect by means of the bites of contaminated mosquitoes we have succeeded in conveying the disease to 6, or 85.71 per cent. On the other hand, of 7 nonimmunes whom we tried to infect by means of fomites, under particularly favorable circumstances, we did not succeed in a single instance.[6]

VII

THE SAN FRANCISCO EARTHQUAKE

Earthquake and fire rocked San Francisco on 18 April 1906. Lawlessness threatened to spread throughout the city. No organized body of men could cope with the emergency except the troops of the United States Army. So rapid was military action that within less than three hours after the catastrophe struck, General Funston, the same individual who captured Aguinaldo, controlled the city and troops strode through the streets. The Army, not satisfied just to patrol, helped contain the fire, fed the starving, and supervised the hospitals.

Generals Funston and Adolphus W. Greely report the measures taken to limit the calamity.

[*Funston*] I was living at 1310 Washington Street, near Jones, and was awakened by the earthquake shock at 5.16 A.M. of April 18th. Realizing from the intensity and duration of the shock that serious damage to the city, with attendant loss of life, must have occurred, I dressed and, finding that the street cars were not running, hastened on foot toward the business part of the city. My route was down Jones Street to California and along that street to Sansome. That portion of California street between Jones and Powell being one of the most elevated in the city, I had noticed that columns of smoke were arising in various localities, particularly in the region south of Market street.

Soldiers guarding ruins of building after San Francisco Earthquake.

Refugee camp set up by the Army after the earthquake.

Reaching Sansome I saw that several fires were already burning fiercely in the banking district and that the firemen who were on the scene were quite helpless owing to the lack of water.

This, in connection with the number of fires I had seen from the higher part of California Street, convinced me that a most serious conflagration was at hand and, owing to the great extent of the area in which fires had already appeared, the police force of the city would be totally inadequate to maintain order and prevent looting and establish and hold the proper fire lines, in order that the fire department might not be hampered in its work. By this time the streets were full of people, somewhat alarmed but by no means panic-stricken. Encountering a patrolman I inquired of him how I could most quickly communicate with the Mayor or Chief of Police, and was informed that the entire telephone system was paralyzed, but that he felt sure that both of those officials would immediately repair to the Hall of Justice on Portsmouth Square. I requested this man to hasten to the Hall of Justice and leave word for the Chief of Police that I would at once order out all available troops and place them at his disposal.

There being no means of transportation available and quick action being imperative, I ran from the corner of Sansome and California streets to the Quartermaster's stable on Pine between Leavenworth and Hyde, a distance of slightly more than a mile, directed my carriage-driver to saddle a horse, and while he was doing so, hastily wrote on a leaf from a notebook a brief note addressed to the Commanding Officer, Presidio, directing him to turn out the entire garrison and report for duty to the Chief of Police at the Hall of Justice. The man was directed to stop at Fort Mason on his way to the Presidio, and give a verbal message to the same effect to the commanding officer of that post.

From here I proceeded on foot to the Headquarters of the Department of California, Phelan Building, at the corner of Market street and Grant Avenue, a distance of about a mile. Here I found several officers of the staffs of the Pacific Division and the Department of California, as well as a number of clerks and messengers who had already, under the direction of the Chief Clerk, engaged in getting the more important records in shape for removal from the building, if necessary. At about 7.45 A.M., arrived the first troops from Fort Mason. These troops had already been reported to the Mayor and the Chief of

Police, and had been directed by the former to guard the banking district and send patrols along Market street to prevent looting. The arrival of these troops was greeted with demonstrations of approval by the many people now on the streets. At about 8 A.M. the garrison from the Presidio . . . began to arrive. Detachments were sent to guard the Mint and Postoffice, while the remainder assisted the police in keeping the dense crowds of onlookers away from close proximity to the fire and in patrolling the streets to prevent the people breaking into stores and saloons. Most fortunately the latter had already been ordered closed by the Mayor, so that one source of danger had been removed. . . .

I have no doubt, and have heard the same opinion expressed by scores of citizens, that had it not been for the prompt arrival of this large force of regular troops, who were acting under orders to shoot all looters, the saloons would have been broken into and then, the crowd becoming turbulent, would have begun sacking the banks and jewelry stores. The city police, however brave and efficient, would have been totally unable, from mere lack of numbers, to have dealt with such a situation.

By 9 A.M., the various fires were merging into one great conflagration, and were approaching the Palace Hotel, Grand Hotel, Call Building, Emporium and other large buildings from the south. Before this time the task of removing from the Phelan building the records of the Department of California and from the Grant Building the records of the Pacific Division had begun, and was carried on under great difficulties, owing to the fact that the elevators in these buildings were not in operation. . . .

Early in the morning, shortly after it was seen that a serious conflagration was at hand, the acting chief of the fire department had sent a message to the Presidio, requesting that all available explosives, with a detail to handle them, be sent to check the fire, as the earthquake had broken the water mains and the fire department was practically helpless.

The Commanding Officer of the Presidio ordered Captain Coleman, Post Ordnance Officer, to provide the necessary explosives. Under these instructions, 48 barrels of powder in field battery caissons were sent to the Mayor. As the caissons were not suited to carrying large amounts of explosives, two large wagons were procured and in them was loaded the powder, with about 300 pounds of dynamite procured from the civilian employees of the Engineer Department. Captain

Coleman at once proceeded to the Hall of Justice, and reported to the Mayor. Shortly afterward a large amount of dynamite was obtained from the California Powder Works and Captain Coleman and Lieutenant Briggs, acting under directions from the Mayor and the acting chief of the fire department, engaged in the destruction of buildings. While many of the older and more fragile buildings could be destroyed by high explosives, it was found that the modern steel-and-concrete buildings were practically impervious to anything except enormous charges. In addition to the dynamite used, Captain Coleman used a small quantity of gun cotton, which had been brought down from Mare Island.

The troops continued during the day to assist the police and fire department in every possible manner. The work done by them was effective in keeping the most perfect order and in clearing the streets in the vicinity of the fire of the idle onlookers and anxious citizens, who seemed too dazed to act intelligently in their efforts to save their own property. . . .

About 10 A.M. the Commissary Depot was destroyed, and I wired an estimate of the extent of the disaster. I considered it necessary to make an estimate of the number who would be rendered homeless by the fire in case the conflagration could be checked within reasonable bounds. I asked, therefore, for tents and rations for thirty thousand people.

As the fire progressed, however, it became evident that, not thirty thousand, but probably more than a hundred thousand people would be homeless before midnight. Telegraphic request was therefore made that all available tents and rations be forwarded as soon as possible. This step was considered necessary, as it seemed then that all supply warehouses, not only for food but for bedding and shelter, would inevitably be destroyed, without the hope of saving even a small percentage of their contents. A fact which made the saving of property most difficult was that no wagons of any kind appeared to be in the vicinity of the fire to carry away any goods that it might have been possible to save.

By the morning of the 19th the fire had destroyed the main portion of the wholesale and retail section of the city, and was actively burning on a line from about the corner of Montgomery avenue and Montgomery street southwest on an irregular line to Van Ness avenue at Golden Gate avenue. To the south of this it had crossed Van Ness avenue, and had worked its way up Market street to about Valencia street. That part of the fire line from Golden Gate and Van Ness avenues northeast to the bay at about the foot of Broadway was most actively eating its way against a slight wind into the residence section on Russian Hill. The progress of the fire was very slow. It averaged not more than one block in two hours. At that time I could get no definite reports from the fire on the south side of the city or what is known as the Potrero; but from the fact that the fire had gone up Market street so far, it appeared evident that all the south part of the city would be destroyed. . . .

By the night of the 19th about 250,000 people or more must have been encamped or sleeping out in the open in the various military reservations, parks and open spaces of the city. . . .

On the night of the 19th when the fire reached Van Ness avenue, Colonel Charles Morris, Artillery Corps, in command of the troops in that portion of the city, authorized Captain Le Vert Coleman, Artillery Corps, in direct charge of the detachment engaged in the destruction of buildings, to destroy a number of buildings far enough ahead of the fire to make a clearing along Broadway, Franklin and Gough Streets, which space the fire was unable to bridge, and in this manner was stopped after it had crossed Van Ness avenue and the fire department seemed powerless. It is my opinion that if it had not been for the work done at this place, the entire Western Addition of the city would have been destroyed.

By the morning of the 20th the Western Addition, as that part of the city lying west of Van Ness Avenue is called, was considered safe, except for the danger arising from a very threatening conflagration working along the slopes of Russian Hill toward that part of Van Ness Avenue lying north of Broadway. All day of the 20th an heroic fight was made by soldiers, sailors, firemen and citizens to stop this fire, which had a frontage of about half a mile, and was working its way slowly against the wind.

A number of buildings were destroyed here by high explosives, and back-firing was resorted to. The fight at this place was greatly aided by water pumped from the bay at Fort Mason. For a time grave fears were felt for the safety of the post itself, and I directed that fences and a number of outbuildings be torn down and that men be stationed on the roofs of buildings. The flames, however, did not reach Fort Mason, and by the most tremendous exertions were prevented from crossing Van Ness avenue between that post and the point where it had once crossed and been fought out.

By the morning of the 21st the Western Addition was considered safe and the advancing flames south from the Mission district had been stayed; but a rising wind caused the fire to turn northeastward from Russian Hill, and destroy a portion of the city along the bay shore that had hitherto been spared. . . .

The Division Commander, Major General A. W. Greely, having returned to the city on the evening of the 22nd, I relinquished command of the Pacific Division.

[*Greely*] In the morning I reassumed command of the Division of the Pacific. General Funston then was in a state of nearly physical collapse due to his extraordinary efforts and personal exposure since April 18th. He had worked fifty consecutive hours without sleep, and many of the officers and men were in a hardly less exhausted state.

The conditions then existing in San Francisco were of the most appalling character. . . .

The quarter of a million people driven into the streets by the flames, as a rule escaped only with the clothing they wore. Thousands upon thousands had fled to the open country, but tens of thousands upon tens of thousands remained, generally in stupor or exhaustion after days of terror and struggle. . . .

Until relief stations could be visited and instructed, food in great variety and in excessive quantities was issued to every applicant without questioning. As soon as military supervision began, steps were taken to reduce the food supply to articles whose nutritive value should equal two-thirds of the army ration, an amount which experience has proved to be sufficient for non-workers. Next every applicant was required to state that he was destitute. A guard was placed at each issuing station. Orders were given that a soldier should ask courteously each applicant if he was destitute, and could obtain food only by public relief; adult males were asked whether they were willing to work. Unless satisfactory answer was given, the applicant was put out of the line. . . . The largest camp of refugees were gradually brought under military control. . . . The next step was to establish cheap restaurants, and co-incident therewith the refusal of rations to those living outside military camps except three times a week and then only of bread, meat and potatoes. The cheap restaurants, (meals were furnished on tickets given applicants

U.S. Signal Corps telegraph office with soldiers on duty during San Francisco Earthquake.

who said they were destitute), provided the applicants with good, hot meals for which 15¢ was paid in supplies or in cash. . . .

The promptness of the War Department and the generosity of the American people started enormous quantities of relief stores to San Francisco. With a less able Quartermaster than Major C. A. Devol, congestion and confusion would have doubtlessly interfered with the processes of relief, but he immediately made systematic arrangements in advance to properly care for and distribute these supplies from the best available points. . . .

Medical relief and sanitation was intrusted to Lieut. Col. Geo. H. Torney, Deputy Surgeon General, U.S.A.

The magnificent and well equipped General Hospital under Colonel Torney, with disabled power plant, deprived of its water supply, without telegraphic and telephonic connection, and its buildings more or less injured, fared badly through the earthquake.

These adverse home conditions did not prevent prompt medical relief. On the first day one hundred and twenty seven city patients were admitted to the hospital, followed the next day by one hundred and forty five others from hospitals burned or threatened.

When the capacity of the wards was exhausted, hospital corps barracks were vacated and fitted up for relief work temporarily. In addition, large numbers of refugee patients were received at the hospitals of the Presidio and Fort Mason, and other facilities were extended through tent emergency hospitals. . . .

The services of the Army in San Francisco is a unique page in military history. Despite the strict professional training of the United States Army, it has shown unsuspected powers of adaptability to unprecedented and difficult conditions. Accustomed to supreme command, it has known in a great public calamity how to subordinate itself for an important civic duty, the relief of the destitute and homeless. In this work there were no signs of military degeneration, in officers or men. Thrown into intimate relations with the state and municipal authorities, serving side by side with the National Guard of California, and with the Police Department of San Francisco, cooperating with the great civil organization of the Red Cross, its operations have been free from violence, from quarrels, and even from bickerings.

I do not think it too much to claim that this demonstrates the adaptability of the average American, who makes an unsurpassed soldier without impairing his higher qualities as a man and as a citizen.[7]

VIII

CAPTAIN DOUGLAS MacARTHUR, INTELLIGENCE AGENT

Revolution ripped Mexico in 1911. Revolutionaries and counter-revolutionaries struggled for power. Popular passions drove Mexicans to damage property and kill several Americans. President Woodrow Wilson attempted to avoid intervention and war. When, in 1913, General Victoriano Huerta, an alcoholic and drug addict, seized control, Wilson refused to recognize the new government. Determined to secure Huerta's overthrow, Wilson sent naval units to capture and occupy Veracruz in April, 1914. General Funston and four regiments of infantry hustled into the Mexican port and took command of the city. Nearly three months later Huerta was forced to abdicate and to flee the country.

During the short intervention in Veracruz, Captains C. Cordier, Douglas MacArthur, and William Ball describe undercover work to locate locomotives behind enemy lines.

[*Cordier*] Upon my arrival here I made effort to secure information which might later be of value to our forces. I found that I was not in the position to carry out what I should have liked to have accomplished. Although volunteering to assist the local headquarters, my services were not utilized. Notwithstanding this situation all of my spare time was devoted to mixing with the populace, and some valuable information was in this manner obtained. Shortly after, I ran into MacArthur, who was very glad to avail himself of my services in the very comprehensive secret service work which he was carrying on. As we had had previous talks in Washington regarding a possible similar situation to the one now existing here, we were readily able to coordinate our efforts.

From a questionable source, I obtained information which led me to believe that there might be some valuable rolling stock at or near Alvarado, a point about 35 miles southeast from Vera Cruz, on the Vera Cruz and Alvarado Railway. I spoke of this to MacArthur and he immediately asked whether any locomotives had been mentioned. Such happened to be the case. We were unable, however, to determine the kind, number, condition, and exact location of these locomotives. We discussed the advisability of making a reconnaissance as far as Alvarado; but as I was serving with troops, and inasmuch as the orders of the Commanding General proscribed any member of the re-enforced brigade from going beyond the lines, I was unable to accompany MacArthur, who made the trip practically as we had planned it. . . .

The difficulties in the way of the successful accomplishment of the task seemed almost insurmountable at the time. Not only had he not been over the route, but the conflicting reports of the state of affairs in the back country were very disquieting. Beyond our outpost lines were forces of Mexican Federals, irregular bands, and an armed and hostile countryside. It was even thought at the time by some that we were surrounded by a closed line of the Federal troops. . . .

[MacArthur] The general purpose of the reconnaissance was the location of locomotives suitable for road use on the narrow gauge line of the Inter-Oceanic Railroad. Due to the great shortage of animal transportation the command at Vera Cruz was practically immobile. Freight and passenger cars were in abundance, but no road motive power. Every effort was being made to remedy this state of affairs so that in case of field operation, which appeared imminent, the command would not be tied to Vera Cruz.

Through the maudlin talk of a drunken Mexican, I received an inkling that a number of engines were hidden somewhere on the line connecting Vera Cruz and Alvarado. This man was sobered up and found to be a railroad fireman and engineer on the Vera Cruz and Alvarado railroad. He consented, after certain financial inducements had been offered, to assist me in accurately locating the engines. . . .

The Alvarado Railroad is a narrow gauge road connecting Vera Cruz and Alvarado, distant about 42 miles. The principal towns en route are Tejar, Madallin, Paso del Toro, Laguna, La Piedra, and Salinas. We held the line as far as Tejar, nine miles out. About four miles beyond Tejar, at Paso del Toro, the Alvarado line is crossed by the broad gauge line connecting Vera Cruz and the Isthmus of Tehuantepec. This latter line after leaving Vera Cruz, passes through the town of Boca del Rio, where it crosses the Jamapa River, before reaching Paso del Toro. From Vera Cruz to Paso del Toro, therefore, these two

TO ALL BRAVE, HEALTHY, ABLE BODIED, AND WELL
DISPOSED YOUNG MEN,

IN THIS NEIGHBOURHOOD, WHO HAVE ANY INCLINATION TO JOIN THE TROOPS,

NOW RAISING UNDER

GENERAL WASHINGTON,

FOR THE DEFENCE OF THE

LIBERTIES AND INDEPENDENCE
OF THE UNITED STATES,

Against the hostile designs of foreign enemies,

TAKE NOTICE,

THAT

Tuesday —— *New Jersey* ————— *Tuesday, London-day Thursday Friday and Saturday at Holmes on* ———— with his musfic and recruiting party of ———— county, attendance will be given ———— of the 11th regiment of infantry, commanded by Lieutenant Colonel Aaron Ogden, for the purpose of receiving the enrollment of ———— , company in *Major State* ———— such youth of SPIRIT, as may be willing to enter into this HONOURABLE service.

The ENCOURAGEMENT at this time, to enlist, is truly liberal and generous, namely, a bounty of TWELVE dollars, an annual and fully sufficient supply of good and handsome clothing, a daily allowance of a large and ample ration of provisions, together with SIXTY dollars a year in GOLD and SILVER money on account of pay, the whole of which the soldier may lay up for himself and friends, as all articles proper for his subsistence and comfort are provided by law, without any expence to him.

Those who may favour this recruiting party with their attendance as above, will have an opportunity of hearing and seeing in a more particular manner, the great advantages which these brave men will have, who shall embrace this opportunity of spending a few happy years in viewing the different parts of this beautiful continent, in the honourable and truly respectable character of a soldier, after which, he may, if he pleases return home to his friends, with his pockets FULL of money and his head COVERED with laurels.

GOD SAVE THE UNITED STATES.

railroad lines formed roughly the two halves of an ellipse. We did not hold the Isthmus line beyond the outskirts of Vera Cruz.

Mexican troops in force were reported near Tejar and in order to avoid them I determined to proceed along the Isthmus line as far as Paso del Toro and then change to the Alvarado line. My general plan was to leave Vera Cruz alone on foot at dusk and to join my Mexican engineer who was to have a hand-car in waiting outside of our outpost lines. Thence we were to proceed to Paso del Toro where he had arranged to have a narrow gauge hand-car on the Alvarado line manned by two Mexicans. From there we were to push along the line until the engines were located and their condition ascertained. All three of the Mexicans were railroad men and their affiliations and experience enabled them to obtain the hand-cars and have them at their appointed places. For their services I agreed to give them $150.00 gold, payable only after my safe return to Vera Cruz. Captain Cordier of the 4th Infantry was the only person outside of these men who knew of the plan.

The night was squally and overcast. At dusk I crossed our line unseen near the wireless station, where a detachment of the 7th Infantry was encamped. I was in military uniform with no attempt at disguise and with absolutely nothing on me in addition to my clothes except my identification tag and my automatic revolver with ammunition. I found my engineer with a broad gauge hand-car in the appointed place. I carefully searched him, and after some demur on his part removed his weapons, a 38 caliber revolver and a small dirk knife. As a further precaution against his possible treachery, I had him search me so that he might better realize that there being nothing of value on me, my death would afford him no monetary return. The essence of the transaction for him, therefore, became my safe return to Vera Cruz when he would receive his pay.

We proceeded as far as Boca del Rio without incident, but at the Jamapa River found the railroad bridge down. I decided to leave the hand-car, concealing it as well as possible. After searching the bank of the river for a short distance, we discovered a small native boat by means of which we paddled across landing well above the town so as to escape observation. On landing we located, after some search, two ponies near a small shack and mounted on them we followed the trail along the railway until near Paso del Toro. We then made a detour and hit the Alvarado line below the town. The two Mexican

69TH REG'T N.Y.S.M.

Col. MATHEW MURPHY.

**THIS GALLANT CORPS WILL BE READY IN A FEW DAYS
TO START FOR THE SEAT OF WAR!**

200 PICKED, HEALTHY YOUNG MEN WANTED

To fill the Regiment to its maximum strength.

This Regiment is the FIRST of the IRISH LEGION,
commanded by GEN. MICHAEL CORCORAN.

HEADQUARTERS,
Essex Market, cor. Grand & Essex Sts.

firemen were awaiting us with the hand-car. We secreted our ponies and after I had searched the two newcomers and found them unarmed we pushed on. Mile after mile was covered with no sign of the engines. The line is studded with bridges and culverts and my crew protested violently at crossing them without investigating their condition. Time was so short, however, that I dared not stop for such steps, and had to take them in our stride. I was obliged to threaten my men to the point of covering them with a revolver at the first bridge, but after that I had no further trouble with them. In fact, after getting into the spirit of the thing their conduct was most admirable. At every town we reached I took one man and left the car which was run through to the far side by the other two. I fastened myself by a lashing to the man acting as my guide so as to insure us against separation and together we made a circuit of the town joining the car on the far side. This took time, but was the only way I could avoid detection.

We reached Alvarado shortly after one o'clock and there found five engines. Two of these were switch engines and worthless for our purpose. The other three were just what we needed—fine big road pullers in excellent condition except for a few minor parts which were missing. I made a careful inspection of them and then started back. At Salinas, while moving around the town with one of my men as described above, we were halted by five armed men. They were on foot and wore no uniforms. They were not soldiers and were evidently one of the marauding bands that infest the country with brigandage as a trade. We started to run for it and they opened fire and followed us. We outdistanced all but two and in order to preserve our own lives I was obliged to fire on them. Both went down. I was fearful lest the firing might have frightened away my hand-car men, but after some search we found them awaiting us about a mile beyond the town.

At Piedra, under somewhat similar circumstances and in a driving mist, we ran flush into about fifteen mounted men of the same general type. We were among them before I realized it and were immediately the center of a melee. I was knocked down by the rush of horsemen and had three bullet holes through my clothes, but escaped unscathed. My man was shot in the shoulder, but not seriously injured. At least four of the enemy were brought down and the rest fled. After bandaging up my wounded man we proceeded north with all speed possible.

The contrast between the recruitment posters of the Revolutionary War,
Civil War, and World War I, is shown on pages 281, 283, and above.

Near Laguna we were again encountered and fired upon by three mounted men who kept up a running fight with the hand-car. I did not return this fire. All but one of these men were distanced, but this one man, unusually well mounted, overhauled and passed the car. He sent one bullet through my shirt and two others that hit the car within six inches of me, and I then felt obliged to bring him down. His horse fell across the front of the car and on the track, and we were obliged to remove the carcass before proceeding.

At Paso del Toro we abandoned the hand-car, found the two ponies where we had left them and made the best of our way back to Boca del Rio, where we returned the animals from whence we had procured them.

We found the boat where we had left it and started to cross the Jamapa River, but when near the shore the boat struck a snag in the darkness and sank. Fortunately the water at this point was something less than five feet deep, for in our exhausted physical condition I do not believe we would have been capable of swimming. As it was I was hard put to it to keep my wounded man's head above the water. Day was breaking when we reached the bank, but so wearied were we that we were unable to move on for nearly half hour. We then located our first hand-car and ran in close to Vera Cruz where we crossed the American lines unobserved.

None of the men we encountered were Mexican troops. All were guerillas undoubtedly bent on general mischief. Owing to the darkness I was not recognized as an American soldier and in consequence no alarm was ever felt for the engines. Months later when traffic was partially resumed I saw one of them running to Tejar from Alvarado.

[*Ball*] I learned of the reconnaissance immediately after its accomplishment, but made no mention of the matter; as it was imperative that the information that had been obtained should be kept as secret as possible. This information became practically the basis of our future plans, and our first aggressive steps would have been to seize the engines that Captain MacArthur located, and thus make it possible to supply the column when it advanced. The practical importance of this information, if we had moved into Mexico, cannot be overestimated. I am thoroughly familiar with all the conditions surrounding the reconnaissance, and unhesitatingly pronounced it one of the most dangerous and difficult feats in army annals.[8]

CHAPTER V
1914-1941

The right is more precious than peace
WOODROW WILSON

On 28 June 1914 the assassination of Archduke Franz Ferdinand, heir to the throne of Austria-Hungary, ignited the spark which plunged Europe into World War I. Sympathetic to the Allies, angered by German depredations, the United States still was determined to remain neutral.

In early 1917 Germany proclaimed all-out submarine warfare to cancel Great Britain out of the war. When German U-boats torpedoed and sank four American merchant ships in mid-March, 1917, President Wilson realized that the United States had no alternative but to fight.

While the war-torn British and French checked the enemy's onslaughts, Americans belatedly raised a fighting machine. More than a year slipped by before the American Expeditionary Force under General John J. Pershing arrived in France where, in the fall of 1918, it helped turn the tide.

I

THE LAFAYETTE ESCADRILLE

Prior to Uncle Sam's entry into the war, thousands of young Americans enlisted in the British and Canadian armies, and a group of well-to-do youngsters organized the Lafayette Escadrille in the French Flying Corps.

James McConnell of that outfit writes an article explaining war in the air.

We fly over the Verdun battlefield at the hours dictated by General headquarters. As a rule the most successful sorties are those in early morning. We are called while it's still dark. Sleepily I try to reconcile the French orderly's muttered, *C'est l'heure, Monsieur,* that rouses me from slumber, with the strictly American words and music of, "When That Midnight Choo-Choo Leaves for Alabam' " warbled by a particularly wide-awake pilot in the next room. A few minutes later, having swallowed some coffee, we motor to the field. The east is turning gray as the hangar curtains are drawn apart and our machines trundled out by the mechanicians. All the pilots whose 'planes are in commission—save those remaining behind on guard— prepare to leave. We average from four to six on a sortie, unless too many flights have been ordered for that day, in which case only two or three go out at a time.

Now the east is pink, and overhead the sky has changed from gray to pale blue. It is light enough to fly. We don our fur-lined shoes and combinations, and adjust the leather flying hoods and goggles. . . .

The raillery is silenced by a deafening roar as the engines are tested. Quiet is briefly restored, only to be broken by a series of rapid explosions incidental to the trying out of machine guns. You loudly inquire at what altitude we are to meet above the field.

"Fifteen hundred metres—go ahead!" comes an answering yell.

Essence et gaz! [Oil and gas!] you call to your mechanician, adjusting your gasolene and air throttles while he grips the propeller.

Contact! he shrieks, and Contact! you reply. You snap on the switch, he spins the propeller, and the engine takes. Drawing forward out of line, you put on full power, race across the grass, and take the air. The ground drops as the hood slants up before you and you seem to be going more and more slowly as you rise. At a great height you hardly realize you are moving. You glance at the clock to note the time of your departure, and at the oil gauge to see its throb. The altimeter registers 200 feet. You look back at the field below and see others leaving.

In three minutes you are at about 4,000 feet. You have been making wide circles over the field and watching the other machines. At 1,500 metres, you throttle down and wait on that level for your companions to catch up. Soon the Escadrille is bunched and off for the lines. You begin climbing again, gulping to clear your ears in the changing pressure. Surveying the other machines, you recognize the pilot of each by the marks on the side—or by the way he flies. The distinguishing marks of the Nieuports are various and sometimes amusing. Bert Hall, for instance, has "Bert" painted on the left side of his 'plane and the same word reversed, as if spelled backward with the left hand, on the right—so that an aviator passing him on that side at great speed will be able to read the name without difficulty, he says!

The country below has changed into a flat surface of varicolored figures. Woods are irregular blocks of dark green, like daubs of ink spilled on a table; fields are geometrical designs of different shades of green and brown, forming in composite an ultra-cubist painting; roads are thin white lines, each with its distinctive windings and crossings—from which you deduce your location. The higher you are the easier it is to read.

In about ten minutes you see the Meuse sparkling in the morning light, and on either side the long line of sausage-shaped observation balloons far below you. Red-roofed Verdun springs into view just

es McConnell of the
yette Escadrille stand-
beside his plane. *Below:*
roup of the 103rd Aero
adron, consisting of
from the old Lafayette
drille.

beyond. There are spots in it where no red shows and you know what has happened there. In the green pastureland bordering the town, round flecks of brown indicate the shell holes. . . .

Immediately east and north of Verdun there lies a broad, brown band. From the Woevre plain it runs westward to the "S" bend in the Meuse, and on the left bank of that famous stream continues on into the Argonne Forest. Peaceful fields and farms and villages adorned that landscape a few months ago—when there was no Battle of Verdun. Now there is only that sinister brown belt, a strip of murdered Nature. It seems to belong to another world. Every sign of humanity has been swept away. The woods and roads have vanished like chalk wiped from a blackboard; of the villages nothing remains but gray smears where stone walls have tumbled together. The great forts of Douaumont and Vaux are outlined faintly, like the tracings of a finger in wet sand. One cannot distinguish any one shell crater, as one can on the pockmarked fields on either side. On the brown band the indentations are so closely interlocked they blend into a confused mass of troubled earth. Of the trenches only broken, half-obliterated links are visible.

Columns of muddy smoke spurt up continually as high explosives tear deeper into this ulcered area. During heavy bombardment and attacks I have seen shells falling like rain. The countless towers of smoke remind one of Gustave Doré's picture of the fiery tombs of the arch-heretics in Dante's Hell. A smoky pall covers the sector under fire, rising so high that at a height of 1,000 feet one is enveloped in its mistlike fumes. Now and then monster projectiles hurtling through the air close by leave one's plane rocking violently in their wake. Airplanes have been cut in two by them.

For us the battle passes in silence, the noise of one's engine deadening all other sounds. In the green patches behind the brown belt myriads of tiny flashes tell where the guns are hidden; and those flashes, and the smoke of bursting shells, are all we see of the fighting. It is a weird combination of stillness and havoc, the Verdun conflict viewed from the sky.

Far below us, the observation and range-finding 'planes circle over the trenches like gliding gulls. At a feeble altitude they follow the attacking infantrymen and flash back wireless reports of the engagement. Only through them can communication be maintained when, under the barrier fire, wires from the front lines are cut.

Sometimes it falls to our lot to guard these machines from Germans eager to swoop down on their backs. Sailing about high above a busy flock of them makes one feel like an old mother hen protecting her chicks.

The pilot of an *avion de chasse* must not concern himself with the ground, which to him is useful only for learning his whereabouts. The earth is all-important to the men in the observation, artillery-regulating, and bombardment machines, but the fighting aviator has an entirely different sphere. His domain is the blue heaven, the glistening rolls of clouds below, the fleecy banks towering above, the vague aerial horizon, and he must watch it as carefully as a navigator watches the storm-tossed sea. . . .

Principally our work consists in keeping German airmen away from our lines, and in attacking them when opportunity offers. We traverse the brown band and enter enemy territory to the accompaniment of an anti-aircraft cannonade. Most of the shots are wild, however, and we pay little attention to them. When the shrapnel comes uncomfortably close, one shifts position slightly to evade the range. One glances up to see if there is another machine higher than one's own. Low and far within the German lines are several enemy 'planes, a dull white in appearance, resembling sand flies against the mottled earth. High above them one glimpses the mosquito-like forms of two Fokkers. A-way off to one side white shrapnell puffs are vaguely visible, perhaps directed against a German crossing the lines. We approach the enemy machines ahead, only to find them slanting at a rapid rate into their own country. High above them lurks a protection 'plane. The man doing the "ceiling work," as it is called, will look after him for us.

Getting started is the hardest part of an attack. Once you have begun diving you're all right. The pilot just ahead turns tail up like a trout dropping back to water, and swoops down in irregular curves and circles. You follow at an angle so steep your feet seem to be holding you back in your seat. Now the black Maltese crosses on the German's wings stand out clearly. You think of him as some sort of big bug. Then you hear the rapid tut-tut-tut of his machine gun. The man that dived ahead of you becomes mixed up with the topmost German. He is so close it looks as if he had hit the enemy machine. You hear the staccato barking of his mitrailleuse and see him pass from under the German's tail.

The rattle of the gun that is aimed at you leaves you undisturbed. Only when the bullets pierce the wings a few feet off do you become uncomfortable. You see the gunner crouched down behind his weapon, but you aim at where the pilot ought to be—there are two men aboard the German craft—and press on the release hard. Your mitrailleuse hammers out a stream of bullets as you pass over and dive nose-down to get out of range. Then, hopefully, you redress and look back at the foe. He ought to be dropping earthward at several miles a minute. As a matter of fact, however, he is sailing serenely on. They have an annoying habit of doing that, these Boches. . . .

A pilot seldom has the satisfaction of beholding the result of his bull's-eye bullet. Rarely, so difficult is it to follow the turnings and twistings of the dropping 'plane, does he see his fallen foe strike the ground. Lufbery's last direct hit was an exception, for he followed all that took place from a balcony seat. I myself was in the "nigger-heaven," so I know. We had set out on a sortie together just before noon one August day, and for the first time on such an occasion had lost each other over the lines. Seeing no Germans, I passed my time hovering over the French observation machines. Lufbery found one however, and promptly brought it down. Just then I chanced to make a southward turn, and caught sight of an airplane falling out of the sky into the German lines.

As it turned over, it showed its white belly for an instant, then seemed to straighten out, and planed downward in big zigzags. The pilot must have gripped his controls even in death, for his craft did not tumble as most do. It passed between my line of vision and a wood, into which it disappeared. Just as I was going down to find out where it landed, I saw it again skimming across a field, and heading straight for the brown band beneath me. It was outlined against the shell-racked earth like a tiny insect, until just northwest of Fort Douaumont it crashed down upon the battlefield. A sheet of flame and smoke shot up from the tangled wreckage. I watched it burn a moment or two, then went back to the observation machines.

I thought Lufbery would show up and point to where the German had fallen. He failed to appear, and I began to be afraid it was he whom I had seen come down, instead of an enemy. I spent a worried hour before my return homeward. After getting back I learned that Lufbery was quite safe, having hurried in after the fight to report the destruction of his adversary before somebody else claimed him, which is only too frequently the case. Observation posts, however, confirmed Lufbery's story, and he was of course very much delighted. Nevertheless, at luncheon I heard him murmuring half to himself, "Those poor fellows!"

The German machine gun operator, having probably escaped death in the air, must have had a hideous descent. Lufbery told us he had seen the whole thing, spiraling down after the German. He said he thought the German pilot must be a novice, judging from his manoeuvres. It occurred to me that he might have been making his first flight over the lines, doubtless full of enthusiasm about his career. Perhaps, dreaming of the Iron Cross and his Gretchen, he took a chance and then swift death and a grave in the shell-strewn soil. . . .

Generally the Escadrille is relieved by another fighting unit after a couple of hours over the lines. We turn homeward, and soon the hangars of our field loom up in the distance. Sometimes I've been mighty glad to see them and not infrequently I've concluded that the pleasantest part of flying is just after a good landing. Getting home after a sortie, we usually go into the rest tent, and talk over the morning's work. Then some of us lie down for a nap, while others play cards or read. After luncheon we go to the field again, and the man on guard gets his chance to eat. If the morning sortie has been an early one, we go up again about one o'clock in the afternoon. We are home again in a couple of hours and after that two or three energetic pilots may make a third trip over the lines. The rest wait around ready to take the air if an enemy bombardment group ventures to visit our territory—as they have done more than once over Bar-le-Duc. False alarms are plentiful, and we spend many hours aloft squinting at an empty sky.

Now and then one of us will get ambitious to do something on his own account. Not long ago Norman Prince became obsessed with the idea of bringing down a German "sausage," as observation balloons are called. He had a special device for setting fire to the aerial frankfurters mounted on his Nieuport. Thus equipped, he resembled an advance agent for Pain's fireworks more than an *aviateur de chasse*. Having carefully mapped the enemy "sausages," he would sally forth in hot pursuit whenever one was signaled at a respectable height. Poor Norman had a terrible time of it! Sometimes the reported "sausages" were not there when he arrived, and sometimes there was a superabundancy of German airplanes on guard.

He stuck to it, however, and finally his appetite for "sausage" was satisfied. He found one just where it ought to be, swooped down upon it, and let off his fireworks with all the gusto of an American boy on the Fourth of July. When he looked again, the balloon had vanished. Prince's performance isn't as easy as it sounds, by the way. If, after the long dive necessary to turn the trick, his engines had failed to retake, he would have fallen into the hands of the Germans. . . .

(At a new airfield, McConnell continues his narrative.)

Kiffin Rockwell and Lufbery were the first to get their new machines ready and, on the 23d of September, went out for the first flight since the Escadrille had arrived at Luxeuil. They became separated in the air, but each flew on alone, which was a dangerous thing to do in the Alsace sector. There is but little fighting in the trenches there, but great aerial activity. Due to the British and French squadrons at Luxeuil, and the threat their presence implied, the Germans had to oppose them by a large fleet of fighting machines. I believe there were more than forty Fokkers alone in the camps of Kolmar and Habsheim. Observation machines, protected by two or three fighting 'planes, would venture far into our lines. It is something the Germans dare not do on any other part of the front. They had a special trick that consisted in sending a large, slow observation machine into our lines to invite attack. When a French 'plane would dive after it, two Fokkers, hovering high overhead, would drop on the tail of the Frenchman, and he stood but small chance if caught in the trap.

Just before Kiffin Rockwell reached the lines he spied a German machine under him, flying at 3,500 metres. I can imagine the satisfaction he felt in at last catching an enemy 'plane in our lines. Rockwell had fought more combats than the rest of us put together, and had shot down many German machines that had fallen in their lines, but this was the first time he had had an opportunity of bringing down a Boche in our territory.

A captain, the commandant of an Alsatian village, watched the aerial battle through his field glasses. He said that Rockwell approached so close to the enemy that he thought there would be a collision. The German craft, which carried two machine guns, had opened a rapid fire when Rockwell started his dive. He plunged through the stream of lead, and only when very close to his enemy did he begin shooting. For a second it looked as though the German was falling, so the Captain said, but then he saw the French machine turn rapidly, nose down; the wings on one side broke off and fluttered in the wake of the airplane, which hurtled earthward in a rapid drop. It crashed into the ground in a small field—a field of flowers—a few hundred yards back of the trenches. It was not more than two and a half miles from the spot where Rockwell, in the month of May, brought down his first enemy machine. The Germans immediately opened up on the wreck with artillery fire. Despite the bursting shrapnel, gunners from a near-by battery rushed out and recovered poor Rockwell's broken body. There was a hideous wound in his breast where an explosive bullet had torn through. A surgeon who examined the body testified that if it had been an ordinary bullet Rockwell would have had an even chance of landing with only a bad wound. As it was, he was killed the instant the unlawful missile exploded in his breast.

Lufbery engaged a German craft, but before he could get to close range two Fokkers swooped down from behind and filled his airplane full of holes. Exhausting his ammunition, he landed at Fontaine, an aviation field near the lines. There he learned of Rockwell's death, and was told that two other French machines had been brought down within the hour. He ordered his gasolene tank filled, procured a full band of cartridges, and soared up into the air to avenge his comrade. He sped up and down the lines, and made a wide detour to Habsheim, where the Germans have an aviation field, but all to no avail. Not a Boche was in the air. The news of Rockwell's death was telephoned to the Escadrille. The captain, lieutenant, and a couple of the men jumped in a staff car and hastened to where he had fallen. On their return, the American pilots were convened in a room of the hotel and the news was broken to them. With tears in his eyes, the captain said: "The best and bravest of us all is no more. . . ."[1]

McConnell himself was killed in action, March, 1917. When the United States joined the Allies, French and American authorities decided to ask all men of the Lafayette Escadrille to offer their services to the United States, although allowing them to stay under the tri-color flag if they chose. Most pilots went into the American Army; a few stayed with the French.

II

I WISH THE KAISER HAD GONE TO HELL

The United States entered the war on 6 April 1917. To the tunes of "Keep the Home Fires Burning," "The Long, Long Trail," and "Over There," volunteers and draftees swarmed into jerry-built camps, where sergeants treated them to a dose of high-pressure conditioning.

In his letters, a recruit, Private S. Cillis, recounts the tribulations of training at Camp Upton, New York.

After bidding good-bye left and right to everything and anything including my cat, I left home and reported to the Exemtion Board. There after answering the first roll call (since then I must have answered it about 277½ times from Cillis, Ellis, Silas, Gillis, Cellas, Allis, its anthing but my right name.) Well, then they gave us horns, flags, cigerettes, cigars, good wishes and etc. and escorted us to the assembly room of the school, where the children were waiting for us. They made such a noise when they [saw us] that I thought the building was going to cave in. Thar principal made a short adress, bid us God-speed to be sure to make Kaiser Will feel our might, and left the hall amidst a riot of noise. We then boarded a buss and away we went. We rode down Broadway to 137th St. over to Riverside drive, to 72d St. to B'Way again to 57th st. down 5th aven., across 34th st. to the L.I.R.R. station. All the way the Police gave us the military salute. Some people cheered us and others looked at us as if they felt sorry. But we on the buss made as much noise as we were capable. Some were so crazy about it that when they got off were preety near all in.

At the station there was a mixed scene of joy and sorrow. Pretty near all of Fathers, mothers, sisters, brothers, cousins, nephews, nieces, uncles, aunts, wives, grandpapas, grandmamas, long distance relations, short distance ones, aquaintences, friends, ministers, priests, rabbis, were there to see us off. I even seen some who brought dogs to pet them for the last time. Well, fathers and mothers wept, wives and sisters too. But the blessed singles like me were merry and noisy, and

Camp Upton New York
October 1 1917

Mr. Chasin

Dear sir and friend

After being out
here a week nothing has happened to
make me think I'm in the army, except
that I wear a uniform and makes a
fellow feel tough in it. We live in
wooden houses called barracks, they
ought to call them glass houses. there
are more windows than wood. We sleep in spring beds, a straw mattress and three blankets, no pillows. The food is not what mother
makes, but its fair. The officers are still busy assorting us out, and
have not much time for drilling. We exercise a little in the morning, they take us out marching. in the afternoon, give a few lessons in military manners and so ends the days. I don't think we
will get any real hard work for sometime. I still feel like a boy
wearing his first long pants, am not worring over anything
in particular, even when I heard that after four or five months
training we'll be sent to France and there the'll put the finishing

Manuscript letter from Private Cillis describing training at Camp Upton, World War I.

acted more like children on their way to a pic-nic or ice cream party, than to the stern business of war. (I say war because after passing 11 examinations and measured up for uniform and nothing the matter with me, I'm in it for good, no matter how badly I may feel about it later, though to this writing I have found nothing to make me kick). The train was delayed an hour I thought that the war was over, but such was not the case.

When the train did leave there was some more noise. We soon were swallowed in tunnel and they disappeared from our sight. When we reached Jamaica we changed trains and then the trip for real started. As preety near everybody had flags it was easy for the people to recognize us of the villages that we went by. They were all there giving us the hip, hip, hooray. Even the cows stopped from eating and smiled at us, chickens in farmyards flapped their wings, and the ducks ducked and pigs grunted. A few miles before we reached camp [Upton] the train stopped and officers took charge of us. Here ends the history of my departure.

. . . This soldier stuff I like and I don't. Most of the fellows here gamble, which to me that don't appeal, not that I am a strictly Sunday school product, but that was never a favorite pastime with me. They got fellows here that are as short as you, I was surprized to see them here one of them is so short and fat that he look a comic Valentine. He's an Italian too. The food is not so very bad though its nothing like I use to get at home, that is I miss spaghetti and Italian wine. Do you still sleep in bed or are you afraid of the dark? Whats the name of the latest Chaplin picture, are you still stuck on Mary Pickford Oh! ! ! I'm forgetting you're getting married excuse me, I beg your pardon old top so so long.

After being out here a week nothing has happened to make me think I'm in the army, except that I wear a uniform and makes a fellow feel tough in it. We live in wooden houses called barracks, they ought to call them glass houses. There are more windows than wood. We sleep in spring beds, a straw mattress and three blankets, no pillows. The officers are still busy assorting us out, and have not much time for drilling. We exercize a little in the morning, they take us out marching in the afternoon, give a few lessons in military manners and so ends the days. I don't think we will get any real hard work

for sometime. I still feel like a boy wearing his first long pants, am not
worring over, anything in particular, even when I heard that after
four or five months training we'll be sent to France and there the'l
put the finishing touches behind the front. I fugured out that by next
July or August we'll be in action. The married men and many others
are not so joyful about it. I'ts to late for any one who has passed the
examinations to fake an illness. They examined us so thoroughly
and have got all our history, they took finger prints of all of them, and
some fingers twice. When they vaccinated us a couple fainted, and
to cheer us up some one said, that we would have to go through the
same thing again two more times. Some fellows have fits, they are
sent to the hospital. So far nothing of that sort has happened to me.
At my house they always thought I was weak, and I am a little. But
here there are some weaker then me, and lots of them wearing
glasses too. So far I've not met any one I knew we're all strangers to
each other. The're Greeks and freaks, Irish and Scoth, Italians and
Jews, the fellow next to my bed is an Armenian. They are of all
race, color, religion and opinion. They all don't know [what] the're
going to fight for and many don't care either.

> Lieutenants number ones and twos
> Are drilling us to take off shoes
> Tell us when to hit the hay
> When we are tired at the end of day
> Take along on different hikes
> All the Patricks, Joe's and Ikes
> I sleep in a bed make out of straw
> Without a pillow is their only flaw
> The barracks they are made of wood
> And so tastes our daily food
> Our chef ho, I wish he'd die
> His face reminds me of a half baked pie
> His cooking is, well very plain
> He must have learnt from some old dame
> And when I seen him it bring me grief
> To think I've got to eat his beef
> He'll never make a hit with me
> Cause colored water he calls it tea
> His coffee too is only a bluff

And sugar he never puts enough
Of bread he give us only a slice
I know it woun'nt satisfy a mice
The only thing about the hash
Is that we get it without cash
The steaks are good once in a while
Is the reason why we sometime smile
What I do like is hard to tell
I wish the Kaiser had gone to hell
Or that some unknown guy
Would take shot at his right eye
And sock him with a big strong bat
When he isn't wearing his old spiked hat
Or if he ate the food we get
He'd stop the war I'm willing to bet
And Hindenberg that ugly mutt
I wish some one his nose would cut
I also would if I were near
Help to chop one of his ear
To all of us it would be a delight
To wollop him with all our might
We also have a great desire
To roll his body into some mire
Or give him a bath in good black ink
He too would quit the war I think
I wrote this when I was feeling blue
I hope it won't have that effect on you
You might think I had an easy time
But it was mighty hard to make words rhyme
We have to be in bed at ten
So good night to you and to this pen.

We have been moving again. I have been vaccinated for the fourth time now, and to me it appeared as if the butcher must have driven the needle about three inches deep. I now know that I'm still at this camp but for two days my head felt as if it was a foot ball and being kicked by all the sign hangers of the size of John Medvie. As soon as I recovered they put me at the kitchen police, down here when they want you to do some work that they know it is not liked by the fellows, they give it a nice name, Kitchen police means, that one becomes a kitchen maid, or, as the boys call it, a kitchen slave, yeh I manicured potatoes wrestled with pots and pans, chopped wood for the stove, and then to make matters worse, they gave me a job that brought tears to my eyes I peeled onions, when I got through I did not have to wash my face, but what made me sore was that I had to take orders from a pie faced, frog eyed, long eared, narrow chested, bow legged, long tongued, empty headed shrimp who thinks he is a cook, all he did was to smoke a big cigar with his hands in his pockets and give orders, and got credit for all the hard work that I done.

Whooooo some said that I got to be needled three more times, good night I'm going to desert.

The drillings are still easy, and some times they take us out in the woods to chop trees which I enjoy, the weather is still warm out here, in the morning its just a little bit chilly. The whole place has been growing up since I came here, and its still a going strong, half a dozen buildings go up every day, where ever you turn your head you see them grow, like mushrooms.

Men are still coming here every day from all over the state, and also from some other states. It seems that the nearest to this place were sent first and the ones that are the farthest are coming last. I've heard say that when all of the men are here then they are going to start the real hard training, and those that cannot stand it will be sent home.

I make a little pocket money here on drawing some of the fellows portraits, I must have made a hit cause I have a long waiting list and you oughter see how careful they are that I sign my name to them and the date. Some of them send their pictures home, and when they go home on a pass on Sunday, they tell me that they find the pictures framed. They must be preety good I guess even if I say so my self.

We are allowed to go home on Sundays if we are good, *but its hard to be good.* I've been good only once, and once only, have been home, I don't worry if I'm not good cause on Sunday which is the only day that we can go home is when good meals are served to us, we get chicken and pie, sometimes cakes and cocoa, and not long ago the

captain's mother came to see us and brought us chocolates and cigerettes, so you see down here I don't realy miss any thing except your
cheerful smile.

No I'm not satisfied the [way] I look in a privates uniform and I
won't be happy untill I get in a major generals outfit with gold stars
spur and boots and a gold handled sword at my side and a white
horse to ride, just like the picture I've drawn at the head of this
letter. The work is getting preety hard this afternoon I got a stiff
neck by watching aeroplanes doing stunts in the air, and tonight I
got sore hands by fighting two wild frankfurters for supper, but I'm
not kicking because I expect such things to happen.

There is here a French captain who is demonstrating to the
American officers the French method of constructing trenchs. The
French government is certainly extravagant with gold ornaments. I
seen him one day on a road with a group of American officers and
to me he looked like one of the doormen that stand in front of the
big hotels in the City, his trousers and blouse were very light blue,
his cap black, vermilion, and half a dozen rows of gold stripes, on
his sleeves and arms more gold with ornaments of brass and black
boots. He certainly looked like a dandy in comparison with the
simple uniform that the American officers wore. I think that if they
go that way on the battle field they must be easy prey for German
snipers.

You are right that I have little time to write letters, I am in the
heavy artillery in one of the howitezer sections and as the allies need
heavy artillery most we are going to go first probably next March or
April, so we are being drilled every minute of the day and I am
always tired. I spend most of my time when not drilling in resting,
but I'm enjoying the work just the same. Some of the men still feel
sore that they were drafted, I've heard some say that they would
rather be a live coward then a dead hero, another said that he would
like to exchange all the honor that he's going to get out of this war
if he could get his job back again and other things to that effect. I'm
not worring about my job because I wasn't making much.

I'll give you an idea of what we do. The day after Thanksgiving
we were awakened at 5:30 A.M., washed up, had breakfast, were
given some sandwichs to take with us and by 6:00 all were ready

to leave the barracks, at that hour it was still dark but that did'nt bother the captain or any of the officers, who called us to attention and ordered march. As we went some fell as they could not see the many stumps in the dark that are scattered all around here; by daylight we had walked about four or five miles and found ourselves along side the L.I.R.R. tracks, there we halted, and were told that the L.I.R.R. could not build a bridge over their tracks now or some thing like that. So general Bell had decided to build it himself and gave orders to the engineers to do so in a very short time, and now each day about four hundred men from different regiments are taken there and do the work that the Railroad was supposed to do. As my battery is composed of more than half Irish the rest Jews and Italians, the Irish and Italians felt quite at home with picks and shovel and wheelbarrows so amidst lots of shouting, whistling trains, screeching steam engines, we went ahead and worked like hell. It was a cold day so even the officers digged in order to keep themselves warm. We quit about a quarter to four in the afternoon. It was the hardest work I ever did, I did not feel terrible tired that night but ho the next morning I could not get up I felt 2,755,070 different kinds of aches.

Now thats very cold, we dont do any drilling but are kept indoors, and we are given lectures about everything militaraly some are very interesting and others make me go to sleep as they are about things too deep for me, and which I never studied, geometry, surveying, telegraph operating with the "buzzer" and other things, scientific. But I'm not the only one that gets balled up in those things, its only the college and university students who have it easy when it comes to those subjects.

I'm still contented with my lot out here, and when I here a lecture from a man who has been "over there" and I heard quite a few it makes me feel anxious to be over there; not that I'm anxious to kill or get killed, but the curiosity sometimes in me is very strong. The lectures of gas attacks are interesting, when a soldier can put his gas mask as quick as he can no matter how much gas is shot at him he's safe I can put mine in about ten seconds.

Not long ago we were inspected by the lieut. colonel, the highest officer that we've been inspected yet. He's the most soldierly soldier that I've ever saw. We stood erect in our ranks as stiff as wooden

Indians in front of a cigar store. Well he walked majesticaly along and pointed out to the captain more faults that he ever imagined could be found among us. The greatest fault that he found was that many men had their hair cut like a longshoremen, which he did not like, his eagle eye did not miss a thing, as he passed by me he told me to look him straight in the eye, and he said the same thing to *many* others the reason being that when at attention we look straight ahead. When my coporal calls the roll it sounds like as if he was managing a menegerie three men answer to the name of Tiger, Lyons, and Wolf, we also had fellow named Fox, but he's not with us no more.[2]

Tune "Tipperary"

When the Kaiser started in to split the world in two,
He bit off seven times as much as any one could chew,
So here we are upon our way to join the folks in France
To pin the double cross upon the bosom of his pants.

Chorus: It's a long way to get the Kaiser,
                It's a long way we know,
                But you know we're a whole lot wiser
                Then we were some time ago;
                Good Bye Kaiser Wilhelm,
                You are about all in;
                Don't drop dead before we meet you
                Right in Berlin.

When the war is over and we reckon the expense,
We'll try and "hoch the Kaiser" for as much as fifty cents,
It's more than he is worth, but we'll spend it for Berlin,
To fumigate the places where the royal bunch has been.

Chorus: It's a long way, etc.

Tune "John Brown's Body"

Old Bill Kaiser, we are going to cross the blue;
We got a date with friends of ours who have a date with you.
We're going to bring the wallop that will put the business thru
So we are marching on.

Chorus: Glory, Glory, hallelooyer,
             Bill, old dog, we're going to do yer,
             As we go marching on.

Old Bill Kaiser, do you ever stop to think
Exactly what awaits you and your son, the Missing Link,
When we have a little party up in Potsdam-on-the-Blink,
             As we go marching on.

Chorus: Glory, Glory, hallelooyer, etc.

The partnership of you "und Gott" is dead for evermore;
The devil is your partner and he holds the open door,
Where the trademark "Made in Germany" is stamped upon
    the floor,
             As we go marching on.

Chorus: Glory, Glory, hallelooyer, etc.

The S.O.S.
To the tune of "They'll Never Believe Me."

    And when they ask us how dangerous it was,
We never will tell them—We never will tell them
    We spent our pay in some cafe
    And fought wild women night and day,
Twas the awfullest thing we had to do,
And when they ask us and they are certainly going to ask us
    Why it was we didn't win the croix de guerre
We never will tell them—No we never will tell them
    There was a front,—but damned if we knew where.

Hee-Haw

If you see a man that looks forlorn,
With an old slouch hat and a shirt that's torn,
A pair of fatigues all covered with oil
And hands all calloused with honest toil;
A chew of tobacco in the side of his face,

307

Old hob-nailed shoes with only one lace,
You'll find him smiling, perhaps cussing too;
For his friends are many and enemies few—
A four line driver of two spans of ribbon winners
He'll be one of the Supply Company's mule skinners.

Toast To The Kaiser

Now, here's to the Kaiser, the Limburger cheese—
May the swell in his head go 'way down to his knees—
May he break his neck over the Hindenburg line
And go to Hell croaking "The Watch on the Rhine."[3]

III

NO PLACE FOR A WEAK STOMACH

After conditioning and training, doughboys of the American Expeditionary Force, singing "Good-bye Broadway, Hello France," shipped out. Yanks on board British transports recount their trials.

(Doughboy No. 1)

We did not stay in Camp Mills as long as I would like to have stayed. I was planning to go to N. Y. City the night we left and I can assure you that it was a great dissapointment to me to be so close to the great city and never get to see it. We saw some few sights as we passed down the Hudson river but not to my satisfaction. Our journey across this big pond was very interesting while we were leaving old U.S.A. passing out of the harbor and for a day or so out but things began to grow old after we had explored the boat as far as we were allowed and the water looks the same day after day except some days were colder and the water was rougher with sometimes waves dashing over the decks. Officers and Nurces occupy most of the boat while the soldiers are all crowded on one deck togeather where there is hardly room to stand at nights we occupy the hold of the vessel, a very poor ventilated part of the boat, so smelly at nights that one can hardly breathe and for chow,—it is absolutely unpalitable, I can find nothing to eat except bread and butter the rest of the slop they bring turns my inards—and I have not been see sick at all. On board is where one wishes he were an Officer with a stateroom, all the room on decks that soldiers are forbidden and all the nurces to dance and chat with, a smoking room and parlor and salon and above all some thing to eat, they say the Officers have a Menu to order from and are served as in a high classed hotel, I feel now as if I could put in a large order at their dining room for I am near starved, the boys swear the meat we get every meal is cat meat some even find pieces they claim is the tail of the animal but I think from my experience that it is cold storage jack rabbit altho one sight and a smell of the rotten stuff was enough to satisfy me that I would eat none of it, I only wish our officers had to eat just one meal with us, the *hold* of the ship is filled with long tables which we eat on and at night we sleep in hammocks just above the tables hung from hooks in the ceiling.

I stayed on deck all today watching the manuvers of the convoy and watching for U. boats we are likely to see one any time but night has come again and no subs. I would like to see one appear just to see these gunners blow one up altho I am sure I dont want one too close for this water is sure cold and my only chance of floating is on a life raft and I am not crazy about them.

I was very much surprised that I was not seasick at all, I guess it was because the sea was unusually calm and we are on a good big ship that is an eaŝy rider.

This will no doubt be an old letter by the time you get it as I hear that it takes two weeks for our mail to reach home. I hope you will write often to me for you know what mail is to a soldier in a foreign land, our letters will be limited from now on so you must not expect many from me.

(Doughboy No. 2)

Today is Sat. & a miserable day indeed. For the last few days it has been so fogy that the neighborship can not be seen & the fog horns or whistles are blowing continuesly to prevent collisions.

We are now in the danger zone & 50 men have been selected for submarine lookouts. What our duties are is unknown although we are equipped & in readiness. Expect to know by this eve as to what is what.

Every time we get drafted men to fill the vacancies in our Reg. there is always some kind of decease that spreads. I think the cause all reflects to the unsanitary conditions aboard. The other night I was on guard in the steerage & from what I seen there—am surprised that more men are not ill. Why it is a fright. Always tho't that the English were a clean type, believe me I have changed my opinion. The cooks wore dirty underwear & kitchens dirty. The steerage & 3rd class dining room floors are filthy & the atmosphere is foul. How the men (in hammocks) endure sleeping down there is a mystery to me. I would prefer sleeping on deck regardless the discomforts. The toilets are worse than a fertilizing or soap factory.

Our meals are fit for *dogs only*. Fish one or two times a day & when you examine it you lose your appetite. All I have eaten the last twenty four hrs is—bread; coffee; oleomargarine; one chop and four hard boiled eggs. Last night I fortunately & very secretly bought a bottle of beer (for two bits) which helped to "fill in."

I know when we get *"over there"* our people (U.S.) will feed us better, at least wholesome food which is better than abundance & no good. Have recovered from seasickness & can again feel fine & have lots of "pep."

(Doughboy No. 3)

Needless to tell you of our letters being censored and its really terribly hard to write anything interesting. Well I'll do my best so here goes. Today is our ninth day on the water. The weather has been very fine, with the exception of two days. These days it rained and the sea was usually very heavy. The trip has been very long and tiresome at times but the boys usually play cards, sing, or carry on in a general way.

The boat is a large one but does considerable rocking and just at present its doing her share. The boys get lots of sunshine and God's free air, and I really think that's what is keeping the majority alive. The eats are terrible. They give you about half enough. Imagine, Bessie, for a supper, tea, jams, pickles & chees every other night. The English feed us aboard this boat and the Amer. Govt. should certainly look into it. So if your up around Congress just stop in and let them know. These English people after starving us all day come around usually about 10 oclock at night with sandwiches for ten or twenty cents apiece. So what can a fellow do? They got you by the neck.

(Doughboy No. 4)

I just had to write you to-day, although I am keeping a diary for your eyes alone and I hope to be able to get them to you some day. Darling dear this is the most tiresome trip that I have ever taken or ever expect to take again.

Sophia If I could only get back to you and have some of your mothers regular meals you cannot realize how I would eat. I never thought or believed it possible that a person would have to eat some of the stuff we get here. We have porridge in the morning, with no sugar, and all of it is left. For dinner we have fish, and it is all tainted, the meal they have is not eatable, the only thing that keeps us up is bread, and we eat enough of it to start a Bakery. Our Menu, for Supper is usually a little piece of Brick cheese, plus pickles, tea, and bread. Sophia darling, I certainly will have lots and lots to tell you when I get home to you, It would take reams of paper to partially describe the conditions we have to face on this ship, I know the trenches are no worse.

It seems as fate has dealt us an awful blow, and some times dear, the old tears are bound to come to my eyes, and if I wasn't a man I certainly would cry. If I look at your picture once darling, I look at it thousands of times. It is the only thing that keeps my courage up.

We don't know where we are going or what we are going to do or anything. The only thing we know is that we are on our way.

We have to wear life belts all the time, and have boat drill once a day, also have physical exercises in the morning.

The whole thing seems to be a dream and I cannot realize that I have been taken away from you sweetheart.

Tell all my old friends that I am getting along fine, but don't recommend the Army to any-one unless you want them to feel disappointed in it.

Try to keep your mind off this thing dear or a person will go crazy. Don't worry about me.

(Doughboy No. 5)

Going over on a troop ship has certainly been an experience which none of us will ever forget. There is so much which one cannot say that I scarcely know what *is* permissible. The food has been the main bone of contention on board & has not been up to standard in either quantity or quality, also variety. A small kitchen serves 1800–2000 men and to save food and labor we were put on a 2 meal a day diet, & some of the big men never got enough to eat.

Believe me when I say that the infantry quarters, pressed in like crated cattle, were no place for a weak stomach or an aristocratic nose for a period of several days. The rats seemed to bother some of the men in the hold a bit also, but I think that there were absolutely no bugs of any kind on board. We still have that doubtful pleasure ahead of us.

We have, by orders, been sleeping in our clothes for the last few nights, and some have ever since leaving America & since there have been no baths afforded you can imagine there are various odors afloat. (N.B. I had a fine bath a few day back—sergeants self taken privilege).

We have seen nothing of submarines & things look so peaceful & natural that one can hardly conceive of their presence. Just as I write the story comes that a ship 15 miles away has been torpedoed, so things are not so dull after all. But tonight is our last night on board, so we feel pretty good & do not worry. Some of our men *have* worried however & even slept on deck.

Well, night before last was our first night in the zone of active submarine operations & that & sleeping in our clothes for the first time created a little "atmosphere." I went to sleep about 11 PM & slept fairly well until I was awakened by a loud but slightly muffled explosion followed in about 5 seconds by another. It sounded like a torpedo hitting the rear of the ship. My first fleeting sensation was a peculiar one as I realized what it was that had apparently happened, & especially awakened right out of a sound sleep. I snapped on the electric light at the head of my bed & jumped out. The 2 men opp. me hopped out, grabbed life belts & were out for the deck. I waited for the whistle signal before I moved because I wanted to wake a sound sleeper in the next cabin & didn't want to do so unnecessarily, & knew that if I got on deck & the whistle blew I would never be able to get back to our quarters again. But as I stood in our doorway I was most highly entertained by men flying out of doorways & up the corridor, men dragging coats, even dragging life belts half on, men fully dressed, these the timid ones who were first out of their burrows. The thing was serious & yet comical.

In a minute or two I went on deck. About everybody was there but no sign of damage to the boat, & we understood that one of the destroyers who had met us in the night had fired a couple of depth bombs. The whole affair was the subject of much good natured raillery

& indeed was mighty comical in many ways. Men whom you ordinarily had to shake for 10 minutes to get up in the morning were out of bed & on deck by the time the second explosion occurred, a space of 5 or 6 seconds. Unit Q was speedy for once in its life.

Tomorrow we expect to land & will for the first time come into a close active realization that there is a man killing war on. It seems hard to realize, even among a bunch of soldiers.

Big excitement right here. Some more of the depth bombs right out of a clear sky. 12:30 AM & great excitement. Bright moon, smooth water, ships, destroyers flitting around, etc. No boat signal was given, so the men were kept below, but some of us climbed a ladder in a hatchway & had a fine look around. Nurses & officers out, but all were quiet and calm. Certainly great stuff, this going through the danger zone!!!

Well, must pack my blanket roll so will stop this letter here.[4]

IV

WE DETERMINED TO MAKE THE BREAK

After landing in France, the Yanks moved out for the front. In the summer of 1918, airman George W. Puryear, landed behind German lines and was taken prisoner. After one escape attempt, he and other Americans were sent to a prison in Germany. He takes up the story here.

It was in the afternoon of September 15 that we arrived at Villingen. The camp wasn't at all attractive from the outside, but it proved much better and more comfortable than it looked. It covered an area of about 1000 metres by 250. Barracks were built around the outer edges, with an open court in the centre, in which were a tennis-court, volleyball court, library, reading-room, and assembly hall. Around these, inside the line of barracks, was room for us to walk or run for exercise. This had been a Russian officers' camp but it was being vacated for American officers. There were still two hundred Russians there, and at that time seventy Americans.

The American Red Cross had bulk supplies, both of food and clothing, at Villingen. Food was issued every Monday. . . . We were not bothered with any formal breakfast at all. Instead, they issued us twenty lumps of sugar a week, which pleased us much better. I never ate any of my sugar, but saved every piece of it for rations on my escape.

The Germans took a picture of each of us, after which we could, if we choose, go out of camp for walks, on our word of honor.

We could not walk about at our pleasure, but were allowed to go out at a certain time every day in a group of not less than ten, or more than fifty. A German non-commissioned officer went with us as a guide, and we were subject to his orders. We would be out an hour or two. As we went out we would give our written word of honor not to try to escape, accompanied with our picture; and when we returned, we would take it up again.

The defenses of the camps were as follows. The outer windows of the barracks were barred. Where the barracks did not join, a blind fence with wire on top connected them. A few feet outside the line of barracks and fence came the main barrier, which went all around. This was, first, a low barbed-wire fence; just outside that, a ditch about four feet wide, filled with barbed-wire entanglement; and at the outer edge of this came the main fence, of woven barbed wire, about nine feet high, with steel arms on top of the posts, curving toward the interior about two feet, making the top of the fence lean toward the inside, so that it was impossible to climb from that direction, even with nothing else to bother you. Just outside this was the outer guard patrol. This patrol was doubled before dark every night. There was also a line of electric lights a few feet outside, which burned all night.

The Germans boasted of this as one of the safest camps, and so far as having but one weak point went, I suppose they were justified. To maintain the camp, counting all guard-shifts, officials, and so forth, they used over a hundred men—to hold the 270 of us. Practically all of these men were old and unfit for service on the front. . . .

Seven more fliers had come in from Landshut, making a total of 77 Americans in camp. From them we learned that, a few nights after we left Landshut, four of the fellows had escaped. They had all been caught four or five days later. They made fifteen American officers, who, to my personal knowledge, had escaped, and all had been re-captured. This was a bad average, but none had made the attempt when as near the border as Villingen is.

The weather was already growing cold, and I realized that the time for making the attempt, without hazarding the winter weather, was getting short. In spite of my effort to keep myself in condition, I found that my confinement had softened as well as delayed me. I walked miles and miles inside the camp to harden myself. After a few rainy days it cleared, and I went out on the first honor walk. I learned from the Russians that a few weeks of good weather might be expected. The moon was dark. It would be much more dangerous to go in moonlight, and it would be winter before the next dark of the moon. All these things indicated that now was the time.

I talked to Lieutenant H. C. Tichenor, better known among us as "Tich," and found him of my mind, willing to go any length to try it. We shook hands on it and went to work. It was then Thursday, October 3. Monday we would get a new food issue, and we determined to be ready to break Monday night. We proposed to go right out our window and over the barrier some way; get as good a start on the guard as possible, and chance the rest.

The bottoms of our beds were made of planks running lengthwise. These were strong boards one inch thick, eight inches wide, and seven feet long. From these I thought that we should be able to construct some means of scaling the barrier. Tich was a good engineer; we could not drive nails nor could we make any large show of work—for the interpreter dropped in on us every hour or two, and his eye was keen; therefore we worked out and drew our design on paper. We took the boards out one at a time, while some one stood watch for us; bored the necessary holes and did the necessary cutting on each; and replaced them under the beds, where they remained until the last moment, when we took them out and quietly put them together with wire, like putting up ready-made wooden barracks. Albertson, who was good at map-drawing, drew the map I used. From a Russian officer I bought a Russian overcoat and cap. I considered this a fair disguise because the silhouette at night would be the same as that of the German uniform. Also, if I should accidently be seen in the daytime, a Russian prisoner at liberty is common enough in Germany not to attract suspicion if he does not act suspiciously. Again, in the guise of a Russian prisoner I would not be expected to speak German.

There was in camp a Russian who could produce anything you wanted if you had the price. I went to him for a compass. Tich had a good one, but I thought that we should both be fully equipped. I also bought a big spring-back knife and a twenty-mark bill. For the twenty marks in German money I gave thirty marks canteen money.

There were several other men who were planning to escape, and knowing that, when one escaped, there would be an inspection which would catch those preparing, we determined to make our break all together. Willis and Isaacs had discovered a means to short-circuit all the lights of the camp. We planned to put them all out, and as this was done, to break at once at our different points. They certainly could not stop all of us. Isaacs, Battle, and Tucker were to break out of one window, Tichenor and I another, and a third bunch still another. All three of the windows were along the southern side of the camp. Willis, Wardle, Chalmers, and some others, disguised as Germans, were to slip into the quarters of the guard and await the alarm raised by our escape, and then, as these guards were turned out to chase us, they would rush out the open gate with the Huns.

Almost all the Americans had a hand in it in some way. The men who were to put out the lights were not going to try to escape themselves. As a means of short-circuiting the lights, chains of wire were made, with a weight on both ends. These were to be thrown over the uninsulated wires where they came into camp. It was rather a long throw, but several chains were made in case of a miss. Some other fellows were to raise false alarms at other parts of the camp, to distract the guards.

Sunday morning we learned that all the Russians would be sent away Monday. We knew that this would cause an inspection of quarters and our plans would be discovered. We determined to make the break Sunday night. Having expected to leave Monday night after the food-issue, several of us were short of food-supplies. I had traded off so much of mine for my compass and other equipment, that I had practically none. We could not wait and as it turned out, it was probably a good thing that I was no more heavily loaded, even with food. I had my sugar and from the other boys I got four boxes of hard-tack and one opened can of hash. The lights inside our barracks were turned out every night at ten-thirty. Our plan was to short-circuit the others a few moments after that; and the putting out of the outside lights would be the signal to go.

Sunday night Tich and I had cut loose the bars in our window, had taken the prepared slats from our beds and put them together, making a strong and solid run-board fourteen feet long, and were ready.

At ten-thirty the lights in our quarters went out. I put on my

Russian cap and overcoat, pinning up the tail to prevent its catching on the wire, and slung on my haversack with my small food-supply and so forth. Tich and I took our run-board to the window. A messenger came to ask if we were ready. We told him we were. I was to go out of the window first, with the head of the run-board. Tich was to feed it out the window to me, coming out himself as the back end came out. I was to put the end on the fence and go over, Tich coming over behind me. We had selected a rendezvous outside in case we became separated.

About ten minutes elapsed before anything happened. This time we spent, quite nervously, right at the window. Then the outer lights began to sputter and went out. We pulled the curtain down from the window, bent back the bars, and the window was cleared for the go. The guard, who appeared to have noticed something suspicious about our window during the evening, was standing directly in front. When he saw the lights go out, he knew that something was up, and uttering a little explanation plainly audible to us, who were so near him, pulled his rifle down from his back and got it ready for action. With the lights out, things were not clearly visible, but the outline of a man was easily distinguishable within fifty yards or less.

Seeing that the guard stood right in front, I thought it advisable to wait and see what he would do on hearing the noise of the other parties. In a few seconds I heard the wire screech, and the guard below shoot off his gun and blow his whistle. This guard, however, did not move. I knew then that the time had come to go, or we would soon be caught. I shoved the ladder partially out of the window and jumped out myself. The ground was about seven feet below the window. Tichenor fed the ladder out to me, and came out with the rear end. I threw it against the fence, and immediately started over.

The guard standing directly in front saw me and the instant that I started over the fence challenged me. I paid no attention to him, and he challenged me a second time just as I reached the top of the fence. I jumped down on the outside. I stood just outside the fence, the guard about fifteen feet in front of me and facing me. At an angle to my left, and about half-way between us, stood a large tree. I jumped behind this tree. The guard saw me go behind it and waited. I looked back and saw Tichenor then outside the barracks and inside the fence. I saw the other guard on this beat coming from about thirty yards to the left of me. I knew that I could not keep one tree between me and the two guards very long, and that the only chance that Tichenor possibly had of getting out was to come over while I had the guard occupied.

I did not intend to give myself up, so after a few seconds I jumped out from behind the tree and dashed past the guard. I passed within about three steps of the nearest and about twenty of the other. The nearest guard challenged me just as I dashed by him. I did not heed him, but tried to run in as much of a zig-zag course as I could. He challenged a second time. By that time I had got probably six or seven steps farther, and he fired. The other guard, who had said nothing, also fired. The bullets passed quite near me, but neither touched me. Just as quickly as they could breech their guns, they fired again. I was not standing round waiting for them to breech those guns. Just as the second shots were fired, both at the same time again, I stumbled into a ditch and fell. I was familiar with the where-abouts of this ditch, but under the circumstances naturally forgot it. I fell just at the time of the shots. Probably one or both of them might have hit me, had I not fallen. Also the guard nearest, seeing me fall, evidently thought he had shot me. When I scrambled up, he apparently did not see me. The other guard shot at me twice more; by that time I was out of sight.

I ran only a short distance before I was out of breath, being loaded down with the heavy Russian overcoat, two woolen suits of underwear and two woolen shirts, and my food-parcel. I sat down just out of sight, in order to catch my breath. At this time, all kinds of disturbances and shots were heard, for a dozen men were trying to escape at once. I then got up, but being too tired to run, began walking in the direction of the place where Tichenor and I had arranged to meet. After I had walked about a thousand yards away, my silhouette evidently rose above the sky-line, and one of the guards took a pot-shot at me at this long range. Finding that I was seen, I stooped down, so as not to silhouette myself, and ran on to the place where I was to meet Tichenor. I waited for him fifteen or twenty minutes, according to our agreement. While there, I heard some seventy-five or a hundred shots fired down at the camp. At the end of that time I heard the bugle blown for assembly, and knew that he was not coming. I prayed to the Lord and started for the Swiss border alone. . . .

At first I traveled almost directly west. My compass, being made by hand, was not as convenient and easy to use as an ordinary compass, but it was a good one and never failed me. . . .

Morning found me about fifteen kilometres on my way, west by a little south from Villingen. Toward morning, having walked a little late, though it was not yet light in the forest, I met two wood-cutters on their way to work. My tactics of noiselessness saved me, and I observed their approach before they saw me and easily avoided them. After a little I came to seek a better hiding-place for the day. Just as I rose, I saw, and was seen by, the only human who ever saw me by daylight during my whole trip. He was a civilian, about three hundred yards away, and was looking straight at me. I feigned indifference to him, adjusted my clothes leisurely, and strode away as if he meant nothing to me. Thanks to my Russian costume, he was not suspicious and did not follow.

As soon as the trees hid me, I went faster but still maintained an indifferent manner. In a few minutes I found a good place, and taking off my shoes and putting on a pair of heavy wool socks, which I had brought for that purpose, settled down for the day. The weather was kind to me, and after a few hours the sun brought to me the possibility of food and sleep. During this first day I ate all my hash, because, being opened, it would not keep. It made a reasonably good day's rations. Realizing the swim which was before me, and not having swum in two years, I began the exercises which I used several hours each day. . . .

As evening came on, I was restless to be on my way, and started as soon as it was dark enough to venture it. Soon after starting, while circling a little village, where there was a crowd of people in the street, I came upon what seemed to be a narrow strip of water. When I attempted to jump across it, what appeared to be the other bank proved to be only long grass, and I went into water up to my waist. I was more afraid that the splash I had made would attract attention than I was worried by my wetting. I clambered to the other side and resumed my journey with the water sloshing in my shoes.

I raided my first garden about midnight, filling my little bag. I ate some during the night, and kept a supply to eat during the day, when it would be impossible to search for anything. For the remainder of my journey I lived more upon these raw foods than upon my scanty rations. Each morning, a little before time to hide for the day, I would collect my day's supply. My dry food I ate mostly when I rested during the night. When I was exhausted, I could feel the immediate stimulating effect of a lump of sugar, just like a hot cup of coffee to the tired man.

A few hours after I started, the sky became covered with clouds, and a little after midnight it began to drizzle on me. About four in the morning, while it was still raining, I found the only barn that I ever saw in Germany which was not either partially inhabited by the people themselves, or so near their house as to be useless as a hiding-place. It stood in a pasture, by itself, and looked inviting.

The finding of this barn was but one of the many instances where Providence helped me on my journey. It rained continually until about four of the following afternoon. By this time, as I had walked all the way with wet feet, they were beginning to trouble me, and to have a dry place for the day was a great advantage. Inside the barn I had hopes of finding some hay, but in this I was disappointed. I had a dry floor, and lying down in my wet clothes, immediately fell asleep from exhaustion, but soon woke and found it too cold to sleep any more. When I woke it was getting light. I kept myself warm during the day, taking my swimming exercises, and my clothes soon dried on me, except my shoes, which I had taken off immediately upon stopping. No one came near the barn during the rain, but in the evening the farmers came, and I could hear them talking outside. Once they opened the door of the shed below and came in. For a while I thought it was all up with me; but they never came into the loft where I was hiding. As darkness came on, I put on my shoes and started out again.

I was feeling fine, and after a few hours on the road which was winding down into a mountain valley, I saw before me a town of considerable size. It was the town of Neustadt, the largest through which I passed during my journey. All roads led through the town. I decided to bluff my way through. It was about 10:30 P.M., and though the streets were already mostly deserted, it was not late enough for a wayfarer to be looked upon with particular suspicion. . . .

I buttoned my Russian military coat, which was far from shoddy. I set my military cap in a very severe position on the forward part of my head, and assuming a very dignified and forbidding manner, I walked through this town a rival to the most military Prussian officer ever seen. As I entered, I met a group of four soldiers. I gauged my steps so as to pass them when the light shone in their faces and at my back. When I came up to them, they stood at attention, giving me fully half the sidewalk. I saluted them as a German officer would, and passed by.

I next met a lone woman, who spoke to me; but my bearing was

321

so haughty as not to encourage familiarity. I next passed a hotel, through the windows of which I could see many soldiers in uniform. No one was outside as I passed in front of the brightly lighted door; but after I had gone beyond about twenty-five steps, the door opened and a German officer stepped out and started down the street behind me. In all my experience I have never seen a German walk so fast as he did. . . . I don't think anyone could have out-walked me under those circumstances. The German soon relieved me from the ever-increasing fear that he was following me by turning into another street. Then I met five women coming from their work. These had a pretty good look at me, but I passed the inspection. I heard a noisy party of five or six, but by turning down a dark street, allowed them to pass and returned to my route behind them.

Just at the edge of the town, the road began to climb again into the mountain forest. Here I came up behind an old man carrying a heavy burden on his back. His progress was very slow and appearance quite harmless, so I determined to pass him. As I approached within about five steps, he lowered his burden to the ground, to rest, which caused him to turn and face me. I was by this time beyond the lights, and I passed him without difficulty, grunting, "Guten Nacht."

The road soon began to wind, and after about an hour's walk, climbing all the while, I came out in a clearing on the side of the mountain, overlooking the town, within a stone's throw below. I stopped and rested, realizing that I had used a lot of my strength and gained very little distance on my journey. . . .

While I was sitting here, it began to drizzle again. A clock in the town below chimed the hour of midnight. I turned again into the forest. . . . My road, still climbing the mountain, led south. After a little it began to grow narrower and narrower, until it vanished in the forest. I could not force myself to turn and retrace my steps. With my compass I labored my way on through the forest in a constant rain, hoping soon to hit another road leading down on the other side. I realized the danger of my blind groping. . . . I could only feel my way along. When looking straight up, I could sometimes see the dim glow of the cloud-covered sky above the tree tops.

I realize now that it would have been better to retrace my steps. But the road, even to return, was lost. I pressed on as best as I could. Soon I felt that the rain had turned into snow. Finally, I came out on the flat top of the mountain. Here the forest ended, and I found myself cold and exhausted, and faced by ground grown up with a thick underbrush, absolutely impassable. At each step I was deluged with melting snow.

I was then on the top of Hohfurst Mountain, an altitude about as high as I could have found on my route. . . .

I stepped back into the uncut forest, where, because of the absence of underbrush, I could make my way, and repeatedly tried to skirt this barrier. At every turn it faced me. I would stumble and fall, often lying where I fell, almost dropping off to sleep. . . .Finally, I just stumbled into another road which, though not going in my direction, I unhesitatingly took and started down the mountain. This road conducted me to a highway going in the proper direction, and with what strength I had left I struck out to make as much progress as possible for the rest of the night. After this experience I tried to stick to roads which appeared to be big highways, and a telephone line along them gave me great assurance.

I walked very late that morning. That night (the night of the 9th and 10th), I made my longest stage. I passed through Hausern about 11 o'clock, where, from the road-crossing signboard, I found the main highway to Waldshut. This I followed for the remainder of the night, stopping for the day within a few kilometres of Waldshut. After waking from my first sleep of exhaustion, I found that, where I was lying, I was exposed to the cold mountain wind, and though it was getting light, I walked on for a little distance, in order to find a more protected place to spend the day.

Realizing that I would come to the passage of the last ditch— the Rhine—that night, I ate heavily of my reserve dry strength-producing food. In fact, I had left, when I started that night, only one box of hard-tack biscuits and three lumps of my precious sugar. . . .

Before starting that night, I took off all my clothes and put on first those in which I intended to make the swim, adjusting them very snugly and tightly, taking up all slack with strings. Over these I put on my outer clothing, to keep me warm till the time came.

About eleven o'clock that night of the tenth of October I came to the Rhine at Waldshut. In order to make sure that I was not mistaken in my location, or misled by the signboards along the road, I climbed up on a hill overlooking the city and carefully compared the country below with my map. . . .

From the hill I could get a favorable view of the river for some distance. I risked a place where, because of the bend in the river, I knew that the current after hitting this bank would bound back toward the other bank. I determined to undertake the crossing here, just below the bend, because I knew that at this place near the bank I would find an eddy of comparatively still water, and that as soon as I hit the current it would have a tendency at first to carry me toward the other bank. About a mile downstream, the river took a reverse curve, and here I knew the current would be hard against the opposite bank. I hoped to make the other shore before, or at least by the time, I reached this curve, thus taking the benefit of every possible advantage.

When I approached this place, I found that the descent to the water would be comparatively easy, also. It was well after midnight by now. I ate the last lumps of my sugar and part of the box of crackers. I was nervous to be off, but wanted to make sure. I lay there and watched for about three hours, and during that time no guard appeared near the spot where I intended to start my swim. The only sound that came up to me was the constant voice of the river. The swift current kept up a ceaseless little roar, punctuated by the noise of the whirlpools which came and went here and yonder. . . .

I did not underestimate the crossing of this last ditch. I knew that its swift and treacherous current was made up from the melting snow of the mountains above, and that its temperature was so low that no ordinary constitution was strong enough to withstand it more than a few minutes. I had heard in camp of a little cemetery near Basel, filled with the dead bodies of Russian prisoners who had attempted to swim the river. I had known and considered these things from the beginning. . . .

It was by now about four o'clock in the morning. I took off all my clothes, except those in which I intended to try to make the swim, and one O.D. shirt, which I kept on, to hide the whiteness of my undershirt, but all unbuttoned and ready to throw off very quickly. I put my compass, map, and German pictures, which I wished to carry over with me, in my pocket. I opened in my hand my big knife and started to creep down to the water's edge. . . .

So slow and careful was my progress that it took me about an hour to cover the few yards down to the water's edge. I had to cross a railroad and a road which ran parallel to the river. As I lay just at the edge of the water, like a lizard, with eyes and ears alert ready to slip in, I heard a clock strike five. It was thus that I knew the exact time of crossing the river; I knew also that I did not have much time to spare, for soon the day would begin to break. After that, all was quiet but the river before me, whose voice was never silent as it tumbled on, with a current in the centre of seven kilometres an hour. I got to my feet and, still crouching low, stepped into the water. As I had expected, near the bank it was practically still. The bank went down steeply, and I saw that I could make no distance wading. I stripped off my O.D. shirt, dropping it, with my knife, in the water, set my eyes on the opposite bank, and uttering a short, silent prayer, shoved out into the stream. I knew then that I had my liberty. The chance of recapture was past. . . .

After a few strokes, I saw that my shoes about my neck would be too great a hindrance, and I cast them off into the river. For a while I swam quietly but swiftly, expecting any moment to hear an alarm given and to become the target, under the rays of a searchlight, for the German sentries who were sure to be not far away. But nothing of the kind happened, and after a little I felt myself pass from the eddying waters into the swift current, which picked me up and hurled me on at a tremendous rate. I knew then that the time for my utmost effort was at hand. I knew that the treacherous current, which was now kindly assisting me out toward the centre, would, after I reached that point, have a similar tendency to hold me in the centre. I laid aside my caution, and raising my arms out of the water, put forth my best effort.

By this time I began to be affected by the temperature of the water, my head became dizzy, and for a while I thought I was about to lose my grip on myself. All was confusion about me. I feared that I might mistake the bank I had left for the bank I was going toward. I struggled hard to right things in my head and eyes and maintain control of my body. . . .

After a few moments I felt better and my head cleared. I threw every ounce of my strength into the effort. Though I had won one attack, I felt the temperature taking a firmer hold on me. I knew that at any moment I might strike a whirlpool. So I swam as fast as I could. When within about twenty-five feet of the other bank, which was shooting by like scenery out of any express-train window, my hand touched the bottom. I immediately attempted to land, but, though the water was not waist-deep, I could not stand against it, and my feet not taking firm hold on the bottom, I was thrown full length down the stream. There I got my first ducking. I soon recovered myself, however, and allowing myself to go down freely with the current, kicked toward the bank with one foot on the bottom. With every step I went downstream fifteen or twenty feet. After a few steps, and when very close, the bottom again disappeared, and I had to swim. I was in the bend of the river which I had seen from the mountain on the other side, and the bank, being steep and well washed, was passing me like an express train. At first my grasp at the bank was futile; but I scratched and clawed along for a good many feet, and finally succeeded in stopping the bank.

When I pulled myself out, I was not able to stand up. I was very much afraid of falling back in the river in my dizziness. My physical distress was too great, and my danger still too apparent, to enjoy at first the fact that I had reached the neutral shore.[5]

V

THE LOST BATTALION

In the autumn offensive of 1918, Americans were assigned the Meuse-Argonne sector where, if they were successful, they would snap the German supply line. The first phase of the Meuse-Argonne push lasted from 26 September to the beginning of October. Then came the drive into the Argonne Forest. Its wilderness of trees shaded a dense underbrush which hid the trenches, barbed wire, machine guns, and tunnels.

On 2 October, two days before the advance started, Major Charles W. ("Go-to-Hell") Whittlesey led his battalion into the Forest. His unit had lately come up to the front, and lacked reserves of food and water. The terrain was almost impassable. Suddenly, the Germans trapped Whittlesey and his men in a pocket. For six days the battalion held out. Unknown to Whittlesey, a furious American offensive was pushing past him on either flank. Of the 550 men in his battalion, only 194 walked out when help came. Major Whittlesey, Private Robert Manson, and an airman recite the saga of the Lost Battalion.

[*Whittlesey*]   In the Allied drive which commenced September 26th 1918, the 1st B'n. 308th Infantry was the advance Battalion in the Western Subsector of the 77th Division Sector in the Forest of Argonne; the 2nd B'n., 308th Infantry was in support, commanded by Captain George McMurtry.

On October 2nd these Battalions were at 294.9 – 275.95 (Binarville Map 1/20.000). The advance had been held up at this point on October 1st by machine gun opposition. The terrain was difficult; a ravine running North and South thru the middle of the Regimental Subsector, with steep, thickly wooded hills on either side. The principal resistance had been encountered on October 1st on the west of the ravine where D and F companies were in position.

At 11:35 A.M. the following order was received from Colonel Stacey, Commanding 308th Infantry, "The advance of infantry will commence at 12:50. The Infantry action will be pushed forward until it reaches the line of the road and railroad generally along 276.5 where the command will halt, reorganize, establish liaison right and left and be ready for orders for a further advance. . . . You still leave two companies on your left as a containing force and push forward your right with the remainder of your force, that is the remainder of 1st and 2nd Battalions. The General says you are to advance behind the barrage regardless of losses. He states that there will be a general advance along the line."[6]

[*Manson*]   In the early part of the afternoon, I was in a concrete German dugout with Major Whittlesey, when these orders came from the Colonel to take a given objective and hold it regardless of cost in casualties. At 2:30 that afternoon, October 2, the battalion was to make the drive and they would be supported by flanking regiments and by artillery.

After heavy fighting we penetrated the German line, gaining our objective just at sundown. We were located on the northern slope of a bleak, unsheltered ravine. Some of the men stood guard while the others dug themselves into the hillside for shelter from the shrapnel and bullets. Then night settled over the forest, and we were ordered to be as quiet as possible, as any noise would give away our position to the Hun.[7]

[*Whittlesey*]   *October 3rd.* At day break E Company was

sent back to attack on the West of the ravine which runs North and South, the plan being to assist from the rear in bringing D and F companies forward. Lieut. Wilhelm was in command, Lieut. Leake with him.

At 7:00 A.M. K. Company, 307th Infantry came up, having been sent to follow along our runner posts, with the mission of keeping in contact with the 308th Infantry till the 307th Regiment should come up on the right flank. Captain Holderman, Lt. Pool and about 80 men. Details were sent back for rations as the men had advanced carrying only one day's ration. All reserve rations had been consumed during the earlier phase of the advance. Fortunately water was found in a spring just south of the position. These ration details never returned.

At 8:30 A.M. German Artillery shelled the position but without serious effect owing to the steep reverse slope.

Patrols that were sent out reported Germans on the right and left flanks in small numbers, and the impossibility of establishing liaison in either direction.

At 10 A.M. Lieut. Leake returned with 18 men from E Company, reporting that E Company had been surrounded, and that Lieut. Wilhelm had ordered him to get his platoon out by any means possible. (Lieut. Wilhelm subsequently worked his way through to the South with a few remaining men).

At 10:30 A.M. a report was received that the runner post system in the rear had been broken, two posts having been attacked and scattered by the Germans. A message reporting this fact was immediately dispatched to Regimental Headquarters by carrier pigeon. From this time on it was never possible to re-establish communication with the rear.

At 10:00 A.M. a German trench mortar opened fire from 600 yards to the West. Scouts reported the mortar protected by a machine gun. A Platoon was sent to attack the mortar, but met serious machine gun fire and accomplished nothing.

A prisoner who was captured during the day stated that his company of 70 men had been brought in during the night to take position in our rear.

At 5 P.M. the Germans attacked our left flank (H Company Commanded by Lieut. Cullen). A small force also attempted to encircle the right flank. The attack lasted 45 minutes, and was successfully repulsed. Casualties of the day about ten. The night passed quietly.

[*Manson*]   On Thursday, October 3, we tried to send messages through, but found our runners at the nearest post either killed or captured. Patrols were sent out to reconnoiter, and then we knew that we were completely surrounded; surrounded on a bleak, unsheltered ravine, with the German Army on a cliff above, and with a powerful German detachment deeply entrenched on the other side of the ravine. Enemy troops were so close that we could hear the calls and orders of the men. If we showed ourselves in the openings of the wooded forest, we could be reached by German machine guns, rifles, and trench-mortars.

[*Whittlesey*]   *October 4th.*   The effective strength present, including K Company, 307th Infantry, was now about 520. A constant drain was suffered by patrols killed or captured, as an increasing effort was made, throughout the entire period, to get in touch with Regimental Headquarters in the rear, and with the 307th Infantry which was coming up on the right. These patrols were uniformly unsuccessful as the Germans occupied the heights to the rear in considerable force. . . .

As a result of this day consideration was given to a change of position. It seemed inadvisable: to the West the Germans held a position strongly protected by Machine Guns: to the North and East we feared to encounter a barrage from our friendly artillery, as we had already reported the co-ordinates of our position and had no means of sending further messages. The hills to the South was objectionable as being exposed to German artillery fire which fell there at some time each day. The position which we occupied was well protected from German artillery, and was fairly protected from the trench mortar to the West which fired on our position about twice a day for a period of an hour each—not more than 10% of the shells falling on our position, the rest falling at the base of the hill in the rear.

The men were now suffering from hunger; and the condition of the wounded was very serious. No overcoats, blankets, slickers or shelter halves had been brought, and the cold nights intensified the suffering. However, throughout the entire period the weather was favorable considering the time of the year.

This night we heard the attack of the friendly forces to the South drawing closer and hoped that our own troops would soon break through to join us.

[*Manson*]   On the second day, October 4, no help had come, and, realizing our true situation, runners volunteered to carry tidings back to regiment headquarters. Two brave lads—Private Bottell and Private Frail tried to make their way through. Both were encountered by a number of machine guns and fell to the ground. Frail was killed, but Bottell got back, after a bullet had passed through his helmet, slightly tearing his forehead. Gee, what a close shave!

Patrols were sent out at different times, and in most cases did not return. All day long Jerry kept shooting potato-mashers—machine guns and trench-mortars—from the cliff above and from across the ravine. The German snipers were very active, now and then killing or wounding one of us. At one time a trench-mortar shell hit so close to my hole in the ground that I was completely buried and for a moment or two I thought I was going to a rest-camp (cemetery).

We had sent up pigeons, and it was these couriers of the air that carried the tidings to the other Yanks in the forest. Early that afternoon the American artillery sent over a barrage which lasted two hours. They tried to get the Germans on the cliff above, but they fell short. I am not saying we had poor artillery-support. No! It has been proved throughout the war that a barrage often falls short. It was our business to signal back, "Barrage short," but what signals we had, had already been spent in our advances since September 26.

Sergeant-Major Gaedeke and I were sitting in our hole in the ground at the time the barrage fell. Our dear Major, who was but five feet from me at the time, shouted, "Go to the left, men." Everywhere about us the ground was heaving and shooting up. You can imagine our excitement. It had a Wall Street panic beat a hundred different ways.

It was a case of lambs with us all. Some stayed in their holes, others ran to the left, others to the right. The sergeant-major ran to the right, and the only traces we found of the poor lad after the barrage was his hat and gat (pistol). Under this deadly fire we suffered many casualties. The groans of the wounded and the dying all the time made the place an inferno. Sometimes I imagine I still hear the groans.

330

[*Whittlesey*]   *October 5.*   In the morning our outposts from the hill to the North reported that 200 Germans had been seen moving South to the Hills in our rear.

Encouragement was felt however at our friendly artillery barrage in the early morning, which commenced on the hill to the South, advanced to us, jumped our position, and continued North, showing that our position was understood by our friendly forces.

Our effective strength was now about 375 (including all units present).

Sounds of fighting on the hill to the South were very clear during the day.

At 4 P.M. the Germans played a machine gun on our position for twenty minutes, firing in that time with an intensity difficult to exaggerate. This fire was one of the most unpleasant features of our entire experience, although it caused few casualties as the men stayed in their funk holes well. It was never repeated. It was immediately followed by a potatoe masher attack from the hill to the north. The attack was repulsed. . . .

[*Manson*]   The food problem troubled us on the third day, October 5. What little food we had with us was already disposed of. For water we depended on a muddy stream at the bottom of the ravine, and on one clear, grateful spring that bubbled invitingly. But each trip to it meant exposure to snipers. One instance I remember is when one dough-boy with eight canteens went to fetch some water. He was given a warm reception by the Hun, and returned with two canteens, plugged with holes, from which the water was streaming. More than one lad fell in an attempt to get water. When starting the Argonne drive we discarded our overcoats, raincoats, and blankets. What few blankets we had not turned in, in our rush to carry the ravine, were used for the wounded. At night, or before the fog had lifted in the morning, we would bury the dead that lay on the hillside. The ground was very poor, and in most cases we buried them in their own dugouts. Many of us were too weak to dig the hard soil. Here and there arms and legs could be seen sticking out of the graves.

Still no relief. We could have fought our way back at a great loss, but our Major would not leave the wounded to the mercy of the Hun. He would walk from one to another, giving us good cheer and hope.

[*Airman*]   *October 5th.* Word was sent to the squadron to get into communication with the 1st Battalion of 308th Infantry under Major Whittelsy which had broken liaison, become cut off and surrounded by the enemy. For this purpose four planes were sent out as couriers, two in the morning and two in the afternoon to carry messages to the location which had been sent out from the "First Battalion" by pigeon.

As well as dropping the messages we dropped all the available chocolate and cigarettes on hand.

In general a great deal of propaganda was dropped over German held territory and in our own front lines copies of the Stars and Stripes, late papers, chocolate and cigarettes furnished by the Y.M.C.A. for the purpose. . . .

Day ended with 15 pilots, 16 observers, and 16 machines available after 23 hours service flying and no casualties.[8]

[*Manson*]   Every day planes came over looking for us in the interminable fog. We put out our battalion panels to attract the airmen, but such was the lay of the wooded ravine that the airmen could not see us. And the air was so foggy that we often mistook them for German planes, altho these, too, paid us a call. Several times I saw planes drop packages which I later learned included munition, bandages, and "iron rations"—chocolate, the soldier's delight.

That night Jerry attacked us, but we fought him off.

[*Whittlesey*]   *October 6th.* An exceedingly determined effort was made to get patrols through at this time; for the courage of the men had been shaken by the seeming failure of our troops in the rear to break through. The men were very hungry, and many requested permission to attempt individually to work their way back through the lines at night. Permission was refused. . . .

[*Manson*]   Our casualties increased on the fourth day. The Major, however, was as cool as ever. His hourly message to the men was, "Be patient, help will come." As I watched him from my hole in the ground, I said to myself, "How calm he is." I realize now why they call him "Cool Charles" in civil life.

Just before dawn we were again attacked by the Germans. Again we could hear their orders and commands, hear one Hun speaking to another. Not once did we try to fight our way back. We had been ordered to take the position and hold it, and we were obeying orders. Things looked pretty blue. We knew that efforts to reach us were unremitting. We knew that help would come from the Americans only 1,200 meters away, but we feared that it would not come in time.

Then we heard very heavy firing across the ravine. We were all happy, believing that relief was coming at last, and that the Hun was being chased out from around us by the Americans. But we were in a desperate fix. It was death to stay, and the chances of getting back to our lines were one to a hundred. So nine of the boys decided to leave at sunset, although they had no permission to do so.

[*Airman*] *October 6th.* Visibility as usual very poor.

The one outstanding feature of the day's work was the effort made by our entire available force to carry aid to the "Lost Battalion."

It is to be remembered that the coordinates were sent back by Major Whittelsy via carrier pigeon. Also, there was no way of checking these coordinates as the conditions under which the surrounded men existed prevented them either showing themselves or exhibiting any very noticeable designating panel. For our part therefore we could but use the exact location given as our objective and drop our packages in such a manner that they would fall on an east and west line in the deep ravine at the bottom of which our men were supposed to be. . . .

Every plane flew well under a thousand feet by altimeter which brought them down scarcely above the hill tops over their objective. After it became apparent to the enemy that a determined bid was being made for that certain point—clearly evidenced by the arrival of plane after plane over the same spot—they quite naturally prepared for others to follow and to break up the work if possible. . . .

[*Whittlesey*] *October 7th.* The effective strength of all units present now amounted to about 275.

Discouragement was felt in the morning by shells falling on our position from the South East. This we assumed to be the fire of friendly artillery, although it subsequently proved to have been a German field piece behind us. Fortunately this fire was not prolonged, and was not repeated. . . .

At 4 p.m. a private from H Company reported that he had left without permission in the morning with eight others. They encountered a German outpost, five of the nine were killed, the rest were captured. This man was given by the Germans a demand for our forces to surrender, a copy of which is hereto attached. He was then blindfolded and returned to our lines.

"To the Commanding Officer of the 2nd Bn. 308th of the 77th American Division.

Sir: The bearer of the present, Crowell R. Holingshead has been taken prisoner by us on October —. He refused to the German Intelligence Officer every answer to his questions, and is quite an honorable fellow, doing honor to his fatherland in the strictest sense of the word. He [is] . . . carrying forward this present letter to the officer in charge of the 2nd. Bn. 308th. of the 77th Division with the purpose to recommend this Commander to surrender with his forces as it would be quite useless to resist any more in view of the present conditions.

The suffering of your wounded men can be heard over here in the German lines, and we are appealing to your human sentiments.

A white flag shown by one of your men will tell us that you agree with these conditions.

Please treat the Crowell R. Holingshead as an honorable man. He is quite a soldier, we envy you.

Signed: The German Commanding Officer."

No reply to the demand to surrender seemed necessary.

[*Manson*] Our Major would rather die than surrender. Every time I think of him he reminds me of Custer's last fight. Almost an hour after the Major's refusal, Jerry attacked us. Our stock of ammunition had run low, and we were so weak we could hardly drag ourselves to our feet. What we endured is hardly believable. Some chewed roots of trees, leaves, and tobacco. I never chewed tobacco before, but I tried a pinch of Bull Durham. I felt like a man who is seasick, and wants to throw up, but can't.

Some of us wrote short messages each entrusting his to some pal on the chance that his pal might get through alive. There were some thanks whispered for the little-chronicled deeds of kindness the week had witnessed. Here and there men promised to kill each other rather than be taken prisoner. But we fought off the Hun. In the last attack the Germans were so close to us that we could make them out in the darkness. And we sure did give them a rousing reception! In the last moment of the attack we lost one of our best officers, Lieutenant Schenk, well worthy of decoration.

Then all grew quiet. We lay in fear and dread of another attack, when a call for Major Whittlesey rent the quiet of the night. "We are on your right, the 307th." The Major answered from his hole in the ground. Again the voice rang out, "We have come, we are bringing rations for the men."

It was the happiest moment of my life. I was hysterical. I laughed and cried for joy. I felt like a cat having nine lives. I was not the only one acting that way. When they gave us canned hash I had no mess kit I ate it from my hands covered with blood and dirt. I'll tell the world it tasted like sirloin steak smothered with onions.

The following morning more rations came. Our Major gave out the rations and made sure the wounded were fed first. I was sitting in my dugout when I heard a gruff voice about five feet above me demanding the Major. "Who the hell is calling the Major now?"

Looking up I saw it was some one wearing two stars on his hat. I immediately got on my feet and informed this officer, who, I learned later, was General Alexander, that the Major was on the right. "Shall I call him, sir?"

"No! No! I'll go to him," he replied, as much as to say it was an honor to do so. He then congratulated us, and told us what a load had been on his heart for five days and how the other Americans had fought to save us. He wanted to know why the wounded men were still lying there. He told his orderly to rush every ambulance available. And within three hours more than 160 men were on their way to the hospital. Some of the boys who were not wounded had to be carried out on stretchers too weak from hunger, exhaustion, exposure, and hardships to shift for themselves.

VI

I THOUGHT THAT I WAS A GONE SUCKER SURE

Private Jesse Maxey was also in the Argonne Forest. To his wife, he writes of the fighting.

American Ex. Forces

Dear Wife:

. . . Our front lines was about ½ mile ahead of us. The night of the 24th we moved out to our right and went into some old open trenches which was wet and muddy. We laid in them all night almost froze. Thair was a big frost on us the next morning, we staid thair until the night of the 25th and was issued more ammunition and hand grenades. So we pulled out when it got dark going through our front line trenches out into no mans land and thair we laid down to wait for our artillery to open up which opened up at 2:30 o'clock that night. Well, every thing was very quiet until our artillery opened up, we could hear a machine gun clatter away a little now and then and a few rifle shots. But O, MY. when our guns began to roar which was at the back of us lined up almost hub to hub, at 5:15 we were to start over the top, it was awfully cold out thair as a heavy dew fell on us and some frost. We was almost froze when the time came for us to start. The grass and briers was about up to our waists out thair for thair hadnt been any fighting thair for quite a while.

Well, the time came for us to go ahead so we got up and gave a loud yell and away we went. Our machine guns went too clicking away and our shells singing over our heads. It was not light good when we started and the smoke and fog was so thick we couldnt see more than three or four yards ahead of us. We went a few hundred yards and would drop in old shell holes and lay thair and try and listen and look ahead of us to see if Jerry was trying to come over to meet us. We came to an old trench that was full of watter and thair wasent any way to cross it but to wade it or swim so we plunged into it and the watter came up about to our waists. It was cold believe me, we went a little farther and captured two Huns. They were under an old bridge, they had started out when we first saw them they were about 50 yards ahead of us. We dropped and leveled our rifles on them and they came out with thair hands up scared to death so five or six of us got up and they came on towards us, they seemed simply wild. We went towards them too and they would hang thair feet in an old wire and down they would go and up again hollering for dear life as they made sure we would shoot them if we kept the guns on them. Some of them were hollering "shoot" and some of us was saying don't shoot. I didn't want to shoot them unless they tried to kill us. Well someone taken them back. I don't think they had any guns as I never saw any but when we got up to the old bridge, that barrage was enough to scare any one to death as we was out now to where our shells had been falling. It seemed that our shells had fallen about every six square foot.

We went on over the hills our shells falling on ahead of us and our machine guns clicking away over our heads. You could not hear anything for them as the bullets from our machine guns was singing over our heads like a swarm of bees and our shell whistling way up in the air and we could hear them bursting way on ahead of us.

Finly we came to thair trenches and thair we got lots of prisiners, another fellow and myself got 13 out of one little dugout. We got close up to the dugout, and we seen a machine gun setting in the mouth of the dugout so we stopped and decided what to do. So I asked him what he wanted to do, go up and get the machine gun or stay thair and keep his eye on the dugout until I could crawl up and get the gun, so he decided he would let me go. So he crawled to where he could cover the hole and shoot any of them if they came out. Of course we didnt know whether for sure thair was any one in thair or not, but we could not risk it any way, so I crawled on up to the dugout and got the gun. I did not dare to get up and aim to carry it so I drug it way laying down. Of course I didnt carry it very far, just far enough so no one could step out and get hold of it without us getting him for sure. So the fellow came on up to where I was and we crawled on up to the dugout and got up and hollered for them to come out and here they came with thair hands up hollowing "Kamerad," 13 of them. I wish I had that machine gun back home. We turned them over to a company that was following us up and we went on. We taken the feed box out of the machine gun and threw it as far as we could so if we had left any Germans around thair they could not use it.

I never new the boys name that was with me, as we soon got mixed up with some of the rest of the fellows and you know when we was relieved that thair wasnt very many of us left. Well, we all moved on pretty quick. We came to another line of trenches and thair I saw an awful sight. When we got in about 200 yeards of the trenches an old man came running out hollowing and crying with his hands up. Well, some hollowed shoot him, shoot him we all had our guns on him so I guess he thought we was going to kill him anyway so he just dropped down on his knees when he was about 50 yards from us and stretched his hands up and turned his face to the skye seemed that he was praying. About this time one of our officers ran out to whare he was and hollowed not to shoot. I think he was an old Priest that is, we always thought so any way, he had a long beard on his face and looked to be 60 years old. Well, we got lots of prisiners out of them trenches and got several of our boys wounded thair as the Germans was now shooting at us from on ahead. Thair at that line of trenches in one of the dugouts one the boys on my left threw a hand grenade in on a Hun as he started to come out without his hands up and killed him. The one that he killed was an old man with mustache seemed to be at least 40 years old.

Well, it was along about eleven o'clock now in the day and as we hadnt had any breakfast we were getting quite tired and hungry. After we passed the last line of the Germans trenches we began to come to some of thair artillery which some was turned around as if they were trying to move it and some just as if they had just left thair guns which had quite a bunch of shells by thair sides and others were laying in ditches as they possibly had horses hitched to them but could not make time fast enough with them and had to unhitch and leave them behind as they knew that we was coming right after them. Well, we had advanced so far mostly through open fields and hills but now we came to the big woods or forests and then was when our trouble began. Snipers in trees with machine guns and so on, though they did not kill so many of our men but wounded so many.

We advanced through the first body of woods without very much resistance but by the time we reached another opening things were getting right hot as we now had advanced so fast that our artillery wasnt any more good to us as we were out of thair range so they could not reach over us. Well, we had to stop as the Division on our left had met with such a resistance that they could not keep up with us. We stopped in an old trench at the edge of the woods which we had just come through, an open hill laying before us and thair was a town just over the hill. While we were stopped, of course, the Germans could get thair guns in operation which they didnt fail to do, machine guns and artillery. With this they opened fire on us, in a short while we got orders to move forward so we started to advance and by that time Jerry was sending shells over in a jiffy. But we never reached the top of the open hill, we crawled up as far as we could. Right thair was when I saw what war really was. I got covered with dirt, rocks and pieces of falling shells, I thought every minute that I would get mine. The fellow on my right got hit, I dont know how bad and I dont know what became of him. What few minutes we were up thair we had one Sergeant killed and two corporals and several privates, I think we lost about 15 men.

We got orders to fall back to the edge of the woods in an old trench and wait until our machine guners could get up to help us. The Germans was sending machine bullets over the skye line like a swarm of bees. We fell back to the edge of the woods and thair some of us would lay up on the bank while some would dig in. That is whare I got my gass, thanks to the Goodman I didnt get enough to hirt me very much, though I got enough so that I could not keep my mask on when I did get it. The way it happened, I had been digging me a hole to get in and I taken my mask off and laid it down as it was in my way as we were digging for dear life and then I went up with my rifle and carried my pack with me to lay in front to protect me and when I came back I left my pack up thair. Well, while I was back down in the trench orders came that we could eat some of our iron rations so I went back after my pack and while I was up thair Jerry sent over some gass shells and thair I was, up thair without my mask.

Well, it was my luck to be on an outpost that night as we were looking for Jerry to make a counter attack. We were posted out on an open field in front of our front lines, we were laying down in the field and we thought we saw something like little trees moving to our right but didnt pay much attention to it as we wasnt for sure but in a short while we herd someone digging out to our right but we supposed that it was some of our boys possibly our machine gunners planting thair guns as we knew they had come up. Well the Sergeant decided he would send a couple of fellows out that way to see who it was. The boys had about time to get out to whare we thought they were and it was so dark they could not see who they were without going right up to them, so we heard them hollow "Whose thare?" about that time we herd a few shots and up went a flare which lit the field as light as day. We could see the Germans as plain as day but couldnt see our two boys anywhere. Well, we thought the boys were killed. After a while everything got quiet and one of the boys came crawling up to us, he didnt know what became of the other one. The other boy got lost and crawled the wrong way and finally found another company of the 47th but we never saw the boy for several days. We thought he was killed or captured.

The next morning we were relieved by some other company and we fell back into suport. Thair is lots of days that I have no recollection of as I saw so many boys get killed and so many wounded right by my side that I cannot explain it. Though I recollect mighty well one day and night that I spent.

We were in the front lines again and we got orders to fix bayonettes and advance over a hill that was covered thick with scrubby brush and old brush piles. It was late one evening about five o'clock we moved over the hill through the thick brush and taken a couple of machine gun nests. But all at once we came to some old German shanties when all at once sounded like a hundred Germans cut way at us with machine guns. So right thair we had to get down and it was my luck that I was caught right in an open place so I dropped behind an old stump and thair I had to stay as it looked as if they were going to mow the old stump down. Well, I thought that I was a gone sucker sure as I knew sure if I got up they would kill me and I thought if I laid thair they would come over thair and capture me so thair I was.

I decided to stay, I looked to the right and could see none of the boys and neither to my left. So I unlocked my rifle and thought to myself if they do come over if I see him first I will sure get him. I laid thair until dark looking every minute for Fritzie to sneek up on me but he didnt come and when it got dark enough I raised up a little and looked all around me but I could not see any one so I crawled on back the way I came until I got back into the brush. I went back quite a ways in the brush expecting every minute for my own boys to kill me as I thought they might take me to be a German, as it was quite dark. I came to an old road before I came to anyone so I taken down the road and I spied some one standing in the road but didnt know wheather he was an American or a German but I went on towards him and stopped about ten yards from him and asked who was thair, I thought if it was a German I would have as good a chance at him as he would at me, but thank the Goodman it was an American officer and he told me that my company was out to my right.

It had began to rain in the meantime and when I got out to where

they were they was digging in. They thought that I had been killed
or captured. Well I thought I was captured too, I takened my shovel
and went to digging but when I got a place dug I was miring in mud.
I decided that I wouldnt lay in that mud the rain was bad enough so
I crawled back into a bunch of bushes and laid down. Thair I laid
all night soaking wet and it just pouring down the rain, almost
frozen. We were relieved the next morning and fell back in the
second lines. While we were moving back the Germans got observations on us and they shelled the life out of us, lost a good bunch of
men.

Several days passed that I have no recollection of. A Corporal and
seven of us was sent back about ½ mile to gather up some rifles
ammunition and we had to go over an open hill we went in single
file over the hill with quite a distance between us and the Germans
saw us and threw the shells into us. The Corporal and myself was the
only ones that didnt get killed or wounded. We bound the wounds
of two of the men up which could walk and carried them to a first
aid station and the first aid men taken the other two up on stretchers
and carried them and they other two, I dont know what became of
them as we never did see anything of them for sure as thair was
already so many laying killed about on the ground.

We were strung out in a string I was the second one from the
front one when the shell came. Three shells came all at once right
on top of us. I know the man in front of me fell and the one in rear
of me. The concussion from the explosion knocked me down and
when I went to get up I was bured in dirt and rack I thought I was
killed as they almost knocked me senseless. We went up and taken
over the front lines again in a few days. They had advanced quite a
ways since we were back in suport. We had to go through the
German barrage going up and coming back, we didnt stay in the front
lines but two days that time as we had lost so many men. When we
were relieved again we had just got back in suport when a call came in
for some men to get back up to the front lines and carry some stretchers
and help carry the wounded back as they were wounding so many of
our boys that they could not get them back to the first aid station.

Will leave out quite a bit that I witnessed now as it is too bad to
write. I helped carry men from the first aid stations to whair the
ambulances could get them. I spent some of the awfullest days that
day that I ever did in my life. Carrying wounded isnt any pleasant

task and the Germans were counter attacking so hard that we were ducking from shells all the time almost. Will leave out lots now that I saw and close up until I get home and tell it myself. We had 250 men when we started over the top on the 26th of Sept. and when we came out thair want but about 80 of us left. Gee, I did feel lucky, which all of us did that were still alive. . . .

Hope you will get this letter allright, this is the 4th one.

Your Husband,

Pvt. Jesse M. Maxey.[9]

VII

I THANK YOU FOR YOUR *PATIENCE* AND *COURAGE*

On the eleventh hour, of the eleventh day, of the eleventh month, 1918, the armistice came. On 12 November General John J. Pershing addresses his troops:

GENERAL HEADQUARTERS

American Expeditionary Forces

France, November 12, 1918

General Orders, No. 203

THE ENEMY HAS CAPITULATED. It is fitting that I address myself in thanks directly to the officers and soldiers of the American Expeditionary Forces, who by their heroic efforts have made possible THIS GLORIOUS RESULT.

Our Armies, hurriedly raised and hastily trained, met a veteran enemy, and by courage, discipline and skill always defeated him. Without complaint you have endured incessant toil, privation and danger. You have seen many of your comrades make the Supreme sacrifice that freedom may live.

I thank you for your PATIENCE and COURAGE with which you have endured. I congratulate you upon the splendid fruits of victory which your heroism and the blood of our gallant dead are now presenting to our nation. YOUR DEEDS WILL LIVE FOREVER ON THE MOST GLORIOUS PAGES OF AMERICA'S HISTORY.

Those things you have done. There remains now a harder task which will test your soldierly qualities to the utmost. Success in this and little note will be taken and few praises sung; fail, and the light of your glorious achievements of the past will be sadly dimmed.

BUT YOU WILL NOT FAIL. Every natural tendency may urge towards relaxation in discipline, in conduct, in appearance, in everything that marks the soldier. Yet you will remember that each officer and EACH SOLDIER IS THE REPRESENTATIVE IN EUROPE OF HIS PEOPLE and that his brilliant deeds of yesterday permit no action of today to pass unnoticed by friend or foe.

You will meet this test as gallantly as you have met the test of the battlefield. Sustained by your high ideals and inspired by the heroic part you have played, you will carry back to our people the proud consciousness of a new Americanism born of sacrifice.

Whether you stand on hostile territory or on the friendly soil of France, YOU WILL SO BEAR YOURSELF IN DISCIPLINE, APPEARANCE AND RESPECT FOR ALL CIVIL RIGHTS THAT YOU WILL CONFIRM FOR ALL TIME THE PRIDE AND LOVE WHICH EVERY AMERICAN FEELS FOR YOUR UNIFORM AND FOR YOU.

> JOHN J. PERSHING
> *General, Commander-in-Chief.*[10]

VIII

I NEVER LOST A MAN

Two months after the armistice, Captain Harry S Truman, 129th U.S. Field Artillery, recalls the fighting.

ON ACTIVE SERVICE
With the
AMERICAN EXPEDITIONARY FORCE
Jan 8 1919
Camp La Behalle
Near Verdun France

My Dear Wilson:—

Yours of the 2nd of December came night before last and I was most happy to hear from you. If you have D Battery I know it is the best Battery in the Brigade because I have one of the same letter and you can guess what I think of it.

We went to the Vosges from Coetquidan, and stayed about ten days, then went in to reserve at St. Mihiel having made the most terrific night march I ever hope to make. From there we marched west of Verdun just south of Varennes where we went over the top Sept 26 and moved up for six days breaking all records for swift accomplishment of objectives and came out on October 3 after about one half the Division had become casualities. The casualities in the Artillery were very light. I never lost a man and the regiment only about twenty killed—no officers. Kenady was gassed but not seriously. We got to see and experience everything that there is in war. Aeroplanes bombed us, we were shelled while moving up and some of us got in range of the machine-guns. Leaving Point Smith, Burke and another Wilson we acquired after you left got mentioned in orders as did the whole regiment as a regiment. I was lucky enough to shoot up a German battery in position and one moving down the road on the first day out and also made them desert a large O. P.

After we moved back we rested about ten days and then went into emplacements east of Verdun. My position was not far from Douaumont the most famous fort in the war and on which the Crown Prince killed some 200,000 men trying to take. It was supposed to be a quiet place when we went up there but the Huns used to send over from 1800 to 4000 shells a day on the different forts. My position was about half way between two forts and not far from a cross road that the Hun shelled every night. He never happened to hit any of us though. Salisbury had a couple of men killed on this crossroad on November 2. We fired right up to 11 o'clock on November 11 and the infantry went forward that morning. I fired 160 rounds of "D shell" at a range of 10500 meters.

We have been sitting still in a muddy little old camp not far from our last position ever since Nov 11 hearing rumors one day that we'd go to Germany and the next that we'd go home. We don't do either. We got some good American horses and a lot of new harness the other day and I took the battery out mounted today for the first time since we moved out of position.

I hope we come home soon. Walthers, Maj Gates, Long, Capt Pete and all the rest send best regards. I hope I see you soon on 5th Ave.

Sincerely,

Harry S Truman[11]

IX

GENERAL BILLY MITCHELL, PROPHET OF AIRPOWER

During the peace that followed the war, Army pilots experimented with aircraft. Brigadier General William Mitchell, U. S. Air Service, was positive that the bomber spelled the doom of seapower. His vision of airpower rather than naval power as the defender of America touched off a feud with the Navy. His successful bombing tests against warships intensified the controversy.

In July, 1921, after much haggling, the Air Service and the Navy held a test off the mouth of Chesapeake Bay. Bombers sank three German vessels, including a powerful battleship. In tests off Cape Hatteras two years later, Air Service bombers sank the obsolete battleships Virginia *and* New Jersey. *Mitchell, in his official report, tells of that experimental run.*

The Navy Department was requested to turn over two battleships to the Army Air Service for the conduct of bombing experiments. The ratification of the Disarmament Treaty provided that a certain number of battleships be scrapped; if sunk they must be in not less than fifty fathoms of water.

I desired to have the tests against the seacraft simulate, as far as possible, actual battle conditions and to have the tests take place where the fifty fathoms curve is nearest to the shore, in order not to subject the personnel to unwarranted risk in flying over water. I desired that the Navy Deparment turn over to the Army Air Service two of the sturdiest ships to be scrapped with steam up and magazines filled and equipped with radio control.

The Navy Department agreed to turn over the *Virginia* and the

New Jersey after September fifth at any point designated by the Army
Air Service.

In order to familiarize our personnel with the operation of our
most advanced weapons I was eager to utilize an aerial torpedo in an
attack against these ships. I desired the first attack to be made against
a radio directed battleship by an aerial torpedo controlled by radio. I
then desired the battleship to be attacked by a single airplane carrying
a four thousand pound bomb. It was my intention to use the "Owl"
for this attack. . . .

The program was changed from time to time and that submitted
by the Air Service providing for attacks at regular battle altitudes was
changed by the War Department and attacks ordered at an altitude
of ten thousand feet and over. It must be remembered that we had no
service ship that could attain an altitude of ten thousand feet with its
load of bombs, nor had any practice been held at that altitude by our
Air Service personnel. When this order was received, four days before
the bombardment tests, we had only succeeded in equipping one of
our Martin Bombers with a supercharger capable of carrying loads to
ten thousand feet. By working day and night we had four supercharged
ships ready on the day of the attack.

Personnel was so short that we had to assign certain crews to two
and three missions on the same day. The Bombardment Group really
is not a group, but is merely a detachment of officers and men gathered
together from various places who have not been properly trained as an
organization. The individuals were excellent, however.

The greatest pressure came after Friday, August thirty-first. At
9:15 A.M., Friday, August thirty-first, the Chief of Air Service received
a letter from the War Department changing the previously approved
program for the bombing tests and ordering that the tests be conducted
up to ten thousand feet. This allowed but two days, excluding Sunday
and Labor day, for preparation. It was necessary to change the position
of the radiators on the superchargers, procure bombs from the Ordnance Department, transport them to Langley Field, change the altitude bars in the sights, switch the high altitude sights to the super-
charger planes, and conduct such practice as was possible in the brief
time that intervened.

. . . civilian and enlisted personnel worked day and night, through
Sunday and Labor Day, in a desperate effort to get the equipment into
shape. This entailed double duty on the part of officer personnel . . .

and subjected them to considerable risk in forcing them to fly super-chargers about one hundred and seventy miles, much of which was over water, without an opportunity to properly test them after the radiator installation had been made. The personnel had never taken off a supercharged ship with the load which they were required to carry on the day of the bombing tests.

With proper preparation and organization, the Army Air Service is capable of going to 10,000 feet and higher with the maximum load which the ships will carry and of dropping bombs accurately from that altitude, but no provision had been made for such a contingency in the training program which had been carried out at Langley Field in preparation for these maneuvers.

On September first and second I again checked up on the airdrome at Hatteras and gave Captain Ballard detailed instructions as to where the bombs and fuel for each plane should be placed. The details handled at the meetings of officers held on September first, second and third . . . [covered] each attack and definite instructions were given. . . .

On Tuesday, September fourth, the entire Group, less the super-charger flight of four machines and two machines from Aberdeen which had been assigned to this flight, proceeded to the Hatteras airdrome. Bombs were loaded in preparation for the actual attack.

Tests showed that the two thousand pound bomb racks were not functioning properly and it was necessary to work late into the night before this equipment would function. Even then it was not entirely satisfactory. . . . The superchargers made one practice flight at ten thousand feet against the *Alabama* and dropped two loaded six hundred pound bombs each at that target. They did very well, indeed.

About eight o'clock I got all the personnel on the airdrome at Hatteras together and gave them a brief talk on what was expected, the importance of the test, and what it would mean to the Air Force. . . . I worked with the communications until about midnight and was up at four o'clock the next morning to check up on weather reports. The visibility was bad and a light rain was falling. Small local thunder storms could be seen from the airdrome. The communications system absolutely went to pieces. The land telephone line would not function. The radio was entirely out and it was after seven o'clock before we were able to get word from Langley Field, through the Weather Bureau telephone line, that Lieutenant Austin's flight of supercharged planes had taken off for their objective.

Daybreak at Langley Field found the airdrome wrapped in fog so thick that it was impossible to see the balloon hangar from the bomb dump. This fog rose a little about six o'clock. Lieutenant Austin's flight took off and took a chance on getting through. In the vicinity of Cape Henry they found they could not get under the fog and were forced to turn around and come back about ten miles in order to get over it. They continued on their way and, in spite of unfavorable weather, arrived at their objective within ten minutes of the designated time.

The bombing of this flight from eleven thousand two hundred feet was as good as any during the day and their work as a whole was really remarkable. . . . The members of this flight returned to the airdrome at Hatteras, got out of their supercharged ships and took their places in the formation of eleven hundred pound ships which carried out the bombing during the day. These officers did double duty, one team making three trips over the water. It is too much to expect flying personnel to do double duty on this kind of work. . . .

The second attack with the two thousand pound bombs clearly showed up this condition of fatigue. The personnel was becoming nervous, over anxious, physically worn out, and were evidencing very clearly the severe mental strain under which they were working. . . .

The second attack was made by seven ships, each loaded with one two thousand pound bomb, and one ship which had not arrived in time for the first attack. This ship carried four six hundred pound bombs. One of these bombs dropped off the ship alive on a turn about two miles from the target. It was accidentally released by the bomber. The two thousand pound bombs were dropped sufficiently close to the ship to have sunk it had they functioned as well as in 1921. Two things were obvious on this attack: First, the bombs were sticking in the traps, and, second, either the fuses had deteriorated, or the bombs were not exploded at a proper depth.

The first attack had caused the ship to list a few degrees to port. The two thousand pound bombs, apparently, allowed it to take water on the opposite side and it came back almost to a vertical position. I flew close to the ship before the bombing began and again after the two thousand pound bomb attack. I could see that it had settled considerably and it would have sunk eventually, as the result of these two attacks, although it might have taken some little time. The direct hits by the six hundred pound bombs would surely have put it out of commission and would probably have killed a high percentage of the operating personnel.

Realizing that the ship was doomed, I shifted the eleven hundred pound attack to the *Virginia*. This attack, by Lieutenant Crocker, was better than any other attack during the day. . . . His attack was launched quickly and the bombs were dropped with remarkable accuracy. The attack began at 11:53 and was ended by 12:07. Fourteen eleven hundred pound bombs had been dropped which literally tore the ship to pieces. Formation was reformed and was on its way back to the airdrome at 12:22. In about thirty minutes from the time the first bomb was dropped the battleship was under water. . . .

In case the eleven hundred pound bombs did not sink the *Virginia* I had the two thousand pound bomb flight ready to take off with orders to attack the same target.

I returned to the airdrome and ordered the two thousand pound flight to attack the first target. They had refueled the ships and loaded seven two thousand pound bombs since their morning attack. No one unfamiliar with the amount of work entailed in refueling Martin Bombers with makeshift equipment and in handling two thousand pound bombs on an emergency airdrome can realize how much hard physical labor is involved. . . .

The wind had changed so that it was blowing directly across the airdrome and the sun had evaporated the light rain which had fallen in the morning. This loosened the sand and added further difficulties to the take off. The news of the destruction of the *Virginia* elated the personnel and greately encouraged them. The take offs of the ships with the two thousand pound bombs were successfully effected. By this time we were very short of gasoline. It was necessary to drain some of the ships in order to provide a full charge for two more planes. I selected the best crews and put them on the last two planes and had them loaded with eleven hundred pound bombs.

The two thousand pound bomb flight attacked from three thousand feet. All of the bomb traps stuck a little. Every bomb overshot the target by about the same amount. The shooting was very consistent but not more than three and, possibly, only one bomb was dropped close enough to be effective. No bomb was more than a ship's length away—sufficient to put the ship out of action but not to sink it.

Immediately following this attack the two ships loaded with the eleven hundred pound bombs launched their attack. The first bomb, dropped at 3:22 fell about ninety feet from the ship. The next shot, dropped by the same crew, struck close along side, but was a dud and did not detonate. Lieutenants Cole and Beverly made this attack. Lieutenant Myers with Sergeant Nero, from Aberdeen, followed Lieutenants Cole and Beverly. They made three trips over the target to get the wind direction and velocity exactly right. On their fourth run they dropped one bomb which struck the ship squarely. It tore open the hull and blew one cage mast from its foundation. The ship immediately began to sink and before the plane was able to make the turn and come back to drop the second bomb it had turned over. Lieutenant Myers did not drop his second bomb on the target because of the danger of fragments striking the personnel in the photographic planes. The second bomb was dropped safe. . . .

By seven P.M., September sixth, practically all the planes had returned to Langley Field. . . .

Conclusions

1. Air Forces, with the types of aircraft now in existence or in development, acting from shore bases, can find and destroy all classes of seacraft under war conditions, with a negligible loss to the aircraft.

2. Conditions of weather affecting air and sea conditions do not alter the statement made above, as aircraft can operate under conditions under which seacraft cannot operate. For instance, sixty-mile wind, low visibility near the water, and operations at night are very difficult for seacraft. There are no conditions in which seacraft can operate efficiently in which aircraft cannot operate efficiently. Aircraft, therefore, form an absolutely positive system of defense against seacraft within the radius of their action.

3. The weapons used in the recent exercises against the seacraft were bombs alone. Torpedoes, gas, gun-fire, and mines were not used. The Army Air Service was not permitted to attack the targets as it would under actual conditions.

4. Seacraft are much more vulnerable when they have steam up in their boilers, are moving at high speed in formation, and when they are equipped with ammunition in their magazines and on their decks. A comparatively small bomb will cripple their condensor systems, throw their rudders and propellers out of line, and completely demoralize the operating personnel.

5. The problem of the destruction of seacraft by Air Forces has been solved, and is finished. It is now necessary to provide an Air organization and a method of defending not only our coast cities, but our interior cities, against the attack of hostile air forces. . . .

6. Our scheme of national defense should be revised at once. It should be based on the following principles.

(a) An Air Force should be provided as a means of frontier and coast defense, both against seacraft and against aircraft. . . .

(b) A Navy should be organized and equipped to take the offensive on the high seas, and not be employed along and close to the coast. Such Air Forces should be assigned to the Navy as can go to sea with it and fight with it on the high seas.

(c) Navy control, so far as it affects coast defense, should cease two hundred miles from the coast. Complete control and responsibility for the defense of the land should reside in the Army and it should be organized to accomplish this mission. A Navy driven from the high seas must be protected by the Air Force of the Army.

(d) At present there is a complete lack of liaison or system about our national defense. The duties are distributed between the Army, Navy, the Air Forces, the coast Artillery, the Army Corps Area Commanders and the Coast Guard, in such a way as to make it impossible to function efficiently in an emergency. . . .

An efficient solution of our defensive needs will not exist until a Department of National Defense is organized, with a staff common to all services. Sub-secretaries for the Army, for the Navy, and for the Air should be created. At the present time our aeronautic efforts are dissipated from an inefficient system of command, an inefficient method of handling personnel, and an inefficient distribution of the funds appropriated for the national defense. In the last ten years $1,870,000,000.00 has gone into the creation and maintenance of our Coast Artillery and coast defense. What defense is this against hostile Sea Forces, or against hostile Air Forces? Millions of dollars have been spent for Navy Yards distributed along the seacoasts, few of which have depth of water sufficient to accommodate a wounded battleship limping into port and drawing forty or forty-five feet of water.

A small part of the money which we can save from these useless expenditures, devoted to the creation of an Air Force, would protect our coast against any enemy, either in the air or on the water.[12]

X

'ROUND THE WORLD FLIGHT

Like General Mitchell, other army aviators experimented with air-craft. Believing it possible to circumnavigate the globe by plane, these men studied the problem, gathered information, maps, and data.

In 1923 a committee was appointed to select a route and choose an airplane able to withstand the hard usage to which it would be exposed. This accomplished, the personnel to make the flight volunteered and in December, 1923, the War Department gave permission for the demonstration. Lieutenants Leigh Wade and Lowell H. Smith reconstruct the historic flight which began on 6 April 1924.

[*Wade*] The route was selected and divided into six parts or divisions. An experienced flying officer was put in charge of each to select the landing places, distribute the supplies, arrange for an interpreter, if necessary, billeting, etc. . . .

We had new engines, spare parts and tools distributed so well over our route that we could make any repairs or adjustments necessary. All boxes were packed the same whether in Alaska, India, or Greenland. We could find anything in the dark, if necessary. The wood used in crating the supplies was of spruce, the principal wood used in wooden airplane construction, so that when we needed repairs to wooden parts all we had to do was to take a piece from one of the crates.

When the preliminary work was well underway, the personnel selected to do the flying was ordered to Langley Field for a brief course to familiarize ourselves with the type of plane to be used, meteorology, and navigation.[13]

[*Smith*] The forenoon of each day was given to studies, while the afternoon was spent in going over the maps to be used on the flight and in making tests on the Douglas Cruiser which had been completed and flown to Langley Field for the purpose of making flight tests and for training of personnel. . . .

While in training at Langley Field, numerous flights were made with the Douglas plane, carrying various loads up to a total weight of 8300 pounds, to determine the best suitable type of pontoons and propellers for heavy duty work and to bring out any other weaknesses which would ordinarily develop during hard continuous service. Results of these findings were communicated to McCook Field and to Douglas Aircraft Corporation in Santa Monica, California. The recommended changes were incorporated in the construction of the four planes which were to be used on the flight. . . . After the training was completed at Langley Field, all the maps for the entire route around the world were then studied, lines of flight marked on them, distances and compass courses filled in, together with various notes on harbor facilities and landing fields to be used in case of emergency, and were shipped to Washington to be reshipped to main supply bases of each Division for availability upon arrival of the flight.

On February 16th, the entire personnel of the flight reported to the Chief of Air Service for the final instructions, after which they departed for Santa Monica, California, where their time was spent at the Douglas Plant watching the completion of the planes they were to fly. Each officer had his plane assigned upon his arrival at the factory and the personal interest in the plane that he was to pilot began before the plane had neared completion.[14]

[*Wade*]   On March 17, 1924, we left Clover Field, Santa Monica, for Seattle, Washington. This part of the trip was to fully test out our planes in order to assure ourselves that nothing had been overlooked. The planes were flown over land as land planes.

[*Smith*]   *Seattle, Washington.*
The flight remained in Seattle from March 20th to April 6th. During this period, Planes Nos. 1, 3 and 4 were varnished. Plane No. 3 also changed its motor. Pontoons replaced landing gears, other primers were installed, anchors and ropes were fitted to the planes for emergency use and the final selection of tools and spare parts was made, particularly care being taken to keep down the total weight. . . .

While at Seattle, through arrangements made by the Chief of Air Service, the various planes were designated in a christening ceremony after four American cities; Plane No. 1 being named the "Seattle"; Plane No. 2, the "Chicago"; Plane No. 3, the "Boston"; and Plane No. 4, the "New Orleans."

Seattle, Washington to Prince Rupert, B.C.—   650 miles
                                                       8 hrs. 10 min.

Planes were made ready for the flight to leave on April 4th, but unfavorable weather reports along the line of flight resulted in a delay until April 5th. On this date, the "Seattle" was unable to get off the water, caused by the overloading of the plane for this long flight. After several attempts to leave the water, the propeller had been damaged by the water spray and the repairing of it was necessary before continuing. The Boeing Aircraft Company again came to our assistance, working all night, in order that the start could be made on April 6th. On this date, the "Seattle," "Chicago" and "New Orleans" got away as planned and continued flight to Prince Rupert without the "Boston" which had difficulty in starting and was delayed 40 minutes. The first part of the flight to Prince Rupert was over Puget Sound, Georgia Strait, ramming into fog at Quadra Island, then through Johnston's Strait to Queen Charlotte Sound, where we were forced to the water's level by the fog. Flying was especially difficult because of the glassy condition of the water, it being almost impossible to estimate our altitude. Upon reaching the open sea we left the fog behind, flying over very rough water most of the remaining distance; the weather being squally, making it necessary for us to fly through and around numerous snow storms. . . . The flight landed at Prince Rupert during a heavy snow storm at 4:55 p.m. The "Seattle" made a "stall" landing which broke two outer struts and four verticle wires on the plane. The advance arrangements here were excellent and no especial difficulty was encountered in repairing the plane, except that caused by very severe weather and the necessity of working outside.

[*Wade*] Leaving here, we entered into the hardest part of our journey, because of the meteorological conditions to be encountered. The weather was colder also, which made our work on the planes more difficult.

At Sitka, Alaska, a storm came in on the open side of the harbor, which lasted for two days. The first day, three of the planes dragged anchor and were in danger of colliding before we could reach them. We worked from noon until late in the evening before they were made fast to adequate anchors. The second day, one of the planes broke loose from its mooring. Luckily one member of the flight was aboard who saved the day for all of us. The others were rushing about trying to secure boats to go to the rescue, or were wading out in the water. Just as it was on the crest of a swell, ready to hit the rocks on the next, he managed to get the engine started and pulled the plane out of danger.

The next day we passed by the glacial region but were denied the beautiful scenery by a blinding blizzard. It was just like flying at night; we broke formation, every plane for itself. Fortunately, it ended just south of the entrance to the harbor at Cordova. Had the shore line not been straight, we would have piled up on the rocks, or against any projection or island, as we were following the shoreline very closely. It was a great relief to arrive at Seward in Resurrection Bay.

[*Smith*] *Seward, Alaska to Chignik, Alaska*—   425 miles
                                                            6 hrs. 38 min.

Snow storms delayed the flight until April 15th. One of the planes had some difficulty in getting off the water but at 10:05 all were in the air together and headed for Chignik. Lieut. Nelson had been designated as Flight Leader for the day and took a course south from Seward to a point near Pilot Rock, where he took a direct compass course to Chignik, flying over the tip end of some of the narrow peninsulas near the Seward end of the flight. On several occasions, the "Seattle" dropped far to the rear and upon one of these occasions, although it was being closely watched by the remaining personnel, it was seen to swing over toward Portage Bay. At this time, the other planes were flying directly into very strong head winds and did not have enough fuel to return and still reach Chignik. They were still uncertain as to whether the "Seattle" was really in difficulty or following in the rear. The remaining three planes landed at Chignik in a poorly protected harbor at 4:25 P.M.

A radio station had been established here by Lieut. Clayton L. Bissell, the Advance Officer of the 1st Division, and was immediately pressed into service; first, by requesting United States Destroyers, which were known to be near Seward, to proceed at once to Portage Bay and Kialagnik Bay, advising them of the location where the "Seattle" was last seen and requesting that they start search immediately. A prompt reply was received that they were proceeding at full speed and would reach the points designated shortly after daylight the next morning. Broadcasts were sent out requesting any vessel in the vicinity to assist in the search. The Alaskan Mail Steamer STARR responded and headed for the point, furnishing a great deal of assistance by relaying radio messages to all points in the vicinity so that nothing was left undone to expedite locating the lost plane. . . .

Chignik, Alaska to Dutch Harbor, Unalaska, Alaska—   390 miles
                                                                7 hrs. 26 min.

No attempt was made to leave on April 16th because of the absence of the "Seattle." Upon receiving word of its having been towed to safety at Kanatak, and as it would require several days for repairs, it was decided best for the "Chicago," "Boston" and "New Orleans" to proceed to Dutch Harbor, which was a main supply base furnishing a much more secure anchorage for the planes than the harbor at Chignik. Severe weather prevented the flight from continuing until April 19th. On this date, difficulties were encountered in starting the flight caused by strong winds and rough sea, making it almost impossible to cast off from the moorings, but at 11:01 the flight took off for Dutch Harbor . . . landing at 6:25. . . .

At 3 A.M. the guard, that had been placed over the planes, informed us that one of the planes had broken loose and that another one was drifting dangerously. Temporary precautions were immediately taken to secure them until morning when it was decided to beach the planes on temporary runways. The "Boston" was having motor trouble and decision being made to change, a large freighter, the Brookdale, tied up at the Dutch Harbor pier, volunteered its services and lifted the plane from the water onto the dock, later using its boom to make the exchange of motors. After this work was completed, all planes were placed on the temporary runways on the beach and thoroughly inspected for the Pacific crossing. All work being completed, the flight waited for the "Seattle" until May 2nd, when the following telegram was received from Major General Mason M. Patrick, Chief of the Army Air Service:

LIEUT. LOWELL H. SMITH   MAY 2, 1924
   C.O., ROUND-THE-WORLD FLIGHT
      DUTCH HARBOR, UNALASKA, ALASKA.
DO NOT DELAY LONGER WAITING FOR MAJOR MARTIN TO JOIN YOU STOP SEE EVERYTHING DONE POSSIBLE TO FIND HIM STOP PLANES NUMBER 2, 3 AND 4

TO PROCEED TO JAPAN AT EARLIEST POSSIBLE MOMENT.

PATRICK

Planes were immediately made ready to depart the following day.

[*Wade*]   On attempting to rejoin the flight, Major Martin crashed into the side of a mountain, completely demolishing his plane, but fortunately not injuring either himself or Sergeant Harvey, his assistant and mechanician. After struggling over the mountains, facing snow blindness, living on meagre emergency rations and wild game for ten days they arrived at Port Moller on the Bering sea side of the peninsula. Here a boat picked them up and they returned to the States. . . .

Through the Aleutian Islands we had many things to worry us, such as sudden changes in weather, usually from bad to worse, and peculiar winds called by the natives "woolie wahs" [williwaw]. From a perfect calm, a "woolie" would sweep down, often sweeping everything in front of it. The islands are sparsely inhabited, in most cases of volcanic origin, and without any trees.

Flying along four or five hundred miles, far from civilization, without seeing a human being, only occasionally a few birds, a seal, or whales, makes one lonely. Now and then we would close in our formation for companionship, sometimes with the wing tips almost touching. . . .

Many times when we prepared to leave on a leg of our journey, a stiff breeze would be blowing, necessitating one member of each crew lying flat on the pontoon to free us from the mooring. In doing so we would get the spray from waves breaking on the pontoons. Then we would hop in and fly several hundred miles, our flying garments freezing with a coat of ice, which served to keep the heat in next our bodies.

Our living accommodations in many instances were of considerable contrast to those afforded by our American homes or hotels. We quartered ourselves in traders stores, salmon cannery bunk houses, or on boats with bunks just wide enough so that we had to sleep in one position and which were not long enough to stretch out in. . . .

We enjoyed all of it, and many amusing incidents happened. In one place a fisherman, Jack Toner, had a houseboat which was a saviour to us. Working in the open and becoming cold, we would call on him to get warm. When we departed he asked us to write our names on his front door which he carefully varnished over to preserve. Later, on his return from a fishing trip, he found that someone had stolen his front door for a souvenir. . . .

We had a great problem to complete our flight from Attu Island across the Pacific. The weather never seemed to clear on both ends, that is, at Shimshu of the Kurile group, Japanese territory, and Attu Island. Finally we selected a day, but very shortly on our way we encountered a terrific storm. In attempting to detour around it, we used up our fuel and were forced to take refuge in Soviet territory, on Bering Island of the Komandorski Islands.

Foreseeing such an event, we had sent a boat of the Bureau of Fisheries ahead, taking position just off shore. When they saw us coming in they dashed in and dropped moorings to which we made fast overnight. We received a call from the Soviet Governor General of the Islands on board the boat. Our relations were most amiable but he regretted he could not invite us ashore. Leaving early the next morning, we completed our Pacific flight upon arrival in Japanese territory.

Passing along the Kamchatka peninsula we encountered a very bad storm, which lasted for two days. After leaving our planes to go aboard the U. S. destroyer *Ford,* which with two Japanese destroyers was waiting for us with supplies, we were unable to get near our craft until the following afternoon after the storm calmed down. Then we found the moorings had chafed through and only an emergency rope was holding the planes to the moorings.

By two in the morning we had refilled and were on our way to Yetorfu Island. . . . Ducking from one island to another in fog most of the journey; the only relief was in seeing a few birds taking to the air or sea lions rolling off the jagged rocks into the water as we passed an island.

It seemed like heaven to land at Lake Hittakappu on Yetorfu Island and find green grass, trees, and a large crowd of Japanese in their highly colored costumes. Among them was a group of school children who had hiked overland for three successive days to be there on our arrival.

We arrived at Lake Kasumigauru, just outside of Tokyo. We were thirty-one days behind schedule and had lots of work to do on our planes, such as changing engines, pontoons, etc. We found the

Japanese had planned a two-weeks' welcome for us. Ambassador Woods arranged a condensed schedule, so we left our work and went on a two-day reception, and as warm and sincere a reception as anyone could hope for. Our only complaint was that there were so many meals in one day and that we were not able to eat all the delicious food.

. . . When we arrived at Kogoshima, the last stop in Japanese territory, late one afternoon, we received a surprise and thrill. It seemed as though all of Japan was gathered on the beach to welcome us at sunset; and a band from our Navy played our national anthem, while about fifteen thousand school children sang in our own language.

The next flight was across the Yellow Sea to Shanghai. It was the first perfect flying day since we started. We were greeted by a great mass of people, and were given a magnificent reception in the evening.

Then and there we decided that we must have relays for receptions. We had only our heavy uniforms and we were in the tropics. So afterwards we took turns in borrowing a light suit from someone aboard a boat and going to the receptions.

The method used in propelling boats worried us. In sculling a boat by a long oar around our pontoons, the sides of which were made of a thin veneer, we feared a puncture and delay. As it was we had difficulty enough arising from the water with heavy loads. Therefore, all through the tropics, we sent a boat on ahead with fuel aboard so we could land alongside or near it, to take on the needed supplies.

Leaving Shanghai, we followed the coast line to Amoy, and on to Hong-kong. It was amusing to see the native fishing boats away out to sea, propelled only by man power. Sometimes we came so near them that they scrambled all over the boats in fright.

From Hongkong to Hoiphong, French Indo China, we passed over a group of islands that rival, if not surpass, our Thousand Islands in beauty. . . .

On the next leg of our journey one of the planes was forced down in a lagoon near the shore just east of Hué. The others landed. A new engine was necessary, so on we went to Touraine to order a new one from Saigon. While the new engine was en route, the disabled plane was towed up the river to Hué by native sampans, a subchief in each beating a tom-tom for cadence while their families and hundreds of natives trailed behind in boats. The new engine was trucked over a jungle trail at night to Touraine, was in the plane running in just seventy hours from the forced landing, and on its way to Touraine to join the other two planes. The rapidity with which the repairs were made is explanatory of the work of the organization which planned our trip.

Thence on to Saigon and to Siam, landing in the river at Bangkok. Thinking we were going to be with them for some time, the natives were surprised when informed we were stopping only for one day. However, they wanted to pay a proper tribute and on the eve before our departure invited us to a beheading of two prisoners. . . .

Our next flight took us directly over the Malay peninsula to Burma. It was all very wild country, parts of which were inhabited by an ancient race of pigmies, who still hunt with blowpipe and poisoned dart. On arrival at Burma we found a storm from the Bay of Bengal had blown in and clouds covered the mountain tops. We had a great time picking our way through. One plane was caught in a down current of air and barely escaped crashing in the jungle. It rained until we got to Rangoon, where we remained several days because of repairs to one of the planes, damaged by a native junk boat during the night.

We flew through rain most of the remainder of the way to Calcutta, via Akyab and Chittagong. At Calcutta we changed engines and put wheels on in place of pontoons to fly overland to England. As a rainy season was due, we shipped our engines by rail to Karachi and worked night and day in order to depart as soon as possible. We took off from Maidan Park, in the center of the city, on July first.

Our journey across India took us to Allahabad, past the beautiful city of Delhi, on to Amabala; thence across the Sind Desert, where we encountered a sand storm for nearly five hours before our arrival at Multan. We were coated inside and out with sand. The heat was terrific. We were told it was one hundred and twenty-eight degrees on our arrival, which we had no cause to doubt.

July fourth, en route to Karachi, the *New Orleans* had engine trouble eighty-five miles out, due to a valve breaking. Lieutenant Nelson demonstrated his skill as he nursed it on in to the airdrome. Here we put in our new engines and left India behind as we carried on along the Persian Gulf, at times passing over saw-toothed mountains which were so barren that I doubt if even cactus could grow. We stopped at Cha Bar, Bandar Abbas, Bushire, thence over Basra and on to Bagdad.

We were so anxious to leave the tropics and get home that even though we were near some of the wonders of the world, we did not deviate from our course, only stopping overnight at the Royal Flying Corps Airdrome near Bagdad and thence on to Allepo, Syria.

Our next flight was exciting as we took on sufficient fuel to fly direct to Constantinople. With this heavy load we were forced to wind our way through the Taurus Mountain following a trail. Often we were completely surrounded by mountain peaks and the passages so narrow that we were forced to go through single file. Over the high plateau, passing extinct volcanic craters, past Konia and suddenly a beautiful city, Constantinople, came into view, with the blue Bosphorous, the great wall and many mosques.

After two nights and one day we departed for Bucharest, Roumania, where we spent one night, and continued across Europe over the Franco-Roumanian air route, passing Belgrade, on north to Budapest for, lunch and to Vienna. We stayed overnight and then hurried on to Paris via Strassbourg.

As we were thirty-one days behind schedule at Tokyo we decided to work extra hard and to make up the lost time so we could take a one-day holiday in Paris. We arrived on the fourteenth day of July, having picked up seventeen days. Our holiday consisted of placing a wreath upon the Unknown Soldier's grave, a luncheon, a reception at the Hotel de Ville and by the President at his home, followed by a dinner at the Allies Club. . . .

July sixteenth found us on our way to Croydon, England, thence to Brough on the Humber on the seventeenth. Here we had to prepare for the Atlantic flight, putting pontoons on in place of wheels, new engines and whatever other work was necessary. We had ample time as our supplies had not been fully distributed across the Atlantic.

Our first flight then was to Scapa Flow, where we came in contact with our Navy again, which was to escort us across and render invaluable assistance.

On the first attempt to reach Iceland we encountered fog, and, in attempting to go over it, we were forced to break formation. The

Arrival of Lt. Smith in Paris, Around the World Flight, 1924. *Left:* President Coolidge greeting flyers on their arrival in Washington, D.C.

New Orleans was hit by the propellor wash of one of the other planes and sent down in a tail spin but recovered control just over the water and continued on. The *Chicago* and *Boston* returned to Kirkwall to give out a message of the approximate location of the *New Orleans*. After many hours of suspense we received a message of its safe arrival at Angamasalik, Iceland.

The next day, half way to the Faroe Islands, my plane, the *Boston,* was forced down due to engine failure. We signalled to the crew of the *Chicago* not to land but to send assistance. They continued on and dropped a message to the U.S.S. *Billingsly.* This news was radioed to the other boats which came to my rescue. Nearly five hours after landing on the sea we were taken in tow by an English trawler. The sea was getting heavier and as we rode over the swells, it nearly pulled our plane apart. So it was a relief when the *Billingsly* relieved the trawler, and towed us a brief time, when they turned us over to the light cruiser *Richmond,* on which we hoped to store the plane. However, in the rough sea it was impossible, especially after the boom dropped, damaging the plane and making it necessary to try to tow it to shore in the Faroes. In this attempt the *Boston* was lost, sinking the next morning.

In the meantime the *Chicago* and *New Orleans* took off for Reykjavik on the west coast of Iceland. There they prepared for the crossing to Greenland. . . .

A naval aviator, Commander Leighton, and myself flew in and looked over the harbor at Angmasalik, Greenland, and after considerable thought it was decided to fly direct to Friedrichsdahl, a distance of eight hundred and fifty miles.

It was on this flight that many exciting things happened. As they neared Greenland, a dense fog was encountered. Signor Locantello, the Italian aviator, started with them. When he came into the fog, he turned back out of it and landed at sea. He was rescued five days later by the U.S.S. *Richmond.*

When the others met the fog, they realized that the sea was too rough for them to land, and that they did not have sufficient fuel to return to Iceland, so went on. They remained low over the water and about eighty miles out encountered floe ice, then icebergs, with which they played tag. Flying side by side, swerving from one side to another to miss an iceberg, now and then jumping over them, one came in view too suddenly to turn. This one was so huge that one plane went one way and the other in the opposite direction. Lieutenant Nelson in the *New Orleans* made a circle to permit Lieutenant Smith in the *Chicago* to go on and prevent a collision. Traveling at about ninety miles per hour and the visibility about three hundred feet, they kept on keen edge every moment. As they neared and rounded Cape Farewell they came out of the fog only to find another bank at Friedrichsdahl. Locating the harbor by mountain formations, they found a rift in the fog, Nelson arriving thirty-five minutes after Smith. That evening was celebrated aboard a Danish revenue cutter.

On to Ivigtut and across Newfoundland, down the coast to Picton, Nova Scotia, where Ogden and I rejoined them with the *Boston II*. Thence down the Maine coast, where we were worn out dodging fishing boats, small islands and buoys, in the worst fog we had found anywhere. We finally took refuge at Mere Point, Casco Bay.

The next day we arrived at Boston Airport. . . . During our trip we were totally ignorant of the enthusiasm here in the States, but readily realized it upon finding a huge crowd there to greet us, in addition to the Army and Navy officials.

Leaving our pontoons for wheels we flew overland to the end of the trip. Everywhere we found the same enthusiasm. New York, Washington, D.C., where President Coolidge waited several hours with his entire cabinet in a drizzling rain, Dayton, Ohio, Chicago, and all, on every stop to Seattle. . . .

We were one hundred and seventy-five days en route, making a total of seventy-five flights on sixty-four days of flying. Our total flying time was three hundred and seventy-five hours.

CHAPTER VI
1941-1945

Nothing is easy in war

DWIGHT D. EISENHOWER

The gnawing, worldwide depression of the 1930's accelerated the rise of goose-stepping dictators abroad. When Adolf Hitler invaded Poland in 1939 and plummeted Europe into World War II, Americans wanted to avoid entanglement but feared that if they did not bolster the democracies, the future security of the United States would be threatened.

In the Atlantic the situation with Germany deteriorated. Then, suddenly, in the Pacific, on 7 December 1941, Japan struck a devastating blow at Pearl Harbor, the worst naval disaster in American history. Congress declared war. Japanese bombers hit the Philippines; ground forces landed on the Malay Peninsula and pushed toward Singapore. Other Japanese troops occupied the British Gilbert Islands, Guam, and Wake Island.

I

THE ROCK

In mid-December, 1941, the Japanese executed nine amphibious landings in the Philippines, destroyed planes, and knocked out the Cavite Navy Yard. In command of the Far Eastern forces, General Douglas MacArthur evacuated Manila on 27 December, withdrew his tattered troops to the Bataan peninsula, and established headquarters on the island bastion of Corregidor.

Under severe bombardment, the Americans valiantly held out until May, 1942, when the enemy forced them to capitulate. On the Rock, Colonel Paul Bunker lived through the holocaust. He kept a detailed, day-to-day diary of the events leading to the surrender.

[*Corregidor, 3 January 1942*] At 12:33 the alarm sounded—after we could hear the planes! The first lot of bombs dropped at 12:35, then a few AA shots, then a string of about 18 bombs close together. Could hear them swish about 5″ [minutes] before they hit! Planes came over again at 12:39 but could hear no bombs. . . . Heard planes coming again at 12:50 and our AA opened fire 1½ minutes later; seemingly far off and only a few rounds (or it might have been bombs). *Then* I heard the planes and Swish-Boomety-Boom! the bombs arrived at 12:58 about 18 of them and very strong, especially one of them. The dull drone of the planes continued, instead of fading out as usual. B/60 opened at 1:01 then another battery or two, as the drone became louder. Then the usual "Swish-Boomety-Boom" at 1:03. This was the 3d trip across. Then everything quiet except for the sounds of the bursts of the AA shells. . . .

Got in my car for tour of inspection. Arrived at Barracks at 2:25 and what a scene of devastation met the eye! Huge patches of corrugated roofing missing and scattered in painfully distorted shapes all over front and rear parades. Practically every shell window in the barracks blown out, leaving gaping square empty openings. Capt. Julian met us and smilingly reported "Colonel, I have no office now." A huge bomb had landed just across the car track in rear of his place and blew out a crater 25' deep and 40' across, cutting rails and trolley wires and shattering every window on rear face of barracks. A smaller direct hit on B/59 mechanic shop, where the mech had practically finished making me a filing cabinet! Our Regtl Workshop and Topside Checker burning fiercely and, of course, no water at Topside! One could see, from direction of wind, that it would also burn the other bldgs including the "Spiff Bar" as it later did. I went up into my library and found utter chaos. Glass case containing my shell collection blown to smithereens and thousands of books littering the floor everywhere, even some outside! Going down stairs I found soldiers already looting the PX like ghouls. . . .

[*8 January*]   Turned out early and relieved Edison as Watch Officer and let him sleep in my dug-out. Breakfast at Wheeler and I sure did enjoy wheat flakes! They have improved their latrine but the seat holes are so close together that a customer is apt to wipe the wrong posterior. . . .

At 12:29 the Air Raid alarm sounded. A rumor, current today is that Gen. MacArthur said, 2 days ago, "After 14 more hours, the Japs cannot attack Corregidor unopposed." I wish it were true! Maybe that ties in with the absence of bombing yesterday? "All clear" sounded at 1:15. No bombing of Corregidor or nearby. . . .

[*16 January*]   MacArthur issues exhortation to troops:—No further retreat! Thousands of men and hundreds of planes are en route to help us, but must fight their way, and so will be delayed—etc. (If the Navy is responsible, they'll never get here!) Rumors are persistent that, instead of a 6 month's reserve of food, we have only 3 months! . . .

The Japs bomb the landing field near Cabcaben at least once a day in an effort to prevent our few remaining planes (about 5, they say) from using it. However our field crew get out with their "bulldozers" every night and level off the bomb craters so that, by morning, it is about as usable as ever. The planes, too, are now never left on the field, but are hidden away at a safe distance. What a pity our aviators didn't have sense enough to do that at the start of the War. It is humiliating to think of the number of planes of ours that the Japs destroyed thru our own dumbness and inefficiency. . . .

[27 *January*] Last night our P-40s took off late at night and later much bombing was heard over Cavite way. It is said that some of our bombers came up from the South and bombed Cavite and Clark Field—and that the Japs broadcast "The treacherous Americans bombed an open city" meaning Manila, which they have made *not* an open city—though they bombed it when it *was*. I wish we had bombed the Jap front lines in Bataan, instead. . . .

[2 *February*] For today the news arrived that the Japs have driven them [the British] back into Singapore itself—that the British retreated across the causeways, blew them up, and are now holding only Singapore—but the Limeys are already whimpering that the Japs can now bombard their airfields, etc. but that they will "hold out." They sure are great at letting other people do their fighting for them!

Note that Pres. Roosevelt's latest speech guarantees that we will redeem the Philippines' INDEPENDENCE! Gratuitous, unnecessary and dam bad strategy. . . .

[6 *March*] Strange as it seems, reports say that the Japs have or are getting air supremacy over Java. Where are all the Allied planes— retreated to Australia? If true, that bodes ill for the future. Another report says the Japs are preparing to invade India!

Why don't the Allies do a little "invading" on their own hook? Japan proper hasn't been touched once, yet. . . .[1]

II

WE BOMBED OUR TARGET EXACTLY AS PLANNED

While the Americans struggled to defend the Philippines, the Army was planning a raid against the Japanese Empire. After Pearl Harbor, the forces in the Pacific could not generate large scale offensives, but flew hit-and-run raids with carrier-based planes. The most

371

brilliant of these was the air strike on Tokyo delivered by Colonel James H. Doolittle's B-25's from the carrier Hornet *on 18 April 1942. The startling news that the capital of Japan had been bombed boosted American morale.*

In their official reports, Colonel Doolittle and Lieutenant Richard O. Joyce describe the raid.

[*Doolittle*]   The joint Army-Navy bombing project was conceived, in its final form, in January and accomplished in April, about three months later. The object of the project was to bomb the industrial centers of Japan. It was hoped that the damage done would be both material and psychological. Material damage was to be the destruction of specific targets with ensuing confusion and retardation of production. The psychological results, it was hoped, would be the recalling of combat equipment from other theaters for home defense thus effecting relief in those theaters, the development of a fear complex in Japan, improved relationships with our Allies, and a favorable reaction on the American people.

The original plan was to take off from and return to an aircraft carrier. Take-off and landing tests conducted with three B-25B's at and off Norfolk, Virginia, indicated that take off from the carrier would be comparatively easy but landing back on again extremely difficult. It was then decided that a carrier take-off would be made some place East of Tokyo and the flight would proceed in a generally Westerly direction from there. Fields near the East Coast of China and at Vladivostok were considered as termini. The principal advantage of Vladivostok as a terminus was that it was only about 600 miles from Tokyo against some 1200 miles to the China Coast and range was critical. Satisfactory negotiation could not be consummated with the Russian Government and the idea of going to Vladivostok was therefore abandoned.

A cruising range of 2400 miles with a bomb load of 2,000 lbs. was set as the airplane requirement. A study of the various airplanes available for this project indicated that the B-25 was best suited to the purpose. . . .

Twenty-four airplanes were prepared for the mission. Preparation consisted of installing additional tankage and removing certain unnecessary equipment. Three additional gasoline tanks were installed. . . .

Two wooden 50 caliber guns were stuck out of the extreme tip of the tail. The effectiveness of this subterfuge was indicated by the fact that no airplane, on the flight, was attacked from directly behind. The lateral attacks were more difficult for the attacker and gave our machine gunners a better target. . . .

When the turret guns were fired aft with the muzzle close to the fuselage it was observed that the blast popped rivets and tore the skin loose. As a result of this it was necessary to install steel blast plates. Inasmuch as it was decided that all bombing would be done from low altitudes and the Norden bomb sight did not particularly lend itself to extremely low altitude bombing, the bomb sight was removed and a simplified sight designed by Captain C. R. Greening was installed in its place. Actual low altitude bombing tests carried out at 1500 feet showed a greater degree of accuracy with this simplified sight than we were able to obtain with the Norden. This not only permitted greater bombing accuracy but obviated the possibility of the Norden sight falling into enemy hands. . . .

Pyrotechnics were removed from the airplane in order to reduce the fire hazard and also for the slight saving in weight. Two conventional landing flares were installed immediately forward of the rear armored bulkhead. This gave a maximum of protection against enemy fire. There was no dropping mechanism for the landing flares. It was planned, if it became necessary to use them, that they be thrown out by the rear gunner. A lanyard attached to the parachute flare and the fuselage would ordinarily remove the case some 6 feet from the airplane. . . .

Inasmuch as it was planned, in the interest of security, to maintain radio silence throughout the flight and weight was of the essence, the 230 lb. liaison radio set was removed.

The lead ship and each of the flight leaders ships were equipped with small electrically operated automatic cameras which took 60 pictures at one-half second intervals. The cameras could be turned on at any time by the pilot and were automatically started when the first bomb dropped. Cameras were located in the extreme tip of the tail between the two wooden 50 caliber guns. . . .

All special equipment such as emergency rations, canteens, hatchets, knives, pistols, etc. were made secure before take-off.

Special 500 lb. demolition bombs were provided. These bombs were loaded with an explosive mixture containing 50% T.N.T. and 50% Amatol. . . .

The Chemical Warfare Service provided special 500 incendiary clusters each containing 128 incendiary bombs. . . . Several tests were carried on to assure their proper functioning and to determine the dropping angle and dispersion. . . .

A special load of 50 caliber ammunition was employed. This load carried groups of 1 tracer, 2 armor piercing and 3 explosive bullets.

The twenty-four airplanes for the Tokyo project were obtained from the 17th Bombardment Group. Inasmuch as the airplanes had been obtained from this group and there were, therefore, crews available without airplanes, together with the fact that these crews were experienced in the use of these particular airplanes, the crews were also obtained from this source. It was explained to the Commanding Officer of the 17th Bombardment Group, Lt. Colonel W. C. Mills, that this was to be a mission that would be extremely hazardous, would require a high degree of skill and would be of great value to our defense effort. Volunteers for this mission were requested. More people than we could possibly use immediately volunteered. Twenty-four crews were ordered to Eglin Field for a final course of training. These crews together with the ground maintenance men, armorers, etc., proceeded to Eglin Field, Valparaiso, Florida, as rapidly as the airplanes could be converted and made available. The first of them arrived just before the first of March and the rest just after.

Concentrated courses of instruction were given at Eglin Field. The instruction included carrier take-off practice under the supervision of Lt. Henry Miller of the U. S. Navy. This practice was carried out on one of the auxiliary fields near Eglin. White lines were drawn on two of the runways of this field. Take-off practice was carried out with light load, normal load, and overload up to 31,000 lbs. In all cases the shortest possible take-off was obtained with flaps full down, stabilizer set three-fourths, tail heavy, full power against the brakes and releasing the brakes simultaneously as the engine came up to revs. The control column was pulled back gradually and the airplane left the ground with the tail skid about one foot from the runway. This appeared to be a most unnatural attitude and the airplane took off almost in a stall. In spite of the high wing loading and unnatural attitude the comparatively low power loading and good low-speed control characteristics of the airplane made it possible to handle the airplane without undue difficulty in this attitude. Only one pilot had difficulty during the take-off training. Taking off into a moderately gusty wind with full load, he permitted the airplane to side slip back into the ground just after take-off. No one was hurt but the airplane was badly damaged. While we do not recommend carrier take-off procedure for normal take-offs, it does permit of a much shorter take-off, and may be employed in taking off from extremely short or soft fields. . . .

Special training was given in cross country flying, night flying and navigation. Flights were made over the Gulf of Mexico in order to permit pilots and navigators to become accustomed to flying without visual or radio references or land marks.

Low altitude approaches to bombing targets, rapid bombing and evasive action were practiced. Bombing of land and sea targets was practiced at 1500, 5000 and 10,000 feet. Low altitude bombing practice was specialized in. One hundred pound sand loaded bombs were used in the main but each crew was given an opportunity to drop live bombs as well.

Machine gun practice was carried on, on the ground and in the air. Ground targets were attacked and it was intended to practice on tow targets as well but time did not permit. In order to get practice in operating the turret, pursuit planes simulated attack on our bombers and the gunners followed them with their empty guns.

The first pilots were all excellent. The co-pilots were all good for co-pilots. The bombardiers were fair but needed brushing up. The navigators had had good training but very little practical experience. The gunners, almost without exception, had never fired a machine gun from an airplane at either a moving or stationary target.

In spite of a large amount of fog and bad weather which made flying impossible for days at a time and the considerable amount of time required to complete installations and make the airplanes operational at Eglin Field the training proceeded rapidly under the direction of Captain Edward York. In three weeks ships and crews were safely operational although additional training of the crews and work on the ships would have improved their efficiency.

On March 25, the first of 22 ships (one airplane . . . was wrecked during take-off practice and another airplane was damaged . . .) took off from Eglin Field for Sacramento Air Depot where the airplanes were to have a final check and the remaining installations were to be made. On March 27, all airplanes had arrived.

On March 31 and April 1, 16 planes were loaded on the U.S.S. *Hornet* alongside of the dock at the Alameda Air Depot. Although 22 planes were available for loading there was room on deck for only 15. 16 planes were actually loaded but it was intended that the 16th plane would take off the first day out in order that the other pilots might have an opportunity to at least see a carrier take-off. A request had previously been made of Admiral W. F. Halsey, who was in charge of the task force, to permit each one of the pilots a carrier take-off prior to leaving on the mission or to permit at least one pilot to take off in order that he might pass the information obtained on to the others. Admiral Halsey did not agree to this due to the delay it would entail. He did agree to take one extra plane along and let it take off the first day out or the first favorable weather thereafter. It was later agreed to keep this plane aboard and increase our component from 15 to 16.

Training was continued on the carrier. This training consisted of a series of lectures on Japan given by Lt. Stephen Jurika, Jr. of the Navy, lectures on first aid and sanitation by Lt. T. R. White, M. C. our flight surgeon, lectures on gunnery, navigation and meteorology by members of our own party and officers from the *Hornet,* and a series of lectures on procedure by the writer.

Actual gunnery and turret practice was carried on using kites flown from the *Hornet* for targets.

Celestial navigation practice for our navigators was supervised by the *Hornet* navigating officer. Star sights were taken from the deck and from the navigating compartment in the airplanes. In this way a high degree of proficiency was developed and satisfactory optical characteristics of the navigating compartment window were assured.

A great deal of thought was given to the best method of attack. It was felt that a take-off about 3 hours before daylight arriving over Tokyo at the crack of dawn would give the greatest security, provide ideal bombing conditions, assure the element of surprise and permit arrival at destination before dark. This plan was abandoned because of the anticipated difficulty of a night take-off from the carrier and also because the Navy was unwilling to light up the carrier deck for take-off and provide a check lite ahead in these dangerous waters.

Another plan was to take off at crack of dawn, bomb in the early morning and proceed to destination arriving before dark. This plan had the disadvantage of daylight bombing presumably after the Japanese were aware of our coming and the hazards incident to such a daylight attack. The third plan, the plan finally decided on, was to take off just before dark, bomb at night and proceed to destination arriving after daylight in the early morning. In order to make this plan practical one plane was to take off ahead of the others arrive over Tokyo at dusk and fire the most inflammable part of the city with incendiary bombs. This minimized the overall hazard and assured that the target would be lighted up for following airplanes.

Despite an agreement with the Navy that we would take off the moment contact was made with the enemy and the considerable hazard of contact being made during the run in on the last day we still decided to gamble in order to get the greater security of a night attack. As a matter of fact, contact was made in the early morning and we took off several hours after daylight.

The first enemy patrol vessel was detected and avoided at 3:10 A.M. on the morning of April 18. The Navy task force was endeavoring to avoid a second one some time after daylight when they were picked up by a third. Although this patrol was sunk it is understood that it got at least one radio message off to shore and it was consequently necessary for us to take off immediately. The take-off was made at Latitude 35° 43′N Longitude 153° 25′E approximately 824 statute miles East of the center of Tokyo. The Navy task force immediately retreated and in the afternoon was obliged to sink two more Japanese surface craft. It is of interest to note that even at this distance from Japan the ocean was apparently studded with Japanese craft.

Final instructions were to avoid non-military targets, particularly the Temple of Heaven, and even though we were put off so far at sea that it would be impossible to reach the China Coast, not to go to Siberia but to proceed as far West as possible, land on the water, launch the rubber boat and sail in.

Upon take-off each airplane circled to the right and flew over the *Hornet* lining the axis of the ship up with the drift sight. The course of the *Hornet* was displayed in large figures from the gun turret abaft the island. This, through the use of the airplane compass and directional gyro permitted the establishment of one accurate navigational course and enabled us to swing off on to the proper course for Tokyo. . . .

In spite of the fact that at least one radio message was gotten off prior to our take-off by the Japanese patrol boat that was later sunk—that we passed a Japanese light cruiser (thought by one of the pilots to be a tanker) about 700 miles East of Tokyo—a Japanese patrol plane or bomber headed directly for our task force about 600 miles from Tokyo (this plane turned around and followed one of our airplanes so we know we were observed by it) and innumerable Japanese patrol and fishing boats from some 300 miles offshore until crossing the Japanese Coast, the Japanese were apparently entirely unprepared for our arrival. Inasmuch as messages must have been received at some message center, we can only presume poor dissemination of information or the complete failure of their communication system.

[*Joyce*] I turned west and flew over that short neck of land to Tokyo Bay at 3500 feet altitude. When I reached the bay I dove out of the clouds and located my target and lined up on course with the target at 2400 feet indicated and 210 MPH indicated with the bomb doors open. I encountered no pursuit until I was over the target and no AA fire until I was over the bay. An Aircraft carrier was steaming out of the bay toward the Yokosuka Naval base and opened up on me with AA guns of presumably small caliber. That fire was very ineffective and inaccurate. I dropped two 500 lb. dem. bombs on the Japan Special Steel Company main plant and both were direct hits. One bomb hitting directly in the center of a big plant and the other landing between two buildings destroying the end sections of both.

The third dem. bomb and the incendiary were dropped in the heavy industrial and residential section in the Shiba Ward about ¼ of a mile in shore from the bay and my target. My primary target was right on the shore of the bay. I encountered heavy AA fire over my target and since I took a long straight run on the target by the time my bombs were out I found myself in an AA bracket with the puffs and bursts coming very close but generally behind but catching up fast. At that time a formation of nine zero fighters came in above me and a little to my right in front. I increased power and went into a steep diving turn to the left to escape AA fire and pursuit. The fighters peeled off in attack and followed me but I dove in underneath them and for the moment eluded them. I got out of the AA fire. I indicated as high as 330 MPH in the dive and leveled out very close to the ground and hedge-hopped all the way out to the sea at about 275 indicated air speed.

I saw three Nakajima 97s above me and to the left who pursued me but could not keep up with my speed. The zero fighters, however, had a big altitude advantage and followed me. I shook all but three as I headed west toward the mountains. They did not seem too eager to come in too close to me as my rear gunner was firing his guns at them from time to time. One pursuit came along side of me and above me when I turned south at the mountains to go out to sea and we fired at him with everything we had and I believe that we hit him but none of us are sure whether or not we knocked him down. I believe not. He was in a very good spot to deliver an attack but he did not and instead broke off combat and peeled off and left us. We released our bombs at approximately 13:40 o'clock ship time.

I saw no barrage balloons anywhere over Tokyo, nor did my crew, however, there might have been some that we did not see since our attention was concentrated on our target and then in escaping the AA fire and pursuit airplanes and we did not have much of a chance to look at the ground. I encountered no machine gun fire from the ground to my knowledge. I left the mainland of Japan about 10 miles west of Yokohama. I encountered light AA fire again there but it came from some distance and was ineffective since I was flying very low and very fast. I was picked up and pursued by three pursuit which met me as I was leaving the mainland. I had begun to throttle back when they came in to attack and I increased power and climbed up into some clouds at 3000 feet and eluded them. I sustained a climb of 2000 feet per minute and outclimbed them. I left the mainland at about 13:55 ship time.

[*Doolittle*]   Encountered nine fighters in three flights of three. This was about ten miles north of the outskirts of Tokyo proper.

All this time had been flying as low as the terrain would permit.

Continued low flying due south over the outskirts of and toward the east center of Tokyo.

Pulled up to 1,200 ft., changed course to the southwest and incendiary-bombed highly inflammable section. Dropped first bomb at 1:30 (ship time).

Anti-aircraft very active but only one near hit.

Lowered away to housetops and slid over western outskirts into low haze and smoke.

Turned south and out to sea.

Passed over small aircraft factory with a dozen or more newly completed planes on the line. No bombs left. Decided not to machine gun for reasons of personal security.

Passed on out to sea flying low.

Was soon joined again by Hoover who followed us to the Chinese coast.

[*Joyce*] I flew out to sea about 30 miles, out of sight of land and then headed south for the Oshima Strait a heading of 244 degrees true. I sustained one anti-aircraft hit on my plane in the fuselage directly ahead of the horizontal stabilizer. It tore a hole in the fuselage about 7 inches in diameter. I also was hit in the left wing tip by machine gun bullets presumably from the pursuit but the damage was very slight. There were no injuries to my crew or to the engines. I sighted no enemy aircraft between Tokyo and China where I abandoned my plane. I sighted no enemy surface sea craft between Tokyo and the Chinese coast other than small fishing boats of which I saw many both between Tokyo and the Oshima Strait and between Oshima Strait and the China coast.

On approaching the coast of China I encountered adverse weather conditions namely fog and rain. I was forced to go on instruments about 100 miles from the China coast and remained on instruments until the time of leaving the ship. I had previously attempted to use my automatic flight control equipment but it was not functioning properly and I had to fly the ship manually all the way. I made the trip from Tokyo to China at about 500 feet altitude and 1300 RPM and started at 29 inches of mercury and gradually reduced to 25 inches as my gas load reduced. I indicated about 160 to 165 MPH. I picked up a strong tail wind across the China Sea which enabled me to go as far as I did. I held a course of 261 degrees true from the Oshima Strait to China.

About the time that my navigator estimated that I should begin to gain altitude for the mountains on the coast we were low enough to the water that we spotted an island and got a few glimpses of land as we came in over the coast. It was getting dark and still foggy and raining and getting worse. There was an overcast above us. We crossed the coast at about 20:40 o'clock ship time and I believe about 40 miles south of the entrance to Hangchow Bay. I climbed to 4,000 feet over land and continued on course. I figured I had enough gas to just get me about as far as Chuchow and not much further. I figured my consumption roughly at about between 65 and 70 gallons per hour. I know it was less than 70 gallons per hour after leaving Tokyo.

As we neared our ETA at Chuchow I realized that the weather was such that we could never expect to make a landing so I told the crew to get ready to bail out and I slowed the ship up to 125 MPH. I climbed to 9,000 feet with about less than 15 minutes of gas left and told my rear gunner to jump which he did, we then released the escape door in the front when we were sure that it would not hit the rear gunner and the engineer-gunner, navigator, co-pilot and myself then jumped in that order. I rolled the stabilizer back to keep the ship from gaining too much speed and then I worked myself around to get out of the cockpit and had some trouble in squeezing between the armor plate back of the pilot and co-pilot seats and had to keep pushing the stick forward to keep the ship from stalling. I had little time to do anything after I got in position to jump. I gathered some food and equipment and jumped out through the escape hatch in the navigator's compartment where the rest of the crew had left except the rear gunner. I left the engines of the ship running.

I dropped clear of the ship and pulled the rip cord and the chute opened and functioned perfectly except that the metal sheared on one of the leg strap buckles and the leg strap on my left leg parted and almost dropped me out of the chute. I slid down and the chest strap came up and smacked me in the chin with a stunning blow and at the same time jerked my pistol out of my shoulder holster and tossed it out into space. I was swinging quite badly and had some time to stop that but finally did. I estimate that I floated about one minute. I heard the plane below me and it hit the side of a mountain and exploded and burst into flame. A few seconds later I hit the ground . . . quite suddenly as I could not tell when I was going to hit. I was not very far from the airplane but I realized that I was on a pretty steep slope and could see very little for the fog and rain. I was uninjured. I got out of my chute and got my mussette bag and wrapped myself up in my parachute and tried to sleep and keep warm and dry.

The next morning it was still foggy and when it cleared enough for me to see I started for the wreck of the plane. I had to go up over the mountain I was on. I had landed on top of a high mountain on a steep slope with many boulders and cliffs. I realized that I was quite lucky that I was not seriously injured. The plane was only about a mile away but it took me four hours to get to it. When I arrived at the scene of the crash which was also very high up in the mountain I found a number of Chinese were there picking in the wreckage. I hailed them and made them understand that I was an American. They were friendly towards me. The plane had hit the side of the mountain and sprayed over a large area and had burned. I was able to salvage nothing from it. It was a total loss. The Chinese farmers led me to a small village that day and the next day I met some Chinese soldiers who held me for a day and then led me over the mountains for two days until I reached Tunki Anhwei and the Military police there got me a ride on a truck to Tanki and I took the train from there to Kimwa to Chuchow. I stayed at Chuchow three days then went by train to Ningtu from there to Hengyang by bus which took three days and then a plane picked us up at Hengyang a day later and took us to Chungking.

[*Doolittle*] Navigator plotted perfect course to pass north of Yaki Shima.

Saw three large naval vessels just before passing west end of Japan. One was flatter than the others and may have been a converted carrier.

Passed innumerable fishing and small patrol boats.

Made land fall somewhat north of course on China coast.

Tried to reach Chuchow on 4495 but couldn't raise.

It had been clear over Tokyo but became overcast before reaching Yaki Shima. Ceiling lowered on coast until low islands and hills were in it at about 600'. Just getting dark and couldn't live under overcast so pulled up to 6,000 and then 8,000 ft. in it. On instruments from then on though occasionally saw dim lights on ground through almost solid overcast. These lights seemed more often on our right and pulled us still farther off course.

Directed rear gunner to go aft and secure films from camera (unfortunately they were jerked out of his shirt front where he had put them, when his chute opened.)

Decided to abandon ship. Sgt. Braemer, Lt. Potter, Sgt. Leonard and Lt. Cole jumped in order. Left ship on A.F.C.E., shut off both gas cocks and I left. *Should have put flaps down.* This would have slowed down landing speed, reduced impact and shortened glide.

All hands collected and ship located by late afternoon of 19th.

Requested General Ho Yang Ling, Director of the Branch Government of Western Chekiang Province to have a lookout kept along the seacoast from Hang Chow bay to Wen Chow bay and also have all sampans and junks along the coast keep a lookout for planes that went down at sea, or just reached shore.

Early morning of 20th four planes and crews, in addition to ours, had been located. . . .

Discussed possibility of purchasing three prisoners on the seacoast from Puppet Government and endeavoring to take out the three in the lake area by force. Believe this desire was made clear to General Ku Cho-tung (who spoke little English) and know it was made clear to English-speaking members of his staff. This was at Shangjao. They agreed to try purchase of three but recommended against force due to large Japanese concentration.

Left airplane about 9:20 (ship time) after 13 hours in the air. Still had enough gas for half hour flight but right front tank was showing empty. Had transferred once as right engine used more fuel. Had covered about 2,250 miles, mostly at low speed, cruising but about an hour at moderate high speed which more than doubled the consumption for this time.

Bad luck:

(1) Early take-off due to naval contact with surface and aircraft.

(2) Clear over Tokyo.

(3) Foul over China.

Good luck:

(1) A 25 m/h tail wind over most of the last 1,200 miles. . . .

Before leaving China, arrangements were made with General Koo Chow Tung and Madam Chiang Kai-shek to endeavor to ransom the prisoners who had fallen into the hands of the puppet government. Some consideration was given to attempting the rescue of the prisoners that had fallen into Japanese hands in the vicinity of Payang Lake but it was indicated, due to the strong Japanese position, that at least two regiments would be required and the chance of the prisoners being killed during the action was so great that the idea was abandoned. Negotiations were being carried on, when the writer left China, to the end of offering small guerilla bands a certain amount of money for each prisoner that they could bring out of Japanese occupied territory alive.

Several outstanding lessons may be learned from the flight. First, sufficient modern airplanes and competent pilots should be retained within the territorial limits of the United States to assure her adequate defense. Second, an absolutely infallible detection and communication system must be provided. Third, efficient utilization of small surface craft, such as fishing boats equipped with an extremely simple radio could, through the use of a simplified code, send messages to a message center indicating the type, position, direction of approach, speed and altitude of any enemy attacking force. Fourth, the necessity for suitable camouflage and adequate dissimulation. Fifth, the highest possible degree of dispersal in order that a bomb attack, if successful, will do the minimum amount of damage.

The desirability of stopping an enemy bombing raid *before* arrival over target is obvious. This can be accomplished only with a preponderance of fighters.

The successful bombing of Tokyo indicated that, provided the element of surprise is possible, an extremely successful raid can be carried out at low altitudes with great damage and high security to equipment and personnel.

WAR DEPARTMENT
HEADQUARTERS OF THE ARMY AIR FORCES
WASHINGTON
May 7, 1942

Memorandum For The President:

Subject: Doolittle Project.

1. Summary of the Doolittle project:

Crews taking part	16
Accounted for and all safe	10
Accounted for but all injured	1
Accounted for all safe but 1 dead	1
Accounted for but 1 man missing	1
Accounted for in Siberia	1
Accounted for in Japanese hands in China (2 reported killed)	1
Not accounted for	1
Total	16

2. Of the crew in the hands of the Japanese, 2 are reported dead. General Doolittle is endeavoring to ransom the other 3, and made

arrangements prior to departure from China. General Doolittle left May 5th.

3. Summary of final report on operations:
    a. Planes performed very well. All pilots over China jumped in parachutes
    b. All planes completely destroyed to prevent information reaching enemy hands.
    c. Antiaircraft over Japan was active, but inaccurate.
    d. Barrage balloons in use but many destroyed by Japanese enemy aircraft.
    e. Following targets hit:
        Yokosuka—Naval station.
        Nagoya—Barracks, oil and storage warehouse, and military arsenal
        Mitsuibishi—Aircraft factory
        Shiba (Ward of Tokyo)—Steel plants
        Tokyo—Industrial Area
        S.E. Tokyo—Steel works, gas plant and Chemical works
        Yokohama Area—Warehouse, railroad siding, refinery, tank farm, Industrial Area, oil refinery and storage
    f. Royal Palace—Many fires started in densely populated district 2 or 3 miles north of Royal Palace.

H. H. ARNOLD
Lieutenant General, U.S.A.
Commanding General, Army Air Forces[2]

III

A CLAY DUCK IN . . .
THAT AERIAL SHOOTING GALLERY

Halfway around the world at air bases in Great Britain, planes of the United States Air Force took off for German-occupied Europe. A copilot tells of the raid against Regensburg, 17 August 1943.

When the 100th Group crossed the coast of Holland south of The

Hague, at 1008 hours at our base altitude of 17,000 feet, I was well situated to watch the proceedings, being copilot in the lead ship of the last element of the high squadron. The Group had all of its 21 B-17F's tucked in tightly and was within handy supporting distance of the 95th Group, ahead of us at 18,000 feet. We were the last and lowest of the seven groups of the 4th Air Division that were visible ahead on the south-east course, forming a long, loose-linked chain in the bright sunlight—too long, it seemed. Wide gaps separated the three combat wings. As I sat there in the tail-end element of that many miles long procession, gauging the distance to the lead group, I had the lonesome foreboding that might come to the last man about to run a gauntlet lined with spiked clubs.

At 1017 hours, near Woensdrecht, I saw the first flak blossom out in our vicinity, light and inaccurate. A few minutes later, approximately 1025 hours, two FW-190's appeared at one o'clock level and whizzed through the formation ahead of us in a frontal attack, nicking two B-17's of the 95th Group in the wings and breaking away beneath us in half-rolls. Smoke immediately trailed from both B-17's, but they held their stations. As the fighters passed us at a high rate of closure, the guns of our group went into action. The pungent smell of burnt powder filled our cockpit, and the B-17 trembled to the recoil of nose and ball-turret guns. I saw pieces fly off the wing of one of the fighters before they passed from view.

Here was early action. The members of the crew sensed trouble. There was something desperate about the way those two fighters came in fast, right out of their climb without any preliminaries. For a few seconds, the inter-phone was busy with admonitions: "Lead'em more . . . short bursts . . . don't throw rounds away . . . there'll be more along in a minute."

Three minutes later, the gunners reported fighters climbing up from all around the clock, singly and in pairs, both FW-190's and Me-109G's. This was only my fourth raid, but from what I could see on my side, it looked like too many fighters for sound health. A coordinated attack followed, with the head-on fighters coming in from slightly above, the 9 and 3 o'clock attackers approaching from about level, and the rear attackers from slightly below. Every gun from every B-17 in our group and the 95th were firing, criss-crossing our patch of sky with tracers to match the time-fuze cannon shell puffs that squirted from the wings of the Jerry single-seaters. I would estimate that 75%

B-17 over Poland in World War II.

of our fire was inaccurate, falling astern of the target—particularly the fire from hand-held guns. Nevertheless, both sides got hurt in this clash with two B-17's from our low squadron and one from the 95th Group falling out of formation on fire with crews bailing out, and several fighters heading for the deck in flames or with their pilots lingering behind under dirty yellow parachutes. Our group leader, Major John Kidd, pulled us up nearer to the 95th Group for mutual support. . . .

It was 1041 hours, over Eupen, that I looked out of my copilot's window after a short lull and saw two whole squadrons, 12 Me-109's and 11 FW-190's climbing parallel to us. The first squadron had reached our level and was pulling ahead to turn into us and the second was not far behind. Several thousand feet below us were many more fighters, with their noses cocked at maximum climb. Over the interphone came reports of an equal number of enemy aircraft deploying on the other side. For the first time, I noticed an Me-110 sitting out of range on our right. He was to stay with us all the way to the target, apparently reporting our position to fresh squadrons waiting for us down the road. At the sight of all these fighters, I had the distinct feeling of being trapped—that the Hun was tipped off, or at least had guessed our destination and was waiting for us. No P-47's were visible. The life expectancy of the 100th Group suddenly seemed very short, since it had already appeared that the fighters were passing up the preceding groups, with the exception of the 95th, in order to take a cut at us.

Swinging their yellow noses around in a wide U-turn, the 12-ship squadron of Me-109's came in from 12 to 2 o'clock in pairs and in fours and the main event was on.

A shining silver object sailed past over our right wing. I recognized it as a main exit door. Seconds later a dark object came hurtling through the formation, barely missing several props. It was a man, clasping his knees to his head, revolving like a diver in a triple somersault. I didn't see his 'chute open.

A B-17 turned gradually out of the formation to the right, maintaining altitude. In a split second, the B-17 completely disappeared in a brilliant explosion, from which the only remains were four small balls of fire, the fuel tanks, which were quickly consumed as they fell earthward.

Our airplane was endangered by various debris. Emergency hatches, exit doors, prematurely opened parachutes, bodies, and assorted fragments of B-17's and Hun fighters breezed past us in the slip-stream.

I watched two fighters explode not far beneath, disappearing in sheets of orange flame, B-17's dropping out in every stage of distress, from engines on fire to control surfaces shot away, friendly and enemy parachutes floating down and, on the green carpet far behind us, numerous funeral pyres of smoke from fallen fighters, marking our trail.

On we flew through the strewn wake of a desperate air battle, where disintegrating aircraft were commonplace and 60 'chutes in the air at one time were hardly worth a second look.

I watched a B-17 turn slowly out to the right with its cockpit a mass of flames. The copilot crawled out of his window, held on with one hand, reached back for his 'chute, buckled it on, let go and was wisked back to the horizontal stabilizer. I believe the impact killed him. His 'chute didn't open.

Ten minutes, twenty minutes, thirty minutes, and still no let-up in the attacks. The fighters queued up like a bread-line and let us have it. Each second of time had a cannon shell in it. The strain of being a clay duck in the wrong end of that aerial shooting gallery became almost intolerable as the minutes accumulated toward the first hour.

Our B-17 shook steadily with the fire of its .50's and the air inside was heavy with smoke. It was cold in the cockpit, but when I looked across at Lt. Thomas Murphy, the pilot, and a good one, sweat was pouring off his forehead and over his oxygen mask. He turned the controls over to me for a while. It was a blessed relief to concentrate on holding station in formation instead of watching those everlasting fighters boring in. It was possible to forget the fighters. Then the top-turret gunner's twin muzzles would pound away a foot above my head, giving a realistic imitation of cannon-shells exploding in the cockpit, while I gave an even better imitation of a man jumping six inches out of his seat.

A B-17 of the 95th Group, with its right Tokyo tanks on fire, dropped back to about 200 feet above our right wing and stayed there while seven of the crew successively bailed out. Four went out the bomb-bay and executed delayed jumps, one bailed from the nose, opened his chute prematurely and nearly fouled the tail. Another went out the left waist-gun opening, delaying his 'chute opening for a safe interval. The tailgunner dropped out of his hatch, apparently pulling the ripcord before he was clear of the ship. His 'chute opened instantaneously, barely missing the tail, and jerked him so hard that both his shoes came off. He hung limply in the harness, whereas the others had showed immediately some signs of life after their 'chutes opened, shifting around in the harness. The B-17 then dropped back in a medium spiral, and I did not see the pilots leave. I saw it just before it passed from view, several thousand feet below us, with its right wing a solid sheet of yellow flame.

After we had been under constant attack for a solid hour, it appeared certain that the 100th Group was faced with annihilation. Seven of our group had been shot down, the sky was still mottled with rising fighters and it was only 1120 hours, with target-time still 35 minutes away. I doubt if a man in the group visualized the possibility of our getting much further without 100% loss. . . . Our group fire power was reduced 33%, ammunition was running low. Our tail-guns had to be replenished from another gun station. Gunners were becoming exhausted and nerve-tortured from the prolonged strain, and there was an awareness on everybody's part that something must have gone wrong. We had been the aiming point for what seemed like most of the Luftwaffe and we fully expected to find the rest of it primed for us at the target.

Fighter tactics were running fairly true to form. Frontal attackers hit the low squadron and lead squadron, while rear attackers went for the high. The manner of their attacks showed that some pilots were old-timers, some amateurs, and that all knew pretty definitely where we were going and were inspired with a fanatical determination to stop us before we got there. The old-timers came in on frontal attacks with a noticeably slower rate of closure, apparently throttled back, obtaining greater accuracy than those that bolted through us wide out. They did some nice shooting at ranges of 500 or more yards, and in many cases seemed able to time their thrusts so as to catch the top and ball turrent gunners engaged with rear and side attacks. Less experienced pilots were pressing attacks home to 250 yards and less to get hits, offering point-blank targets on the break-away, firing long bursts of 20 seconds, and, in some cases, actually pulling up instead of going down and out. Several FW pilots pulled off some first rate deflection shooting on side attacks against the high group, then raked the low group on the break-away out of a side-slip, keeping the nose cocked up in the turn to prolong the period the formation was in their sights.

I observed what I believe was an attempt at air-to-air bombing, although I didn't see the bombs dropped. A patch of 75 to 100 grey-white bursts, smaller than flak bursts, appeared simultaneously at our level, off to one side.

One B-17 dropped out on fire and put its wheels down while the crew bailed. Three Me-109's circled it closely, but held their fire, apparently ensuring that no one stayed in the ship to try for home. I saw Hun fighters hold their fire even when being shot at by a B-17 from which the crew was bailing out.

At 1150 hours, one hour and a half after the first of at least 200 individual fighter attacks, the pressure eased off, although hostilities were still in the vicinity. We turned at 1154 hours with 14 B-17's left in the group, two of which were badly crippled. They dropped out soon after bombing the target and headed for Switzerland, one of them, "042" carrying Colonel William Kennedy as tail-gunner. #4 engine was on fire, but not out of control. Major William Veal, leader of the high squadron, received a cannon shell in his #3 engine just before the start of the bombing run and went in to the target with the prop feathered.

Weather over the target, as on the entire trip, was ideal. Flak was negligible. The group got its bombs away promptly on the leader. As we turned and headed for the Alps, I got a grim satisfaction out of seeing a rectangular column of smoke rising straight up from the Me-109 shops, with only one burst over the town of Regensburg.

The rest of the trip was anti-climax. A few more fighters pecked at us on the way to the Alps. A town in the Brenner Pass tossed up a lone burst of futile flak. Colonel Le May, who had taken excellent care of us all the way, circled the air division over Lake Garda long enough to give the cripples a chance to join the family, and we were on our way toward the Mediterranean in a gradual descent. About 25 fighters on the ground at Verona stayed on the ground. The prospect of ditching as we approached Bone, short of fuel, and the sight of other B-17's falling into the drink, seemed trivial matters after the vicious nightmare of the long trip across southern Germany. We felt the reaction of men who had not expected to see another sunset.

At 1815 hours, with red lights showing on all our fuel tanks in my ship, the seven B-17's of the group who were still in formation circled over Bertoux and landed in the dust. Our crew was unscratched. Sole damage to the airplane: a bit of ventilation around the tail from flak and 20 mm shells. We slept on the hard ground under the wings of our B-17, but the good earth felt softer than a silk pillow.[3]

IV

WE AWOKE AND ALL HELL WAS
BREAKING LOOSE

In the Mediterranean, Allied troops had landed in Sicily in July, 1943 and, supported by superior air power, conquered the island in August. On 9 September the British Eighth Army hit Calabria, Italy, as the Americans stormed ashore near Naples. Enemy opposition to the American Fifth Army was severe and the GI's barely escaped catastrophe on the beaches of Salerno. In a surprise assult at Anzio near Rome in January, 1944, the Fifth Army threatened the Germans to the southward, but the enemy's defense of the Gustav Line delayed the occupation of the Italian capital for nearly six months.

Pfc. Harvey Hamilton of the 84th Chemical Mortar Battalion hit the beach at Salerno and, with his outfit, trudged northward.

We awoke and all hell was breaking loose. We had arrived at our destination, Salerno, Italy. The big troopship couldn't move in close to shore, it had to stay out of shell range. They gave us pills to keep us from getting seasick, then loaded us on small boats, LCP's (landing craft personnel), and lowered us to the water. There were about twenty-five in each boat. The sea was very rough and it tossed us around like chips while waiting for the signal to come ashore.

Some of the boys were terribly seasick, one boy was vomiting on my feet, another vomiting over the side of the boat and others trying to vomit, so it was pretty much of a mess. One fellow was so sick he tried to jump overboard and we had to hold him in. As we came in, the battleships and destroyers were shelling the mountains trying to knock out the German guns that were shelling the beach. Finally we reached shore and saw boats torn up, turned upside down and helmets floating around in the water and that told us lots of our boys had lost their lives. We waded through water above our knees getting to shore and as we came onto the beach things had quieted down some. We saw lots of fellows sitting by slit trenches but we found out later that they were dead and had been fixed like that so it wouldn't look so bad to

Fifth Army digging out of the mud during World War II.
Below: General Dwight D. Eisenhower.

the troops coming in. We were hiking to our assembly area and had stopped to take a breath and smoke a cigarette by some fig trees. We were standing around eating figs when here came a bunch of Jerry planes strafing us. Boy, did we scatter. We finally reached the assembly area which was a cornfield and tomato patch by a nice farmhouse. . . .

The first few days at Salerno were rugged. We had about three air raids every day and about that many at night. We had good air cover, but just as soon as our planes left the Jerries would sneak in to bomb and strafe. The antiaircraft gunners were trigger happy and excited and they shot down more of our planes than the Germans. . . .

I saw three of our boys killed by a tank and one of them had seven .50 calibre bullets through the front of his helmet. It sure is a gruesome sight to see lots of American boys lying in a row dead and covered with blankets. As you know, our weapon is the 4-2 chemical mortar which shoots a shell weighing between twenty-five and thirty pounds. It is good for mountainous terrain and will reach spots the artillery can't touch. The artillery shells go over the hill and into the valley but with our mortars we can shell the reverse side of a hill from top to bottom and also drop shells in ravines that the artillery can't get. It was sure noisy at Salerno. The navy shells whistled over our heads all night. . . .

After we got our mortars we moved to another area to move out to a gun position. That night we had a big air raid and they hit a German plane. We could see it when it got hit and also a little ball of fire. In a few seconds the entire plane was burning, then it turned and came straight towards us. I had been standing in my slit trench watching the fireworks and as the plane came toward us I didn't know whether to run or stay. Some of the boys were running around and didn't know what to do or where to go. I was standing with one foot in and one foot out wondering what to do, when suddenly the plane turned and crashed about two miles from us and we breathed a sigh of relief, in fact, we started breathing again.

Our first gun position was in the bed of a dry canal. We were set up in a defensive position just waiting for the Germans to break through. It was here that an 88 landed within six feet of me. It didn't go off.

The photographers were up in trees taking pictures of the big tank battle that was raging just in front of us. The next day we moved to another position in an open field behind a few blackberry briars. We were drinking water out of a stream. We couldn't move out of our holes in the daytime so at night we would fill our canteens and walk around a little. . . .

We stayed there for a few days, then one Sunday morning about four o'clock we started moving cross-country, pulling our carts, one loaded with ammunition and the mortar on the other. That was sure a tough pull over irrigation ditches and through briars and bushes. There were many dead cattle lying around and the fields were full of shell holes. About noon we crossed a blacktop highway torn up with shells and bombs. We stopped in a ditch about one hundred yards from the highway in a clump of wild bushes. We were all so tired we just slid down any place. There was a farmhouse between us and the highway, so my buddy and I took our canteens and started to the house for water.

We heard airplanes when we were about halfway to the house. They were Jerry planes trying to bomb the highway. They dropped two large bombs but missed the highway and came so close to us that the shrapnel and dirt was singing over our heads like a swarm of bees. We were really hugging the ground. They then dropped personnel bombs at the other boys. The personnel bomb weighs about twenty-five pounds. A large chunk of dirt hit one boy on the leg and put him in the hospital. Another one hit a case of rations and splattered meat and beans and stew every place.

We then moved to a very beautiful orchard of oranges, tangerines, lemons, grapes, figs and apples. . . .

We were here a few days then moved up by a little town, but now the Germans were moving so fast that we had a hard time keeping up with them. We slept under some apple trees and there were so many apples on the ground that we had to scrape them to one side so we could lie down to sleep. We passed through so many towns I have forgotten the names of most of them. . . .

We kept moving until we reached the Volturno River. We had our gun position on a high mountain and we had to pack the ammunition about a mile. We packed two rounds at a time in a shell carrier made for that purpose, so that was about sixty pounds we were packing. You might have read about the smoke screen that was laid across the Volturno while the engineers built the bridge. Well, we were the ones that laid it. While we were on those mountains we could look down the valley, green with grass or alfalfa and full of shell holes. They were so thick you could almost step from one to the other. On the night of October 13, we crossed the Volturno and stopped by a farmhouse. We again were the first troops there since the infantry had passed.

It was so dark we couldn't see a thing so we just laid down and went to sleep. The next morning we woke up and dead Germans were all around us. They had pulled out in a hurry and left lots of machine guns and ammunition. They had killed a hog but didn't have time to eat it and had hidden it in the house. There was one Jerry that was killed in the garden right by the house. We buried him and hung his dogtag on the cross over his grave. The ditches around were full of dead Germans. . . .

We passed through many towns and villages, all of them bearing the scars of war. On the night of November 7th we were supposed to meet the infantry and go with them on a mission but it rained just as we started. The roads were all dirt and our trucks lacked about six miles getting us there. We started out pulling the mortars up hill and down hill and so dark we couldn't see a thing and all the time the rain was coming down by bucketfuls. When we got to our destination we were several hours late and the infantry had gone ahead. They told us to lie down and make ourselves comfortable.

We were soaking wet and water was standing all over the ground so you can imagine how comfortable we were. I had a change of clothes in my bedroll so I put them on, got in my bedroll, pulled the end of my shelter half over my head and said, "Let it rain." One boy laid down as soon as we stopped and it started raining harder. He had laid in a low place and a stream of water was running over him. It rained about all night and when I awoke the next morning I was wet again, so we built a fire and dried our clothing. That night we were on the move again and when we stopped the Germans were shelling our area. We found a cistern about ten feet deep and jumped in. Later we moved into a house. Some of us fellows slept downstairs on the rock floor and the family slept upstairs. Before the Germans had retreated they told the family to go with them or the Americans would kill them, so they were suspicious of us for a while. They soon got over that.

The day of November 11th we were issued our winter wearing apparel, consisting of woolen underwear, overcoat and gloves. The next morning we moved out with the infantry and passed through the town of Pozzuoli which was about seven miles north of Venafro. Fires were still burning in the town as we passed through and as we walked along the road we saw lots of signs warning us of mines. . . . The Germans had the road camouflaged so good it looked as if it ran up to the end of a hollow and stopped. As we moved up the hill we saw a German gun that had been firing on the town but it was destroyed and there were five fresh graves with their helmets hanging on the crosses. . . . The Germans were shelling the hill as we moved up and wounded many of the infantry boys. We were so close to the Germans we couldn't pitch a tent so we just spread our blankets out and went to sleep.

The next morning it started raining and we got wet again. It rained about three days before we could put up our tents and by that time the mud was shoe deep. That was the beginning of the rainy season and it rained almost every day. We got soaking wet almost every day packing ammunition. We had to go to bed so our bodies could dry our clothes by the next morning, then we would start all over again. We went to bed about four o'clock and got up about nine o'clock the next morning if we weren't awakened by shells. We stayed on that hill thirty-eight days and shot four thousand rounds of ammunition. That's sure a lot of war bonds.

The mountain was so steep a mule couldn't climb it, but we packed ammunition up in the mud and rain, sometimes 'till twelve o'clock at night. On steep hills the Italians have made terraces to keep the soil from washing away and walled up with rock. At night we would sit by the wall waiting for the shells to come in before going to bed. They threw a big barrage at us one night and as I ran out of my tent a shell exploded upon the hill in front of me and blinded me for a few seconds. The powder smoke was so thick we could hardly breathe. We stood on the mountain and watched shells explode in the valley below.

One night it was raining and some medicos were sleeping in the ambulance when someone opened the door and said, "Kamerad." It was two Germans giving up. They were sick and wanted treatment. I saw them bring in some prisoners there who still had hand grenades in their pockets.

One Saturday night we got orders to move forward again. So about midnight we started out. As we pulled our carts along the road we saw lots of mines that had just been taken up and also dead Germans lying in the ditches. We had to wait about two hours for the engineers to build a bridge so we just lay down in the road and went to sleep. As soon as the bridge was built we moved on and met the boys using the mine sweepers. A fellow sure steps light when he's traveling a road and doesn't know whether the mines have been taken out or not. We didn't get much sleep that night and the next day we dug our slit trenches.

Late that afternoon the Germans threw over a smoke shell, they were ranging in on the road. That night about nine o'clock they started throwing in the shells. That was the first time I had seen shelling that looked like the picture shows of war. The shells were coming in so fast it looked like the whole hillside was on fire. I had a slit trench that was hardly big enough for me but when the shelling started another boy jumped in with me. How we both got in there I don't know. . . .

In a few days we were relieved, after one hundred eighteen days of steady combat. The day of January 6th we moved back for a very short rest, in fact, two weeks. Then I was able to take my under-clothing off that I had been wearing since November 11th.[4]

V

ON THAT MORNING SIX MEN WERE BURIED WITHIN THE PERIMETER

In the China-Burma-India theater of operations, the Japanese had occupied Burma and severed the supply line to China. To feed supplies to China, GI's built the Ledo Road in 1943–44 from northeast India to a junction with the Burma Road near the Chinese border. From India over the Himalayans, the "Hump," Americans flew supplies.

British Tommies entered Mandalay and, simultaneously, Chinese troops captured Lashio, the old terminus of the Burma Road. The British took Rangoon in May, completing their conquest of Burma and reopened the road to China.

The best-known American account of mass suffering and endurance in this theater is the tale of Merrill's Marauders, an outfit of gallant men who operated behind the Japanese lines in Burma, 1944. Captain Henry Stelling of the Medical Corps, and a combat historian relate the adventures of the Marauders after they marched down the Ledo Road and the subsequent fight at 'Nhpum Ga.

[*Stelling*]   It cannot be overemphasized that this is the first time in the history of modern war that so many men so heavily laden, have been called upon to march so rapidly and so long, over such high mountains and through such thick jungles, on inadequate diet, in pursuit of such a tenacious enemy. . . .

Never before has severe exhaustion syndrome been so manifest on such a large scale as it is manifest most astoundingly throughout the men and officers of the 5307th. Before the third month of combat . . . blacking out and dizziness were common in spite of adequate salt and vitamins intake and an almost passable but still inadequate diet. Lack of muscle tone accentuated diarrheas already present in over 90% of the men. . . . Weight loss averaged twenty pounds per man and in many cases reached as much as fifty pounds. This in spite of the fact that the men were trained down to the point of no excess fat early in the campaign. Failure to regain the usual physical rebound in strength and endurance after a day or two rest every ten to thirty days was universal. The comparatively delicious ten in one ration which was dropped to us occasionally during these short day or two rest periods failed to give us the rebound energy expected. The men continued to decrease in strength and endurance and their physical and mental lassitude and exhaustion continued to increase until the very last.

It is a fact that the morale and spirit de corps which reached their height following the first two major combat engagements in which the men fought magnificently and withstood assault, and in the second engagement accounted for over 200 of the enemy for every American killed or wounded, that this wonderful fighting spirit as a unit gradually dwindled due to exhaustion [and] false promises. . . . The spirit and will to go on became purely a matter of getting out of Burma as soon as possible rather than that of a fighting unit proud of its record and desirous of increasing accomplishment to add to its laurels. Toward the last it became a matter of getting over one more hill and still another mountain over and over again with the certain knowledge that by no other means could we ever hope to terminate the torture. . . .

This was no little march of a week or a month or of a few hundred yards of fighting for ten days or so without packs. This was a long grueling campaign. . . .

Early in February the regiment arrived at Margherita near Ledo. After a days unpacking and packing the packs for the animals and those for our own backs, we started down the Ledo Road. The first days march of over twenty miles resulted in many sore backs for animals and men and many blistered feet and other ailments for the men. . . . About twenty of the men had to be ridden on trucks because of their condition following this first days march. Several, including a medical officer, were sent to the 20th General Hospital for treatment on the second day of the march. We continued from ten to twenty miles per day down the Ledo Road until we had covered practically its full length to about the 100 mile marker in ten days. Of course all the men carried full packs. . . .

After starting into the jungles we failed to make our objective the first day so our Battalion Commander decided to continue in the dark along a very narrow jungle trail without lights of any kind. The trail went across several muddy stream beds and two or three flimsy bamboo foot bridges. In the pitch black dark only those who have attempted to do so can possibly appreciate the utter impossibility of keeping a column of loaded pack animals and men moving along such a trail with thick vines and bamboo and underbrush growing up to the very edge of a narrow winding trail and with fallen logs and roots every few feet. With just a little light or in bright moon light it can be done, but with no lights at all and men falling and stumbling and animal packs getting caught in vines and stuck between and under limbs of trees, it is an impossibility to move over a few feet a minute. It takes hours to move even a half mile. . . .

During three days rest at the end of the ten day Ledo Road march, and after part of a day and a night and another part day march to our first stopping place in the jungle, we received our first air drop and packed rations and ammunition in addition to regular packs for our start into deeper jungles to our first engagement with the enemy; every few days we received air drops of food and ammunition and other supplies when needed. This was to be routine during the four months of the Burma Campaign. The Air Corps working in conjunction with the men of the rear echelon coordinated by regimental and combat headquarters did an excellent job without which the campaign would have been impossible. . . .

The 2nd Battalion fought through four major engagements and three minor ones and several skirmishes during the four months of the Burma Campaign. 55 men were killed in combat or died of wounds and 175 of the wounded are still living. Two died accidental deaths out of combat. . . .

It should be borne in mind that only once were we taken totally by surprise by the enemy. Excellent scouting and patrolling and general reconnaissance by our own men and accurate and timely information by the Kachins assigned to us and the excellent work of the OSS mostly done by Kachins kept us well posted. Of course this information came to us mostly through Regimental Headquarters. Only one out and out catastrophe occurred due to failure to guard a trail. But none of the enemy ever forced their way through our perimeter.

The worst combat ordeal for the battalion and the one catastrophe referred to which caused the highest number of casualties came when we were completely surrounded by what later proved to be a reinforced battalion of Japs as we were holding rear guard for the regiment at Nphum Ga. We were surrounded here on this hill for fifteen days. The conditions were horrible in the extreme. . . .

[*Combat historian*]   A captured sketch indicating that the enemy was making a wide enveloping movement up the Tanai Valley, with a reinforced battalion, which threatened the Chinese left flank at Shadusup, came to combat headquarters and Gen. Stilwell ordered Merrill to block this thrust.

A good trail which ran through Npum Ga and Janpan to Shadusup seemed the logical route for the enemy to follow on such a mission so Gen. Merrill directed Col. Hunter to move with all haste to Npum, at which place he was at the moment located.

At 0930 the 2nd Bn. arrived at Auche. The 3rd pushed on through them and Orange CT [Combat Team] continued to Npum Ga while Khaki [Combat Team] stopped along the trail between. Contact with the Japs was momentarily expected from the direction of Warong so a defense perimeter was dug in, and precautions taken against possible infiltration.

No action materialized during the bivouac and at 0600 Khaki CT started toward Npum Ga. Blue CT followed closely. At 0630 Battalion headquarters and Green CT started up the trail. As they were filing out of the village two shells landed at the edge of the town, uncomfortably close. A moment later two more came closer.

The situation was very unsatisfactory. Between Auche and Npum Ga the trail followed the crest of a narrow ridge. Its precipitous sides, covered with rank growth, left no place for dispersal. It soon became evident that Jap artillery in the vicinity of Warong was indulging in observed fire.

Lt. Col. McGee [Commanding 2d Battalion] radioed the head of the column to put on all possible speed. As the tail cleared Auche the third pair of shells came whistling over and had found the range. One man and several animals were hit. Then a steady stream of artillery fire poured into the area and searched the trail. It was four miles, mostly uphill. Mud was ankle deep and so slippery that animals frequently fell and before they could be righted had to be unloaded, and then repacked. Word to "move faster" kept being passed up the column which was already going at an awkward, slithering run. Medics were ordered to the rear, and were kept busy. The battalion made the distance, in one and a half hours.

Npum Ga is situated at the top of a mountain and offered some protection from the shelling. Gen. Merrill met McGee and directed him to hold there. At 1800 a radio from the General, who had now moved 2½ miles farther on to Hsamshingyang, directed McGee to block trails in the Kauri-Npum Ga area and prevent any movement north of Npum Ga, paying special attention to the west flank where a usable trail ran along the Hkama river.

A suitable tract was available at Hsamshingyang for the dropping of supplies and the 3rd Bn. took up a position from which to protect it, sending out patrols and stationing road blocks which would prevent any surprise from the north.

The exertion of the last few days had told heavily on the men. In addition to the 70 odd miles marched, they had crossed a river or stream 51 times and the last uphill dash through mud and bursting shells was particularly exhausting. However they quickly whipped the hilltop into a tenable position and established a perimeter defense. . . .

Sharp, thin ridges surround Npum Ga. To the north the elevation continued for about half a mile then tapered gradually down toward Hsamshingyang. To the east there was a sharp decline cut by several projecting fingers, flanking ravines which led down to the Tanai river, a couple of miles away. The Hkada Hka (river) paralleled the Tanai generally, about the same distance to the west. Here too the ground sloped sharply away and was covered with hillside bamboo and dense jungle growth.

There was water at the base of a point that jutted out to the northeast. A narrow trail led down to it. To take advantage of the best terrain, and to include the water supply, necessitated a perimeter that was roughly heart-shaped with a small salient protruding sharply eastward. Blue CT occupied the southern, larger half of the position; Green the northern, slightly shorter line.

At this time Gen. Merrill, who had been sick for several days and under a doctor's care, became very ill. The unit surgeon insisted that he be evacuated to a hospital along with the casualties which were even then being flown out of the air strip at Hsamshingyang but he refused. His condition was so serious that Col. Hunter privately advised Gen. Stilwell of the situation, who radioed directing the evacuation of Merrill at the earliest moment thought safe. General Merrill still refused to go until the last wounded man was removed and this did not occur until the 31st of March. By then he was helpless on a stretcher. The unit surgeon considered further delay to be inadvisable. Col. Hunter assumed command. . . .

Mar. 31st began with the usual barrage, however the attack that followed came from three points at once; from the south, the east and the northwest. The principal effort struck from the east, and was directed at isolating the water hole. After an hour of hot fighting, they succeeded in cutting it off. A Marauder counter-attack failed. The enemy had established a strong position on a little ridge commanding the hole and by this time McGee did not have sufficient men to hold the place, even if he could have recaptured it, without weakening his defenses at some other point. Every available man, including mule skinners and headquarters personnel was in foxholes on the perimeter. The water hole was lost.

About 1000 oclock McGee received a message that the trail to Hsamshingyang had been cut. 3rd Bn. patrols were trying to dislodge the block, and hoped to do so by noon—but they didn't. Fighter-bombers appeared and were directed to known Jap positions by radio.

Weather conditions had not been favorable for the past few days and the air force had not been able to help much.

McGee decided to try to cut through the Jap block and open the trail to supplies at Hsamshingyang. For this he carefully thinned out his entire line, accumulating a task force which approximated a reenforced platoon. It struck out viciously under mortar and machine gun support. Within 200 yds it struck strong dug-in positions and was thrown back with several casualties. . . .

An air-drop arranged to hit within the perimeter included plenty of food and ammunition, but the water shortage was serious. Some rain moisture had accumulated in a hollow where several dead mules lay. The pioneer troops managed to contrive a shallow pit to conserve this brakish fluid which tasted horribly of decomposed flesh.

A strong Jap patrol moved up the trail toward the vital air strip. They were met by an Orange CT patrol on the way. The sound of firing quickly brought reinforcements from Major Lew and the Japs were pushed back after a sharp fight in which several Marauders were killed and 12 wounded. Col. Hunter decided to risk weakening the defenses at Hsamshingyang and use these men in an attempt to open up the trail to Npum Ga. He selected Orange CT for the task, and ordered Khaki to take over all patrols and the defense of the airstrip.

On the morning of April the 1st, the 2nd Bn. at Npum Ga defense was treated to a welcome "April Fool." The usual Jap artillery salute to approaching daylight was missing. Their patrols, however, established the fact that the enemy had dug in on the high ground east of the water hole, and they laid a mortar concentration on it. At 0900 Jap big guns answered again. This time from positions much closer. During the early hours they had evidently displaced to Kauri and were now firing at a 1000-yd. range. After a relatively light barrage, the enemy launched a simultaneous attack from east and northeast. It failed.

More bodies of the dead Japs and animals now added to the nauseating aroma that shrouded the mountain top like a heavy fog. The shortage of water had become dangerously acute. In desperation McGee requested an air-drop of 500 gallons in plastic bags. The grave water shortage prevented the doctors from making plaster casts and they were administering sulphadiazine dry to the patients.

McGee sent out patrols to try to locate weak spots in the Jap line, but everywhere they tried, except in one place, they found a complete barrier. This one exception was an extremely steep and rough descent on the west side of the perimeter defense leading into a gorge through which possibly they could reach the river a mile or so away. The remnants of the 3rd Bn. platoon, which had been cut off when the trail to the air strip had been blocked the day before, elected to attempt a breakthrough to the west, by way of the river. Splitting into two sections, they started at twenty minute intervals. One group reached the river just at nightfall and the next day made their way upstream to Hsamshingyang. Just as the second group started, they ran into Japs and dispersed into the jungle. After innumerable narrow escapes, and almost superhuman effort, they accidentally bumped into the leading platoon of Orange Combat team which was engaged in attempting a break through the encirclement. The Orange Team now, finding itself cut off from the rear, in turn took to the under-brush, and circled back to the air strip at Hsamshingyang.

The mission on which Hunter had dispatched Orange CT in a desperate effort to penetrate to the 2nd Bn. was unsuccessful. . . . Here again the Japs displayed ability to make full use of the terrain and cleverly anticipated flanking movements, establishing protective positions in their path. . . .

At Hsamshingyang [3 April] Col. Hunter called a staff meeting at 1500. Information of enemy in strength moving up the Tanai River valley to the south and east had been received. This did not improve the outlook any. The urgent message to the 1st Bn. had been delayed a day and a half due to a combination of radio trouble and mistakes in encoding and decoding. No help could be expected from the 1st Battalion for at least four days.

After discussing all aspects of the situation Col. Hunter made his decision in these words: "Gentlemen, in the morning we start an attack that will drive through to the 2nd Bn. It may take two or three days but we *will* get through. All troops except the sick and the mule skinners will be withdrawn from the air strip. Large patrols will be called in and Kachins substituted where ever possible. To-morrow, as soon as we can get ready, Orange CT will attack due south along the trail. Khaki CT will leave their heavy equipment here, march due south behind Orange until they are 400 yds. from Jap positions, then turn west down the mountain and attack the Japs on their west flank. The artillery will be moved up to where it can fire point blank into the Jap bunkers and pill boxes. Every man of the gun crews volunteered to do this this afternoon. The attack will be tentatively set for 1200 to-morrow. Ruses, feints and anything else you can do to fool the Japs is in order. A fake message will be dropped from a plane so as to fall in the Jap lines. This message will be to the 2nd Bn. and will say that a battalion of parachutists will be dropped between Kauri and Auche at 1700 hours to-morrow (Apr. 4). If possible we will have a dummy drop in that area to fool them."

At Npum Ga Apr. 4th dawned with the situation unchanged. It was the eighth day of the battle and the fifth of the siege. Some of the wounded, who could not be evacuated, had died. On that morning six men were buried within the perimeter. A large proportion had dysentery and stomach disorders. Another heavy artillery shower killed 3 and wounded 12 more.

The success which the battalion had had in repulsing the repeated Jap assaults was due in great measure to the work of Sgt. Matsumoto, who had tapped the line at Walawbum. Working his way close to the Jap line, he constantly reported on their activities and foretold coming attacks which enabled the defenders to concentrate their weapons accurately at the threatened point and prepare in advance for the shock. In one instance when the Japanese struck at a portion of the perimeter that stuck out on a nose of the mountain the attack met no resistance at all and the Japs promptly jumped into the empty foxholes—all of which had been booby-trapped. Well-placed machine gun fire accounted for the survivors. The following platoon was hitting the ground behind when Matsumoto ordered them to "Charge" in their own tongue. Many did, directly into the band of machine gun fire. 54 dead, including two officers resulted. Matsumoto was indefatigable. He crawled from side to side of the perimeter and listened to conversation and orders. At night he inched his way out in front and got more information, keeping the combat team commanders and McGee nearly always ahead of the situation.

The requested air-drop of water was successfully arranged and relieved the most desperate aspect of the situation. Rations and ammunition were received satisfactorily, some of each going to the Japs but not in serious quantities. However, all attempts to break the encirclement met with failure.

At Hsamshingyang preparations for an all-out effort went

forward. . . . Col. Hunter himself joined Orange CT which was to attack astride the trail. Overhead, planes were dive bombing and strafing where ever they could find a target or where they could be directed to unseen targets by radio.

At 1100 it was evident that the attack could not jump off at 1200, so Col. Hunter rescheduled it for 1600. He wanted to make his maximum effort with all the power he had or not at all. The delay was due to the difficulties Khaki CT had in making their way through the jungle.

The plan included a fake battle staged by the pioneer and demolition platoon of the Orange at some distance to the west of the actual point of attack. It was hoped that this diversion would draw Jap fire from the immediate thrust. Dummy runs of the dive bombers were also arranged in conjunction with the mortar and artillery fire. The bombers were to follow the barrage with two live bombing passes then the artillery and mortars would cease as the planes came around for the third time. Orange CT would rush forward while the enemy were still seeking cover from the expected strafing.

At 1530 the fake fight started and the Japs obligingly shifted their mortars to throw fire in that direction. At 1545 the planes were on hand and at 1605 the artillery and mortars opened up. The attack followed exactly as arranged and was successful in gaining relatively considerable ground. The Jap force that was blocking the trail was blasted out of their strong position and pushed back until it merged with the enemy line that surrounded the 2nd battalion. Orange CT was now within 1000 yds of the beleagured Blue and Green.

While this attack was going on, the Japs made a heavy assault on the west side of McGee's position and succeeded in gaining a slight penetration. A few of the enemy actually got into some foxholes that had become vacant through attrition. A two man counter attack with hand grenades wiped out the penetration quickly and the defenders took a new grip on themselves. The dangerous incident was believed to have been caused by some mule skinners, who were now all in the line, taking advantage of a lull to leave their positions.

At 0200 and again at 0430 on the 5th assaults were made on the west side of the perimeter. Reported in advance by Sgt. Matsumoto, both were dispersed. During the day no further attempt was made but artillery fell on the position intermittently. It appeared that the 3rd Battalion push had relieved the pressure considerably.

On Apr. 6th they followed the same tactics. McGee was unable to spare anyone from his defenses to assist. Although the defenders had a very welcome respite from the vicious assaults on their position, there was no assurance that it would continue. Since evacuation had been choked off they had accumulated 17 dead, 97 wounded and 4 missing.

The 3rd Battalion gained another 200 yards on the 6th, most of it due to the extraordinary fire direction of Lt. Woomer, platoon leader from Co. K. He had worked his way to within 25 yards of a Jap position where two machine guns had been holding up the progress for hours and with his SCR 300 radio directed mortar fire until it was landing just over the target. Then he calmly gave the order: "Deflection correct. Bring it in 25 yards and if you don't hear from me you'll know you came this way too far. Then shift it back just a little and you'll be right on it."

The guns were knocked out in the next rounds and Lt. Woomer was unhurt. . . .

On the 7th, Orange and Khaki continued attacking. Their tactics did not vary from those of the previous two days, but they had more high explosive ammunition to use. The total advance for the day was 300 yards. The Japs attacked Npum Ga twice more during the night and early morning hours, but without the ferocity and vigor that had characterized nearly all of the earlier ones. A good deal of their automatic fire was engaged against Khaki CT now boring in from the northwest. Orange held to the ground gained through three days of hard fighting. Only 500 yards separated them from McGee, but they could not gain another inch. . . .

At 1700 on Good Friday, Apr. 7th, Osborne's 1st Battalion appeared on the scene after a forced march of nearly four days duration. They were well used up, but very welcome.

At 1930 Col. Hunter held a staff meeting and laid out the operation for the following day. The 3rd Battalion would again attack along the Npum trail. Those of the 1st Battalion men who were capable of continued exertion, (250 were selected) under Capt. Senff, would move to the southwest until in rear of the enemy and create a diversion.

Apr. 8th was just like the four preceding except for the additional activity from Capt. Senff's force. They proceeded to the designated point, meeting occasional patrol resistance. Blocking the trails as he went along, he bivouacked at about 1815 on a piece of high ground approximately 850 yards from the 2nd Battalion perimeter. A small Jap patrol ran into the bivouac during the night and another of 12 men disturbed them 0530 in the morning.

After moving a short distance to the southeast they came under harassing fire from the direction of the Kauri-Npum trail so Col. Hunter directed Capt. Senff to retrace and contact the enemy to the north. He did so, placing blocks at all usable trails as he went. Sniping and patrol clashes continued all day.

In the afternoon a draw was mortared, where enemy were suspected of being in ambush, and the action brought down enemy fire which landed on their own men.

By that time the siege was over. Apparently the Japanese had become jittery over the reinforcements just arrived, which were taking toll of their patrols in all directions. The ring around Npum Ga simply dissolved. Rice still cooking and abandoned equipment attested to the suddenness of their departure.

Easter Sunday of 1944 will probably remain the happiest in the remembrance of every surviving member of the 2nd Battalion.[5]

VI

NEXT TIME I'M GOING TO CARRY A .45

While the Marauders fought at 'Nhpum Ga, air raids on France and Germany softened the way for the invasion of Europe, 6 June 1944. Swarming ashore on the beaches of Normandy, Americans took Cherbourg as the British captured Caen. After devastating fighting, the Yanks marched into St. Lo on 18 July.

Captain A. Blatt of the Medical Corps and Chaplain Francis L. Sampson, a Roman Catholic padre, tell of that night of 5–6 June when, with the paratroopers, they dove out of their planes behind German lines.

[Blatt] The afternoon of June 5th was a little cloudy and windy but we knew that we were going that night. After supper we

409

put on all our equipment and were lined up in plane loading order when General Eisenhower inspected us and he spoke to me as he went by.

When we marched out to the hangars to meet our guides all the pilots and crew chiefs were wearing .45's. We went out to the plane, got our chutes on, got in and warmed up and took off. It was just dusk then, and shortly after we were airborne and in formation it got quite dark. Through the door of the plane I could see the lights of other planes in our serial. They were all getting into formation. So far it was just like the ordinary problem, and then the next time I looked out the lights were out—and that meant we were over the Channel.

We flew for what seemed about an hour and just when we got the signal that we were twenty minutes away from the target area, I saw a sudden flame appear behind us, then dive down and disappear. I didn't know whether it was a transport or escort or enemy—and then the coast appeared beneath us in the moonlight and there were sparks and flashes all along us. They were the flak guns. About that time the flak started flying past the door. (I remember hoping to myself that it was not flak but sparks from the engine.) I could see the fields and rivers below in the moonlight and here and there on the ground the flash of the guns.[6]

[*Sampson*] The ack-ack was terrific. The plane was hit many times and one boy had a bullet go right through his leg. As we stood up and hooked up, the plane was rocking badly in a strong wind. The green light came on and the jump master pushed our equipment bundle out and we went out as fast as we could, my assistant right behind me. Our jump was a surprise all right . . . for us! The Germans were waiting for us and they sent such a barrage of bullets at us that it will always remain a mystery to me how any of us lived. The tracer bullets alone made it look like the Fourth of July. I collapsed part of my chute to come down faster.

I lit in the middle of a stream over my head. I grabbed my knife and cut my bags from me . . . but could scarcely move to free myself. The canopy of my chute stayed open and the strong wind blew me down the stream about 100 yards and into shallow water. I lay there a few minutes exhausted and as securely pinned down by equipment as if I had been in a straitjacket. None of our men was near, and it took about twenty minutes to get out of my chute (it seemed a year, with German machine gun and mortar fire sweeping the area). I crawled back to the edge of the stream near the spot where I landed, and started diving for my Mass equipment. By pure luck I recovered it after the fifth or sixth dive. The whole area was swamp, and as I started getting my bearings I looked for the lights to assemble on. I learned later that they were shot out as soon as they were turned on and the men in charge mostly killed or wounded. Very luckily I spotted my assistant not very far away, still struggling to get out of his chute. We got together and made for the nearest hedgerow that would offer cover. We no sooner got there than a plane on fire came straight at us. The plane crashed about eighty yards in front of us and threw flaming pieces over our heads. We saw two more planes go down not far away. Neither of us had a weapon so we welcomed two of our men who came crawling along the hedgerow.[7]

(*On his plane, Blatt was ready to jump*)

We got the red light, and rather quickly . . . the green light flashed and I followed Captain Smith out the door. The plane was going fast and the opening shock was terrific. The force of it broke my chin strap and one of the metal fasteners on the helmet and the ground came rushing up so fast I wondered whether or not I should pull my reserve when CRASH—I landed. (The reason the ground came up so fast was because we jumped at about three hundred feet instead of the six hundred feet that we jumped on problems.) I hit the ground so hard that I thought I had broken my back for a few minutes, but I could move my arms and legs O.K., so I started to get out of my harness. I was in a field all by myself, and as I lay struggling in my harness, I could see other planes going over and the flashes of guns all around me shooting at them and I saw two sticks jump and I could see the tracers going up at their canopies. I couldn't unfasten the buckles.

Just then I saw a figure coming along the hedgerow. He came out of the gloom holding a rifle. I spoke the password and clicked the recognition signal on the little metal cricket we all carried and got a good hold on my trench knife. (Next time I'm going to carry a .45 come hell or high water.) But, to my profound relief, he answered properly. It was Sergeant Wood of headquarters company. He helped me out of my harness and we went along the hedgerow. Machine guns

411

and ack-ack would splutter in the other fields as some of the planes came back flying low and fast on their way back to England. Once or twice the whole sky would light up momentarily and that meant a plane going down in flames. At the corner of the field about six of our men had gathered. None of us knew where we were and my back hurt so badly that I could not carry all my equipment. J. E. Turner, the dentist, was in the group, and he took one of my bags, Major Ginder another, Corporal Boney another, and I carried the fourth. Altogether in a short time there were about thirty of us and we took off in the direction that someone suggested. Then all of a sudden I was with another group and Turner and Ginder had disappeared. The night was starry and fairly clear where I was and then suddenly I was going down a road with still another group. Every once in a while a machine gun would open up and we would scatter— then a grenade or two would put the machine gun out of action and then suddenly it was starting to get light and visibility was increasing. A machine gun opened up at a crossroad. Dodson, a bazooka man, put it out of action and we crossed the road into a field and there were two dead paratroopers and a dead German. There were only about twelve of us then—three were medics—so we all got in a ditch and put a couple of men out on the snipers who were getting in pot shots at us. My back was hurting pretty bad so I got a grenade I jumped with out of my pocket and waited for day to break.

[*Sampson*] Our little group got together and started toward the place we judged our troops might assemble. We moved slowly under concealment of hedgerows, and welcomed the sight of half a dozen paratroopers running down the road ditch. They were not of our Regiment but told us where we might find the 501st or a part of it. We went in the direction they pointed until we came under heavy enemy rifle fire and I approached a nearby farmhouse. I walked in and found the house full of wounded paratroopers . . . about twenty-five of them. It was just a three room house and the French farmer, his wife and child were there. Chaplain McGee—a splendid Protestant chaplain—was giving first aid as best he could. He had run out of bandages and since I, my assistant, and the Medic were well supplied he was very happy to see us. We all worked with the men for the better part of the day. A boy came in wounded telling us of his buddy who was shot in the back in the tall weeds about 100 yards from the house.

Chaplain McGee and I decided to try and find him. Just as we stepped out of the house (front door) a German mortar hit the back door and killed the French woman and the little girl. The poor farmer nearly went out of his head.

[*Blatt*] Lieutenant Lepsher, a demolitions officer who had taken charge, went off on a reconnaissance to see if he could locate any other paratroopers. The rest of us waited in a ditch and the day grew brighter. There was machine gun and rifle fire in the distance. . . .

When Lieutenant Lepsher came back it was about eight o'clock and bright daylight. We heard the bombers pounding the beach about three miles to our east and we could still hear machine guns and rifle fire, but the snipers around us had either withdrawn or were waiting for us to show ourselves, because no one was firing at us right then. I put on my Red Cross brassard (we had not worn them on the jump because at night the white band is too good a target). Lepsher had contacted some of the first battalion about half a mile away so we sneaked down the ditch and hedgerow back to the road right beside the machine gun that Dodson had knocked out a few hours before and started south.

At another road junction about one-half mile away, we came on about sixty paratroopers coming down the road. It was so wonderful to be back in the fold and not to feel as though one were entirely surrounded by enemies. We joined them and went down the road. We knew where we were at last, just about one mile north of where we wanted to go. As we were walking down the road, one of the flank scouts came back to the road and said there was a man with a broken leg two fields away. I left the column, and with two men to act as protection against snipers, I went over to see him. He had a fractured leg all right, but had already been given morphine. I put a splint on him, and fixed him up generally and noted his position on the map so we could pick him up later. Some sniper fired once but my riflemen scared him away. We then cut down the field to the third battalion assembly area, but there was no one there at all. However, out on the road about three hundred yards away were some Americans, both our division and the 82d, so after taking care of a couple of them, I went on down the road planning to go to the place where regimental headquarters was to be.

When I arrived, Ramey and Colonel Michalis were there. They

told me that Colonel Mosely had a broken leg and that they were leaving to go to the regimental objective—a gun position near the coast. Elements from the regiment had cleared the opening of the beach—the sea-borne troops were landed even then, and we had broken up any organized resistance in our area. They had some wounded there, and they turned the two aid stations over to me and two third-battalion medics. All the regiment personnel was going back to the beach. The farm where we were was under enemy fire especially from snipers, but they left about six riflemen as protection. All afternoon we gave plasma and put on splints and dodged the sniper fire. We wanted to clear out the wounded and get back nearer to our own people, but we had no means of evacuating the wounded, no place to send them that we knew was in operation, and besides, the whole yard of the farmhouse was filled with enemy ammunition, both small arms and mortar. It was too heavy for us to carry and we were afraid to leave it, because then the snipers would come in and take it. About four in the afternoon some gliders were towed right over us west toward Ste. Mère Eglise; it sure looked good to see them and to know that we had such air superiority that we could bring them in safely by daylight. About five miles to the west of us the gliders cut loose, and then the planes came right back over us on their way back to England. By that time we had everyone taken care of—the walking wounded were in a barn, the litter wounded in rooms of the farmhouse. Everyone had been fed and we had blacked-out one room for us during the night.

Shortly after that the first of the sea-borne troops came by. They said the road back to the beach was entirely in our hands, although there were still enemy patrols firing here and there. . . .

[*Sampson*] About six p.m., some of the patients getting worse, I decided to try to find a doctor, so I went looking for our Regimental Aid Station. I left my assistant with Chaplain McGee. After going about a mile I found a patrol of our men and they told me where to go. Since the area was under fire I avoided the road and went by way of the swamp. The deep swamp was filthy and cold but afforded good cover. I finally reached the Regimental Aid. There was quite a fight going on there. The enemy had dug in well on the high ground about 300 yards from us, and were picking off some of our men.

The enemy was gaining strength and we were losing, so about 8:30 the Officer in Command decided to withdraw to safer ground a couple of miles away. The wounded that could walk would go with them . . . the others must be left behind. The Medical Aid men drew straws to see which one remained with the wounded. A boy named Fisher drew the short straw. I told the Regimental Surgeon that I was staying with the wounded. The Germans had perpetrated so many atrocities that I thought I might be able to keep the men from getting panicky and possibly keep the Germans from adding another crime to their list. As soon as the last of our forces had left I made a white flag from a sheet and hung it out the door. One boy had just had a hand grenade go off in his pocket and the doctor, before he left, told me that only a miracle could save the boy's life. I gave the lad two blood plasma units at once and spent all night running between the seriously wounded patients and the white flag. Every fifteen minutes I would go out and wave the white flag, because I was afraid the Germans, suspecting a trap, would fire hand grenades and mortars into the house before approaching it.

All night long this went on. The boy with the grenade wound died about four a.m. in my arms. . . . The Medic and myself changed all the bandages of the men, and as I was cooking some hot chocolate I looked out and saw Germans set up a machine gun in the front yard. I grabbed the white flag and went out. A German jumped at me and stuck a gun in my stomach.

Well, a couple of paratoopers (German) marched me up the road about a quarter of a mile. One of them pushed me against a hedgerow and the two stepped back about ten feet and pulled back the bolts of their weapons. I said a quick Act of Contrition. . . . Just then there were some shots fired just a few feet over our heads. It was a German noncom firing to attract the attention of the men I was with. He came running down the road and stopped when he reached us. He was a fine looking tough soldier about twenty-five. He spoke to my two captors and told me in broken English to come with him. I told him I was a Catholic priest and showed him my credentials. And to my real amazement he snapped to attention, saluted, made a slight bow, and showed me a medal pinned inside his uniform. . . . He took me a little farther down the road to a German officer, who in turn called an Intelligence man. I explained that I was a Chaplain, knew nothing of military value and requested to be allowed to stay with my wounded men. The officer permitted this and my noncom friend took me back. The German paratroopers had ransacked the house of the little food we had, and picked up all the hand grenades that our men had left. The noncom, in a very friendly way, told me to stay with my "comrades" and that a German doctor would come in a day or so. I had to show him the wounds of all the men and practically every square inch of the house. . . . Then he left. But the paratroopers (German) dug in about the grounds and in the adjoining fields.

The wounded men had been frightened almost to death. One German had put a gun to one of the boys' head and pulled back the bolt; all the others turned their heads away. Another had shot the ceiling full of holes. The men were weak from fear and I told them that I had been too, but they were all quite calm. I spent the next few hours changing bandages and giving plasma, and fixed a bit of chocolate and what few rations we could scare up. The Germans were constantly running around outside the house, and apparently were planning to stay permanently.

The men gradually fell asleep and about ten p.m. I did so too. Just about midnight heavy shells began to fall and were landing on every side of us. One of the boys said it must be our own artillery trying to root the Germans out of this strategic high ground. The whole house bounced and shook for four hours. I put three of the men under the beds; the plaster was dropping all over the place, and the window glass had sprayed all over the room. Fourteen of the men were in one room, most of them very seriously wounded. Two men with sprained ankles were in the kitchen, and a Medic was in the barn holding down a boy who had gone out of his head, and who was trying to run out to the Germans.

About 2:30 a.m. three shells made a direct hit on the house all at once. Half of the house completely collapsed on the two boys in the kitchen. I heard one of them call out "Father Sampson," and just as I got to the door the rest of the ceiling came down on the boy. I held his head in my arm and cleared away debris till I could touch his back. I felt his heart pump very hard for about one minute and then stop. I dug in the debris until I could touch the other boy. He was crushed beyond help and was dead. The roof of the kitchen and the entire wall was blown out. . . .

I had the boys take turns in leading the others in the Lord's Prayer. . . .

A flashlight had been blown out of the house and somehow turned on. It flooded the remainder of the house in light and was sure to draw fire both from our artillery and from the enemy, so I went out to turn it off. Just as I stepped out a German soldier brushed past me running for all he was worth, and as I reached to turn out the flashlight I saw another German in the creek about five feet away. He moved a bit, and when I lifted him up he died. I gave a quick absolution, and when I turned around to go back into the house I saw a German kneeling on one knee and leaning against the house. He had a machine gun across one knee pointing straight at me. I said what was supposed to be an Act of Contrition and ran into the house. The next morning when I came out the German was still there, in the same position. He was dead.

How we ever survived that night I shall never know. . . . After the artillery was through our infantry (501st) came up to close in. The house was riddled with rifle and machine gun fire. A tracer bullet ricocheted off the ceiling, grazed my leg and set my pants on fire. I saw an American lieutenant sneaking upon our building with hand grenades. It turned out to be Lieutenant Blackmon, an All American end for Alabama, who had taken over command of company B after Captain Bogart was killed. I ran out and stopped him, yelling for all I was worth. He said that he thought there were Germans in there. The Germans who were not killed were captured. Ours was the only room left standing in the entire village. . . .

The air was scarcely empty of parachutes before General Dwight D. Eisenhower, commanding the Allied Expeditionary Force, sent word to the peoples of occupied Europe.

People of western Europe! A landing was made this morning on the coast of France by troops of the Allied Expeditionary Force. This landing is part of the concerted United Nations plan for the liberation of Europe, made in conjunction with our great Russian allies. I have this message for all of you. Although the initial assault may not have been made in your own country, the hour of your liberation is approaching.

All patriots, men and women, young and old, have a part to play in the achievement of final victory. To members of resistance movements, whether led by national or outside leaders, I say, "Follow the instructions you have received." To patriots who are not members of organized resistance groups I say, "Continue your passive resistance, but do not needlessly endanger your lives until I give you the signal to rise and strike the enemy. The day will come when I shall need your united strength. Until that day, I call on you for the hard task of discipline and restraint."

Citizens of France! I am proud to have again under my command the gallant forces of France. Fighting beside their allies, they will play a worthy part in the liberation of their homeland. Because the initial landing has been made on the soil of your country, I repeat to you with even greater emphasis my message to the peoples of other occupied countries in western Europe. Follow the instructions of your leaders. A premature uprising of all Frenchmen may prevent you from being of maximum help to your country in the critical hour. Be patient. Prepare.

As supreme commander of the Allied Expeditionary Force, there is imposed on me the duty and responsibility of taking all measures necessary to the prosecution of the war. Prompt and willing obedience to the orders that I shall issue is essential. Effective civil administration in France must be provided by Frenchmen. All persons must continue in their present duties unless otherwise instructed. Those who have common cause with the enemy and so betrayed their country will be removed. As France is liberated from her oppressors, you yourselves will choose your representatives, and the government under which you wish to live.

In the course of this campaign for the final defeat of the enemy you may sustain further loss and damage. Tragic though they may be, they are part of the price of victory. I assure you that I shall do all in my power to mitigate your hardships. I know that I can count on your steadfastness now, no less than in the past. The heroic deeds of Frenchmen who have continued their struggle against the Nazis and their Vichy satellites, in France and throughout the French Empire, have been an example and an inspiration to all of us.

This landing is but the opening phase of the campaign in western Europe. Great battles lie ahead. I call upon all who love freedom to stand with us. Keep your faith staunch—our arms are resolute—together we shall achieve victory.[8]

VII

IF YOU MAKE THE SLIGHTEST ERROR, SOMEONE DIES

Southward in the Italian Alps, OSS agent, Captain Roderick Hall,
wrote letters home concerning his mission. He deposited these with
partisans and with nuns at a convent to be mailed after the war.

Hallowe'en
Oct. 31, 1944
Andrich, Cadore
Italy

Dear Mother and Family,

Your last letters, all written in July and August, arrived in a
bunch—by parachute! The heavy cases of arms and explosives and
supplies came floating down silently through the night; and among
them was a package (with its own 'chute) which carried all the news
from home. There were birthday cards from you and Bruce, family
letters from Betsy and the Lougees and Leadbeaters, a clipping of
Wells Lewis, and lots else.

I was the only one of our team who got mail, so I read some of the
paragraphs to the others to give them a little taste of home—they were
pretty disappointed—all about Father's big tomato in the garden, and
the water shortage this summer, and the busted outboard of Bruce's.
We all got a big laugh out of the clipping which showed the chart on
the wall "My Draft Status!" and had the caption, "They were certainly breathing down my neck there for a while!" We were definitely in
a situation where "they were breathing down our necks," and could
enjoy that one heartily. However, for security reasons, I had to burn
all the mail, much as I hated to, keeping only the birthday cards, which
I have carried with me ever since.

You see, we were some 250 miles behind the front in Italy and
actually right up against the border of Germany itself—in the Italian
Alps where, as you know, I'd always wanted to fight my tiny part of
this war, anyway. The letters appeared out of the dark over a wide

419

place in the bed of the Tagliamento River near a village called "Enemonzo," about 10 miles east of Ampezzo and the same distance west of Tolmezzo. At Tolmezzo were 11,000 Nazi troops and mongoloids [Mongolians] from Turkestan, picked up in the German retreat from the Caspian and now serving as mercenaries.

We used the river flats for over 12 "supply drops," although our flaming signal fires were in full sight of Tolmezzo, on the nights when we got the signal over the regular commercial program from London to expect a plane-load. To get to the dropping zone we rode in a huge truck (captured from the Nazis) which roared down thru the winding gorges of the Tagliamento at terrific speed from Ovasta. We went so fast because it was a race to a certain road fork. We had to make it before the Germans did, if they should ever get it into their thick skulls to investigate what was going on. I believe they knew; but psychology was on our side; they imagined our partisan bands of Italian patriots so strong that any attack by them would be suicidal. Actually we had less than 100 men in our command; and the Nazis waited 'til he had the garrison in Tolmezzo built up to 14,000 men before he struck. But that happened much later.

At Ovasta, a medieval hamlet lodged on a shelf overlooking the River and ringed round by the gigantic spears and flakes of the Carnic Alps, we had our "Base" Headquarters. We had a powerful short wave set with which to communicate with Army HQ way to the south; and a room or two; and a tobacco supply composed of old "butts" and cornsilk.

I was at the Base very little, spending my time in long swings—by trail, or motorcycle, or bicycle, or climbing rope deep into zones crawling with Germans but where unarmed groups of patriots waited for help. So my returns to "Base" were always occasions for mutual celebration; it was good to get back to a bed and hot food, after sleeping in haybarns or caves and eating mushrooms and cold cornmeal, with an occasional squirrel thrown in. The days went very fast then. At "Base" there was corn on the cob, and American radio programs, and "Smitty" (Major Lloyd C. Smith, State College, Pa.) had arranged a deal with a prewar ice cream freezer in Ovara, so we had ice cream now and then—all we had to do was climb down 1500 feet to the valley floor and then climb up again.

But I'm getting 'way ahead of things. The peaks are plated with ice now; there are drifts in the passes and snow powderings in the valleys. August, everything was green and warm—we took our showers in waterfalls, went roaring up and down the village streets singing Yankee songs to the delighted grins of the war-weary people who were fed to the ears with the grim and cruel Nazi soldiers.

You know how long I'd worked on this Alps thing—well, I finally sold it to GHQ. . . . We put together a team of five: Major Smith, who'd won the DSC getting 13 stranded nurses out of Nazi hands in Albania; 1st Lt. Joe Lukitsch—a paratrooper who came over on the boat with me; Sgt. Victor Malespino, interpreter who worked for me when I was chief instructor in the Spy School in the mountains outside Algiers; 1st Cl. Seaman Stan Sbeig from Bridgeport—radioman.

Smitty was to organize and direct partisans in Carnia; and I was to do the same in Cadore, having also the mission of closing the Cortina road. Once inside German-occupied territory, we were entirely on our own, as autonomous as soldiers-of-fortune in a Chinese war or banana republic revolution. But I guess General Devers and General Alexander had faith in us because they okayed the deal, 100%, one afternoon on the shores of Lake Bolzeno, where I'd gone to explain the project.

Of course it wasn't as easy as that; the project had to be drafted as carefully as a case before the Supreme Court; and the preparations were as detailed as an expedition to Everest—maps, sleeping bags, foreign money, climbing gear, radio cyphers, medicine, and just about a thousand damn things—all weighed and triple checked.

Finally, the night of August 1st, we gathered under the wing of a big 4-motored Lancaster at Brindisi airport. We had on "Strip-tease" suits, against the cold at 10,000 feet, and looked like Eskimos. We sweated rivers—and froze later over Udine.

The ride was painful for we were cramped in amongst the containers of our supplies, and the roar of the engines was overwhelming— also, naturally, the prospect of a parachute jump into enemy country at night, or any other time, is none too comforting.

I realize this sounds like a story, but it's about the way it happened (leaving out the gaudier details); and I know you've been wondering why you haven't heard from me for the last three months. Naturally we couldn't tell anyone what was up.

At Brindisi we did not know just where we'd drop. A couple of places I'd been counting on were ruled out in the last two days because of Nazi troop movements. We climbed up thru the small hole in the bottom of the plane and found we were bound for Mt. Pala in the foothills of the Alps of Carnia, bad news for me, as it was some 85 miles from the Cortina area. Smitty and I squabbled for the privilege of being "first out" on the jump, but he outranked me.

We nearly did not make it, as the pilot could not find the right pattern of ground fires in the right place. Jerry, was, aside from shooting at us with flak, apparently lighting a few signals to decoy us. Finally the word came back over the inter-com that the right fires had been spotted, but in the wrong place. One of the crew opened the hatch, and after a dying run by the plane, Smitty, Vic, and Stan disappeared thru the hole—just like that. Joe Lukitsch and I swung our legs into the hole and looked down. With a full moon the tumbled hills far below looked eerie; the fires looked small and distant—they were, about 2500 feet. Suddenly the green light blazed and the bell rang on the wall of the ship, and I dropped thru, Joe right after me. The 'chute opened with a crack, but I had a bad spin and the shroud lines were twisting rapidly—if they twist enough, the 'chute collapses. I fought for about 1000 feet before the twists came out.

Then I looked around. With the night breezes Joe sailed past like a shot out of a cannon. Below, there was nothing but hill, woods and rocks. It looked like a trap. I was sure it was when I landed—between two wicked spikes of limestone, doing a couple of back somersaults down a gully into some saplings. There wasn't a person around, just complete silence. I cut my way out of the 'chute and got out my automatic. For twenty minutes there wasn't a sound. Then I made for a low, bare hillock near by and in a little while the others came up. It was 2 A.M. The fires were phony all right. Smitty had landed near them and seen a man running away.

About 700 yards away a fire shone on the side of Mt. Pala, but we couldn't find the path; which was lucky as the fire came from a house the Germans were burning, we found out later. They were too drunk to pay any attention to the drop.

We hid in a deep swale until dawn, and then I went to a farmhouse to ask questions. By noon we had made contact with some local partisans and later were on our way back into the mountains. We felt that we had been granted a miracle. The whole operation was in full sight of Nazi observation towers in the plain below; and the lack of reception and the hideous rock pile we landed on should have made us all casualties and easy prisoners. Aside from cuts and bruises we were O.K. It took the Nazis a week to start chasing us.

On August 12th I started out alone for the "Cadore," about 30 miles from Ovasta, crossing Lavardet Pass; made contact with the partisans around San Stefano, and started work. The Cadore was tough, because there were Nazi garrisons in all the towns, and the area was much more populated and desirable to Jerry than desolate Carnia. Cortina alone had 1000 picked troops to guard the 5000 wounded Nazis in the hotels and hospitals there.

The Air Corps would not "drop" to me in Cadore—mountains too high; altho I spent 18 days at a dropping zone on the Austrian border (the Val Visdende)—watching the Army build its "Alpine Line." Whatever you've heard about that in the papers is direct intelligence I gathered. Finally we rigged a system for back-packing arms and explosives across the ranges from Carnia. I traveled back and forth and round about all over the area, always in uniform, often 500 yards from Nazi garrisons, or walking past their front doors at night, and earned a pair of legs like cast iron.

So, by the end of September, I had been able to get an organization of 500 men on its feet, despatch reams of important intelligence to GHQ, blow out the standard gauge R.R. from Venice and the electric R.R. through Cortina to Austria, and eleven highway bridges, effectively blocking all routes through the Alps north of Venice. Mr. Nazi was proportionately furious, the more so when we attacked three garrisons, taking around 187 prisoners.

But by the end of September there was snow on the highest peaks, and the campaign in Italy had changed to a holding action, designed to keep as many Nazi troops there as possible, so they wouldn't reinforce the other fronts. Our time-schedule was badly upset. We got the terrific news, too, that Jerry planned to turn over Carnia to the savages from Turkestan, who would massacre all the Italians and take the farms for themselves—thus giving future Germany an area deep into Italy, populated by a solid block of pro-Nazi Mongols.

Smitty worked himself green, getting in arms for the poor Italians and begging to have Tolmezzo bombed—but GHQ wouldn't bomb, for some unknown reason. All things taken together, we felt we had to stay until the front had advanced considerably, so as to help the Army as much as possible in cutting the supply lines.

In spite of the shadow that hung over Carnia, everything was going very well in the upper Piave River valley in Cadore. At the end of September I heard about a large group of Italian patriots—all ex-

Alpini soldiers—on the *other* side of Cortina, over near Selva-di-Cadore. They needed help. So I made up my pack and started out, contouring the peaks just at the line where the bare rock jumps from the steep scrub slopes. It took three days to make the 55 miles and involved 32,000 feet of climbing. But from August 12th 'til now (3 months, or a little less) I'd been living and working at 7000 feet and often going to 9000 feet on reconnaissance, so it wasn't too tough. I lost some time skirting the Marmarole range and Mt. Antelao, as I had to slip through patrols of 500 Nazi Alpenjaeger who were out hunting partisans. And the last day was in a snowstorm and a foot of new snow over the flank of Mt. Pelmo.

This group was all I'd heard, being all ex-officers and non-coms of the Alpini troops who knew every trail and crag of all the Dolomites. Their HQ was only four hours by foot from Cortina, just over the range I had skied in 1937–38. I got a message back to "Base" requesting a drop. The plane came, two weeks later, in the middle of a Nazi drive on partisans around Cortina, so we did not get the drop, being unable to light signal fires. We climbed up in the rock of the precipices for five straight days and watched the Nazi hunting for us in the forests below. Each evening they fired cannon and machine guns up into the rock gullies—just in case; and we watched the tracers smack on the rock all around us. We couldn't do anything, having no guns. But they never really saw us, and finally went away.

Then I got crushing news: the 14,000 troops at Tolmezzo had over-run Carnia from the south, while 3000 Nazis, brought in from Austria, attacked from the North. Smitty and the rest were caught between the two forces, and I haven't heard a whisper about them since—over three weeks. I feel sure he must have got through and escaped toward Yugoslavia, that being one of our exit plans before we started.

But for three weeks now I've been the only Allied Officer in the whole Alps—and without a radio. Just waiting for some break and trying to keep up the partisans' courage. Not that the time has been wasted. I managed to get contact with certain people in Bolzano and perfected a plan for blowing out one of the tunnels on the R.R. through the Brenner; sent the explosives off to them disguised as crates of jam last week!

Then, too, I managed to sign up a couple of electrical engineers and we worked out a scheme for crippling the entire telephone and telegraph net in the Alps here—important, because, of the Alpine Line fortifications Jerry is working so feverishly on. And of course there's been a wad of intelligence coming in: for example, by a stroke of pure luck, I got the map of the Nazi troop dispositions as planned for the defense of the Brenner—stuff like that; another case, the HQ of the Japanese secret service (Hotel Corona, Cortina).

It has snowed every day for three weeks, and is still at it, so movement is out of the question, as Jerry can track you too easily in the snow. However, recently I made contact with an officer (Captain Joe Benucci) down in the Venetian plain below Belluno; so things are looking up. He has a radio.

At present I'm in the tiny hamlet of Andrich, part of the community of Vallada, three miles west of Cencenighe; whiling away the hours reading *Ivanhoe* and some 1939 copies of *Collier's* someone dug up! The fine Italian family here with whom I'm staying will mail this after the war.

The position is really good, as it's plunk in the middle of the Alpine Line the Nazis are building. They're laboring over some beautiful targets for us to blow up when and if we get a "drop." But you don't need to worry: we're getting to be old hands at the art of running in under the Nazi's nose and blowing the shoestrings out of his boots before he knows what's happened. If he ever catches up with me, all he'll find is another Yank who parachuted from a crashing plane—of whom there are many hiding away in the Alps—and waiting for the end of the war.

How I'll get out, I don't know, although I wish I could give you some assurance. The possibility of crossing the Swiss frontier is out of the picture now because of the snow (it came a whole month early this year). Carnia is solid Nazi, now, so a dash to Yugoslavia—150 miles—is none too good. So it looks like North or South. North, to fall back with the Nazis when they retreat from Italy and take up this line; South, to try to filter through and meet the Allies when they advance. Either possibility isn't bad. But the best one is, of course, the end of the war before the Nazis move back here in force. That's what I'm hoping for.

No matter what, it may be some time after the Armistice before I get out to wire you—having to hide and linger around awhile before showing myself. So that's why I'm writing this—the family here will mail it with the Armistice.

The mission (called Mercury Eagle) has already paid for itself and been a success. We got a lot more accomplished than anyone thought possible; luck has been with us all the way, it looks like. If Smitty is O.K., everything is all right; and I have high hopes for the future. Luck has really played a big part, with countless hair-breadth escapes from Mr. Hitler's animals, and universal success in whatever we undertook. It's only regretted that we did not get even more support from Rome, for opportunities were boundless in August and September.

It would be a lie for me to say that this had been an adventure or good time for me. True, at times there have been light moments, a few; and at other times the work has been long and exhausting. I've seen more gorgeous scenery than three men will in a lifetime—sunrises and sunsets among the peaks, moonlight glimmering on glaciers, storms swirling around tremendous pillars of rock, cataracts, forest glades, ancient villages.

But full enjoyment is not truly there when you are on eternal guard against guns appearing behind every rock and shadow. The "threat" never leaves you, asleep or awake; and I have not lain down yet to sleep without a cocked pistol at my right hand.

In a land where you regularly have to hike and climb eleven miles to reach a point only three miles away by road, there's usually more to occupy the mind than breathless vistas of beauty. You are usually "breathless" from the close acquaintance with the bare bone and sinews of that which makes up this magnificent scenery—as seen at a distance.

It has not been sport, but rather a deadly business—an unending struggle to plan each tiny detail for days ahead, when you really don't know what's going to happen in the next fifteen minutes. If you make the slightest error, someone dies; I found that out quickly. It seems as though life and death has been in my hands since this started, for as only representative of law and order wherever I've gone, I have to sit as judge at trials of criminals and spies; to determine the fate of prisoners taken; to issue orders for the general good that yet meant violence to someone along the line before they were consummated. It was the one feature of this job I did not foresee, and would have avoided with all my heart. I have saved many, many lives that would otherwise have been lost—Nazi prisoners, circumstantial cases, petty cases—for the law of the partisans before I arrived was death for anything or anyone shady. But, for the rest, and for my mistakes—well, I guess I've forgotten how to smile. My hair is quite grey, now.

Militarily, I've thought of it as a game of chess, with the whole

Alps as a board, whereon you try to outguess the enemy and move always into a square where he won't come. The feeling of being hunted is something that can never leave you; it's very tiring, and requires fierce self-control when you have so much else that requires the best sense and judgment you can exert. This village of Andrich happens to be a square where Mr. Nazi won't think of looking for awhile.

If there has been any recompense for us, it has come, not from the scenery, but from the reactions of the people—persecuted, starved and enslaved by the Nazis. We've been able to bring them medicine; a few of the comforts of life (cigarettes, coffee, sugar); a little money; but mostly *hope*. There's nothing anyone will ever be able to say or show that will make me think there's anything good about a German. The atrocities are true; I've seen them; and they're universal. Villages burned, children hung, men tortured, old people turned out in the snow, civilians shot for sport—I've seen those things with my own eyes. These hideous acts yield a crop of men whose fury knows no bounds— they make up the partisan bands I've helped organize; they're the sword of God, if there ever has been one in history.

If any of you ever travel to these parts in the future, don't be afraid to mention my name. It's known from one end of the Alps to the other (a fame far out of proportion to what I've been able to do). You'll receive hospitality undreamed of, assuming you're in the little inns and with the real inhabitants.

This job hasn't been world-shaking and may never be recorded even in Army records. But I've told about it, so that you will know, even if it hasn't been as much as many, many others have done in this war, at least I've done something.

Love to all,
Steve

January 1, 1945

Dear Family

There wasn't much chance to wish you all the Season's Greetings, but you know I was thinking about you, each and every one. Base Headquarters 'way down in Southern Italy advised me they had sent you a letter in my behalf. I hope it got to you in time to make Christmas free of doubt and worry. That's one big, tough trouble with this game—the secrecy. But somebody has to do this work, unsung and wearing as it may be—just like your job at the Signal Corps, Mother;

or Bruce's job at GE. It's all important. Somebody has to do it. . . .

My Christmas was mostly work, of the unpleasant, desperate kind. The night of December 23rd I got word in my shack Hq. up on the side of a mountain which looks like Bartlett Mountain, that the Air Corps had made a drop of supplies for us the day before 6 miles down a valley toward a big Todt camp. Next A.M., before dawn, we started off on skis to pick up the boodle. It was strictly a race between us and Mr. Nazi, as he knew all about the drop by then of course.

We went up over Fernazza Pass at about 6500 feet and swooped down the valley to the Drop Zone. I got the peasants to help and we got all the supplies out of the danger zone by noon, on sleds. No Nazis in sight—only a ski patrol of two men who blundered in as we were working. I scared them away by making faces and other threatening gestures. Maybe they figured I was German, in this paratroop uniform —anyway, no one unfriendly came around afterwards.

Once the crisis was passed I succumbed to a heavy fever and decided to rest in the village nearby, Nazi or no Nazi. So with the local Hitlerites digging the jive at a dancehall a mile and a half down the road, I spent a delightful Christmas Eve with an old friend, the Countess. Cookies, tea, apples—and at midnight candles on the tree. We talked about our respective families so far away. By morning the fever was gone and I left to follow the men.

The Countess has been my link with the Nazis. She's Swiss or Argentinian, or something—anyway neutral; and a confidante of the Nazi Political Administrator for Belluno Province. This bird, Dr. Lauer, runs around in a Farnum automobile with a bodyguard of 30 Nazi toughs. Thru the Countess I've been working on him and have him to the point where he's neutral! At least he and the Countess agreed over the phone to delay the official report of the "drop" until after Christmas; that's what gave us time enough to salvage the supplies! I sent Lauer a message, that I'd guarantee his personal security any time he wanted to take a powder and escape the Gestapo. I understand he laughed and said right now I was the one to watch out.

Also on my hook is the local chief of the Gestapo! When the Nazis picked up a couple of Limeys and one of our head civilian officials in the Comitate of National Liberation, we persuaded this Gestapo man to rig up a fake prison escape for them. I realize "You can't do business with Hitler," but in this game you sometimes have to. This sounds like story-book stuff, but actually it's rather prosaic. They're all worried over their own skins, and it's just a matter of picking on the ones who are most worried—and most useful. I've become something of a myth to them—"the American who has been here five months that no one can catch" so that helps. They're all so frightened they cling to anything that looks good.

Well, since my last letter (now reposing in a bottle under five feet of snow) there's been a lot of hard work and ups-and-downs. If the war continues I'll have buried bottles all over the Alps, for many of my maps and secret documents are so cached.

I left Andrich November 17th and went up over the flank of Marmolada Peak again to rejoin the Brigade. An exhausting trip of 13 hours. Have to use this route to avoid the big Nazi garrison at Alleghe. A request had arrived asking me to blow out the Cortina railroad. I had just 40 lbs. of plastic, but figured I could get into the machinery of the electric sub station at Cortina. We made the plans. And a couple of nights later the Fascist Secret Service picked up one of my key men! Under threat of torture he turned yellow and led Nazi patrols to the hiding places of eleven of his men. Two nights after that he returned with twenty Nazis to the house where I was staying, but of course I had cleared out. They beat up my hosts, an elderly couple, and stole all the food, but did not burn the house down—their usual custom. This man Tell was then told to write down all he knew—it took him five days—so now the Nazis have the complete goods on me. This plays in my favor, as now I can play in the open without the bother of airtight secrecy. Tell found he could *not* do business with Hitler; they're going to shoot him without trial. Worst feature of all this was that Tell also handed over to Jerry all the plastic, thus delaying the R.R. job.

We set up Brigade Hq. at Fontana Fredda—which means "Cold Fountain"—a cow barn in a hidden basin which used to be one of Civetta's glaciers. The night of November 25th a plane came over at 3:30 A.M., but I had my suspicions and told the men *not* to light the signal fires. It was a tough decision to make. Next day we packed up and moved five miles to another cow shed, this one under the big glacier on Mt. Pelmo. Name was "Fiorentina," which means "Little Flower Meadow"; but it was just another icicle shop to us. Very cold with 5 feet of snow. An hour after we moved three groups of Nazis appeared over the rim of the basin at Fontana Fredda; they were investigating the plane business. Seeing a dead camp, they came no nearer to investigate, which was lucky.

Then for three weeks we made the trip every night to Fontana Fredda to have a crew always ready in case of a drop. It was tough work for me without skis the first week: ten miles a night in 2 feet of loose snow. Finally Ettore, the Brigade Commander, found some skis.

About December 15th we heard that the Nazis were going to send a big force into the area to try to pick us up. So we moved again, to the hut deep in the forest up on the side of Mt. Fernazza. We still manned the DZ every night. I had had a message from Rome December 12th which promised an immediate drop from fighter bombers. But by December 23rd I figured the deal had fallen through. The men were in bad shape from all the work; we had influenza, dysentery, frostbite, and bloody feet. So at 4 P.M. I made the decision that all must go home.

I promised to try to get a radio and said maybe in a month we could start work again. They did not want to quit, but I knew that their weakened condition was too dangerous for the situation. They sang the "Mountain Aria" for me, most beautiful of all the Alpini songs and which always brings tears to my eyes. Then, they trailed out into the dusk. An hour later, as I was gloomily contemplating the fire alone, a courier stumbled in the door and said there had been a *day* drop by five fighter planes the day before. You know the rest.

We got mortars, funny papers, machine guns, soap, carbines, cigarettes, explosives, and a pile of assorted stuff. One was a very special secret item made by the Automatic Signal Corporation, which will be an enormous help to us, saving hours and hours of work and much danger! It was a great Christmas for everybody.

We hid all the drop material and scattered to hide and wait and see what the Nazis would do about it. To date, they haven't done anything!

I went off alone to duck into my den in Andrich, and made the trip up over Marmolada again with skis. This time I froze both feet literally as hard as boards. It was on a stretch of 1000 yards, up a concave north slope where the sun does not hit. Snow was 5 feet deep and absolutely loose all the way to the bottom. Took me five and one-half hours to make that 1000 yards, even with skis. I'm getting a bit fed up with that Marmolada trip.

Have been in bed for a week with feet packed in grease. Feeling has returned and it looks like good luck again. In bed, I designed a newspaper which the CNL is going to print for the entire Alps area.

Also, directed search parties for three bomber crews who bailed out over here the other day. We've found only two men of them, but I have hopes to get the others before the Nazis do. Expect to rejoin the Brigade for the attack on Cortina in a couple of days. I knew where the Hq. for the Jap Secret Service is hiding there, and believe I will hand them a New Year's present to improve friendly relations—a 50-lb. time bomb.

The little brown brothers will no doubt be annoyed to see their dinner table sailing through the room one evening soon around 8 P.M. But, then, they always were ungrateful for free presents from us.

"That looks like the top of the news from here," as Fulton Lewis says. Maybe in my next I can give you a more exciting installment—this past period has been mostly hard work and heartbreak. Oh yes—the plane which hovered over our DZ that early morning Nov. 25th—it was Fascist, sent out as a decoy! Probably loaded with bombs, which was not what we were waiting for, exactly. So the fateful decision was right, after all.

You've probably heard that my Captaincy came through—Dec. 7 —Pearl Harbor Day. If you're interested in ribbons and such stuff: I've picked up three "Action" stars on the Italian Campaign ribbon and will probably get the Purple Heart, deaf in my right ear from a shell blast and had my left wrist scratched up by fragments—like the feet, minor things anyone could get, but they seem to hand out medals for nothing these days.

If this war doesn't end soon, I'm going to register for voting up here. I've grown and shaved off five moustaches out of sheer boredom. My Italian—incorporating all the bad grammar of my teachers and innumerable cuss words—is quite fluent. The French is more grammatical, but suffers from a lack of profanity.

Well, family, I hope I beat this letter home. Friends are going to mail you my map-case which contains diary and other things.

All my best love and affection to all,

Steve[9]

(On his last mission, with both feet badly frozen and swollen, Captain Hall was picked up by the Fascist police, turned over to the Nazi SS guards, and was tortured for two weeks before his death on 20 February 1945.)

VIII

YOU WOULD BE PROUD OF THE
AMERICAN SOLDIER

In the Central Pacific, the American thrust toward Tokyo had begun with the Gilbert Islands in November, 1943 and, by the summer of 1944, had expanded through the Marshalls to the Marianas, within range of Japan itself. Troops stormed Saipan, recaptured Guam, battered the Palu group, and cleared the way for MacArthur's return to the Philippines.

Ground forces landed on Leyte, 20 October 1944. With the occupation of Mindoro, GI's swept down on Luzon and entered Manila, 6 February 1945.

In a letter to his aunt, Protestant Chaplain Stewart W. Hartfelter recounts the action in the Philippines.

No one should sell the Jap soldier short. In the two previous campaigns in which our division participated, the Japs we met were poorly fed, were suffering from disease and jungle rot, were poorly equipped and had low morale. The latter we learned from the prisoners we captured. But here in the Philippines the Jap is a different soldier. He is nasty and rugged; he is a savage fighter; he is well equipped; he is efficient in the use of arms; he is in excellent physical condition; he is very much a formidable foe. Our liberation of these islands is not an easy task and simply because Manila has been turned over to the Filipino government does not mean that these islands have now been completely liberated. True, the Japs have withdrawn from the valleys, but they have gone to the mountains where, for the past three years, they have dug elaborate caves and tunnels in which to store their supplies, ammunition, and weapons. These also serve as entrenchments for themselves where they are fairly safe from our air power and much of our artillery.

If you will look at a map and study it, you will notice that hundreds of square miles of these Philippines are made up of mountainous regions. These mountains rise sometimes to a height of 4,000 feet and

General Douglas MacArthur. *Below:* GI's raise the flag on Leyte in the Philippines.

are steep, rugged, and have very little foliage which our men can use for cover as they scale the mountain. The infantrymen have to move forward in the open in the face of fierce Jap machine gun, sniper, and mortar fire. So when you read that our casualties are light, it simply means that they are light in comparison with those suffered by the Nips. We are losing a goodly number of men, but we are getting more than ten Japs for every one of ours which they get.

Though the infantryman is the one who has to take the final inches of ground, and much of it has to be won in vicious hand-to-hand fighting with bayonets, yet too much cannot be said for our American artillery. Their accuracy is phenomenal and is far superior to the Jap artillery. The Jap 77 mm. gun is their best artillery weapon. The American infantryman could never move forward if he did not have the artillery covering him. The American superior air power is of inestimable value, for our ground forces can now fight without fear of attacks from the air. The Japs bomb us occasionally at night, but their attacks are small and do very little damage. . . .

Let me now give you a word picture of the civilians here in the Philippines and the kind of an existence they have had during the past three years. . . .

In the rural areas they [the Japs] confiscated food and livestock, stole clothing and especially blankets, raped the women and especially the young girls of 14 and 15 years of age, and forced the men to labor for them without paying them even so much as a starvation wage. These are the people I have met and seen. All of these Philippine Islands are primarily rural areas. Most of the children I have seen are suffering from extreme cases of malnutrition, tuberculosis, and malaria run rampant; people are pleading for blankets to keep them from suffering from the cold, chilly nights. I have seen tiny children who have been orphaned when the Japs slew their parents for objecting to their taking food, clothing and stock. No American living in our native land can ever understand what these people in occupied lands have gone through and suffered.

Naturally, you have been asking yourself, "Well, I wonder what the United States is doing now to help these destitute people? . . ."

A few days ago one of our patrols came back from the mountains. The men were tired, tattered and torn, unshaven and dirty. There is nothing about that which is unusual. But tenderly cuddled in the arms of one of these men was a nine-months-old baby girl. Her mother and daddy had been slain by the Japs and she had been left lying in the brush. She was suffering from severe exposure and hunger, having been there for about three days. Our public relations officer here at headquarters immediately contacted nearby civilian families and found a home that could adopt her.

What about the needed medical care of the civilians in general? Our army doctors are doing the best they can to take care of the most needy cases. This means an extra burden on our doctors, as they are kept exceedingly busy taking care of our wounded, but they still find time for this clinical work. Just a couple of evenings ago a young mother carrying her baby stopped in my tent and asked if we had a doctor near. Her baby was running a temperature. Our medical officer lives in the next tent to mine, and hearing what she said, he came over and took the mother and baby to our dispensary and gave the baby the best of medical attention. I have seen old men and women, young children and older children, receiving care in our army hospitals for sickness and sometimes for wounds received from the Japs. You would be proud of the American soldier if you could see the way he opens his heart to those in distress.

How are these civilians able to earn a living? The American Armed Forces are now employing hundreds of civilian workers to labor in our camps and build installations. For example, at our headquarters in the rear fifty men were employed for three weeks to build a chapel of bamboo. They were paid a standard wage as skilled carpenters, and the chapel is beautiful in its quaintness. . . .

The last picture I want to paint in words is a hasty sketch of what my ministry has been like here in the Philippines. I have five services on Sundays. My first is at 8:30 here in our lovely chapel at head-quarters. From here I go to the portable hospital which is attached to our division. My third service is with our engineer battalion and the fourth and fifth are with our quartermaster and ordnance units. During the week I have held as many as nine services. These have been with the combat troops. In addition to this I visit the hospitals at least five times a week and there I spend worthwhile hours talking to my wounded men. It is a great source of satisfaction to see that these men receive such splendid and expert care. None of us will ever know the great number of lives which have been saved by blood plasma, the sulfa drugs, and penicillin. Then, too, I have my sad work at the cemetery and keeping the records of the burials of my men.

Our United States cemeteries are hallowed ground, and when I look on the row on row of white crosses they represent more than the markings of a number of graves. . . .

Perhaps you have been wondering more about what kind of services I hold for our combat troops and the conditions under which these services are held. . . .

For three days several of our rifle and heavy weapons companies had been fighting inch by inch up the steep side of a mountain ridge. The Japs were well dug in and were entrenched in their caves and tunnels. They rained machine gun and mortar fire down on our men. The sun beat down with vengeance and for thirty six hours our men had to fight without water. But as casualties fell they still moved forward and near the crest of the range they engaged the Japs in hand-to-hand fighting. Early in the morning the crest was reached and secured. First the men buried our dead in temporary graves, then lay down to rest. A few days later these men buried on the mountain were removed to one of our United States Armed Force's cemeteries. . . .

That afternoon Father Rogers and I climbed to the top of the range to see our men and hold services for them. From the crest we could look down across the opposite valley and see the enemy there in their dug-in position. On the crest one was within range of enemy machine gun and sniper fire.

My Protestant men kept watch from our secured positions while the Catholic men dropped back below the crest and attended mass. Then the Catholic men held their positions as my men dropped back to attend my service and receive communion. That was an unforgettable moment. Every man on that mountain that day attended either the Catholic mass or my Protestant service.

No words can hope to describe what I felt in my heart as I looked into the faces of those men, faces that had been unshaven for days, faces into which had been ground the grime and dust and sweat from hours and days of desperate fighting, faces that were drawn from exhaustion and fatigue, eyes that were bloodshot from the tortures of battle, lips that were cracked from those thirty-six long hours without water, and clothes that were torn by death that passed by. . . .

As evening hastened on and the men began preparing to dig in their foxholes, Father Rogers and I started down the mountainside. At the foot of the mountain we stopped in our battalion aid station to see the wounded that had been brought down from a nearby mountain. There we found six civilians also waiting for treatment. They were refugees from the mountains. One was a woman, thin and pale. Two were men, weakened from long hours of forced labor. The other three were children. Their big, brown eyes were filled with fear and terror. To them strangers had come to mean suffering and pain. One little five-year-old girl had a compound fracture of the right arm, the five-year-old boy had an infected foot, and the other, a little six-year-old girl, had been shot through the right shoulder twenty-five days before by a Jap sniper. As I started to leave and passed by a stretcher where one of our wounded men lay, he took me by the hand and said, "Chappie, if we have to go through all this hell to prevent all this suffering by tiny, innocent children, then it is worth it."[10]

IX

DIG IN!

General George S. Patton's Third Army had swept across France. The Yanks entered Paris on 25 August 1944. British and Canadian soldiers hit the Netherlands as the Americans swung north into Belgium and Luxembourg. Other GI's plunged ashore in southern France in August, struck Toulon and Marseilles, and moved on up the Rhone Valley. Supported by the French Underground, the Americans crossed the Vosges Mountains and joined the northern armies on the Rhine. France and Belgium were liberated by the end of October, 1944.

The Germans, displaying desperate fighting ability, counterattacked into Belgium and Luxembourg in December. But the heroic stand by the forces at Bastogne and the Allied attack from the north and south contained the German breakthrough in the Battle of the Bulge.

Noncom Richard H. Montgomery of the 75th Infantry Division describes the fight at Wy, Belgium.

The regiment arrived in Hasselt on the night of December 19th. We marched all that night and finally at dawn arrived at our bivouac area in a large farmhouse. We spent all day parking our extra equipment and moving it into a large storage room in Hasselt. The night of the 20th we loaded on trucks and headed in the direction of the barely audible cannon fire. It was a cold all-night ride in which nobody could get any rest, the fourth such night, as the crowded 40 and 8's had been equally as miserable. By this time we heard a rumor from the civilians that the Germans were coming. We laughed, as that was ridiculous and impossible, and everybody knew it.

In the morning we stopped by some 155's which were bellowing interminably and had some heated C-rations prepared by the kitchen. Our last hot chow had been in France some time back. We waited most of the day for orders and finally marched up in front of the 155's about five hundred yards and dug in, not too deeply at first, and soon we could hear a terrific artillery barrage out in front of us and began to get scared, too scared to sleep, although we had arranged for a change of the guard. By morning the holes were pretty deep. Some of the boys had hit water.

It was very cold but we still had all our equipment, shelter halves and blankets, and sleeping bags. That same morning, the morning of the 21st, about 10:00 A.M., a German paratrooper killed a civilian some place in front of our positions. Still there was no military or official information concerning a German offensive. We spent the day digging new foxholes fifty yards in front of the old ones. (Some damned officer thought we didn't have enough to do.) By this time everybody was at the other person's throat. We were all dead tired and the boys were beginning to rebel. The captain arranged for us to get some sleep in a barn with only a skeleton force out in the foxholes to guard the front.

I pulled early guard that night, and this was our sixth night without sleep, from 7:00 P.M. to 11:00. We moved out at midnight, back up to the crossroads near the 155's. Here we dropped packs, and hand grenades were issued. There we stood in ranks until daylight, waiting for trucks which apparently were lost. When the trucks did come it started to rain and I was in an open truck. We rode all day in a tremendous convoy which seemed to go through the same town every three hours regularly. We were fooling hell out of somebody. My truck got lost from the outfit but not from the convoy. We were very miserable. Our feet seemed to be a part of the steel floor bed of the truck. The cold was unbearable. We had some compensation though—the 1st sergeant was in the back of the truck with us and just as miserable as the rest.

All that night the convoy rolled on. The rain turned to wet snow. Finally at dawn we halted on what appeared to be a logging road. We dismounted and formed a column on both sides of the road with five-yard intervals between men. My squad went off to the right flank looking for snipers. We didn't find them and reformed on the road where the general was passing out hand grenades to the men. I was already carrying a B.A.R. (Browning Automatic Rifle) and all the ammunition my frozen feet could move so I didn't take any. We moved up a mile or so and dug in a perimeter defense around an antiaircraft battery. There wasn't anything between us and the enemy, but nobody told us. About noon our air force started coming over very high and in endless procession. The first group immediately began to draw German A.A. fire and about ten planes came down in flames, apparently disintegrating completely in the air. We didn't see many parachutes. Then the Jerry planes started coming in groups of four and flying low. Some dog fights developed with our fighters. A P-47 came over us about one hundred yards in the air with a Messerschmitt right on his tail. Our A.A. battery swung their machine guns at him—but too late. The P-47 crashed and exploded. The Jerry tried to pull up but he crashed too. Then a P-38 started down. We could almost feel the pilot trying to turn his plane over so he could bail out, but the controls wouldn't respond. He tried three times and then crashed and exploded.

We got out of our holes to move out and were lined up in the field. A P-47 dived on us as if to strafe but he didn't, Thank God! We moved to a new location and dug in, stayed here for two hours or so and moved back to a new place and dug in. About dark we started marching. It was Christmas Eve. We walked to a new position up a long hill. I threw away my gas mask on the way up the hill. We were all very disgusted, tired and cold. The officers halted us at the top of the hill and brought up hot chow and plenty of it—our first hot meal in a long time and our last for a long time, forever for some of us. The colonel came up and gave us a short pep talk. It didn't do much good, at least not as much as the hot meal by a long shot. Lt. Dowler sent me out to the right flank as security with orders to shoot at anything that moved. I did and almost got a second lieutenant. (Most of the boys seemed sorry that I had missed and expressed their regrets.) We stayed there for what seemed like a long time and finally we moved out with as much silence as possible and started a long slow march through the woods. We crept along, for hours it seemed, until the men were going to sleep every time we stopped. I saw General Mickle walk past once. He had on a soft cap which stood out as everyone else had on steel helmets. We had been briefed slightly and knew that we were supposed to move into a town where our reconnaissance had reported there was no opposition. It was a poor job of reconnaissance we found out later. Finally we came to a complete halt and received orders to dig in. Everybody dropped in his tracks and immediately went to sleep despite the intense cold.

We were awakened by a short artillery barrage which was bursting high over a few houses which we could see in front of us. Then our heavy machine guns opened up about one hundred fifty yards to my left and the attack commenced. Nobody could find anybody. The Germans replied to the machine guns with a few rounds of 88's and immediately silenced them. I heard shrapnel flying through the trees for the first time. My squad was together—too much together—and Sanchez, our first scout who had seen action before on Attu, was trying to spread them out. We hit the open field in front of us on the double and in short rushes advanced on the town [Wy]. There was a company in front of us and they had already penetrated into the first street and had pushed on by the time my platoon got there. We reassembled on the street and the officers came up and told us to dig in—in the middle of the street! This was madness and we tried to tell them, but they just became more insistent. The 88's started coming and I ran in the nearest house where I stayed, as my squad was supposed to remain there. Sanchez took off toward the Burp guns which were winging bullets our way. S/Sgt. Uhler, squadron leader, and his assistant, Dodd, were attempting to dig in alongside a small building outside.

I was pretty hungry and with my little knowledge of French talked an old lady into frying some ham and eggs for me and my assistant B.A.R. man, Dawson Jack Brown. They surely tasted good and I began to feel a little better. My feet commenced to thaw a little and pretty soon Jack and I went outside and started to dig in. Lt. Hipp came along and told us to move after we got a good hole started. I had a few words with him and he got pretty mad, so I moved and as soon as he left we went back in the house. The old lady went out to get us some more eggs and was wounded in the foot by an 88. Pretty soon we heard the cry, "Retreat, tanks are coming." This retreat cost us plenty. We ran out of the town and an airplane came down over us and dropped three bombs which to this day I feel were meant personally for me. I looked over my shoulder and saw them coming just in time to dive face down into a little stream.

We were ordered to dig in out in the open field. Jack told the lieutenant he wasn't going to dig his own grave and to hell with it. We retreated back into the woods. Equipment was falling left and right, ammunition, rifles, overcoats, arctics, machine guns, gas masks, and even helmets. Men were running everywhere for their lives. All semblance of organization disappeared. Finally, I heard T/Sgt. Tupper calling in his inimitable voice for the first platoon to reassemble. I threw my overcoat away as did Brown and headed for him. The lieutenant and three others went back into town to carry out some wounded. One was Red Collins, an Indiana boy and a good friend of mine. Tupper led the rest of us back into the town. There weren't many in the platoon who came.

Then Tupper and I went out to gather up rifles and ammunition for the men who were still in the town. Tupper led me over to where our 3rd squad had been ordered to dig in. Two of the boys were still there, blown to Kingdom Come by an 88. I looked at them, but didn't recognize either one. Tupper told me who they were. I still couldn't recognize them. Bloody helmets and rifles were lying in the street and in the yard where they were. Nine men in the third squad had been put out of action by that one 88. Collins died, making three dead out of the nine. Tupper and I took their rifles and ammunition. I remember one rifle which had part of a man's forearm blown into the stock. Tupper wanted me to get it, but I took one look and told him I didn't think the rifle would work! We went down to the town church and put one man up in the steeple as a sniper. Some of the boys had brought in about eight prisoners and we had them lined up in the street. Then Tupper led Sanchez, Brown, Gerstle and me out to the last house in town, that is the house closest to the enemy, and told us to stay there. A mortar section was setting up on the street as we went inside the house. The house was strewn with German equipment. . . . There were two civilians in the house, one a boy and the other an old woman, evidently his grandmother, who was obviously out of her mind, probably from the shells.

A few shells came in and we ran for the basement. We were all in it and Gannon came running into the house to tell us that they had retreated again and nobody was left in the town except us. What he said was pretty close to the truth and it scared hell out of us. Just then some one of us detonated a Jerry concussion grenade which had been rigged up as a booby trap in the basement. It paralyzed Brown's left arm and just about put the finishing touches on the rest of us. Our nerves were almost gone. We decided to get out. We opened the door of the house and there was the mortar section spread out all over the street, all wounded, dead or dying. Sanchez stopped to help the wounded and I went with Gannon to look for Tupper. We found him and he reassured us and sent us back to the house, promising to bring help for the wounded and support for us. We went back then and set up our B.A.R.'s—Gerstle was a B.A.R. man also—on tables looking out of the windows on the ground floor. One side of the house was completely blind; that is, it had no windows and that side faced the enemy. We were expecting a counterattack at any minute, but with the number of shells coming in we were afraid to occupy the top floors of the house and it seemed like suicide to go outside and try to dig in. The ground was frozen solid as a rock and snipers were still firing at us occasionally. A building nearby had served as an ammunition dump for the Jerries and it had been set on fire, and besides all the explosions, the fire was casting light all over the street in front of our house. We talked the little boy into getting us some straw with which we covered the basement floor and after discussing surrender and a few other items among ourselves we decided to let two of us get some sleep.

Brown and I took the first shift on guard from seven to nine. It was one of the most terrifying experiences I have ever had. I was so tired I was almost unable to stay awake in spite of the danger. It was necessary to keep extremely quiet and the floor being covered with glass and grenades, etc., this was very difficult. Brown yelled for me once and told me there were about fifteen men outside and he didn't know whether they were ours or theirs. We didn't shoot and they disappeared. I went back to my window and settled down. A German sniper took off to my right and ran a full clip down a hedgerow in front of me. I swung a B.A.R. on him but it was too late. He had hit the ground. I was afraid to dust the area for fear they would see my muzzle blast and blow our house down *toute de suite*. Then I heard a sound directly beneath my window. I thought they were crawling up to throw a hand grenade in the window. I picked up a grenade and, shaking like a leaf, bent forward to see. It was a large pig which was rubbing his back on the bricks under the window. The pig went a little farther and started munching on a German body, one Sanchez had shot with his grease gun in the afternoon.

The moon had come up and it was pretty clear in the field in front of us. All of a sudden Brown called me and I jumped to see what he wanted. He said there was somebody outside. We waited in silence and with our weapons ready. A civilian came around the corner of the house and Brown covered me while I grabbed him and dragged him inside. I tried to tell him in French that it was dangerous to be on the street. I was so nervous I couldn't think of the words and my attempt was almost useless. Brown tried but we couldn't make him understand. Finally we turned him loose and went back to our vigil. The moonlight made things look human in the fields and I tried to watch carefully for any movement. We knew that if they counterattacked we didn't stand a chance. The quiet settled again and then was broken by three rapid shots and the most terrifying scream I have ever heard. This scream was followed by some soul-tearing moans, and then the poor man cried for his wife two or three times and the gun opened up again. During this I was frozen stiff with fear. We found out later some of the boys had shot a civilian. They had moved up and into the houses near us, but we weren't sure which ones.

By this time it was about 9:00 o'clock and we went down to awaken Sanchez and Gerstle and told them what had happened. They relieved us, and Brown and I went down to get some sleep. The bed in the straw wasn't bad. We had some German blankets and it was warmer in the basement. Brown and I both took off our shoes as we figured we could never leave the house anyway in case of an attack. We were so mad, mostly at our own officers, that we would have surrendered probably at the first opportunity. Brown used to say, "Be the first to see the sunny Rhineland" and go through a pantomime of meeting a German soldier trying to surrender and throwing his rifle down first. It is impossible for anyone to realize the feeling of despair which grips a man when his comrades abandon him. We went to sleep immediately and were awakened by Tupper who told us before we were fully awake that we were going out and dig in in front of the town. I choked back some tears and told him that this was suicide, but the officers were back in the town now and they wanted a place to sleep. The basement we were in looked pretty good to them and they started gloating over it before we were out. This only served to make my anger worse. We moved out about twelve and that ended the battle of Wy, Belgium. . . .[11]

X

WE SANG *SILENT NIGHT* WITH THE
ROAR OF PLANES OVERHEAD

During the stand at Bastogne, the Germans captured Chaplain Francis L. Sampson, the same priest who jumped into Normandy on D-Day.

. . . We had walked from Belgium, all the way across Luxembourg, and on the 24th of December we walked (without breakfast or dinner) to Prum in Germany. We were herded (800 of us by now) into the upstairs auditorium of a school where Hitler's and Goering's pictures covered the front wall. We were told that we were going to be fed— supper was being prepared now. We sort of expected that even the Germans would remember that this was Christmas eve. Our supper consisted of one half boiled turnip and a cup of warm water— nothing else. The men were in a mood to riot. I suggested to the colonel in charge that I hold service. It was a pitch-black night and the city was being bombed all night long (I hadn't known before that our fighter planes bombed at night.) The Germans had placed us in the most dangerous place in the city—even a near-miss would collapse the building. We sang *Silent Night* with the roar of planes overhead and bombs dropping very close. I said a prayer, and then spoke for about a half hour. . . .

Christmas Day we were given one slice of bread as we started on our way—no dinner and no supper. We marched about twenty miles to the town of Gerolstein. There was a group of 700 Americans about an hour ahead of us. All 1500 of us were pushed into a two-story building. But just before we went in American bombers came overhead. We prayed that they would keep on going and just as we thought they had passed us up without any unwelcome Christmas gift we heard the terrifying whistle of bombs falling. We hit the ground, just as the most terrific blasts you can imagine bounced us up in the air. They hit about 200 yards away but flying debris killed 8 and a direct hit on the group a couple hundred yards ahead of me killed, I believe, about 30 of our men and wounded others. Some of the bombs hit the local hospital in which we had several Americans. The Germans sent the wounded Americans down to our building, and although we were so packed in that we couldn't budge, let alone sit or lie down, we had to make room for a hundred wounded. I shall never forget it—the filth and misery of the place. A lieutenant with his leg blown off just below the hip told us to take care of the other men first. Our aid men had practically nothing left to care for the wounded, and the Germans laughed at requests. A number of men were sent out to clean up the bombed city, and they were abused unmercifully.

We were given nothing to eat that night, or the next morning, or the next afternoon. We were allowed out one at a time—1500 of us. I was allowed out to bury the men in the local cemetery—the Germans were much more solicitous about the dead than they were about the living. As I got back to the building, I saw a German guard stop every American who came out. I watched for a bit before going back in. The guard offered a slice of bread for a wrist watch. I saw one American make the exchange and the German made the same offer to the next man. Finally an American came out who had a Parker pen but no watch. He offered that for the bread, and the German took the pen, tore the slice of bread in two and gave the American a *half* slice for it. That night the first group were sent down to the depot, which had been bombed that day, and were placed in boxcars and sealed in. It was still early evening, and a P-47 came over, strafed the railroad yards and killed eleven more men (Americans). Gerolstein will always remain in my mind as a city of misery. The next morning each man received a cup of soup, and a fifth of a loaf of bread and two inches of liverwurst. The Germans told us that this was to be our rations for two days, but every man was so starved that he bolted the whole ration almost at once.

We walked for the next two days from dawn till dark, and

without food. American fighter planes would swoop down at us, but we stayed in formation and waved whatever we had. They would recognize us as Americans and tip their wings and wave and leave. Often as we approached a town it would be just getting a going-over by fighter planes and dive-bombers. We would have to wait at the edge of the town until it was over. You can be sure that we were not royally welcomed. I had an aircorps leather jacket on and a civilian seeing this ran up and cracked me with a shovel. It didn't hurt very much but I was careful to wear my trenchcoat over the leather jacket after that when we went through towns.

On our march through this part of Germany we saw dozens of buzz bombs take off from their camouflaged ramps on the other side of the hills that paralleled the road. They made a noise like a broken-down 1928 Dodge truck, and an orange flame poured out the rear end. They looked like giant birds with tails on fire. Not infrequently we could see ten or twelve in the air at the same time. I must say that they at least diverted our minds from our aching feet. . . .

On the second night out of Gerolstein we stopped at the little village of Bos. And here the townspeople went all out to feed us as best they could. Every housewife made soup and sandwiches and hot coffee (even ersatz coffee tasted good). These people were very kind, and when they found out that I was a priest they offered me anything they had. I couldn't quite understand why the people of that town were so different, until one of the women informed us that the town's Catholic pastor had told all his parishioners to do what they could for any prisoners who passed through.

Many of the men were getting footsore and had difficulty keeping up. We marched till dark, and were put in a warehouse, but it was so bitter cold that the guards decided to march us all night rather than try to sleep on the cement floor of that frame building. At three a.m. we arrived at Koblenz, and a more devastated city you cannot imagine. Another bomb dropped on it would simply have been wasted. This city of 400,000 was absolutely flat. We wandered around the streets for three hours trying to find a way out of town, but debris had blocked every street. Finally, holding each other's hands we had to walk carefully single file across the bombed and wrecked bridge on the Rhine. We had now walked twenty-four hours straight and we had had to drop many of the men at little village hospitals.

About ten kilometers beyond Koblenz we waited for three hours for our rations. Each man received a fifth of a loaf of bread, and then a large number of men shared a quart can of pressed meat. Then they pushed us on with no rest. It was sleeting and we were in wretched spirits and most of the men in very bad physical shape; every step from there on was in misery. At three in the afternoon we arrived absolutely exhausted at Bad Ems. . . . We felt that we could go no farther. But the townspeople would not have us; they refused to allow us to stay in the town stables, which had nothing in them but mighty inviting straw. They herded us in the park in the town square, and the people came in droves to ridicule us and laugh at us. The super-race really showed its true status then, and how contemptibly small it seemed to be. How proud I was to be a member of that tired, worn-out group of Yanks. One of the men called for a prayer. Every man bowed his head as I led the prayer for strength and courage for all of us, and we finished with the Our Father. The hospital there was also the Corps Hdqs. (a violation of Geneva rules), and the German officers refused to speak or listen to our American colonel, and they sent a sergeant out to tell us to get moving. The colonel, one of the two doctors and a couple of majors were through— they had to be helped to the hospital. The rest, about 400 now, went on.

About twenty kilometers on to the next town, which turned out to be Limburg, and we were all finished; we could go no farther. They told us that there was a prison camp only three miles from town. This, we felt sure, must be our destination. Just then the air raid sirens sounded; it was the first warning. A few minutes later a different signal from the sirens indicated that the planes were definitely headed this way. Then came the signal to hit for the air raid shelters. The guards took all of us down one of these huge underground cement shelters. It had dozens of very large rooms deep and safe from anything but a block-buster. The Germans poured in by the hundreds: children and mothers with babes in arms, old folks and sick people, soldiers and ministers, police and prostitutes. There was no panic and everything was done with fine order, as though it had been a daily habit for years. But the look on these poor people's faces was enough to soften even our own bitterness into something like sympathy and compassion. They regarded us with neither fear nor hatred; nor did it seem to occur to them to enjoy seeing us subject to a bombing from our own planes. . . . Then the planes came over. Limburg was apparently not their target for that night. They passed over the city dropping only five bombs as a token that the city was not forgotten and would be taken care of later.

When we came out of the shelter we were told that Limburg was absolutely filled up with prisoners. Major Saunders, the ranking prisoner, told the chief guard that we were incapable of walking further; we must stop here and would be glad to sleep in the air raid shelters. The chief guard went to get instructions; it was three hours before he returned. We were desolate because we were not taken to the Limburg Stalag, but we little realized then how fortunate it was for us that they had no more room. Two days after this, New Year's Day, 1945, the German newspapers and radio carried the story of the bombing of Limburg, and took great delight in describing how one American plane flying above the low fog that covered the town and the nearby Stalag dropped five bombs on the prison camp, killing more than sixty American officers. Nor was this just propaganda. . . .

At last, after walking over 185 miles in the last ten days, they put us in boxcars—sixty men to a French 40 and 8 car (40 and 8 means that it can hold 40 men or 8 horses.) And now we were sealed in these cars for six days and six nights, without a single bit to eat or a drop of water to drink! That seems incredible, but I have 400 witnesses to the fact. There were two little openings at each end of the car. We took turns sitting in each other's laps, for there was no room to sit down.

Our hunger during those first three days seemed more than we could stand. All I could think of was Aunt Millie's rolls and homemade bread and bacon and eggs at 821 West Sixth St. The men couldn't seem to stop talking about food. Everyone became very irritable at times, but generally speaking the men took this hunger trial in stride. We would take turns reaching to scrape the snow off the top of the boxcar. Once, while stopping in a town, we called to a woman to bring us some water. We threw four helmets out to her to bring it in. She came back carrying the water and a fourteen or fifteen-year-old boy helping her. She had just reached us when a guard saw her. He ran up, dumped out water on the ground, and gave the woman a push. The boy went down to the other end of the car to hoist up the water quickly, but he was not quick enough. By this time the chief guard came up, and the two of them pushed the boy against a brick retaining wall and gave him a beating. . . .

We didn't know where we were going. We had passed through Berlin, and were heading north. I discovered later that many of us had the same thoughts, but didn't dare to mention it. We had begun to suspect that the Germans were intentionally starving us to death, and that we would not be brought out of the boxcars alive. But on the sixth day, during a driving blizzard, we were let out of the cars, and told that we had arrived at our destination, Neu-brandenburg, Mecklenburg. We were terribly weak and it was all we could do to walk the four miles to Stalag 11-A—our home for the duration. On the way we ate fistfuls of snow, and icecream never tasted half so good.[12]

In prisoner-of-war camps from Germany to Japan, Americans wrote home.

Dearest Family,   [1942]

Alive and kicking. Did not receive any injuries and have not been sick a day. Work in our garden in the daytime but the bugs and weeds are already ahead of us. Attend a Spanish class six nights a week and am learning quite a bit. We say Rosary every morning. Still have the Rosary and Crucifix that you sent me, Mom, don't know what I'd do without them. Congratulations on your graduation, Bell. Sorry I missed it but I'll make it up to you. Hope you don't go and get married now, at least not before I get home. Say a prayer for me and maybe, if God wills it, this won't last too long. Keep your girlish 122 pound figure Mom, at least till I see you in it.

My dearest Mother and Dad,   [1943]

Well things are still going along all right. I went to Church Sunday. We have a Christian Science service here in camp. . . . We don't have any music but the reader reads the words. It's sure better than nothing. Don't forget to save some white meat for me. I'll tell you that the Red Cross Organization is sure doing a wonderful job. We're mighty grateful to them. I'd like to be going to Lindy's on Wilshire tonight. That's what I miss.

Dear Folks, [1943]

Well hear I am again with a few lines to let youall know that I am getting along very well and hope theas few lines find youall the same. I guess youall know by now that I am in Germany. I been hear about 2 weeks. I still haven't received any mail, but hope to get some real soon. How was youalls crops this year. I hope you had a good cattle crop this year. How is Mike and his faimely getting along. I sure am doing my part of sleeping and eating since I am a prisoner. I hope to hear from youall real soon and lots of news. Tell everyone helo for me.

Dear Folks, [1943]

Well yesterday was Thanksgiving, although we didn't eat turkey. I guess we still have a lot to be thankful for. It seemed sort of funny not being able to sit down to a good dinner with the family.

A few weeks ago we received a complete Army outfit from the Red Cross along with our regular boxes. All the fellows were like kids with new toys. It made us feel like soldiers again to get in our new uniforms.

How is everyone these days? Tell everyone I was asking for them.

Dearest Mother, [1943]

The sweat shirt and cigarettes sure came in handy. Well it won't be long till Christmas. I sure wish I could be with you but I guess that is impossible. Me and some of my buddys had a big cake baked today and it sure was good, but it weighed aboute 20 pounds. "Ha" "Ha" Tell Lester hello.

Dear Folks, [1943]

Mary Xmass to every one. I hope this finds every one well, as I am. I feel very good coues I received six letters from youall to day. Gee thoes young gals sure are getting married. Now Maggie you better keep track of them so when I get back so I know witch ones are married and who is not. ho. ho. I don't give a hoo if they all get marry just so one and the right one won't. ho. No Maggie I haven't received any mail from any gail yet, but maybe some other time. Mike must be rich buying a home now, was glad to hear that. I can speak german pretty good now. Well must cloes for this time and get ready to eat again.

Hello Hale, [1944]

Just a line to let you here from me. I am O.K. Hope you are O.K.

Well Hale are you doing alot of corting. I gues you are from what I here. Hale I have been getting a lot of male. I got the PKGS from mother. Hale if you see AnnaMae and Annie Russell tell them to send me a picture and you send me one to.

My dearest Minnie. [1944]

I am getting along swell. Remember that after you have sent me a clothing parcel send me lots of food in my parcels you are allowed. I have been highly complimented several times in my cooking. I've made some wonderful batches of fudge, and lots of stews. I really love to cook on the side. Please send me cigarette parcels also. Always include dehydrated vegetables, chocolate bars, gum, and packages of soups which I always enjoy.

Dearest Susy, children. [1944]

Hope this finds you well, have you been receiving money I started sending home year ago. Treated well, food good here. Don't worry. Will be home. Hope war will end soon. Find small farm near home. Use own judgement about it. I dream of home nightly. Hope we can be together soon. Love to Jack, Judy, Dick, Sally. Keep smiling kids. Rice diet now fourteen months. Feeling fine. Weigh nine Stone. Most popular book in camp Fanny Farmer Boston Cook Book. All nationalities are in this camp. Send smokes, chocolate, food. Keep chin up.[13]

XI

NO FORM OF DEFENSE IS WORTH A DAM

After their futile counterattack in December, 1944, the Germans retreated beyond the Rhine. With the Americans, British, and Canadians driving in from the north, south, and west, the Russians converged upon and captured Berlin. The Third Reich collapsed and, on 7 May, surrendered.

General George S. Patton and Lieutenant James F. McKillen

relate the push toward the Rhine, its crossing, and subsequent events which led to final victory.

(*Patton*)

Luxembourg, Jan. 24, 1945

. . . At the present moment, we are pursuing the Germans quite rapidly, and it is possible, although not better than that, that our efforts, combined with those of the Russians, may terminate this show sooner than is now anticipated, unless for reasons beyond our control we stop what we are doing now and do something else. On several occasions we have followed this unfortunate policy—or at least it seems so from my worm's-eye-view.

Luxembourg, Feb. 6, 1945

We are having a very funny battle right now. I am taking one of the longest chances of my chancy career; in fact, almost disobeying orders in order to attack, my theory being that if I win nobody will say anything, and I am sure I will win; in which case it may well be that I can turn loose armored divisions and re-enact the Brest Peninsula show—of course not quite so fast as the weather is abominable, but still to a degree.

There is no violation of security in telling you this, because long before you get the letter the event will be history, or it may not even appear in the papers if it fails.

Luxembourg, Feb. 21, 1945

Yesterday, I was on a trip which you would have enjoyed a great deal.

First, I visited the place where we crossed the Sauer and Our Rivers. It was really an incredible feat of arms. The river at the time of crossing was about 200 yards wide and running about 9 miles an hour through a gorge which could be only approached down four gullies.

The Germans were on the far side where they had been constructing pillboxes since 1939. We were on this side.

We attacked with two divisions. The one on the right, the 5th, elected to go by surprise; the one on the left, the 80th, decided on a preparation. The results seemed to show that either system is all right if there are stouthearted men making the attack.

The chief losses, aside from enemy fire, came from the water. One day we lost 139 assault boats. Of course, we did not lose the crews of all of them.

These assault boats would be ideal for coot shooting, but are very poor for river crossings. They hold six men and are practically square and work by paddles, which practically no one knows how to work.

The first time I visited this spot the enemy was still shelling it, and we had to keep up a smoke screen so that he could not see whether he hit the bridges. There were a bunch of engineers building a bridge, and I remarked that I had never seen so many small men working so hard; apparently they overheard my remark. When I was there yesterday, things were somewhat quieter, and they had finished the bridge and had a large sign on it, "The General Patton Bridge, built by the Mighty Midgets." It was really quite a thing to do.

Some of the pillboxes covering the bridge were fantastic in their efficiency. There was one at the end of the Midget Bridge which was constructed out of the hardest concrete I have ever seen, because our 90 mm.'s firing at 400 yards bounced off. However, we got a direct hit through the embrasure and cleaned out everyone inside.

Another one was built inside of a stone house. What I believe the Germans did was to take the house, remove the inside, and then build the pillbox. When the fight started, they simply pushed out or shot out the walls in front of the embrasures and opened fire.

Another pillbox was camouflaged to look like a wooden barn and was perfectly harmless unless you opened the barn door, in which case an 88 mm. gun stuck out through 10 feet of concrete.

However, the whole thing proves that people who build walls or ditches or pillboxes, or think that the ocean can defend them are gullible fools. No form of defense is worth a damn.

We took in this particular place some 200 pillboxes by storm according to the following principles: —

You first locate the pillbox by being shot at from it. You then locate at least three others covering the one you are working on, usually by the same method of being shot at.

You then detail men to shoot at the eye slits of the pillbox, and as soon as you have discouraged the Germans, which is not difficult, because the eye slit or embrasure is sort of a bull's-eye at which anyone can shoot, you then have a soldier go up with about ten pounds of TNT, fastened to a thing which looks very much like a for-sale sign, except with a longer stick. This he pushes up against the two-inch steel door of the back of the pillbox, lights a short piece of fuse, and crawls around the corner, putting his fingers in his ears.

When the explosion takes place, the people inside are either killed or stunned, which in a good many cases means the same thing because soldiers are not too gentle removing people who have been shooting at them.

We next visited the Corps to the north where the roads are terrible. I drove for about five hours along troughs of what looked like rather rich cocoa. However, the American soldier and the American equipment have conquered them. We have cut down whole forests with electric saws and built a corduroy road which we have covered with rock with our bulldozers.

Yesterday we had a very lucky attack and finally succeeded in capturing the so-called triangle between the Moselle and Saar Rivers.[14]

(McKillen)

We reached the Rhine at the city of Rheinberg, Germany, and there the Krauts had their backs against the river with the bridges out and they fought like cornered rats and that was pretty tough. We fought for around two or three days to take Rheinberg, and that is the first place you came close to collecting $10,000 insurance.

I was on reconnaissance one morning in the edge of Rheinberg and had just stopped to get out of the jeep and go into a building so I could get upstairs to get a better view of the situation. There was a German self-propelled 88 mm. gun setting down the street which I hadn't seen, and just as I got out of the jeep they fired on it and scored a direct hit and blew the jeep all to pieces. Jeeps are hard to get, too, so that made me mad. However, one of our tanks was coming into town at the time and got the German gun before they could pull out.

After we captured Rheinberg, we set up defensive positions along the Rhine south of Rheinberg, and that is where I was in the farmhouse that I sent the picture of. Things were pretty hot the first few days we were there, and we couldn't step out of the house in the daytime as we were right on the bank of the river and the Krauts could see every move we made. However, they must have decided to save their ammunition to use against us when we started to cross the river, because they quit firing after a few days and we could move around fairly well.

While we were there we were continuously making night patrols across the river to get information that would help in the river crossing, and I can tell you that regardless of what you read in the newspapers, the 9th Armored Division wasn't the first one to cross the Rhine. By that time I had begun to think I was in the Navy instead of the Army, I had been on so many boat rides. . . .

Just before the Rhine crossing was made, I was transferred to the weapons platoon and had to have my mortars set up to fire across the river while the crossing was being made, so I had a foxhole right on the bank for observation and really had a seat on the fifty-yard line. . . .

That Rhine crossing is something I wouldn't have missed for the world. All that you read in the newspapers about the Navy and engineers copping the show is true, but they didn't give them half enough credit. Those sailors and engineers carried boat load after boat load of doughboys across that river, and did it under terrific artillery fire.

Two of the 9th Army's "Varsity Infantry Division" plus "Old Hell on Wheels" (the 2d Armored Division) were to push through us and make the crossing, and the preparation they had was something. The air corps was out in force all day long the day before the attack was made and they dropped everything on those Krauts but the kitchen sink. At midnight, and H-hour was to be at two in the morning, our artillery preparation fire started and I've never heard anything like it. I don't see how any Krauts could have been alive on the other side of that river, as that artillery barrage lasted for two solid hours right along the river banks.

There was an artillery observer with me at my forward observation post and he told me that we had over ninety battalions of field artillery behind us in that barrage, and there I was trying to see where the shells from my 60 mm. mortars were landing. I finally gave up and told my gunmen to fire up all their ammunition as fast as they could and I settled back to watch the show.

About five in the morning I decided that I'd like to see what was going on on the other side, so I hitched a ride across on a LCVP, and got the surprise of my life. Here it was only three hours after H-hour and those darn engineers were already on the other side building a road and the leadway to a bridge to start bringing armor across.

The Rhine crossing had been a lot easier than anyone had thought it would be and a lot less costly. Of the division that made the crossing through my area, one regiment had only eight casualties and another only five.[15]

(Patton)

Idar-Oberstein (Germany)
March 29, 1945

I don't know what the people at home are saying about it, but the operations of the 3d Army, which culminated on the 22d of March with the complete destruction of the 7th and 1st German armies—in which operations we took 6000-odd square miles of Germany, liberated or captured 3000 towns, including Trier, Coblenz, Worms, etc., and captured over 140,000 prisoners and killed or wounded over 90,000 Germans—are probably the greatest defeat ever suffered by an enemy in the history of war and executed at the lowest cost to us.

General Giraud of the French Army was visiting me yesterday, and I told him that I thought our success had been chiefly due to luck. He replied "No, to audacity," and I believe he was right.

Since crossing the Rhine on the 22d of March (thirty-six hours before the British did and thereby stealing their show) we have advanced about 65 miles and took an additional 8000 prisoners today.

Some days ago I heard of an American prisoner of war camp about [60 miles] to my east, so I sent an armored expedition to get it. So far I have not been able to hear what they did.

We have gone back to living in our trucks as we move pretty often now. . . .

Erlangen, May 1, 1945

The war is sort of dragging itself out to a nonspectacular termination. There is still a possibility that I will run into the Sixth German Panzer Army, but in my opinion, the total strength of that Army does not exceed that of one American armored division, and since I have four armored divisions and thirteen infantry divisions, the Sixth Panzer Army will be in a bad way.

Judging from the last war, when one gets to the point where the enemy starts making rumors of peace, his fighting value completely disappears. We have been taking tremendous numbers of prisoners.

In the last nine days, for example, we have taken 129,000-odd. During the same period, the battle losses of this army have aggregated 1767, the non-battle, 2686, or a total of 4453, so that you can see we are trading pretty well when you consider that the strength of the 3d Army at the present time is slightly in excess of 426,000 men.

Of course the figures I am giving with reference to our own casualties are not for publication. There is no objection to telling people how many of the enemy we are catching. In this connection, our total official bag of enemy prisoners since the first of August, 1944, is 688,984, and we estimate that we have killed and wounded an additional 500,000. In tanks, we are still trading better than two to one; that is, two Germans for one American tank. . . .

HEADQUARTERS
THIRD UNITED STATES ARMY
APO 403
July 13, 1945
General Notes on Remarks to be Made to Divisions

You men have just won a great war. You won it because you were better trained, better equipped, better clothed, and better fed than any soldiers in the history of the world. I sometimes wonder if you fully realize how very great you are.

During combat, I talked to every unit which it was possible to reach, and I told you what to expect in battle and the best methods of rapidly, cheaply, and decidedly defeating the enemy. The record of your achievement speaks for itself. As a moderate estimate, we killed, wounded, or captured ten Germans for every American we lost, killed or wounded. Now that all or nearly all of you are returning to civil life, I believe that I should continue to do my best to instruct you how to save your lives and the lives of your children. I realize that in doing this I shall be criticized, but my conscience will be much clearer in the knowledge that I have done my duty as I see it, and have evoked criticism, than it would be if I avoided criticism and left my duty unperformed.

It is certain that the two World Wars in which I have participated would not have occurred had we been prepared. It is my belief that adequate preparation on our part would have prevented or materially shortened all our other wars beginning with that of 1812. Yet, after each of our wars there has always been a great hue and cry to the effect that there will be no more wars; that disarmament is the sure road to health, happiness and peace; and that by removing the fire department, we will remove fires. These ideas spring from wishful thinking and from the erroneous belief that wars result from logical processes. There is no logic in wars. They are produced by madmen. No man

457

can say when future madmen will reappear. I do not say that there will be more wars; I devoutly hope that there will not, but I do say that the chances of avoiding future wars will be greatly enhanced if we are ready.

At school, the big strong boy seldom gets in fights. His companions know his capacity, and he respects their weakness. A prepared America is a strong big boy; but a big or little boy who is not physically strong, and particularly one who indulges in unsolicited advice, gets into many fights until at last he is so badly mauled that he loses his manhood. Remember this, and remember further that preparedness must be both physical, mental, and spiritual. If we have, as we could have, the greatest Army, Navy, and Air Force in the world, and yet are not mentally and spiritually prepared to do our duty as men, our efforts will be only partially successful. Many of you know by personal experience how difficult it was to adjust yourselves to the brutal realities of battle after a lifetime of being told that there would be no more wars. If we produce another generation similarly indoctrinated, we may not be able to win the battles.

Twice in my lifetime, America, the Arsenal of Democracy, has come from behind to ensure victory. Is it not evident that should another war arise, those producing it will make every effort to see that the Arsenal of Democracy is knocked out in the first round? How this can be done I do not know, but I do know that the progress made in airplanes and self-propelled missles is such that the possibility of an early knockout cannot be discounted.

Perhaps a good illustration of what I am trying to put across to you is this: when I went to school, and I presume it is the same now, all the children were taught how to form in column and march out of the building in an orderly manner in case of fire. This instruction did not, so far is I know produce fires, but when fires occurred, the lives of the majority of the children were saved. If we go to the extreme of saying that preparedness produces wars, then the instruction in fire drill would produce fires. Therefore, we should not teach children that a fire may come, that the building may burn; and as a result, have the sad duty of removing the charred little bodies from the ruined schoolhouse.

You men are all American citizens, and in your generation you will have a very large voice in determining the election of our public servants and the enforcement of our laws. I am sure that you have found out that discipline, self-reliance, and mutual respect and faith are necessary in the Army. These traits are just as necessary in civil life. Laws which are not enforced had better not be promulgated.

Referring again to the fire department aspect of the prevention of war, a very large proportion of the duties of the fire departments in large cities is not the extinguishing of fires, but their prevention through advice and supervision. You men are all potential firemen. You have put out the fire by your heroic efforts. It is now your duty as citizens to see that other fires do not occur, and that you and your children are not again called upon to extinguish them.

I have been speaking to you not as your Commanding General, but rather as an old man to young men. I am in no way trying to propagandize you, but as I said before, it is my considered opinion that my duty demands that I should explain to you things as I see them.

In closing, let me say that it is my profound hope that we shall never again be engaged in war, but also let me remind you of the words attributed to George Washington: "In time of peace, prepare for war." That advice is still good.

G. S. Patton, Jr.
General

Peace had come to Europe. After atomic bombs destroyed Hiroshima and Nagasaki in the summer of 1945, peace came in the Pacific.

Commander-in-Chief, President Harry S Truman states his position in ordering the dropping of the atomic bomb.

August 11, 1945

My dear Mr. Cavert:

I appreciated very much your telegram of August ninth. Nobody is more disturbed over the use of Atomic bombs than I am but I was greatly disturbed over the unwarranted attack by the Japanese on Pearl Harbor and their murder of our prisoners of war. The only language they seem to understand is the one we have been using to bombard them. When you have to deal with a beast you have to treat him as a beast. It is most regrettable but nevertheless true.

Sincerely yours,
HARRY S TRUMAN[16]

Mr. Samuel McCrea Cavert
General Secretary
Federal Council of The Churches of Christ in America

CHAPTER VII
1945-1962

*It should be the policy of the United States to support
free peoples*

HARRY S TRUMAN

With peace restored, Americans dealt with the problems of European recovery, control of the atomic bomb, and the organization of the North Atlantic Treaty Organization (NATO). The policy of containing the Soviets suffered disaster when China fell to the Communists in 1949. A challenge to the United Nations came in 1950 when the North Koreans, reinforced later by the Chinese, plunged into South Korea. Wishing to save collective security and avert a third world war, President Harry S Truman responded to the appeal of the United Nations and intervened. American GI's and South Koreans, with incidental aid from fifteen allies, fought the Communists up and down the Korean peninsula. The war was deadlocked when, on 27 July 1953, a truce put an end to the military conflict.

I

THEY GOT A BELLYFUL

The "police action" in Korea was one of the cruelest wars in United States history—the biting cold, the fierce snowstorms, the rugged terrain, the fanaticism of the enemy, and the bloody engagements exacted a staggering price.

Sergeant John N. Southern, Pfc. Leigh Sullivan, Corporal Josh Willoughby, Sergeant Tom N. Simonson, and Pfc. Raymond D. Hendricks describe the struggle.

[*Southern*]   . . . The man I'm talking about was a company commander of mine . . . I'll call him Capt X. . . .

We had just completed the first phase of an attack on a hill mass, and so dug in for the night. We received lots of fire from mortars and machine guns as we were attempting to prepare our positions. Capt X ordered us to tighten our perimeter and get ready to stay. During the night, our artillery bombarded the hill. We had no enemy contact.

Next morning, the platoon for which I was acting platoon leader was ordered to assault and take the hill. A 57mm rifle section and a 60mm mortar was attached for support.

There was a heavy fog over the hill and surrounding terrain. We advanced up the steep slope to a point about 200 yards from the top when we received fire from two enemy machine guns and other small-arms. I had two men wounded. The rest of the platoon hit the ground. I attempted to work some men around the flanks, but enemy fire and steep slopes stymied that move.

I radioed Capt X and asked for mortar support. The gunners tried

463

it, but we were so close to the target area, they couldn't get in on it effectively. Then Capt X told me to try a frontal assault. We tried with two squads with a LMG in direct support. It was no good. We couldn't get at those two enemy machine guns. I had more casualties and we fell back.

I radioed back that time and requested permission to withdraw and place artillery fire on the Chink bunkers. The answer I got was to stay put, form a skirmish line and attack. Capt X came right back on the radio with something like. "Nuts, there's not such a thing as 'pinned down.' Stay up there on that hill and get that attack started."

It was then that my temper started coming to a slow boil. I tried to line the men up for another attack, but it was hard as hell to get them to stick their heads up to fire, let alone try another attack. I kept hollering at them and running around trying to get organized. At the same time, my radio man kept yelling at me that Capt X ordered an immediate assault. By then, I was madder'n a wet hen. It looked to me as if it must be pretty easy for him to sit on his can back *there* and tell me he wanted an immediate assault up *here*.

Finally, about six men got lined up. We fixed bayonets and charged the hill screaming "shaw-nee" (Chinese for "kill with sharp knife"). The Chinks did a little shooting and abandoned their positions. The rest of the platoon came on up and we continued the assault. We took two more hill masses with only light resistance.

When things settled down that day, I was still hot. It was the truth, I hated that captain's guts.

A few days later, we were in another attack. It was another hill and a rough one. Capt X moved the whole outfit across open ground to a sort of dike at the base of the hill. The Chinks were throwing plenty of stuff down on us. The Captain takes a look around and then took a blue scarf from around his neck. We still had our heads down behind the dike. He told us to watch that blue scarf. When he waved it, we were going up the hill after them. We were to keep watching for it because that was where he would be.

Up to then, I'd still been mad at the guy, didn't think he was any good, but I began to watch him a little more after he said that. First time I'd seen anybody do that. The blue scarf made him an outstanding target. Pretty soon, he waved it, and over the dike we went—and fell in a little stream on the far side that was narrow but deep. We hadn't even seen it. We scrambled out and charged up the hill and there was

WONJU II- CHIPYONG

Soldier-artist Robert C. James' drawing of war in Korea.

that captain out in front where everyone could see him, waving that scarf and going up the hill like a monkey up a grape vine. Fire was heavy and we were losing some men. We were only part way up when I got hit in the legs and down I went. Last I saw of the Captain, he was still chugging up that hill waving the scarf.

[*Sullivan*] Company G moved into its new positions on November 22d. I was attached to the company as radio operator for the forward observer, SFC Mahen. Both of us were from the heavy weapons company.

We had been warned before moving up that the Chinks in the new area were hotter'n pistols. Everyone was wondering just how much trouble we were in for.

We rode up to the dismount point in trucks, then walked the rest of the way up the hill. On the way up, we passed the British troops we were relieving. You didn't need a crystal ball to tell they were happy to be getting out of there. I asked 'em what their big hurry was. They answered, "You'll soon find out."

We moved into our new positions, and the first thing we noticed was that there were only bunkers enough for about half of us. The reason for that was that the British companies are a lot smaller than ours.

Well, we were sort of out on a point from the main part of the position. By the time we got everything set up, it was too late to really get a good hole dug, so Sgt. Mahen and I pitched a tent over a hole about two feet deep. I had to work all that night in the rain laying wire, so when I did get a chance to sleep, I didn't worry too much about what I had over my head.

About nine o'clock the next morning, one of the boys from the company came over to our hole and told us the kitchen crew was going to bring up Thanksgiving dinner at one o'clock. We said, "Good deal!" and rolled over to sleep until one.

But at one o'clock, the Chinese started pouring artillery in and what happens but a shell blows our Thanksgiving chow all over that hill. It was getting bad. The bunkers were caving in with the pounding they were getting, and we were losing men. Then their infantry started moving in about four o'clock.

Out where we were, the Chinks had just about cleaned us out. We had a lot of wounded and dead and couldn't hold off another Chink attack there. We had to pull back to the top of the hill, a distance of about 300 yards.

All the time the Chinese were pounding us, an aid man named Rogers worked until I thought he would cave in. With all that stuff flying around that hill, he moved wherever he was needed just like he was takin' a walk in the park only maybe a little faster. He saved a lot of lives up there.

Sgt. Pitman, he's a lieutenant now, kept moving around from hole to hole, and he finally told us we were going to bug out and move back up to the main positions. He sure did a wonderful job there. If he had any fear, he didn't show it. I don't know if I showed it or not, but I had plenty for both of us.

Then we received orders to destroy our equipment and begin to move out. I wrecked my radio so the Chinese couldn't use it, grabbed a dead GI's rifle and started back up the hill. It was on the way up that Sgt. Mahen got hit in the legs. He must have been hurting bad, but he didn't let out a whimper.

After we reached the top of the hill, we dug in and held.

A sergeant I knew was there. He was due to go home on rotation. Well, our artillery was just barely clearing the top of the hill so they could get down into the Chinese below us. One of the rounds didn't quite clear the hill. It killed the sergeant and another guy, wounded five others. Those things happen. If it hadn't been for the artillery, the Chinks would have clobbered us good.

The Chinese kept up their attack until the next morning. I guess they got a bellyful because they pulled back.

It was a good thing they did. We were about out of ammo. My buddy and I only had 38 rounds and 6 grenades between us. But we weren't pushed off the hill even though we lost a lot of men.

Early that morning we found our Thanksgiving dinner scattered around in the snow. It was dirty and frozen, but we brushed it off and ate it. It was good.

A little later, I was told to help wounded men off the hill, and then go back to my company and pick up another radio. They were all walking wounded. We got down off the hill and got on the road and about 15 rounds of artillery landed just across the ditch. None of us were hit, but it sure beat us up. After that, I didn't feel much good.

I got back to the company and the company commander told me to stay back for a couple of days. I stayed.

[*Willoughby*]   We did quite a bit of fighting in the spring—May and June it was.

One time, my company pushed for four days and nights. There wasn't any letup, no rest. I was radio operator in our platoon and, at the end of the four days, there weren't many of us left. There'd been an awful lot of men hit. But we had done everything we were supposed to do except get one hill. Just that one hill was all that was left. It was hard to judge if we had one more hill left in us or not. Anyway, we had orders to jump off the next morning at 0400, and take that hill no matter what the cost.

We jumped off, what there was left of us, at 0400. There were Chinese on that hill, "toksan" (Japanese for "many") of them. We cleaned 'em all out except in this one big bunker. We lost some more men. One of my buddies got shot in the mouth. He fought to stay alive, gasping and fighting for every breath, but he died.

But that big bunker had us stopped. We were getting fire from rifles and automatic weapons, and would get sprinkled with grenades every time we got in close.

Finally, the two lieutenants, my officer and the one leading the other assault platoon, just pulled us back and we sat down. We were just about done, but we had to get that big bunker. The two officers talked. They decided they'd rush the bunker from two flanks while the rest of us would cover them. Several of the men said that, "no, they couldn't do that by themselves. If they wanted to rush it, everybody would rush it." The officers said, "Knock it off, we'll do it our way. Just cover us when we go in."

The men talked under their breath a little bit. Those two officers hadn't been with us long but all of us liked them 'specially after those four days. They were good Joes.

They got their heads together and talked some more. They checked their watches to make sure they were together. Then my officer called me and we went around the top of the hill toward the other side of the bunker. The other one went the other way.

We got to where the rest of the platoon was and the lieutenant told them what we were going to do. I stood behind him with my radio. Then he stopped talking, and just stood there. He'd take a look at his watch every now and then. Finally, he unhooked a grenade from his belt and checked it, looked at us, took a last look at his watch, and lit out running for that big bunker. The Chinks opened up and so did we. He got in pretty close, raised the grenade to pull the pin, and the Chinks flipped out about a dozen grenades and they went off all around him. They just about tore him apart.

About the same time, we heard grenades go off 'round on the other side.

We got him out of there and got him on a litter. He was still alive, torn up bad, but he wasn't hurting any. He didn't know anything. After a little bit, he died there on the litter. We felt awful bad, felt sick. Some of the guys stared down at him and then turned their faces away so the rest of us couldn't see them cry. We were just about paralyzed, I guess.

But the next ranking man stirred around after a few minutes and began to get us squared away. We got around the other side of the knob, and the other platoon had their lieutenant there too. He was dead like our's. Both his legs were gone. The Chinks had done that with grenades too.

We got a 57mm rifle up on that hill and blasted that bunker. Then we moved in. There weren't any Chinks got away.

I hope that hill was valuable for sure. If it wasn't then, it is now because we paid a big, a mighty big price for it. I never saw so much blood. I felt awful bad about those two lieutenants. They were fine men, good Joes, both of 'em.

[*Simonson*] One night early in June, around the 6th I think it was, a bunch of us were sitting around chewin' the fat after knocking off work for the day. Word was put out that volunteers were wanted for a job. At first, nobody said anything. Then, the lieutenant, our platoon leader, said that some men were needed to help the infantry get across the river to the north bank. I couldn't see why they needed volunteers to do that. Didn't sound like much of a job. Why didn't they just line up a detail and go do it? Anyway, I said I'd go.

Next morning, bright and early, we took off from the company area and went over to the 65th Inf. We stuck around there for awhile waiting for the doggies to move out. We all got down to the river bank about ten o'clock.

The river didn't look too bad. We knew it wasn't very deep here, about shoulder deep in spots, but the current was really rough. Some of us in the engineer detail shucked off some clothes and started across with the rope for the infantry to hang onto so they wouldn't get swept off their feet. It looked like a cinch. But we got only about half way across the river, paying out the rope as we went, when a Chink machine gun opened up on us. We stopped for a little trying to figure things out, but there didn't seem much to figure. It was the first time I'd been shot at.

The future didn't look 'specially bright, but I wasn't much worried. Didn't seem to be anything else to do, so we took the rope on over, got it anchored, and the infantry started across. Then that Chink gun really got hot. I went back in the river, and was out in the middle on the upstream side of the rope trying to help the guys on the bank get some more slack out of it. Bullets were splashing close, but I didn't think much about it—too busy I guess. Some of the infantry men got hit though.

Then one right next to me got shot in the leg. I was in water about to my waist, and the lieutenant on the bank yelled at me. "Simonson, get your damned fool head down." After awhile, he told me to come on out.

After I got out on the bank and looked back and saw those bullets chopping up the water among the doggies, I got scared. I got to thinking about all the places I might be hit. It was bad.

We sat there on the bank awhile and it began to rain, and before the middle of the afternoon, the river had come up several feet. Flash floods roll in quicker'n scat in this country. About dark, the volunteers were relieved by some other men from the company. They said they were going to put a foot bridge across. They did all right: had it in before morning, but the Chink artillery zeroed in during the night. They kept shooting the next day too. During the morning, the 65th started coming back across. Guess they found more than they looked for over there, and just couldn't get the stuff across to handle it without a road and a bridge that would carry trucks. Anyway, they started back across, and they had quite a few wounded guys with them. Then, too many of them got jammed up on the footbridge, and it collapsed. I think some of the men on it drowned. I was in the company area when it happened.

Next afternoon, all the men left in the company moved out to help the 65th get across the river. They still were over there and having a pretty rough time.

We were going to try to get boats across the river. Trouble was, we had to lug'em across about a half a mile of rice paddies before we could get to the river bank. After all that rain, those damn paddies were hip-deep in mud and water, but we started out dragging the boats in the dark. We were almost there when I stumbled and nearly fell on my face, all tangled up with somebody's feet and legs. Everybody got excited. We had the boat right on top of a couple of guys. Turned out they were from the 65th. They'd set up a perimeter and these characters thought we were Chinks and they'd kept quiet and let us haul the boats up on 'em.

We finally got the boats down to the river, but it was too high and swift for 'em.

They just couldn't make it. We had to get a line across someway, so an L-19 airplane came up and strung some combat phone wire across. We hauled a rope across with the wire, hauled the boats over on the rope, loaded up with wounded and made the return trip. We made several trips like that with the Chinks dropping artillery all over the place, but the 65th all wound up on the south bank.

While we were working around there, I saw this man walking around with nothing on but a blanket and a pair of combat boots. Somebody said he was a lieutenant with the 65th who had swum the river several times helping wounded men get across. He was still there taking care of his men and giving orders to get things straightened out. I had a lot of respect for that guy. He was a regular Joe.

We wrapped it up finally and took off for the company area. That didn't make me mad. I'd had it and so had everybody else. There wasn't anyone in the outfit with any "go" left in 'em. Eighteen men didn't go back with us. Two of 'em were dead. The others were wounded.

That sack never felt better than when I crawled in it that time.

But I kept thinking for awhile about those bullets splashing in the water so close, and remembering it made me sweat.

I kept thinking about that lieutenant too. Never did hear his name, but he sure was a fine man.

[*Hendricks*] Things being what they are over here, there are bound to be some lousy jobs come up now and then that have to be done. But just a day or so after Christmas (1951), I had one that was a blue ribbon stinker.

I was point man with a patrol that left our lines at 0500 in the middle of a big snow storm. We were headed for a Korean village quite a little hike away. The patrol had the mission of bringing in all the civilians in the village and destroying the houses. The idea was to get the civilians out of a target area where they wouldn't get hurt, and destroy the houses to keep the Chinks from using them for supply points and shelters.

We moved up on the village at about 1100 and right away I spotted a Joe Chink leaning up against a hut with a rifle in his hands. He was quite a way off though at one of the farther houses. There was only about half dozen of them.

We got ready to move in. I was scared and cold and started to cough. Pruitt, the panel man, gave me a stick of gum. The squad leader, Ray Gonzales, put his men in position to give supporting fire and told me to take three men and enter the first hut. By this time, we'd spotted seven Chinks but none of them near the hut we were going into. The radio operator reported this back to the lines.

Pruitt, Don Childs, Youngblood, Cummings and I entered the first hut which was close up under a hill, and the only one that didn't have a guard. Pruitt and I went in while the other two guys covered us. There were eight Koreans in there, 3 men, 4 women and 2 children.

One of the old women saw me and started yelling and tearing her clothes off. I guess she thought I was gonna rape her. I felt like a fool. We had a helluva time getting her to put her clothes back on and getting 'em started out of there.

We hooked up a WP grenade to burn the place while they were getting themselves gathered up. Then we found out that one of the old men was crippled and couldn't walk. We couldn't figure what to do with him. We couldn't transport him. We couldn't put him out or he'd freeze and we couldn't leave him inside or he'd burn. The rest of them already were moving up the ridgeline to where the main body of the patrol was. We carried the old man outside and thought we'd pick him up on the way back. The fuze on the grenade was already burning.

The four of us moved out to go to the next hut about a half mile away across an open field when the squad leader gave us the word to come back. He said we had received orders to withdraw and not burn the village. We hurried back and pulled the grenades and then put the old man back in the house.

By that time, things were really fouled up. Two of the women were very old and they had flat refused to walk out, so they came back in the house. Two of the little girls belonged to one of the women and she was pregnant.

One of the kids took off all of a sudden and headed on the run across the paddy for the nearest house. Then we got orders to bring the civilians we had with us. The woman wouldn't go because of the little girl who had run away. I didn't blame her; she was the kid's mother. I know my mother would fight to keep from leaving one of her kids. She wouldn't let us touch the other little one either. Finally, we picked up the baby and put her on one of the Korean's back and tied her there so he could carry her better. Then Pruitt and I had to half carry, half drag that woman for a ways. She cried and fought us for about a mile before she decided she'd walk. We all felt like we'd just crawled out from under a bunch of rocks. The little girl didn't have any shoes, so I took my mittens off and put-em on her feet. One of the men gave the woman his field jacket. We got back to the company about the middle of the afternoon. When that woman and her little girl and the rest of them were turned over to someone who'd take 'em back to a camp and take care of them, I felt one hundred percent better. We'd all been feeling like a bunch of gangsters taking those people away from their homes. I know it was right to get those people out of there. For their good and ours, it had to be done. But we sure loused up the job, and felt terrible about it. Of course, the people who were on the other end of the radio couldn't see what we were seeing. They had orders same as the ones they were giving us. But knowing that didn't help. We felt like we'd committed a crime.

I think, later, they planned it so those things weren't so likely to happen. I mean, they set up transportation for the old people and sent interpreters along with the patrols so the civilians would know what was happening.

I just don't know about that little girl who ran away. I don't know if the rest of the people in that little village were brought in or not. I hope they were, but I hope it was done better than we did it. I wish I knew that woman had both her kids with her. I know that several of the fellas who made that patrol said prayers for them.

Say, you know the supply sergeant is trying to get me to sign a statement of charges for the pair of mittens I put on that kid's feet. He doesn't know it, but he's got a long hard way to go before he gets my "John Henry" on that dotted line.[1]

473

II

BECAUSE WE LOVED THESE MEN VERY MUCH

The burden of Korea fell unequally upon Americans. Many were hardly affected and their complacency was difficult for the families of those who bled and died to endure. Mrs. Eleanor S. Hardaway, wife of a West Point graduate, underscores the tragedy of Korea.

Only a short time ago we were telling our husbands not to be heroes. Probably every wife has told her husband not to be a hero ever since men started going off to war. But now our husbands have been cited for heroes' medals—the Congressional Medal of Honor, the Distinguished Service Cross and the Silver Star—the highest awards for valor in battle. They died fighting in Korea, and fourteen wives of the West Point class of 1949 now mourn them as widows.

The word "widow" didn't occur to us for several weeks after we got those telegrams from the Adjutant General. Widowhood came to older people, we thought, not to young women in their early twenties. But today our husbands of so few wonderful months are gone, and we wonder that the young and brave go first, knowing that our husbands were very brave.

At this writing, twenty-one men of the class of '49—fourteen married, seven bachelors—have been killed in action in Korea, or have died of wounds. (Five additional Air Force graduates of '49 were killed in training.) All these men served as lieutenants, most of them as infantry platoon leaders, and they were therefore the most expendable of soldiers. They were given the best military training this country has to offer—at West Point, Fort Riley and Forts Belvoir, Bliss and Benning. But as second lieutenants, the most maligned of military ranks, they were called on for the highest sort of leadership in posts of greatest danger. Their pilgrimage into battle must have meaning to all Americans they fought for, not merely to the wives they left behind. For that reason, I write this article.

As Army wives, of course, we are no less vulnerable to grief than any other wives. One by one, we opened the fateful telegrams. Lt.

Ralph Buffington, of Arlington, Virginia, had seemed so lucky—he and Barbara were the only couple in our class who sailed together for Japan. When they reached Yokohama on July 8, 1950, Ralph immediately got his orders for Korea and had to leave his new bride stranded in a strange new country. Ralph was killed at an engineer roadblock on August twelfth, the first of the class of '49 to die in combat. Babs got her telegram in Japan.

Back home, Nina Magruder was next to hear. The Munro Magruders were married only two weeks before Mac left for overseas from Reno, Nevada, Nina's home town. Then came my telegram that Tom Hardaway, of Wheat Ridge, Colorado, was killed on September eighth.

Week after week, the casualty list has grown and the wives of West Point '49 have read their husbands' names, strangely formal in the official telegrams—Lts. Courtenay C. Davis, Jr., of Horse Creek, Wyoming; William Stanley Kempen, of Wilmington, Delaware; Jerome Jay Paden, of Los Angeles; Fenton McGlachlin Odell, of Lafayette, California; William McCoy Wadsworth, of Gadsden, Alabama; Cecil E. Newman, Jr., of Cuero, Texas; Samuel Streit Coursen, of Madison, New Jersey; Leslie W. Kirkpatrick, of Montgomery, Alabama; Harry Winfree Ware, Jr., of Los Angeles; William Robert Pennington, of Tacoma, Washington; and, only last March, William Douglas Bush, Jr., of Tampa, Florida.

Two years ago this week, the class of 1949 ended the long, hard pull at West Point. June 7, 1949, was a glorious day, the day our men got their shiny gold bars. For some of us, June Week meant not only graduation but weddings as well. Barbara Duquette had a traditional West Point chapel wedding, complete with arch of swords, when she married Ralph Buffington, as did Janet Vroom when she married Harry (Hap) Ware in the Catholic chapel. There were dozens of June brides that year. June seventeenth was the compromise date for my marriage to Tom Hardaway at State College, Pennsylvania, where my father was professor of history at Penn State. Tom wanted to be married sooner. My mother wanted even more time to arrange the wedding and prepare the bride. On June thirtieth, Evangeline Sprague, a tall, pretty blonde, married Sam Coursen, one of the tallest boys in the class. These weddings were all high-spirited affairs. When Mary Stokes and Bill Kempen were married at Sea Girt, New Jersey, they left for their honeymoon on horseback.

. . . Each of us can now remember how we met our cadets. I met Tom Hardaway in 1946 when his class was at Camp Buckner, New York, for summer training. I was then a Mount Holyoke sophomore, spending my summer as counselor at Camp Quannacut, a Y.W.C.A. camp on a pine-wooded lake near Buckner. Tom knew one of the Quannacut counselors and asked her to bring two friends as blind dates to a cadet dance.

I won't forget how he looked then—nor will my bobbysox campers whom he later escorted on a private tour of West Point. He was six feet two, with light curly hair, gray eyes with black eyebrows and a handsome, broad-shouldered build. He moved slowly, but with a self-assured slowness. "He walked like a general," one of his fellow cadets once told me. From the time he was ten, Tom wanted to go to West Point. He was an "Army brat," born and raised on Army posts, the son of Brig. Gen. Robert M. Hardaway, MC, USA, retired, and Mrs. Hardaway. During active military service, Tom hoped to go to Yale, for graduate work in foreign service, because he believed that the military and diplomacy were two sides of the same coin.

We corresponded that fall when I went back to Mount Holyoke, and through the next year we dated rather steadily. At Christmas in 1947, Tom gave me his Army A pin, and the following year he gave me an engagement ring and later a miniature of his class ring, with the same tourmaline stone he wore in his own. We noted at the time that while the class of 1949 had only 576 cadets, 578 miniature rings were ordered. It was a class of masterful men.

Now I met some of Tom's classmates who were later killed in Korea, and the girls they married. I met Evie Sprague, who would marry Sam Coursen, while we were sitting on the iron railing outside the barracks, waiting for the boys to come out. "Big Sam" had discovered Evie at Virginia Beach in the summer of 1947. Evie, after graduation from college, was working during vacation at a summer hotel when Sam and his classmates arrived for combined cadet-midshipman amphibious training. As Evie explained it, she was on her way to buy ice cream when Sam rushed up, declared he had to catch a bus, but wanted her permission to call sometime. Sam called.

Sam was one of Tom's close friends at West Point. He'd prepped at Newark Academy, where he'd been captain of the football team and president of his class. At West Point, however, he was a "goat" of the class, at the lower end scholastically. Another close friend was

Munro Magruder, a six-foot-two boy with a prominent nose, which caused his classmates to dub him "The Nose." Mac had a resonant bass voice and British-accented speech he probably acquired as a youngster in Geneva, Switzerland, when his father, Brig. Gen. John Magruder, was military attaché. At Tom's request, I brought Mac blind dates from Mount Holyoke, among them the prize beauties of the class. Mac remained a determined bachelor, however, until two weeks before he left for Korea, when he married Nina Garner.

Now it seems that none of us ever had quite enough time. Tom and I were engaged in the fall of 1948. I'd graduated from Mount Holyoke and taken a job teaching the fourth grade at the Hartridge School in Plainfield, New Jersey. No town within range of West Point had trouble finding young college graduates for weekday jobs— provided they could see their cadets over the week end.

I lived with two other teachers in the third-floor apartment of a Plainfield house owned by the kindly but watchful Mrs. Fred Moses. Mrs. Moses was so taken by Tom that she allowed him to come up to our kitchen for meals, recognizing that we couldn't often afford restaurants, and she rented Tom a room for one dollar a night, half the usual rent.

After Tom's graduation and our marriage, we began our first and last wonderful year together. All of it seems important now, the kind of perfect year so complete that it must have been fated to end the way it did. Leaving West Point, we were given until August eighth to report to Fort Riley, Kansas, where the brand-new lieutenants were assigned to the Ground General School. For Tom and me, this meant two months of honeymoon. We stopped off in Junction City, Kansas, to case the housing situation on our trip out west, driving a new 1949 club coupe. Apartments were so scarce that we stopped amiable Kansans on the street, and finally found a civic-minded wonderwoman who turned up a basement apartment for us. We deposited our first month's rent before leaving town.

Into our honeymoon and later trips we compressed some of the major wonders of America. We set out for Pikes Peak and got there, although we ran out of gas on the way up; we dined at the Broadmoor Hotel in Colorado Springs, and later at Arnaud's famous restaurant in New Orleans; we went to a rodeo in Cheyenne, and we took a terrifying back road to Central City, Colorado, past abandoned gold mines, to see Mae West play in Diamond Lil.

In August, we set up housekeeping in Junction City, along with the Coursens and Wares, the Buffingtons, Kempens and Wadsworths. On week ends we went to dances. On week nights the boys studied their lessons. When Tom would bring home guns to disassemble, I'd read out the directions from his field manual while he took them apart and tried to get them together again. Once we lost a firing pin about a millimeter wide in our overstuffed chair. Although we disassembled the chair to find it, the pin didn't turn up—Tom went back to class next day with the gun parts wrapped in a paper bag.

Junction City was our first real home. Tom and I both loved our basement quarters, but I think we would have been happy in the middle of the Sahara Desert that year. When the men were away at their classes, Evie Coursen, Janet Ware and I began learning how to be wives in general, as well as Army wives in particular. Mr. Wiley, the most patient butcher in Junction City, lectured us on the difference between rump roasts and rib roasts, and spare ribs and short ribs. Believing modern wives should be moderately familiar with their husbands' work, one day we persuaded M/Sgt. H. L. Morse to teach us marksmanship at the Riley practice range. The sergeant was not merely kind, he was also a genius. Three of us qualified as marksmen, astonishing our husbands when they came home that night.

While most of us went to Fort Benning after Riley, a few were assigned elsewhere. At Benning, most of the married West Pointers of 1949 moved into the Camellia Apartments on Wilson Drive, just outside the main gate to the post. The apartments, of course, were unfurnished, renting at forty-five dollars and up a month, and we all spent anxious hours shopping for furniture we could afford. At Riley, Tom and I had bought an extra-long double bed for Tom's sake, a rug and a chair, and borrowed an old dining-room table, a chest of drawers and straight-backed chairs from our families. Even with these remarkable items we still needed plenty of furniture. . . .

Meanwhile, our soldier husbands were nobly improving our lives. They set to work building bookshelves and outdoor fireplaces, planting flowers in our muddy doorways, turning crates into end tables, and making our rented quarters as much like home as any home we'd ever know. They were eager helpmates. One day, for example, Molly Davis came home from a post fashion show, raving to Court about a gorgeous dress she'd seen. The next evening Court called

Molly to inspect their clothes closet. Inside hung the coveted dress.

As winter passed, our little group showed signs of growth. The Wares, Kempens and Coursens had all begun building their families, and in April, Evie and "Big Sam" Coursen became parents of a nine-and-one-half-pound baby boy, named for his father. Young "Sambo" was several weeks overdue, causing considerable tension in the Camellia Apartments. As a result, Sam and Evie just missed winning the West Point loving cup given to the parents of the first son born of the class. An Air Force classmate won it with a youngster born a week before Sambo Coursen.

Soon after, Janet and "Hap" Ware, and Mary and Bill Kempen had little girls, inspiring more enthusiastic baby showers. Tom and I had discussed starting our family at Benning, but we wanted to be sure we'd get overseas together as soon as possible and so decided to wait. It's my one regret of that wonderful year that we waited.

Soon there were long, tense bull sessions in the Camellia Apartments as our husbands chose their first overseas assignments. It was no less agonizing than room-choosing time at a girls' college. Tom and I had talked about serving in Germany or Austria, but we'd heard that duty there required frequent maneuvers, which would separate us. We talked about duty in the Canal Zone and Hawaii, but Tom finally decided, and I agreed, that Tokyo would be more interesting. In Japan we would find a completely different culture. Tom elected Tokyo and we waited for orders.

In mid-June, 1950, we left Benning to start our leaves before the overseas assignments. That summer four more of Tom's classmates got married. Fenton McGlachlin Odell was a tall, lanky, easygoing bachelor until he met Leslie Tibbetts at the swimming pool in the Officers' Club at Benning. Leslie was the lovely daughter of the colonel who ran the club, but Mac Odell was despondent because he thought she was married. Two weeks after he corrected his intelligence report, however, they were engaged. Mac and Leslie were married at Benning on June 30, 1950.

Lt. Leslie W. Kirkpatrick was the big-time operator of the class of 1949 and unquestionably a general in the making. He'd been a battalion commander at West Point, one of the highest honors, and he'd commanded the entire student detachment at Fort Riley. Kirk, with his Alabama drawl, was a natural leader who could work his way around any situation. He met Kitty Rose Wills during graduation leave in the summer of 1949. They were married in June, 1950, in Little Rock, Arkansas, after Kirk's orders were already cut for overseas.

Lieutenants Jerry Paden and Mac Magruder were both married in July, at the last possible moment before they left for Korea. Jerry had known his bride for three years. They'd met at West Point and their romance was as filled with scenes of West Point's famous Flirtation Walk and Kissing Rock as any movie ever filmed about the academy, Elaine Harper, in fact, got her class ring from Jerry in the moonlit shadow of Kissing Rock. They had one month together before Jerry left for Japan.

Mac Magruder finally surrendered unconditionally in what even we West Point wives would call a quick marriage. But we all loved Nina Garner, whom Mac met in April and married just after he'd finished his air-borne training at Benning. As far as we were concerned, "Hard-Luck" Magruder had ended his unlucky streak with Nina. They had only two weeks together before Mac went overseas. Compared with what Nina and Mac had, Tom and I were spendthrift with our time. . . .

We were at Damariscotta, Maine, on June twenty-fifth, the day the newspapers bannered the outbreak of fighting in Korea. Both Tom and Court Davis had their orders for Japan, but Molly and I were sure that meant Korea. Molly and I read the newspaper dispatches, describing the fearful odds against our forces and the pell-mell retreat of our outnumbered troops. But we never talked about it with our husbands. Tom never brought up such matters. He kept telling me I ought to study stenography, and when he left for Seattle and Japan, he urged me to stay at State College and wait for my orders to join him.

Finally the cadets of 1949 had gone to battle, and on both sides of the ocean we waited for mail. Today, most of us have little packets of letters from our men, written when the going was roughest. Tom wrote almost every day of the month he was in battle. Some of his classmates, however, were in combat so short a time that the mail from home never caught up with them. Courtenay Davis never knew that Molly had a baby on April 26, 1951—in fact, he never knew for certain that she was going to.

Now, like the other wives, I can still follow my husband's pilgrimage to the front through his letters. It must have been terrifying for Tom, seeing the first artillery flashes at night, taking charge of a new platoon that had just lost its officer, persuading tired and frightened men that he, a newcomer to war, was fit to lead them.

The letters have the pace of inevitability. "We landed at Pusan this morning," says one, "and move out to join our divisions this afternoon. At present we are in a replacement battalion." . . . "We are about fifteen miles behind the front lines at the 24th Division Replacement Company. I still don't know what regiment I will get, but hope I have time to get straight on the ground before we go into the line." . . . "The orders came through last night and I am assigned to the 21st Infantry Regiment."

"One other boy from Benning, Harry Maihafer and I were assigned to I Company of the 21st Infantry Regiment. We went right to the front and were placed on top of a mountain ridge. We are so high up it is much too far to bring water or hot meals, so we get water from a spring and eat our C rations." . . . "This will probably be the last note written in ink for a while. Ink is one thing we don't have up on this hill." . . . "In four more days I'll have my Combat Infantry Badge, and without a shot being fired at me. . . . Soon after that, my promotion to 1st Lieutenant should come through. . . . It shouldn't be long before we are ready to start back up the line. . . ."

"We still haven't had an attack, although we shoot a few gooks every day. At least half of us have diarrhea and consequently we feel pretty low." . . . "We are supposed to be getting iced tea and cake this afternoon. Some war! We just got a new mess sergeant!" . . . "I think you had better wait on Japan until we see what is going to happen. A lot of people think the Russians are going to call off the North Koreans." . . . "I just got my first mail from you, four letters at once! . . ."

"Now we're near a stream, which makes it better than our hill, but we're also getting artillery fire and gook patrols. Normally, the American soldier is kind of lazy and doesn't like to dig foxholes, but now you can hear shovels all over the area. . . ."

And then came Tom's last letter, written on September fourth or fifth—he wasn't quite sure which day it was. He agreed with a thought in one of my letters about starting that course in stenography. "That would open up a lot of opportunities," he said.

"It looks like a good Air Force day and we should have plenty

481

of support," he wrote. "This will have to be quick, because we move out pretty soon. We are making limited advances in our regiment now, and I Company regained two hills yesterday. We didn't have too many casualties. We will probably continue the attack today. . . . The outfit on our right has been hit pretty hard and hasn't been able to continue the attack, so we may be held up a little. It all goes to show you that you can't fight a war without infantry, and that infantry is the only way to capture and hold ground. . . ."

That was my last letter from Tom. These letters we all cherish, hoping that their deaths were worth while. As Evie Coursen wrote to me after Sam was killed: "If Korea brings peace—and I pray it may—the sacrifice that Sam and Tom and the others were forced to make is worth it for the world. But if it does not, then I am in despair. I want Sam's death to be a banner for peace—that only will reconcile me—nothing else."

After Tom's last letter there were many letters—from his men, his fellow officers and his company commander. Capt. Floyd Gibson, of Stamford, Connecticut, was deeply affected by Tom's death, as he was by the death of every man who served under him, as though there were something more he might have done to save them. This burden is too heavy for Captain Gibson to bear and it doesn't belong to him. It belongs to all of us.

Captain Gibson recommended Tom for a posthumous award of the Silver Star. Tom and his platoon were on the company's left flank when heavily armed North Koreans infiltrated their position. "Lieutenant Hardaway," as Captain Gibson recorded it, "immediately led a squad of his men to face the enemy. . . . He attacked ahead of his men with grenades. Through his repeated grenade attacks many of the enemy were killed and his squad successfully repulsed the hostile attack. During this gallant action Lieutenant Hardaway was killed."

In his letter to me, Captain Gibson added: "Tom was such an outstanding officer and I was so very fond of him. A commander, even a small, minor one like myself, is not supposed to have favorites, but, unfortunately, the military books by which our lives are governed fail to consider personalities and the heart."

Tom's platoon sergeant, M/Sgt. C. F. Martin, was a veteran of many campaigns. Ernie Pyle wrote him up during the last war, making him famous as the "Gypsy," and Sergeant Martin wore his emerald earrings during the battle in which Tom was killed. Sergeant

Martin was a "character," but also a brave soldier, according to Captain Gibson. Sergeant Martin wrote to me after Tom's death: "Tom and I were more than comrades, there was a love sprang between us as brothers. He was the best officer I've known in my seven years of Army."

I am writing this today for Tom Hardaway and for Sam Coursen, for Kirk Kirkpatrick, Mac Odell, Ralph Buffington, for all this little-recognized band of second lieutenants who laid down their lives in Korea. They became heroes in spite of all our words of caution.

Take Sam Coursen. He hadn't done too well at West Point, but in battle he did magnificently. He loved people and it was typical of him that he died because he was trying to save a wounded soldier's life—a scout he had sent out to probe the enemy's line. When the soldier was hit, Sam went to his rescue and got himself into hand-to-hand combat with the North Koreans. They even succeeded in getting his gun away, but Sam killed seven of the enemy before he was shot in the head. His commander has recommended him for the Medal of Honor.

Or take Fenton McGlachlin Odell. Mac joined his platoon as a replacement only three days before he was killed. Mac's bravery was testified to by his sergeant, who told how Mac was assigned to take a crucial hill in the battle north of Taegu. Mac didn't like the schoolbook tactics, so he recalled how the Americans beat the British during the American Revolution by "walking fire."

Mac gathered his men around him. "If they hit the man in front of you," he said, "just keep walking and firing. We've got to take that hill."

Mac was the man in front. Being only a second lieutenant, he didn't lead his men from headquarters, but walked ahead of them all, firing as he walked. He was still firing when the enemy got him with a grenade, but his men walked on to take the hill.

It's been hard to piece together what happened to all of our husbands, although most of us wives have corresponded eagerly with one another since the telegrams came. We've managed to collect some of the information. Les Kirkpatrick, we know, was killed while serving with Company E, 19th Infantry Regiment, 24th Infantry Division. Two months later only four men of Kirk's original platoon were still in action.

Ralph Buffington, who'd brought his wife to Japan, was an engineer officer sent to the front to repair a radio. He repaired the radio and then got to work adjusting a machine gun. While he was at work the enemy opened fire and hit him with three rounds. Court Davis, husband of Molly, was killed on September thirteenth. His platoon's attack had bogged down. Court got it going again by going in front and pulling the men after him. Just before reaching his objective, according to one letter Molly got, he was killed. Court's baby, Courtenay C. Davis, III, was born on April twenty-sixth.

There were acts of courage around the deaths of all these men, but it won't help much to give all the details now. We know, for example, that Bill Kempen died in the slaughter at the Changjin Reservoir in North Korea, and that Jerry Paden died under enemy fire while serving as forward observer for the 61st Field Artillery. We know that Cecil Newman and "Hap" Ware, Bill Wadsworth, Bill Pennington and Doug Bush are all gone now, mourned by their wives and their classmates of West Point 1949.

Their wives, we'd want them to know, are trying to do what they would want us to do. Nina Magruder has gone back to the University of Nevada to continue her college education, and Molly Davis may go back to college when the baby is older. Kitty Kirkpatrick is now a ward secretary at the Veterans' Hospital in Little Rock, Arkansas, while Leslie Odell is working as information specialist at Fort Benning. Wes Newman is also at Benning, Babs Buffington has taken a job in Washington, D. C., and Elaine Paden is working at her mother's store in Waverly, New York. Mary Kempen's second baby girl has arrived. And Evie Coursen is building a duplex home in Auburn, Alabama, planning to rent half of it to help support herself and little Sambo.

Evie wrote to me recently, talking of Sam's death. "My greatest fear is that heaven will be a sort of abstract place and not a replica of Camellia Apartments, 136 Wilson Drive, Columbus, Georgia. We were so very happy there."

Would I have asked Tom to wait if I'd known what lay ahead of us? The more I thought about it, the more I know I wouldn't have traded that wonderful year at Riley and Benning for all the world. Our marriage never reached maturity, but, in a sense, Tom achieved it himself, rounding out his life in total bravery and nobility. I only hope that my country knows what it lost in Tom and his comrades; that it knows truly what it must pay for victory and peace.

I write this as a West Point widow, but our story must reach beyond West Point to all soldiers joining the ranks, to their parents and their friends. I write this particularly because I know that if Tom had lived, many more people would have known him, and I want him to live a little longer for them now. But I write this primarily for those of us widowed by the Korean war, whether we come from Reno or Little Rock, from Dayton or State College, because we loved these men very much.[2]

Following the truce in Korea, the nation entered an era of uneasy peace, an era of crisis—tension in Berlin, Egypt, Formosa, Hungary, Argentina, Lebanon, Pakistan, Tibet, Guatemala, Israel, Laos, The Congo, Cuba, Vietnam. Although Western policy had sought to create a peaceful world, Americans were rediscovering that "To be prepared for war is one of the most effectual means of preserving peace."

I BID YOU FAREWELL

On 12 May 1962 General of the Army Douglas MacArthur addressed the cadets of West Point upon his acceptance of the Sylvanus Thayer Award.

. . . As I was leaving the hotel this morning, a doorman asked me, "Where are you bound for, General?" and when I replied, "West Point," he remarked, "Beautiful place, have you ever been there before?"

No human being could fail to be deeply moved by such a tribute as this. [Thayer Award] Coming from a profession I have served so long, and a people I have loved so well, it fills me with an emotion I cannot express. But this award is not intended primarily to honor a personality, but to symbolize a great moral code—the code of conduct and chivalry of those who guard this beloved land of culture and ancient descent. That is the meaning of this medallion. For all eyes and for all time, it is an expression of the ethics of the American soldier. That I should be integrated in this way with so noble an ideal arouses a sense of pride and yet of humility which will be with me always.

Duty—Honor—Country. Those three hallowed words reverently dictate what you ought to be, what you can be, what you will be. They are your rallying points: to build courage when courage seems to fail; to regain faith when there seems to be little cause for faith; to create hope when hope becomes forlorn. Unhappily, I possess neither that eloquence of diction, that poetry of imagination, nor that brilliance of metaphor to tell you all that they mean. The unbelievers will say they are but words, but a slogan, but a flamboyant phrase. Every pedant, every demagogue, every cynic, every hypocrite, every trouble-maker, and, I am sorry to say, some others of an entirely different character, will try to downgrade them even to the extent of mockery and ridicule. But these are some of the things they do. They build your basic character, they mold you for your future roles as the custodians of the nation's defense, they make you strong enough to know when you are weak, and brave enough to face yourself when you are afraid. They teach you to be proud and unbending in honest failure, but humble and gentle in success; not to substitute words for actions, nor to seek the path of comfort, but to face the stress and spur of difficulty and challenge; to learn to stand up in the storm but to have compassion on those who fall; to master yourself before you seek to master others; to have a heart that is clean, a goal that is high; to learn to laugh yet never forget how to weep; to reach into the future yet never neglect the past; to be serious yet never to take yourself too seriously; to be modest so that you will remember the simplicity of true greatness, the open mind of true wisdom, the meek-ness of true strength. They give you a temper of the will, a quality of the imagination, a vigor of the emotions, a freshness of the deep springs of life, a temperamental predominance of courage over timidity, an appetite for adventure over love of ease. They create in your heart the sense of wonder, the unfailing hope of what next, and the joy and inspiration of life. They teach you in this way to be an officer and a gentleman.

And what sort of soldiers are those you are to lead? Are they reliable, are they brave, are they capable of victory? Their story is known to all of you; it is the story of the American man-at-arms. My estimate of him was formed on the battlefield many, many years ago, and has never changed. I regarded him then as I regard him now—as one of the world's noblest figures, not only as one of the finest military characters but also as one of the most stainless. His name and fame are the birthright of every American citizen. In his youth and strength, his love and loyalty he gave—all that mortality can give. He needs no eulogy from me or from any other man. He has written his own history and written it in red on his enemy's breast. But when I think of his patience under adversity, of his courage under fire, and of his modesty in victory, I am filled with an emotion of admiration I cannot put into words. He belongs to history as furnishing one of the greatest examples of successful patriotism; he belongs to posterity as the instructor of future generations in the principles of liberty and freedom; he belongs to the present, to us, by his virtues and by his achievements. In 20 campaigns, on a hundred battlefields, around a thousand campfires, I have witnessed that enduring fortitude, that patriotic self-abnegation, and that invincible determination which have carved his statue in the hearts of his people. From one end of the world to the other he has drained deep the chalice of courage.

As I listened to those songs of the glee club, in memory's eye I could see those staggering columns of the First World War, bending under soggy packs, on many a weary march from dripping dusk to drizzling dawn, slogging ankle-deep through the mire of shell-shocked roads, to form grimly for the attack, blue-lipped, covered with sludge and mud, chilled by the wind and rain; driving home to their objective, and, for many, to the judgment seat of God. I do not know the dignity of their birth but I do know the glory of their death. They died unquestioning, uncomplaining, with faith in their hearts, and on their lips the hope that we would go on to victory. Always for them—Duty—Honor—Country; always their blood and sweat and tears as we sought the way and the light and the truth.

And twenty years after, on the other side of the globe, again the filth of murky foxholes, the stench of ghostly trenches, the slime of dripping dugouts; those boiling suns of relentless heat, those torrential rains of devastating storms; the loneliness and utter desolation of jungle trails, the bitterness of long separation from those they loved and cherished, the deadly pestilence of tropical disease, the horror of

487

stricken areas of war; their resolute and determined defense, their swift and sure attack, their indomitable purpose, their complete and decisive victory—always victory. Always through the bloody haze of their last reverberating shot, the vision of gaunt, ghastly men reverently following your password of Duty—Honor—Country.

The code which those words perpetuate embraces the highest moral laws and will stand the test of any ethics or philosophies ever promulgated for the uplift of mankind. Its requirements are for the things that are right, and its restraints are from the things that are wrong. The soldier, above all other men, is required to practice the greatest act of religious training—sacrifice. In battle and in the face of danger and death, he discloses those divine attributes which his Maker gave when he created man in his own image. No physical courage and no brute instinct can take the place of the Divine help which alone can sustain him. However horrible the incidents of war may be, the soldier who is called upon to offer and to give his life for his country, is the noblest development of mankind.

You now face a new world—a world of change. The thrust into outer space of the satellite, spheres and missiles marked the beginning of another epoch in the long story of mankind—the chapter of the space age. In the five or more billions of years the scientists tell us it has taken to form the earth, in the three or more billion years of development of the human race, there has never been a greater, a more abrupt or staggering evolution. We deal now not with things of this world alone, but with the illimitable distances and as yet unfathomed mysteries of the universe. We are reaching out for a new and boundless frontier.

We speak in strange terms: of harnessing the cosmic energy; of making winds and tides work for us; of creating unheard synthetic materials to supplement or even replace our old standard basics; of purifying sea water for our drink; of mining ocean floors for new fields of wealth and food; of disease preventatives to expand life into the hundreds of years; of controlling the weather for a more equitable distribution of heat and cold, of rain and shine; of space ships to the moon; of the primary target in war, no longer limited to the armed forces of an enemy, but instead to include his civil populations; of ultimate conflict between a united human race and the sinister forces of some other planetary galaxy; of such dreams and fantasies as to make life the most exciting of all time.

And through all this welter of change and development, your mission remains fixed, determined, inviolable—it is to win our wars. Everything else in your professional career is but corollary to this vital dedication. All other public purposes, all other public projects, all other public needs, great or small, will find others for their accomplishment; but you are the ones who are trained to fight: yours is the profession of arms—the will to win, the sure knowledge that in war there is no substitute for victory; that if you lose, the nation will be destroyed; that the very obsession of your public service must be Duty—Honor—Country.

Others will debate the controversial issues, national and international, which divide men's minds; but serene, calm, aloof, you stand as the nation's war-guardian, as its lifeguard from the raging tides of international conflict, as its gladiator in the arena of battle. For a century and a half you have defended, guarded, and protected its hallowed traditions of liberty and freedom, of right and justice. Let civilian voices argue the merits or demerits of our processes of government; whether our strength is being sapped by deficit financing, indulged in too long, by federal paternalism grown too mighty, by power groups grown too arrogant, by politics grown too corrupt, by crime grown too rampant, by morals grown too low, by taxes grown too high, by extremists grown too violent; whether our personal liberties are as thorough and complete as they should be. These great national problems are not for your professional participation or military solution. Your guidepost stands out like a ten-fold beacon in the night—Duty—Honor—Country.

You are the leaven which binds together the entire fabric of our national system of defense. From your ranks come the great captains who hold the nation's destiny in their hands the moment the war tocsin sounds. The Long Gray Line has never failed us. Were you to do so, a million ghosts in olive drab, in brown khaki, in blue and gray, would rise from their white crosses thundering those magic words—Duty—Honor—Country.

This does not mean that you are war mongers. On the contrary, the soldier, above all other people, prays for peace, for he must suffer and bear the deepest wounds and scars of war. But always in our ears ring the ominous words of Plato that wisest of all philosophers, "Only the dead have seen the end of war."

The shadows are lengthening for me. The twilight is here. My days of old have vanished tone and tint; they have gone glimmering through the dreams of things that were. Their memory is one of wondrous beauty, watered by tears, and coaxed and caressed by the smiles of yesterday. I listen vainly for the witching melody of faint bugles blowing reveille, of far drums beating the long roll. In my dreams I hear again the crash of guns, the rattle of musketry, the strange, mournful mutter of the battlefield.

But in the evening of my memory, always I come back to West Point. Always there echoes and re-echoes Duty—Honor—Country.

Today marks my final roll call with you, but I want you to know that when I cross the river my last conscious thoughts will be of The Corps, and The Corps, and The Corps.

I bid you farewell.[3]

ACKNOWLEDGMENTS

The material for this book was made possible through the help of the following individuals: Victor Gondos, Jr., John Taylor, Elmer Parker, Sara Taylor of the National Archives; Alan Thompson, Manuscript Division, Library of Congress; John Pomfret and staff, especially Miss Mary Isabel Fry, Henry E. Huntington Library; Major James Sunderman, Major Gene Guerny, and Captain Joseph A. Skiera, United States Air Force; Mrs. Frances R. Biese, Air Force Museum, Wright-Patterson Air Force Base; Lieutenant Colonel L. Gordon Hill, Jr., United States Army; Watt P. Marchman and staff, Rutherford B. Hayes Library, Fremont, Ohio; Kenneth Duckett and Conrad Weitzel, Ohio Historical Society; Eugene Holtman, The Ohio State University Library; Egon Weiss and John Parker, United States Military Academy Library; Richard E. Kuehne, The West Point Museum; Mrs. Frances H. Stadler, Missouri Historical Society; Clyde C. Walton, Margaret A. Flint, and staff, Illinois State Historical Library; Donald C. Anthony, New York State Library; Wilbur Leech, Arthur Breton, and Arthur Carlson, New-York Historical Society; Philip T. McLean and staff, The Hoover Institution on War, Revolution, and Peace, Stanford University; William S. Ewing, William L. Clements Library, University of Michigan; Robert W. Hill and Jean McNiece, New York Public Library; Mrs. Eleanor S. Webster of Glen Ridge, New Jersey.

SOURCES

The introductory notes to the selections are based on the following sources: Thomas A. Bailey, ed., *The American Spirit,* 2 vols. (Boston, 1963); Wesley M. Gewehr, *et al, The United States* (New York, 1960); LeRoy R. Hafen & Carl Coke Rister, *Western America* (New York, 1941); Samuel Eliot Morison & Henry Steele Commager, *The Growth of the American Republic,* Fifth Edition, 2 vols. (New York, 1963); Colonel O. H. Spaulding, *The U.S. Army in War and Peace* (New York, 1937).

CHAPTER I

1. Henry Dawson, *Battles of the United States* (1858), I.
2. Henry True, *Journal and Letters* (1900).
3. *Essex Institute Historical Collections* (1912). By permission of the Essex Institute, Salem, Massachusetts.
4. *New England Magazine* (1899).
5. *Essex Institute Historical Collections* (1912). By permission of the Essex Institute, Salem, Massachusetts.
6. Isaac J. Greenwood, ed., *The Revolutionary Services of John Greenwood* (1922).
7. John C. Fitzpatrick, ed., *The Writings of George Washington* (1932), VI.
8. *New England Magazine* (1899).
9. General James Wilkinson, *Memoirs of My Own Times* (1816). Reproduced by permission of The Huntington Library, San Marino, California.
10. William L. Stone, *The Campaign of Lieut. Gen. John Burgoyne* (1877).
11. *Pennsylvania Magazine of History and Biography* (1897).
12. Alexander Hamilton Papers, Manuscript Division, Library of Congress.
13. Henry B. Dawson, ed., *Record of the Trial of Joshua Hett Smith* (1866).

14. Richard Rush, *Occasional Productions, Political, Diplomatic, and Miscellaneous* (1860).

15. James Thacher, *Military Journal of the American Revolution* (1862). Reproduced by permission of The Huntington Library, San Marino, Calif.

16. Adam Walker, *A Journal of Two Campaigns of the Fourth Regiment* (1816). Reproduced by permission of The Huntington Library, San Marino, Calif.

17. *Indiana Quarterly Magazine of History* (1906).

18. Brigham's and Orr's accounts in Walker, *Journal.*

19. Florence G. Watts, ed., "Lieutenant Charles Larrabee's Account of the Battle of Tippecanoe, 1811," *Indiana Magazine of History* (1961). Reproduced by permission of the *Indiana Magazine of History.*

20. Diary of Nathan Newsom, Ohio Historical Society. Reproduced by permission.

21. *Historical Magazine,* new series (1871). Reproduced by permission of The Huntington Library, San Marino, Calif.

22–23. *Magazine of History,* extra no. 31 (1914). Reproduced by permission of The Huntington Library, San Marino, Calif.

24. H. S. Knapp, *History of the Maumee Valley* (1872). Reproduced by permission of The Huntington Library, San Marino, Calif.

25. Logan Esarey, ed., *Messages and Letters of William Henry Harrison* (Indiana Historical Commission, 1922), I.

26. Knapp, *Maumee Valley.*

27. *American State Papers. Military Affairs* (1832), I.

28. Charles Gardner Papers. From the original in the New York State Library, Albany.

29. *A Compendious Account of the Late War* (1817).

30. Jesse S. Myer, *Life and Letters of Dr. William Beaumont* (1912).

31. *American State Papers. Military Affairs* (1832), I.

32. Mary Hardin McCown, ed., "The J. Hartsell Memora': The Journal of a Tennessee Captain in the War of 1812," East Tennessee Historical Society, *Publications* (1939).

33–34. John Spencer Bassett, ed., *Correspondence of Andrew Jackson* (1926), II.

35. *Louisiana Historical Quarterly* (1926).

CHAPTER II

1–2. Black Hawk War Collection, Illinois State Historical Library, Springfield, Ill.

3. Speech in U.S. House of Representatives, 27 July 1848, *Congressional Globe* (1848).
4. Manuscript collections, United States Military Academy Library. Reproduced by permission.
5. Army-Air Force Branch, National Archives.
6. J. Jacob Oswandel, *Notes of the Mexican War* (1885). Reproduced by permission of The Huntington Library, San Marino, Calif.
7. Indiana, Adjutant General's Office, *Indiana in the Mexican War* (1908).
8. Miscellaneous Mexican War Papers, Ohio Historical Society. Reproduced by permission.
9. *Letters of Zachary Taylor from the Battle-Fields of the War* (1908).
10. Carr White Papers, Ohio Historical Society. Reproduced by permission.
11. Dunbar Rowland, ed., *Jefferson Davis* (1923), I.
12. Army-Air Force Branch, National Archives.
13. J. William Jones, *Life and Letters of Robert Edward Lee* (1906).
14. Army-Air Force Branch, National Archives.
15. Nathaniel Hawthorne, *Life of Franklin Pierce* (1852). Reproduced by permission of The Huntington Library, San Marino, Calif.
16. Army-Air Force Branch, National Archives.
17. [George Ballantine], *Autobiography of An English Soldier* (1853). Reproduced by permission of The Huntington Library, San Marino, Calif.
18. George T. M. Davis, *Autobiography* (1891). Reproduced by permission of The Huntington Library, San Marino, Calif.
19. Winfield Scott, *Memoirs* (1864).
20. Army-Air Force Branch, National Archives.
21. Manuscript collections, United States Military Academy Library. Reproduced by permission.

CHAPTER III

1. Abner Doubleday, *Reminiscence of Fort Sumter and Moultrie* (1876).
2. J. William Jones, *Life and Letters of Robert Edward Lee* (1906). Reproduced by permission of The Huntington Library, San Marino, Calif.
3. William T. Sherman Papers, Ohio Historical Society. Reproduced by permission.
4. *Mahoning Register* (June-September 1861). Microfilm copy, Ohio Historical Society. Reproduced by permission.

5. Rutherford B. Hayes Diary, Rutherford B. Hayes Library, Fremont, Ohio. Reproduced by permission.
6. *Official Records of the Union and Confederate Armies* (1882) series 1, VII.
7. Ulysses S. Grant, *Personal Memoirs* (1886), I.
8. Miscellaneous Civil War Papers, Ohio Historical Society. Reproduced by permission.
9. Manuscript diary as transcribed by Mr. Eldon H. Brown of Columbus, Ohio, published in *Sunday Magazine (Columbus Dispatch)*, 8, 15 April 1962. Reproduced by permission.
10. William E. Barton, *The Life of Clara Barton* (1922), I.
11. *Wisconsin History Commission Reprints,* No. 1 (1908).
12. *Official Records of the Union and Confederate Armies* (1891), series 1, XXXVIII.
13. William T. Sherman, *Memoirs* (1875), II.
14. Miscellaneous Civil War Papers, William L. Clements Library, The University of Michigan. Reproduced by permission.

CHAPTER IV

1. Henry Ware Lawton Papers, Manuscript Division, Library of Congress.
2. *Scribner's Magazine* (1899).
3. Webb C. Hayes Diary, Rutherford B. Hayes Library, Fremont, Ohio. Reproduced by permission.
4. William Harley Papers, New-York Historical Society. Reproduced by permission.
5. Army-Air Force Branch, National Archives.
6. *Annual Report of the Board of Regents of the Smithsonian Institution* (1901).
7. Adolphus W. Greely Papers, Manuscript Division, Library of Congress.
8. Army-Air Force Branch, National Archives.

CHAPTER V

1. *World's Work* (1916–17).
2. Private S. Cillis Papers, New-York Historical Society. Reproduced by permission.
3–4. Army-Air Force Branch, National Archives.

5. *Atlantic Monthly* (1919).
6. Army-Air Force Branch, National Archives.
7. *Literary Digest* (1919).
8. Army-Air Force Branch, National Archives.
9. Manuscript letter of Jesse Maxey, Virginia State Library, Richmond, Virginia. Reproduced by permission.
10. World War I Papers (mimeographed copies), Ohio Historical Society. Reproduced by permission.
11. Harry S Truman Library, Independence, Mo., National Archives. Reproduced by permission.
12. Army-Air Force Branch, National Archives.
13. American Academy of Political and Social Science, "Aviation," *The Annals* (1927). Reproduced by permission.
14. "Report of the Commander of the World Flight, 1924," Air Force Museum, Wright-Patterson Air Force Base, Ohio.

CHAPTER VI

1. Colonel Paul Bunker's manuscript diary, United States Military Academy Library. Reproduced by permission.
2-3. Army-Air Force Branch, National Archives.
4. Howard H. Peckham & Shirley A. Snyder, eds., *Letters from Fighting Hoosiers* (Indiana War History Commission, 1948).
5. General Joseph Stilwell Papers, The Hoover Institution on War, Revolution, and Peace, Stanford University. Reproduced by permission.
6. Peckham & Snyder, *Fighting Hoosiers.*
7. Chaplain Francis L. Sampson, *Paratrooper Padre* (Washington, D.C.: Catholic University Press, 1948). Reproduced by permission.
8. Army-Air Force Branch, National Archives.
9. Leonard F. Lawrence, *Phillips Academy, Andover, in World War II* (1948). Reproduced by permission of Mrs. Milton Dana Morrill.
10-11. Peckham & Snyder, *Fighting Hoosiers.*
12. Sampson, *Paratrooper Padre.*
13. Miscellaneous letters, Manuscript Division, Library of Congress.
14. *Atlantic Monthly* (1948); Copyright © 1957 by Theodora Duer Codman. Reprinted by permission of Little, Brown and Co.—Atlantic Monthly Press.
15. Peckham & Snyder, *Fighting Hoosiers.*
16. Harry S Truman Library, Independence, Mo., National Archives. Reproduced by permission.

CHAPTER VII

1. Captain Max W. Dolcater, ed., *3d Infantry Division in Korea* (1953).
2. Eleanor S. Hardaway, "We are the Widows of West Point '49," *Saturday Evening Post,* 9 June 1951. Reprinted by special permission of *The Saturday Evening Post,* (© 1951) The Curtis Publishing Company.
3. Reproduced by permission of General of the Army Douglas Mac-Arthur.

INDEX

499

INDEX

INDEX

PRINTED IN U.S.A.